D0888565

THE TEXTILE ARTS

THE TEXTILE ARTS

A HANDBOOK OF WEAVING,
BRAIDING, PRINTING, AND
OTHER TEXTILE TECHNIQUES

Verla Birrell

SCHOCKEN BOOKS • NEW YORK

First SCHOCKEN PAPERBACK edition 1973

Third Printing, 1976

Copyright © 1959 by Verla Birrell
Library of Congress Catalog Card No. 58-8363
Published by arrangement with Harper & Row, Publishers
Manufactured in the United States of America

I wish to dedicate this book
to my sister,
MARGARET BIRRELL LEONARD
(1910–1948),
whose personal beauty
and artistic ability
were an inspiration to all who knew her

Contents

Preface

This book considers all phases of fabric formation and decoration, but especially emphasizes the various textile hand arts and hand skills. The important textile tools and processes are traced from their simple forms and ancient origins to the mechanical methods employed in industry today.

The book has been compiled to serve the needs of a variety of interests. The *student of textile design* has received special consideration, and complete instructions are given for each of the various textile design processes; the tools and other materials needed for these processes are also listed and described. Because textile techniques are also carefully analyzed and classified, the *archaeologist* will find this book a standard general reference, a reference text for classes in primitive technologies, and a help with problems of textile identification. The book will also serve the *weaver*, and classes in weaving; the *recreational director*, and classes in craft work; the *art teacher*, and classes in art crafts; the *home economist*, and classes in textile structure and design; the *homemaker*, and those interested in art needlework; the *home craftsman;* and those interested in various hobbies. Finally, the book is directed to all who wish a better appreciation of our heritage in the field of the textile arts.

My interest in the various phases of textile design was stimulated by my university teaching in the departments of art and home economics, of such subjects as history of ancient art, interior design, textile design, and textile chemistry. When I became interested in archaeology and made several research trips to Central and South America, I found many interrelations between the studies of textiles and archaeology. This book resulted from such research.

I wish to express my appreciation to all who have directly or indirectly helped in the compilation of this book. I am especially indebted to Mrs. Mary M. Atwater, the outstanding American weaver, who assisted me in solving many of my weaving problems. I also wish to thank Junius B. Bird, archaeologist, American Museum of Natural History, New York City, for reviewing the archaeological portions of this book and for supplying me with publication data.

VERLA L. BIRRELL

June, 1958
Salt Lake City, Utah

Editor's Introduction

Many books have been published on weaving, on historic textiles, on textile design. This particular one is unique in combining in one definitive volume these several aspects of the textile arts and in relating them to the significance of textiles in the study of archaeology. For the story of textiles is a portion of the story of the development of the cultures of mankind. Through the ages men have employed textiles for the dual purposes of utility and as a means of artistic expression. In the preparation of this book, Miss Birrell has drawn from her experiences as college teacher, student of the history of textiles, and research worker in archaeology investigating ancient textiles.

It is unusual to find a book that is equally appealing and useful to a specialized group, such as college students studying the textile arts, and to a large segment of the public having other varied interests. For one who has an interest in historic textiles, in textile design, or for the hobbiest who enjoys creating textiles, this book offers hours of fascinating reading and a wealth of valuable information. The practitioner—weaver or textile designer—will find it a helpful source of directions and definitions, and will use it as a handbook on fabric structure and design processes.

One of the admirable qualities of this book is its correlation of the various features of textile structure and design; the text presents a unified picture of the textile arts. In the field of education, the division of subject matter into a growing number of discrete courses, each dealing with an individual phase of a larger problem, has been severely criticized in recent years by many professional educators and college administrators. Faculty members in some institutions have responded by reuniting courses into broad areas of study in an attempt to help the student explore an aspect of life as a part of an interrelated whole. Familiar examples of the result of such reëvaluation are courses in communications, the history of civilization, unified biological sciences, and the like. There is some justification for the pursuit of a number of separate courses for the student who is preparing for professional specialization and who has need, therefore, for concentration in the separate aspects of a field of knowledge. Indeed, much of this expansion has occurred as a natural consequence of the rapid growth of information resulting from an expanded program of research. But for the nonspecialist who is seeking an overview of an area, this separation of subject-content into small parts is unsatisfactory.

Home economics faculties, too, are attacking this need for subject-matter integration in various ways: some by the merging of several individual courses into one of broader scope and increased credit in which many aspects of a subject may be studied as a whole, others by a concerted effort to interrelate the material that is taught by several instructors in separate courses. It has been difficult to find textbooks to aid in such integration. This text on the textile arts will be very helpful in the broad course designed to consider textiles from the standpoints of design, fabric structure, weaving, history, and cultural anthropology. It will be equally useful as a basic text for a series of separate courses covering these several phases of the subject, for it provides a unifying link that will aid instructors in achieving the desired integration.

HELEN R. LeBARON

THE TEXTILE ARTS

Fabric Formation and Textile Design

The making of utilitarian fabrics has been a concern of man for thousands of years; he also discovered, long ago, that textiles offered a means of aesthetic expression. Through the centuries there has been a consistent development in both the structuring of fabrics and their design. A glance at the history of textiles even suggests a close correlation between man's accomplishments in these arts and his progress in other phases of his culture. Indeed, we have only to compare the rough weaves of prehistoric peoples with the silk brocades of the Renaissance to realize that we have before us a tangible record of man's progress through eons of time.

If for no other reason, a study of fabric formation and design can be undertaken for the express purpose of gaining an insight into the achievements of cultures other than our own. It is often by actual participation, by attempting to reconstruct the arts of a people, that we are able to gain a full appreciation of the quality of their accomplishments. For example, by attempting to duplicate the intricate patterns of Guatemalan weavers, we are amazed at the high level of attainment reached by these otherwise rather primitive people.

Many people have turned to weaving and the other textile arts for the feeling of satisfaction they derive from these skills. Many find in textiles an aesthetic outlet for their creative talents; others turn to the textile crafts for pure leisure-time recreation. An increasing number of people are utilizing the textile arts and crafts as a means of regaining mental health; weaving is being prescribed in many rehabilitation programs because of its therapeutic values. Last, but by no means least, the number of weavers engaged in hand weaving for economic profit is steadily increasing. In fact, the fruit of the loom is, more often than not, worth the effort.

1

1. Fabric Formation

Fabrics have personality. Some are basically ornamental; others are chiefly functional. Some are fine and beautiful; others are crude and coarse. Some are artistic achievements, resulting from the work of man; others are the products of nature and are used in their raw or natural state.

Some of the methods used to make cloth are very old. Impressions of fabrics on clay, excavated from old habitation sites, show that prehistoric peoples knew such techniques as knotting, coiling, wrapping, twining, looping, and braiding—as well as some of the simple weaving processes.

A classification of the various processes of textile fabrication is presented below.

NATURAL FABRICS

Nature has provided man with a number of "prefabricated" textiles. Chief among these are the skins of animals, including sea mammals, which, in the form of furs or leathers, have served man's fabric needs for untold centuries. From plants have come other ready-made fabrics: large leaves, such as banana and fig, the last mentioned in Genesis, have been used for clothing and as substitutes for paper; the lace tree of Peru and certain barks have fabric qualities which have proved useful.

MATTED AND FELTED FABRICS

Felts are made by matting together plant, animal, mineral, and synthetic fibers either separately or in combination. Plant fiber felts have been made for many centuries. A long time ago, primitive peoples in Africa, on the South Sea Islands, and in certain sections of the Western Hemisphere discovered that the inner bark of some trees, especially the paper mulberry (moraceae) and a few varieties of fig, could be pounded into a cloth known as tapa cloth. To make it, the bark is soaked, strips of it are overlapped, and the mass is placed on the top of a log and pounded with a long clublike mallet until the fibers are matted into a thin paperlike cloth. Tapa cloth is often ornamented with painted, stamped, or burned designs. (See Fig. 1.)

Paper making is another felting process. In this case, cellulose fibers—cotton, flax, wood, hemp, etc.—are finely cut and floated in water in a flat sieve frame. When the sieve is lifted out of the water, the water drains out and the fibers gradually settle to the bottom of the sieve, eventually forming a thin sheet. This sheet is then removed from the sieve and pressed. Kleenex and other similar tissues are cotton felts manufactured somewhat the same way as paper.

The felting of wool has been an important fabrication process since antiq-

2

uity. The barbs along the shaft of the wool fiber make it particularly adapted to felting. In this case the felting is accomplished by treating layers of cleaned and carded fibers, which have been laid at right angles to one another, with moisture, heat, and pressure. India has long been famous for her felted and richly embroidered Numdah rugs. Felt making is a major industry in Tibet and other parts of Asia, where it is used for clothing and many other purposes, and where primitive techniques are still in use. Thus they roll and unroll a sheet of dampened woolen fibers until the fibers are compressed into a compact felt. They also form felts by pounding dampened fibers with a stone or beating them with a stick.

Fig. 1. Tapa Cloth. Bark cloth from the islands of the southwest Pacific.

Felts are now being made commercially from synthetic fibers. The thermoplastic qualities of these fibers make them adapt easily to felting processes. These synthetic felts, Pellon, etc., have become important to the fashion industry. Synthetic fibers are also being mixed with woolen fibers to make a combined fiber-felt; the fabric which results is thin, compact, durable, and may be very attractive, depending on the color quality.

NONWOVEN MESHLIKE FABRICS

There are many interlacing and interlocking textile processes: Knotting, looping, braiding, mesh making, net making, knitting, crocheting, and lace making are all nonweaving techniques. In some cases the fabric produced closely resembles a woven fabric; this is especially true of some of the plaiting processes. Chapter VIII treats these techniques in detail. Weft twining, another nonweaving technique, is discussed in Chapter III.

WOVEN FABRICS

More fabrics are made by weaving than by any other one process. Although some looms are especially adapted to certain weaves, most weaves

3

can be woven on any of the different looms. Some very ornate weaves were made in ancient times on simple primitive looms. Modern hand looms, with their mechanical devices and other improvements, make weaving much easier. Various types of weaves are described in Chapter VII and in the Glossary at the back of the book (see pages 225, 469).

2. Design Form and Structure

HISTORIC AND REGIONAL TEXTILE DESIGN

A look at the historic influences which have affected textile design shows both differences and relationships between the designs of different periods and places, suggesting that one culture has borrowed from another. We will also note that the borrowers have usually altered patterns in accord with their own interpretations, each group acquiring a characteristic manner of expression which distinguishes its work from that of other cultures. It is true that differences in detail are found in the work of individuals within a group, but the work of all is likely to possess a certain kinship, a set of common traits. In addition to regional variances which occur, the design traits of each area gradually change through time. Historic design, and this includes textile design, is said to have a space and time-depth relationship. Textile designs may therefore be classified into regional and historic categories. The historic divisions usually coincide with the major historic periods in the following order: primitive, archaic (sometimes called the Bronze and Iron Ages), Classic, Middle Ages, Renaissance, and Modern. Generally, however, historic textile design is divided into closer

Fig. 2. Inca Tapestry. Poncho from Titicaca Island, Bolivia. (Courtesy, The American Museum of Natural History.)

regional and shorter time interval categories, such as Egyptian Old Kingdom, Middle Kingdom, etc. Archaeology is even more specific and attempts to associate textile artifacts with smaller area sites and shorter sequences of time. It is possible for even the inexperienced to distinguish the differences in design in the major historic periods, but it takes an experienced archaeologist to differentiate between design traits which appear in adjacent levels of a stratigraphic cut. The illustrations presented in this Introduction and in Chapter I constitute a small exhibition of the transition in textile design; these should be studied in the sequence given.

Although many design traits are specific for a period and an area and exert little influence beyond the local limits, others consistently run through centuries and exhibit great influence over wide areas. The weaves of China and Persia and the prints of India were traded in the Near East shortly after the time of Christ; they were eagerly collected by the Crusaders, were copied by the Renaissance craftsmen, and are still cherished today with almost as much fervor as they were 2000 years ago. Textile designs from the Orient and the Near East have reappeared continuously in textile designs of Western cultures; the rosette, palmette, and artichoke motifs are typical designs. (See Chapter I.) A textile design copied from a design of a particular period is generally named after that period; for example, a design which simulates the qualities of a French Renaissance design, though created in our contemporary period, is still designated as a French Renaissance design.

Fig. 3. Coptic Tapestry. Fourth-century piece with linen weft pile. (Courtesy of the Metropolitan Museum of Art.)

Textile designs are limited by their media of expression. The early designs tended to be motifs which were separated into unit areas because such weaves as tapestry and swivel-inlay were used. (See Figs. 2, 3, and 80.) Later, design motifs were placed within a series of roundels, ogival forms, lozenged networks, and various geometric shapes. (See Figs. 4 and 5.) In time designs became more naturalistic, finer in detail, and lighter in color. The use of the draw loom, the brocade weave, finer yarns, and better dyes made this possible. There is, then, a correlation between the tools and the methods employed and the kind of design which can be created. (It is the conviction of the author that there is also a correlation between the advanced social structure of a culture and the complexity of its textile expressions.)

5

This brief summary of historic textile design suggests only the vast amount of material which has been published about the subject. A thorough study of this phase of design would take the student into the fields of history, art, and archaeology.

A complete classification of period textiles into their proper historic and regional categories is beyond the scope of the present volume. Any serious student of textile design will, of course, consult various texts which deal with this subject and will acquaint himself with the textile design trends of the important historic epochs. A useful bibliography is included at the end of this book (see page 493).

BASIC QUALITIES OF TEXTILE DESIGNS

A good textile pattern should conform, in general, to the regulations required of any good design. Much of the success of any design depends upon the clever handling of such elements as line, shape, color, and texture. The qualities of balance, center of interest, repetition, rhythm, and contrast, when used skillfully, are as useful tools to the textile designer as to the painter and the sculptor. Since it is impossible to cover completely the subject of design in this book, the student of textile design should consult texts that do handle this phase of art. However, the qualities which particularly affect textile designs are discussed briefly below.

When a design is to be printed, lines should never be stiff, jerky, or box-like, but should exhibit continuity, variation in width and length, and should possess "character." In these designs, shapes should have interesting contours, should be treated freely, and should be correlated. In a woven pattern, the weave structure often controls the direction of line. For the most part, lines in weaving tend to follow horizontal or vertical directions, depending upon whether they originate in the weft or the warp. Shapes, too, necessarily tend to be more regular because of the limitations of various weaves.

Since color greatly affects the appearance of a design, colors should be carefully selected and combined. The color quality of a fabric should be fluid—that is, there should be good transition between the areas of color. It should be kept in mind that colors appear brighter in hue and lighter in value on dark backgrounds than they do on light ones, that they appear to increase in intensity as the size of the area increases, and that colors in close association tend to modify the value, hue, and intensity of each other. In printing and painting, color is said to build up: color placed on top of the same color appears brighter; placed upon top of a related color, it changes in hue; placed upon its complement, it appears brownish and dull. Colors have a greater tendency to bleed or run when dyed or painted over large areas than when applied to small areas. In weaving, the intermeshing of yarns tends to modify their color: yarns of two different colors produce a two-tone effect; when bright color is woven into white, grey, or black warp, the brilliance of the color is reduced.

The pattern unit in a textile design is often called the figure. Figures or design units may be arranged in panels, rows, borders, isolated areas, and/or in allover patterns. When a border design is combined with an allover pattern, the design units in the two areas must be related in subject and character, and the border units must be either smaller or larger than those in the adjacent allover pattern. Design motifs may also be arranged in horizontal, vertical, or diagonal columns. For certain types of fabrics, such as those to be used as drapery materials, strong horizontal and vertical arrangements of pattern are difficult to handle. Therefore, design repeats for most allover patterns are placed in half-drop or stair-step positions. It is comparatively easy to achieve this effect in painted and printed patterns, but often difficult or impossible in weaving. Design units in many of the pattern weaves, however, may be arranged in diagonal positions, as in colonial or overshot weaving, discussed in Chapter VII.

From the point of view of subject matter, designs may be classified as being naturalistic, realistic, conventional, geometric, abstract, or nonobjective. A textile design to be printed may be converted into any one of these styles; one that is to be woven is more generally either geometric or conventional. In damask, brocade, and tapestry weaves, however, the designs may approach realism. Modern textile designs have been greatly influenced by the styles and rendering techniques used in modern painting. Some modern artists have begun to design textiles, literally transferring the compositions of their paintings to fabrics. This transference is easy if the silk-screen process is to be used for reproduction, but more difficult if the pattern is to be set up for weaving. Only a few weaves are versatile enough to handle such difficult compositions. These modern designs could be set up on a Jacquard loom and woven in brocade, though this is not being done. Many modern artist-weavers have turned to tapestry as the best medium to express their art; we are, therefore, witnessing a current revival of interest in tapestry weaving.

In addition to the qualifying elements just listed, a textile design is affected by the mechanical limitations of available equipment. In the case of printing, the fabric to be printed must be considered, as well as the printing method and the type of equipment to be used. For example, small details which look well on smooth surfaces cannot be printed on rough-textured surfaces. Other production problems that affect the size of the repeat of a design are the following: for the roller printing process, the circumference and length of the rollers; for the silk-screen process, the size of the screen; and for the block printing process, the dimensions of the block. As suggested above, the character of the design is also affected by the reproduction process used. A design for a block print must of necessity be more rigid than one to be reproduced by the tusche process of silk-screen printing. Production limitations placed upon a pattern for weaving are even more stringent. They include the type and size of the loom, the quality of the yarn, and the structure of the weave.

In the foregoing discussion attention has been called a number of times to differences between textile patterns designed for printing or other applied processes, and those designed for weaving or other construction processes. It is therefore apparent that textile designs may be divided into two categories according to their eventual use: if they are to be applied to the surface of a fabric, as in printing and dyeing, their purpose is said to be *nonstructural;* if, on the other hand, they are to be incorporated into the mesh of a fabric, as in weaving, their purpose is said to be *structural.* Part Three of this book treats the nonstructural applications of textile design, and Parts One and Two the structural applications, including instructions for plotting designs for weaving.

In summary, it can be said that the subject and treatment of a textile design should be in harmony with the method used for reproduction, with the type of fabric which is to be either decorated or constructed, and with the intended service for the fabric. A good textile design is one that has a unified composition, serves the purpose intended for it, and represents the culture that created it. It may echo the past or anticipate the future, but it must above all else reflect the actual source of its origin.

3. Professional Textile Design and the Designer

The fact that many outstanding artists have recently commenced to design for textile manufacturers indicates that the textile industry is recognizing the need for trained artist-technicians. As a result, opportunities for specialists in textile design are increasing.

Anyone planning to become a professional textile designer needs to be aware of the training necessary for such a career. A good background in historic design and thorough training in art are necessary. A good textile designer must not only be able to create original and dynamic textile designs, but must be aware of the limits of the textile trade. The textile designer must, indeed, be a many faceted person: he must travel, study, and be vitally aware of major current events in and out of the art field; he must be aware of public opinion and current accepted styles; he must understand market trends and how these fluctuate, thus affecting design trends; he must know that there are different design levels for different economic levels and for different regions; he must understand the limitations of the various methods of production; and he must know the specifications which certain manufacturers require, such as style of art, size of pattern, and manner of presentation. He must, in other words, be a very vital person.

The tools and equipment needed for textile design work include the following: a tilt-top work table, mechanical drawing tools and equipment, transparent tracing paper, medium pencils, assorted flat and round sable brushes, opaque paints and waterproof inks, trays large enough to mix sufficient color, and a right-angled mirror. (Placed in the corner of a repeat, this mirror will show the effect of the intermeshing of repeats on the finished fabric.) The tracing paper is used as a tool: a design may be built up by superimposing many parts, all of which will show through the transparent paper. Although most textile designs are rendered in opaque tempera or casein paint, occasionally chalks and Conté crayons are used. Usually only one full repeat of the design need be painted. Tabs of the colors appearing in the design should accompany each textile design plate. (See Fig. 216.) Obviously, in addition to tools and equipment, the textile designer needs ideas and the ability to carry them to a satisfactory, tangible completion.

A final word to the novice who is on the threshold of becoming a professional textile designer: since a manufacturer can know what type of work a designer can produce only by the work which is produced, the novice should keep a portfolio of his designs. Before presenting any work to a manufacturer, it is best to find out the type of work he accepts and how he wishes it presented. Design plates should be mounted attractively and arranged in the portfolio so that a good design is placed first and the best design last in the group to be shown. Occasionally, designs are submitted by mail; in this case the manufacturer should be consulted before designs are sent. All of the foregoing concerns the work of the free-lance designer. It is, however, usually to the advantage of a person starting out in the field of textile design first to seek employment as a designer in a textile manufacturing firm, thus gaining experience before attempting to establish a career as a free-lance designer.

DESIGNING WOVEN FABRICS

In addition to the art background and experience already discussed, it is apparent that a person who is determined to design woven fabrics needs a loom; actually, several looms of different sizes are needed. Small looms are

9

used to make test samples. The designer will also need a large assortment of variously colored and composed yarns. Sample pieces of weaving to be used as a basis for future orders must be at least 3 yards long, in order to demonstrate the appearance of the fabric when draped or folded.

If the designer is going to undertake creating complex pattern weaves for commercial production, he or she must be fully aware of the limitations of the industrial looms which will be eventually used for weaving the material. In designing individual fabrics which will be woven in limited quantities on hand looms, the problem is somewhat different, because the weaver can manage many novel effects by picking up, crossing, or looping certain yarns by hand.

For the creative weaver as well as for the professional textile designer, a thorough knowledge is needed of the methods employed in plotting various drafts for weaving. Planning weave designs and plotting drafts are discussed in this volume. The experienced designer should be able to analyze the weaves of all types of fabrics and should be able to reconstruct these weaves on graph paper.

PART ONE

WEAVING

CHAPTER I

History of Weaving

Since remote antiquity man has expressed himself through the medium of the textile arts. Each textile formed has a complex set of traits which give to it a certain character. Certain qualities of design, color arrangement, yarn content, or fabric structure may be so pronounced as to identify a textile fabric specifically with a particular region or period. A visit to any exhibition of modern textiles, for example, will not only show a variety of weaves and print patterns, but will also forcibly demonstrate that a certain overall sameness, a direction of interest, is common to the entire group.

There is, however, paralleling this stability, a great versatility in the textile arts. No two weavers want to weave the same design, nor does the individual weaver wish to repeat exactly his own performance. At times in history this feature of human personality has reached peaks of creative endeavor. The incentive behind such performance is not always understood. One wonders, for example, what was responsible for the great urge for individual expression which resulted in the remarkable textile achievements of the peoples of ancient Peru; whatever the cause, there must have been a vital motivation.

There is another phase of fabric formation and design that should be considered. The textile arts are so closely associated with other fundamental aspects of culture that a study of these arts often opens up vistas far beyond the borders of the textile field. Intergroup, national, and international relations, in both ancient and modern times, have often depended upon the uninterrupted flow of textile products. The various textile processes—fiber preparation, spinning, dyeing, weaving, and clothing construction—broadly indicate the amount of energy man has expended to supply his basic textile needs. Though recent mechanical inventions have released man from the bondage of the loom, they have not lessened his needs for the products of this loom.

1. Weaving in Ancient Times

Long before man made his first rudimentary attempts at weaving, he had discovered that he could use animal skins, bark cloth, and twined vegetable fibers to supply his limited clothing and fabric needs.

Somewhere in the rich river valleys of China, India, Mesopotamia, or Egypt, the discovery of the potential qualities of certain textile fibers challenged man to improve his crude methods of fabricating cloth and eventually led him to the discovery of the loom. Many anthropologists feel that weaving originated in the Mesopotamian area earlier than 5000 B.C. and diffused from this center to other parts of Europe and Asia. Others feel that weaving processes were independently invented in various parts of the world. This last theory is based upon the fact that spindle whorls and other weaving tools have been found to have such a wide distribution. Irrespective of the point of origin of weaving and spinning, the invention of the spindle and the spindle whorl immeasurably aided in the development of weaving and increased the momentum of man's development toward civilization.

Information concerning prehistoric and early historic weaving techniques has come to us from ancient writings and archaeological excavations. From Job, one of the oldest books of the Bible, comes the quotation, "swifter than the weaver's shuttle." Ancient clay tablets incised with cuneiform writing, found at Ur, record weavers in that area about 2200 B.C. The well-protected tombs of ancient Egypt have preserved mural paintings which illustrate various weaving activities of long ago: in the tomb of Beni-Hasan (*ca.* 2500 B.C.) murals show weavers using both vertical and horizontal looms. Also found in ancient Egyptian tombs are carved wooden and clay models which show weavers at work. (See Fig. 20.) Archaeologists working at the ancient site of Mohenjo Daro in the Indus valley found scraps of cotton cloth preserved in association with copper, which they date as of the second or even the third millennium B.C.

In ancient Greece the origin of weaving was accredited to Minerva and Arachne. Virgil described contests between these two weavers, relating that in the end Arachne was transformed into a spider, to spin and weave forever. Homer wrote of the experiences of Penelope, who, while awaiting the return of Odysseus from Troy, about 800 B.C., warded off her suitors by vowing that she would not marry until her weaving was completed. At night she secretly unraveled her work. Herodotus, describing the weaving methods of his period said: "Other nations make cloth by pushing the woof upwards, while the Egyptians, on the contrary, push it down." From this description the

14

ancient Greeks used a vertical, warp-weighted loom. (See Fig. 28.) Greek weavers eventually organized into guilds to protect their rights.

Persia, continuing her Mesopotamian heritage in weaving, experienced a revival of creative activity about 226 A.D., under native Sassanian rulers. Silk yarns, arriving over old trade routes from China, were woven into beautiful brocades, brocatelles, damasks, and taffetas. The weavers of Persia and those of Damascus in Syria soon became famous for the rare textiles they produced. Their diagonal-grid and roundel designs set a precedent. See Figs. 4 and 5.

The Romans were quick to utilize the weaving arts of the lands they conquered. Large quantities of cloth were needed for the army as well as for civilian use. Greek weavers were brought to Rome; Coptic weavers (see p. 155) were sent to Gaul; Egyptian weavers supplied Rome with linen thread and linen cloth; and the weavers of the Near East turned out luxury fabrics for the nobility of Rome.

On the Western Hemisphere are other evidences of ancient weaving. In Peru, painted vases found in ancient graves picture women weaving on two-bar back-strap looms. Because the coast of Peru has such an arid climate, many beautiful fabrics which were buried there long ago have been recovered intact. Intricate tapestry and other weaves, embroideries, needle knitting,

Fig. 4. Sassanian (Persian) Fabric. Sixth century, silk compound twill. (Courtesy of the Metropolitan Museum of Art.)

knotting, and other textile techniques taken from these tombs never cease to amaze specialists. Practically the only types of weaving not known to these ancient Peruvians were the Oriental knotted-pile weaves. Cloth several yards wide and 20 or more yards long has been found in mummy bundles. Brown and white cotton, llama and alpaca wool, and some sisal-like fibers were the principal textile fibers used.

In Central America, the Aztecs were weaving interesting fabrics when the Spanish arrived in the New World. It is said that they learned weaving from

15

the ancient Toltecs, who, in turn, may have learned the art from South America or from the Mayas. Very little is known about ancient weaving in Central America, but judging from the elaborate costumes pictured on Mayan sculpture, murals, and in codices, certain tribes must have been skilled in the textile arts. Among the textile fibers used by the Aztecs were sisal, hemp, cotton, hair of certain animals, and silk of a species of wild moth.

Fig. 5. Syrian Roundel. Sixth century, silk twill. (Courtesy of the American Museum of Art.)

In North America the weaving arts were not too well developed. Weaving is thought to have been introduced from Mexico into the southwestern part of North America. The Indians in this area used the hair of the bison, dog, mountain goat, and rabbit in their weaving, as well as certain plant fibers such as yucca and, later, cotton. For the most part their textiles were simple, but some tapestry weaving has been found in the Southwest. In the northwestern part of North America, the Indians used the twining technique to construct blankets from bark fibers.

2. Weaving in Europe During the Middle Ages

After the fall of the Roman Empire, many of the weaving centers established by the Romans in southern Gaul continued to turn out cloth. In 629, Dagobert, King of the Franks, established a yearly fair at Oddia, which became one of the great cloth markets of Europe. Later Paris became another important center.

Wool and linen were the two most important textile fibers in use, but silk and cotton were woven in ever-increasing amounts, as described in the next chapter. Burre, the common cloth of the masses, was the most important cloth of the early Middle Ages. This plain woven fabric was usually brown in color and was woven of coarse wool. Serge, a woolen twill fabric important in Gaul, continued to be woven during the Middle Ages. Other weaves of this

16

period were: linsey-woolsey; biffe, a striped fabric; Baptiste de Cambrai, a fine linen cloth; and brunette, a plain cloth. Fabrics woven in the latter half of this period were: scarlet, a Persian broadcloth; drap, an undyed, velourlike cloth; frisia, a friesé; camelin, a napped cloth made of camels' or goats' hair; camelot, a fine cloth made from the hair of stillborn kids from Tibet; and Coacus, a brocade containing threads of Cyprus gold. The tapestry weave, used at first for narrow braids and later for larger pieces, had been introduced into southern Gaul by Coptic weavers during the period of the Roman Empire.

The Crusaders, returning to Europe after expeditions in the Near East (1096–1270), took home quantities of the beautiful textiles they found there. These fabrics, often scented with rare oriental perfumes, were enthusiastically received and were soon being carried along the trade routes from the Near East to supply the demands of the peoples of Europe. Fine cloth from the Mohammedan weaving center at Alexandria, Egypt, also found a market in Europe.

The history of the medieval textile industry correlated closely with the political, economic, and social events of the time. Revenues received from the taxation of textile products helped finance wars and maintain governments. Jealousies over textile enterprises caused both internal and international feuds. A primary cause of the Hundred Years War between England and France (1339–1453), for example, was a textile monopoly agreement between England and Flanders. Laws in France prohibited dyers from weaving and weavers from dyeing fabrics, limited each weaver to two looms—one for broadcloth and one for narrow cloth—allowed certain privileged individuals monopoly rights for the distribution of certain dyes, and bestowed upon the nobility the right to wear certain fine fabrics and laces. The textile industry became one of the most important enterprises of the Middle Ages and directly affected the lives of the people.

3. Weaving During the Renaissance

Until about 1250 A.D., most of the elaborate textiles used in Europe were imported from the Orient, from the Near East, and from lands bordering the Mediterranean. Slowly Europe became independent of southern and eastern sources, began to weave her own fine fabrics, and finally mastered the intricacies of the textile arts. Events that led up to the European production of fine textiles read like fiction.

ITALY

Italy, on the crossroads between Europe and the Near East, was able to gain an early lead in textile production because of its fortunate position. The

Crusaders helped to open up trade routes between the East and the West, and many trading centers were founded in the cities of northern and central Italy. Even before this time, events had brought weavers to the Italian peninsula. For example, during the Roman Empire, weavers were brought into Rome from various lands bordering the Mediterranean. However, it was the Saracens, who had been brought to Sicily from Byzantium and Persia during the Arabian occupation, about 827–1140 A.D., who were the real initiators of the great textile trends of the Renaissance. The traditions they founded slowly spread northward into Europe, as we shall see. When the Norman conqueror, King Roger II, took Sicily in about 1140 A.D., he brought other skilled weavers from the Near East and set up additional workshops there. Sicily became a center of the weaving arts, but when this island was conquered by the Franks under Charles of Anjou, many of the skilled weavers fled to Lucca, Italy.

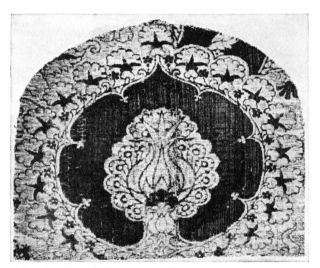

Fig. 6. Spanish Renaissance. Fifteenth century, cut-pile velvet. Artichoke pattern. (Courtesy, Cooper Union Museum.)

Here these craftsmen continued to excel until 1315, when the Florentines captured the city and took many of them back to Florence. The city of Florence soon became an outstanding center of fine fabrics. However, in 1530, Florence fell to the Prince of Orange and Pope Clement VIII, who approached the city crying, "Prepare, Florence, your brocades of gold; we are coming to purchase them with the measure of our pikes." During the sixteenth century, Venice and Genoa began to overshadow Florence in the production of fine fabrics as the textile arts moved northward. The artichoke motif was widely used during this time. See Fig. 6.

FRANCE

The first weaving centers in Gaul had been established by the Romans at Reims, Metz, Journay, Lyons, Arles, and Arras. Later the textiles of Italy greatly affected France. When the Pope went to live in Avignon in 1308, he took a number of spinners and weavers with him. In 1492, Charles VIII invaded Italy and brought back to France 40 tons of fine Italian cloth as well as many Italian artisans and weavers. In 1507, the silk weavers of Lyons were copying the tapestries of Florence, the velvets of Genoa and Milan, and the damasks of Venice and Lucca. In 1520, Francis I brought many skilled weavers from Italy and Flanders and put them to work in France. Naturally, with so many influences from Italy, French fabrics could scarcely be distinguished from those of Italy. Not until the reign of Louis XV did the French find freedom of expression in textile design.

During the reign of Louis XIV, the French tapestry weavers were united into one group, the Gobelin Factory, named

Fig. 7. Renaissance Satin. Italian or Spanish, late sixteenth century. (Courtesy, Cooper Union Museum.)

Fig. 8. Italian Satin. Seventeenth century, silk and linen. (Courtesy, Cooper Union Museum.)

after Jehan Gobelin who had founded a dye works in the fifteenth century on the same site. Tapestry weaving became one of the most important textile enterprises of France and of the Renaissance.

France unwittingly helped spread her weaving arts to other European countries when oppressive edicts forced many weavers to leave their homes and to look for refuge in other lands. Regulations imposed on Arras by Louis XI forced many to leave. Likewise, when Louis XIV revoked the Edict of Nantes, many weavers fled to Flanders; others—the Huguenots, etc.— went to England and America.

19

As a result of importations by the East India Company, printed textiles became popular. Those printed at Jouy, the "toiles de Jouy," were outstanding. (See Fig. 215.)

Fig. 9. French Brocaded Satin. Eighteenth century, Louis XV style. (Courtesy, Cooper Union Museum.)

The Jacquard loom, the culmination of the efforts of a number of men, was invented in 1804. By means of this mechanical device, brocades, damasks, and other difficult weaves could be woven with comparative ease.

20

THE TEXTILE ARTS

ENGLAND

The textile industries of England were substantially built up by refugees from the continent. For example, Philip Augustus passed laws which forced many Flemish weavers to migrate to England. In 1343, Edward III invited Flemish fullers and dyers to move to England. Foreign influences continued to affect the textile industry of England for many, many years. It should be

Fig. 10. French Brocade. Eighteenth century, Louis XVI style. (Courtesy, Cooper Union Museum.)

remembered that the Romans were perhaps the first "foreigners" to set up looms on British soil.

Through numerous inventions of her own, England was able to gain a foot-hold in textile manufacturing. John Winchcombe, also known as Jack of Newberry, who died in 1520, is said to have organized the first textile factory recorded in England, according to Walton (*64*);[1] Winchcombe is also supposed to have invented an extra-wide loom which took two men, one on

[1] The italic numbers in parentheses refer to the References at the back of the book, pages 493–500.

either side, to throw the shuttle in order to weave "broadcloth." Thomas Cole of Reading was the first person to produce cloth on a large commercial scale in England, and Thomas Blanket invented the woolen blanket.

In the meantime, England was welcoming many skilled weavers from the Continent. By 1573, brocades and other fine fabrics were being woven in England. In 1575, the knotted-pile method of weaving was introduced from the Near East. In 1584, Queen Elizabeth granted a charter to a group of Dutch weavers who established an industry in Norwich which soon became famous for its damasks and flowered silks. In 1629, James I of England assisted some Huguenot refugees from France to establish a silk manufacturing industry. In 1685, after the revocation of the Edict of Nantes, many of the 50,000 refugees who left France settled at Spitalfields, near London, which became one of the leading European centers in the production of silk damasks and brocades. Manchester and other towns also became known for their textiles.

Fig. 11. French Brocaded Satin. Nineteenth century, ordered by Napoleon I. (Courtesy of the Metropolitan Museum of Art.)

England also became interested in the textile printing industry. In the decade between 1621 and 1631, the East India Company secured permission to bring cotton, India prints, and "chints" into the country. Soon after this, England established her own printing industries. By 1700, it was found necessary to pass laws to protect these industries, and it became unlawful for the people of England to wear printed calicoes from China, Persia, and the East Indies. A year later the importation of silk fabrics from the East was also forbidden.

Mechanical weaving devices began to appear in England early in the eighteenth century. A gauze-weaving loom was imported from Italy in 1732. In 1735, John Kay invented the fly shuttle, and in 1760, his son, Robert Kay, invented the equipment and started the use of multiple shuttle boxes. In 1787, a minister by the name of Dr. Cartwright invented and patented an automatic loom which changed the shed and threw the shuttle when the reed was operated. Cartwright called his loom the "iron man." Weavers tried to destroy his loom, because it could do in one day what a weaver could do in a week, but in spite of opposition toward new inventions, improvements in weaving equipment continued to be made. Spinning equipment was also being mechanically improved. Chapter II provides an account of the historic development of spinning processes.

Because of the great progress made during the Renaissance, England was in a position to become one of the leading textile producers in the nineteenth and twentieth centuries.

UNITED STATES

Starting not long after the voyages of Columbus, colonists from all parts of Europe began arriving in America. Many came to find permanent homes and brought spinning wheels, looms, and other weaving equipment with them. For some time most of the raw materials—cotton, wool, etc.—used for weaving had to be imported. Although some flax and wool were produced in the colonies before the Revolution, cotton was not grown to any extent until later. The first weaving factory in the United States was established in 1638 by Master Ezekiel Rogers at Rowley, Massachusetts. Twenty families were brought from England to assist in this enterprise. Gradually other textile factories appeared in cities in the neighboring states. William Penn helped establish a factory in Philadelphia. The cloth woven in these factories was simple, durable, and practical. It was not long before weaving gradually moved from the home to the factory.

Soon after the American Revolution, textile machinery was smuggled into America from England and France. Technical knowledge of textile processes was brought by weavers seeking new homes. In 1792, the cotton gin, a machine which mechanically removed the seeds from cotton, was invented by Eli Whitney, a New England school teacher then teaching in Georgia. In 1793, Samuel Slater, coming from England and bringing with him the principles of the Arkwright spinning frame, established the first cotton mill in America at Pawtucket, Rhode Island. In 1794, in Byfield, Massachusetts, the first wool carding machines were invented and operated by Arthur Schofield. Carpet weaving was first attempted in 1774 in Philadelphia.

4. Weaving in the United States Since 1800

Time continued to bring new and exciting developments to the processes associated with weaving. Inventions, many of which had their roots in the eighteenth century, led to new methods of cultivating and processing, better machines for weaving and printing, new synthetic fibers, new dyes, and new fabric finishes. A few of the many important inventions of the nineteenth century are the following: A power loom for weaving checks was invented by Alfred Jenks (1810); the sewing machine was invented by Elias Howe, with the assistance of the Frenchman, Themonier (1830); improvements to the sewing machine were made by Isaac Singer (1851); James H. Northrop, an Englishman working in America, perfected the Northrop loom, which completely mechanized the processes used in plain weaving (1889). His loom was equipped with automatic controls which stopped the loom if a thread broke during weaving. (Some information on new fibers and new fabric finishes is to be found in Chapter II, and on new synthetic dyes in Chapter X. New inventions of spinning equipment are also described in Chapter II.)

At the beginning of the nineteenth century, textile machinery was driven by water power, and manufacturers therefore began looking for mill sites along the rivers in New England. Important mills were built at a number of places in Massachusetts—at Lawrence by Abbot Lawrence, at Fall River by Colonel Joseph Durfee (1811), at New Bedford by Dwight Perry, at Manchester, and at Amsterdam; mills were also built at Providence, Rhode Island, Paterson, New Jersey, and a number of other sites. When Francis Cabot Lowell returned to America after studying the textile industry in England, he established at Waltham, Massachusetts, in 1813, the first textile mill in the United States that combined in one establishment the full manufacturing processes necessary for converting raw fibers into finished fabrics. In 1824, this Waltham Company secured land and water rights at Pawtucket Falls, named the site Lowell, and built a mill there. Lowell eventually became a great textile center. The textile fibers used in these mills were cotton, wool, and linen, important in that order. Silk weaving was undertaken in 1838 by the Cheney brothers in Manchester, Connecticut.

Some of these early mills continued to be important centers of textile production well into the twentieth century. In the second quarter of this century, textile mills were established in areas in the southern states; these mills grew rapidly because the availability of raw materials and cheap labor gave the southern states advantages over those of the north. This general shift toward the south has had disastrous effects on many textile centers in New England. Textile producing and manufacturing enterprises were also taken up and promoted by other states: Texas, Arizona, and California are now successfully growing and processing cotton.

Although the cutting and garment manufacturing industries still center in New York City, Los Angeles is fast becoming an important center. Other cities in which the garment manufacturing industry is making great headway are St. Louis, Kansas City, Dallas, and Phoenix. It is interesting to note that the textile industry, with all its divisions and subsidiaries, is the second largest industry in the United States. The total income in 1957 was $13,000,-000,000.

The sweeping changes which took place in methods of textile production from the Renaissance and through the middle of the twentieth century, have brought about progressive mechanization of textile equipment. (See page 40.) These changes have principally affected the tools and materials used in weaving; weave structures have changed very little since the beginning of the Renaissance. The simple standard weaves are still the backbone of the textile trade. The rich ornamental weaves—the damasks, brocades, and other weaves that had their origins in the Near and Far East long before the Renaissance—are now woven on Jacquard looms and are still considered precious commodities in the textile market.

Although improved machinery does increase the output of woven fabrics, it does not necessarily improve the quality of these fabrics. The charming character of hand-woven materials cannot often be duplicated in machine-woven fabrics. A reëvaluation of the merits of hand-woven cloth has probably been an important factor contributing to the current renaissance in hand weaving. More and more people are taking up hand weaving as a leisure-time activity. Between 1940 and 1950 the number of people engaged in hand weaving in the United States doubled. It is estimated that some 300,000 hand looms are now in operation in this country.

CHAPTER II

Textile Fibers and Yarns and Their Uses

Introduction

The fundamental principles of spinning and weaving,[1] which were well understood by ancient peoples long before the historic era, are still basic to these processes, though the tools and techniques used have been improved to the point that machine spinning and power-loom weaving have replaced most earlier hand methods. In many parts of the world, however, native groups may still be seen using primitive methods of handling the growing, processing, spinning, and weaving of their textile fibers. By visiting these peoples and observing their methods, we are often afforded a glimpse into the handicrafts of the past.

The first fibers employed for structuring utilitarian articles were undoubtedly used in their natural state. Baskets were constructed of reeds and grasses, and mats were plaited of palm leaves and rushes. Human hair was frequently used for braided cords and handles, or was bunched and tied together for cordage. Then, at some unknown period in the ancient past, it was discovered that stronger strands could be made by twisting reeds or other types of fibers into multiple-strand cords. In ancient archaeological sites are found many pieces of crude cordage formed by twisting together two or more reeds or rushes.

When and where it was discovered that wool, cotton, and linen fibers could also be twisted into comparatively strong strands that could be combined into fabrics is not known. It is possible that the discovery was made independently in various parts of the world. Nor is much more known about the time

[1] Since it is necessary to understand the terms used in weaving before undertaking a study of the weaving processes, it is suggested that the beginner turn to the Glossary at the back of the book for explanations of technical terms. (See pages 469–490.)

and place of the origin of the spindle; spindles were usually made of wood which has long since disintegrated. On the other hand, spindle whorls, the weights placed on the ends of spindles, have been preserved in many ancient sites; there is evidence that these were used as early as the fifth millennium B.C.[2]

1. Textile Fibers

Many types of fibers are used in the manufacture of textiles. A classification of these fibers and a brief discussion of their historic background are given below. A complete study, including information concerning the source, distribution, cultivation, and processing of these fibers, is beyond the scope of the present volume.

Ancient peoples discovered at a very early date the usefulness of such coarse plant fibers as jute, hemp, yucca, palm, and grass. Long before the invention of the loom these fibers were intertwined into cordage, baskets, sandals, fans, mats, and fish nets.

Flax may have been used for weaving in the Nile Valley as early as 4000 B.C. Pieces of linen cloth found in Egyptian tombs date as far back as 2500 B.C. This cloth was finer than any linen woven today. Some of it contained 540 threads to the inch and was 60 inches wide and 6 or more yards long.

Cotton is believed to have been first grown in India. Ancient graves at Mohenjo Daro, in the Indus Valley, have yielded cotton samples which may have come from the third millennium B.C. Although Alexander found cotton in India in the fourth century B.C., it is thought that cotton was not grown in the Mediterranean district until several centuries later. The Romans were using cotton awnings at the time of the Apollinarian games, 63 B.C. When the East India Company brought cotton to England in the seventeenth century, the fiber was called "wool grown on trees" by Sir Martin Noel.

Silk, the most beautiful of the natural fibers, was discovered in China by a Chinese princess. According to legend, this was about 2640 B.C. Sericulture was a secret enterprise; the knowledge of this process gradually spread around the world. Many ingenious methods were used to smuggle the knowledge of sericulture out of China. One story tells of a Chinese princess journeying to India to be married, who carried in her elaborate coiffure a packet which contained the eggs of silkworms and the seeds of mulberry trees. Other stories have this same princess, or perhaps other princesses, carrying this precious cargo to other areas. It is alleged that the Japanese learned sericulture from

---

[2] Carbon 14 tests of samples from Jarmo indicate the site as one of the earliest villages in western Asia, located in the vicinity of Kirkuk, Iraq. See Libby, Willard, *Radiocarbon Dating,* University of Chicago Press, 1955.

captured Chinese, or possibly Korean, maidens. When Alexander the Great (356–323 B.C.) and his men returned from India, they brought back the knowledge of silk culture. Aristotle described the silkworm and mentioned that the island of Cos was a center of silk manufacturing (Walton, *64*). Greek historians tell of silk caravans traveling from China in the third century B.C. (Baity, *5*). Justinian, wishing to initiate silk cultivation and processing in the Byzantine Empire, sent two Persian monks to the Orient to secure the necessary materials and information. These monks returned to Byzantium about 536–552 A.D. with the eggs of silkworms and the seeds of the mulberry tree hidden in the hollows of their walking staves (Walton, *64*).

About 827 A.D. the knowledge of sericulture was carried from Byzantium to Sicily by Saracen weavers. After the conquest of Sicily by the Franks, these Saracens moved on to Italy, from which France gained knowledge of this art about 1080 A.D. The secrets of silk culture were carried to England by the Hugenots when they fled from France after the revocation of the Edict of Nantes. The knowledge was carried to Spain by the Moors. Thus eventually the guarded secret of sericulture passed from China to the world at large.

Wool could easily be considered the most important of the natural fibers. The structure of the fiber with its overlapping scales makes it the easiest of all fibers to felt and to spin. It must have been cherished anciently for these very qualities. Woolen clothing was worn in the early cultures of Asia, Asia Minor, Assyria, Persia, Mesopotamia, Palestine, Egypt, and Greece. The Egyptians considered wool impure and would not allow its use for burial purposes.

China grass, also known as ramie, is a linenlike bast fiber which has been grown and used for centuries in China and is now being grown in the United States.

Miscellaneous fibers of various types have served the needs of man since prehistoric periods. Principally used for cordage and for mat making, these fibers include hemp, jute, yucca, henequen, maguey, palm leaves, and milkweed.

CLASSIFICATION OF TEXTILE FIBERS

Fibers are generally classified as being either natural or man-made. The natural fibers are divided into four groups—vegetable or plant, animal, metal, and mineral; vegetable and animal fibers are classed as organic, and mineral and metal as inorganic. Man-made fibers are classed as organic and are designated as either regenerated or synthetic. A more detailed classification of all of these fibers is presented below:

NATURAL FIBERS

Plant fibers come from the following sources:
>   *bark:* redwood, mulberry (Moraceae), and some species of fig
>   *stem* or *bast:* flax (linen), jute, hemp, ramie, milkweed, and nettles
>   *leaf:* sisal (or agave, maguey, aloe, yucca, henequen), pineapple (or piña), abaca (or Manila hemp, a species of the banana tree), New Zealand flax-bush, and palm leaves
>   *fruit:* cocoanut husks (coir fibers)
>   *seed hairs:* cotton (sea island, Egyptian, upland, peeler, Peruvian, and Asiatic), kapok, and milkweed
>   *sap:* rubber (latex)

Animal fibers come from the following sources:
>   *wool:* sheep
>   *hair:* camel, cameloids (vicuña, alpaca, llama, etc.), goats (angora, mohair, and cashmere), rabbit, horse, and other animals
>   *silk:* silkworms, moths, and spiders

Mineral fibers come from *asbestos* and *silicate* (glass or fiberglas).

Metal fibers are made from strips of *gold, silver,* and *copper.*

REGENERATED FIBERS

Cellulose regenerated fibers are rayon, acetate, etc.

Protein regenerated fibers come from the following sources:
>   *vegetable:* soybean (soylon), peanut (ardil), corn or zein (vicara)
>   *animal:* casein (aralac, etc.), gelatin, albumin, etc.

SYNTHETIC FIBERS

Nylon was one of the first successful synthetic fibers. Since 1940, research scientists have been able to produce a number of other synthetic fibers which have been well received. The synthetic fibers are organic compounds of high molecular weight and are formed by polymerization. Dacron, orlon, dynel, nylon, and other synthetic fibers are known to the public by their trade names. An accurate classification of these fibers must, however, designate their actual chemical names. The following classification, suggested by the author, divides synthetic fibers into two groups on the basis of whether they are formed by condensation or by addition reactions.

Synthetic fibers formed by *condensation* reactions are the following:
>   *polyamide:* nylon (adipic acid and hexamethylene diamine), etc.
>   *polyester:* dacron (ethylene glycol and terephthalic acid), etc.

Synthetic fibers formed by *addition* reactions are the following:

29

TEXTILE FIBERS AND YARNS AND THEIR USES

vinyl: vinyon (vinylchloride and vinyl acetate, known as vinyon H-H), darvan (vinylidene dinitrile), etc.

acrylic-vinyl: dynel (vinyl chloride and acrylonitrile, known as vinyon N), etc.

acrylic-nitrile (polyacrylonitrile): orlon, acrilon, verel, creslan, etc.

urethane (polyurethane): perlon U (hexamethylene di-isocyanate and tetramethylene glycol), etc.

2. Spinning and Related Processes

Most fibers must be spun into yarns before they are ready for weaving. Spinning includes four processes:

attenuation: the fibers are pulled out of the distaff or from a ball of roving into a strand of the desired diameter

stretching: the fibers are pulled taut while spinning

twisting: the fibers are twisted together to form single and plied yarns

winding: the finished yarn is wound onto a bobbin and secured against unraveling.

When the spindle with its whorl is used in hand spinning, it assists in the last three of these processes.

Hand spinning can be carried on with rather simple equipment. Although it is possible to spin fibers without any of the processes listed below, the ordinary procedure takes place in the following order:

Carding and Combing

In order to produce good quality yarns, cotton and woolen fibers are usually combed and carded. Combing separates the longer from the shorter fibers; the longer fibers are combed away from the shorter ones. Carding aligns or straightens the fibers, by brushing them between two cards—flat paddlelike brushes with wire bristles. (See Fig. 12.)

Distaff, Slivers, and Roving

After they are combed and carded, the fibers are called slivers. These slivers may be wrapped around the forked end of a stick or distaff (see Fig. 12), rolled into a large ball, or pulled out into a thick ropelike strand known as roving, which is either wound into a ball or coiled into a skein. When a ball of roving is used in spinning, it is generally placed in a round bowl or gourd to prevent it from rolling around at random; a skein of roving is usually placed on a skein winder. The use of the distaff and roving in spinning is discussed in the next section.

30

The Spindle and the Spindle Whorl

Although yarn can be made without the help of a spindle, a spindle with its weight or whorl considerably facilitates the spinning process. The invention of the spindle, which made possible the utilization of the softer textile fibers, can undoubtedly be considered one of the greatest inventions in the history of the world. Its actual effect on human progress is beyond all calculation.

There are various types and sizes of spindles and spindle whorls. The most commonly used hand spindle is the stick spindle, a small, smooth, thin, straight wooden stick, generally tapered at both ends; it averages 12 inches

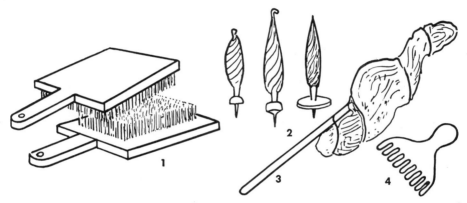

Fig. 12. Tools for Yarn Preparation. (1) Cards. (2) Spindles with spun yarn and spindle whorls. (3) Distaff with carded fibers. (4) Comb used in weaving and in separating fibers.

in length, varies in diameter according to the length, and is regularly weighted with a spindle whorl. The spindle also acts as a bobbin upon which the finished yarn is wound. (See Fig. 12.)

The spindle whorl may also vary in size and shape, but it is ordinarily a small disc-shaped object made of baked clay, wood, metal, or bone. Some spindle whorls are beautifully carved and ornamented. The whorl acts both as a weight and as a flywheel, helping to maintain the motion of the spindle. Its location on the spindle depends upon the manner in which the spindle is used: the whorl may be placed near the lower end, near the center, or near the upper end of the spindle.

Eventually the hand spindle with its whorl was replaced by the spinning wheel, which in turn was put aside when power-driven spinning machinery made spinning a factory-operated mechanical process.

THE DEVELOPMENT OF THE SPINNING PROCESSES

In early prehistoric periods, native peoples in different parts of the world devised simple ways and means of twisting fibers into yarns and cordage. Since that time improved methods have gradually been adopted by most of the civilized cultures, as indicated in the following brief history of the spinning processes.

MAKING YARN WITHOUT A SPINDLE

Undoubtedly the first spinning was done without tools; it is therefore hard to reconstruct the methods used by our primitive forefathers. We can, of course, visit remote primitive tribes of the present day and from their handiwork visualize the processes used of old; this often helps us solve such a problem.

Use of Both Hands

Early primitive peoples undoubtedly first learned to twist rough plant fibers into cordage by rolling these fibers together between the palms of both hands.

Use of Hand and Thigh

A common method of forming cordage—one still used in many parts of the world—is the hand-and-thigh method. Here the fibers are placed on the right thigh and the palm of the right hand rolls them into a yarn. A plied yarn can be made by placing two columns of fibers a few inches apart on the top of the thigh and fairly close to the knee; the palm of the right hand draws these strands toward the hip and forms two Z-spun single yarns. By quickly reversing the direction, the two strands are combined into an S-spun two-ply yarn. (Z-spun and S-spun yarns are explained on pages 41, 42.)

Pictures on Greek vases show spinners sitting on low stools and using the hand-thigh method of spinning. Greek spinners used a pottery shield or knee guard, sometimes called an onos or spinning knee and sometimes called an epinetron, to protect the thigh from abrasion during spinning. The ball of roving rested on the ground at the right side of the spinner.

The Tlingit people of the northwest coast of North America and some of the Philippine tribes still use the hand-and-thigh method of spinning.

Use of Two Men

Yarn can be formed by twisting a strand of fibers between two people.

The Whirl System

Some spinners in the Himalayan mountains form cordage by whirling around and around above their heads a ball of spun cord to which is attached a column of fibers to be spun. This is done in about the same manner as the Western cowboy whirls his lasso.

The Wimble System

The fibers to be spun are attached to a stationary pole or are held by a second person while the spinner twists them with the help of a wimble— a small bow, one end of which is attached to a handle by about 6 inches of cord. In action the wimble resembles a brace used in drilling; indeed, a brace could be substituted for a wimble.

GRASPED SPINDLES, OPERATED WITH BOTH HANDS

Some spindles are operated by twirling them between the palms of both hands. Such a method is used by the Salish Indians of western Canada. The Salish spinner sits upon the ground and holds her large spindle in front of her. This is about 2 1/2 feet long and is equipped with a 6-inch whorl. Above her head is a bar over which the roving is pulled; she spins her yarn by rolling the spindle between the palms of her hands.

SUPPORTED SPINDLES, USING ONE HAND

When the point or side of the spindle rests on or against a support and the spindle is rotated by the fingers or the palm of the right hand, it is said to be supported. When the spindle is used in this manner, the spindle whorl is usually placed near the lower end.

The Kwakiutl Indians of the west coast of British Columbia use an 18-inch spindle which has a wide, flat spindle whorl placed near its center. The spinner sits on the ground with knees drawn up and rotates the spindle between the palm of the right hand and the calf of the right leg. The spindle is held in a slightly forward position, at right angles to the lower leg.

The Navaho Indians of the southwestern part of the United States use an 18-inch spindle which has a wide flat spindle whorl placed near the lower end. The women and men spin differently. A woman rests the point of her spindle on the ground at her right side and lets the shaft rest lightly against her right thigh; she twirls the upper end of the spindle between the fingers of her right hand. (See Fig. 13.) A man places the spindle so that the shaft below the whorl is resting against his right thigh at a 45° angle; he turns it by rotating it between the palm of the right hand and the upper and outer surface of the right thigh.

33

Some of the Indian weavers of Mexico, Guatemala, and along the Amazon River in South America twirl a small light spindle in a shallow bowl or in a half-round gourd placed beside them on the ground. A little water is kept in the bottom of the bowl to moisten the fingers during spinning. (See Fig. 14.)

O'Neale (*50*) describes several methods of using supported spindles in South America. The Chimane spinner sits on the ground and holds her spindle between the big toe and the next toe of the right foot; the point of the spindle rests against a block placed in front of that foot. The Yuracare spinner places her fine spindle horizontally on a wooden block and then rolls it back and forth between the block and the palm of her right hand during spinning. O'Neale calls this last method the Bororo method, and suggests that possibly many of the ancient Peruvians may have employed their fine, beautiful spindles, hundreds of which have been excavated, in this manner.

Fig. 13. Navaho Woman Spinning. Notice loom and partially finished blanket. (Courtesy, Atkins Travel Slides, Inc.)

SUSPENDED OR DROP SPINDLES

A drop spindle is one not supported while in use; it hangs in the air at the side of or in front of the spinner, is attached to the yarn being spun, and is partially free of the spinner. The important feature of the drop spindle is that both hands of the spinner are left free to handle the yarn. This spindle is also known as the Bacairi spindle and as the Andean drop spindle (O'Neale, *50*).

The spinner usually places her distaff, ball of roving or loose ball of prepared fibers—whichever is used—at her left side, gradually pulling the fibers from this source with her left hand as they are needed. The strand of fibers being spun crosses in front of the spinner, passing from left hand to right hand and then downward, and is attached to the spindle which dangles in the air about 12 to 18 inches below the right hand. The right hand twists the yarn and controls the turning of the spindle. The spinner may sit on the ground, kneel, sit on a chair or a high stool, or stand during spinning. Any

34

position which allows the spindle to swing freely is satisfactory.

The drop spindle has been widely used and its distribution throughout the Near East and Asia indicates that the original point of diffusion may have been southeastern Asia. Murals on the walls of Egyptian tombs show ancient Egyptians using drop spindles. The Egyptian spinner placed her ball of roving in a bowl at her right side, allowing the strand of roving to cross back of her and pass over her left shoulder.

Pictures on ancient Grecian vases show women spinning by using distaffs and drop spindles. Some sit while spinning; others stand. (See Fig. 28.)

The drop spindle is still used today in many parts of Asia; it is especially popular among herders and migratory peoples, who spin yarn, but do little if any weaving. They use their yarns for cordage and for embroidering felted fabrics. Three types of drop spindles are used by these peoples, a rock spindle, a crossbar spindle, and a regular stick spindle equipped with a spindle whorl. Caravaneers and herdsmen use the first two types; the women use the

Fig. 14. Above, Spinning Methods Along the Amazon. Peruvian Indian of Iquitos spinning her yarn. Below, spinning equipment from ancient Peru. Basket, spindles, bobbins, gourd cups for spinning, and a warp chain from an ancient Peruvian burial. (Courtesy, The American Museum of Natural History.)

stick spindles. The rock spindle is simply a rock, about 3 inches in diameter, which is tied to the yarn being spun and acts as a weight; when spinning around it acts as a flywheel. As the yarn is formed, it is wound around the rock; a small wooden peg inserted into and over the yarn prevents it from unwinding. Watching a herdsman use a rock for spinning makes one wonder if this method preceded the use of the spindle. The crossbar spindle used by so many caravaneers looks like an inverted "T"; it consists of a wooden rod about 6 inches long which has a small hook at one end; the other end is wedged in a hole in the side-center of a crossbar of wood or stone. This crossbar is also about 6 inches long and has a diameter of about 1 to 1 1/2 inches. It serves as a weight, facilitates the spinning motion, and serves as a bobbin for holding the spun yarn. As the yarn is spun it is wound onto the crossbar in a figure 8 fashion; the hook at the top of the small rod prevents it from unwinding. The women prevent the spun yarn from unwinding from their stick drop spindles by looping the yarn into a half-hitch at the top of the spindle; as more yarn is spun, the half-hitch is undone and the new yarn added to the spindle.

A unique spindle whorl with four projecting arms in the form of a cross is reported from northern China. This spindle is started in its spin as any drop spindle, but is allowed to drop gradually to the ground where it continues spinning like a top.

Another unique device used by Tangut women of the Kansu province in China is an extension stick which allows for a longer length of yarn to be spun at an interval. A straight stick 3 feet long with a small hook in the upper end is placed under the belt in back. As the yarn is spun, it passes up through the hook and drops down where it is attached to the drop spindle.[3]

Various versions of the drop spindle are used by Indians of South America: the Aymara and Quechua use a plain spindle shaft, the Jivaro use a shaft with a small slit in one end, the Carib use a shaft with a hooked end, and the Apinayé use one with a flattened ball on the top end. The spindle whorl is placed near the thickened lower end of the shaft on the first three of these spindles (O'Neale, 50). At the present time, Indian women in Ecuador, Peru, and Bolivia may be seen walking along the highways and byways, spinning as they go; their distaffs can be seen under their left arms, while at the right side a spindle bobs up and down in the air.

The peasant spinners of Hungary and Brittany also use drop spindles. They sit on a chair to spin, each spinner holding her distaff, which is some-

[3] Gösta Montell, "Spinning in Central and Eastern Asia," from Vivi Sylwan, *Woolen Textiles of the Lou-lan People*, vol. VII, No. 2, Sino-Swedish Expedition Publication, No. 15, Stockholm, 1941. A report resulting from the scientific expedition to northwestern provinces of China under the leadership of Dr. Sven Hedin.

times as long as 5 feet, between her knees and letting her spindle drop to the right. Sometimes, she starts the spin of her spindle by rolling it against her right thigh.

FREE-SUSPENDED SPINDLES

A spindle which hangs or is suspended in the air and is entirely free of the body of the spinner is called a free-suspended spindle. Among the spindles used by the ancient Egyptians was one of this type. It was approximately 10 inches long and was equipped with a 3-inch spindle whorl; when in use, the spindle hung in the air beneath a forked stick through which the roving was pulled. The forked stick helped with attenuation; this is the first known use of the principle of the tension ring. The spin of the spindle was started by twirling it between the palms of the two hands; sometimes, it was only rolled between the hands and was not allowed to spin freely by itself.

In ancient times, the Chinese spun silk fibers into ply yarns by using a small spindle weight at the end of each silk filament. Several filaments were grouped together and plied by allowing the spindle weights to rotate, thus wrapping the filaments around one another. Two twining boards—paddles lined with leather—were held on either side of the hanging filaments; the spinning of the spindle weights was begun by rubbing these paddles together.

HAND-PROPELLED SPINNING WHEELS

Many textile specialists today are of the opinion that the spinning wheel was invented in India as part of the cotton complex of that area of the world. The spinning wheels used today in India are practically the same as those used during ancient times, except that the wheels today are equipped with a hand knob on one spoke of the wheel which facilitates turning the wheel. (See Fig. 15.) Some wheels today are said to be equipped with drive shafts. To use this wheel, the spinner sits on the ground and propels the wheel with one hand while attentuating and twisting the yarn with the other. The Indian spinning wheel is placed upon a T-shaped base at right angles to the ground. The spindle is at the heavy end. It is turned by a belt connected to the wheel. A belt running around the outside circumference of the wheel also passes around a horizontally placed spindle located at the narrow end of the base. The revolving wheel rotates the spindle. Similar wheels were, and are, used by the spinners of Egypt and of the Near East.

Fig. 15. Spinners of India. Notice the ground spinning wheel and the large spindle.

The spinning wheel of India was adopted by European spinners, but since the spinner in Europe usually sat upon a chair to spin, the wheel had to be raised to a' convenient level; the base was therefore set upon high leg supports. The European version of this spinning wheel became known as the Jersey wheel.

A FOOT-PROPELLED SPINNING WHEEL

Toward the last part of the Renaissance, improvements were made on the Jersey spinning wheel. First of all, a treadle was added, which greatly lessened the drudgery of spinning. The treadle was attached to an arm which,

Fig. 16. Spinning Wheel. Spinning wheel and yarn swift, Sweden. (Courtesy, Nordiska Museum, Stockholm.)

in turn, was attached to a knob on the drive wheel. In some cases the distaff was attached to the spinning wheel frame, usually at the back, but sometimes on a bar above the spindle. Eventually an automatic winding bobbin was added to the wheel. Baity (5) describes this last device somewhat as follows: In place of the regular spindle, the pulley or drive belt rotates a flyer type of spindle. This is a horseshoe-shaped piece of wood with a

THE TEXTILE ARTS

set of hooks along its inner edge; it is located at the outside end of the rod which also holds the winding spool and two pulleys, in this order. The open end of the flyer faces these items. The fiber strand passes through a hole in the back of the horseshoe curve, runs along one arm of the curve, passes through a hook or hetch at the end of that arm, and then, in the process of operation, winds on the spool. The spool with its own pulley is located between the flyer and its pulley. (The pulley of the spool turns at a different speed than that of the flyer, because the driving pulley is of a different size.) (See Fig. 16.) The revolving flyer twists the yarn at the same time that the spool winds it up. The yarn is moved from one hetch to another on the inside of the flyer to insure even winding along the spool. This new version of the Jersey wheel, with its many improvements, is now known as the Saxony wheel; it became popular in Asia, Europe, and the United States.

JENNY SPINNING DEVICES

As early as 1735, weavers began to plan faster methods of spinning. About 1763 a six-multiple spinning frame with mechanical attachments for pulling out the roving was built in England on the principle of the hand wheel. This machine was known as High's jenny. Sometime between 1767 and 1770, a spinner by the name of James Hargreaves accidently knocked over a spinning wheel and noticed that the wheel spun while the frame reclined on its side. He saw the possibility of a belt turning multiple spindles and Hargreaves' spinning jenny resulted. The first yarns spun upon Hargreaves' jenny were only strong enough to be used as weft.

THE WATER FRAME AND MULE SPINNING DEVICES

The next development came in 1769 in England, when Richard Arkwright and others invented a water-frame spinning machine which spun hundreds of spools of yarn simultaneously. Built on the principle of the Saxony wheel, the machine was operated at first by horse or mule power and later by water power. A decade later, Samuel Compton invented the hand mule, which spun a very fine yarn. This machine was named mule because it was a cross between the jenny and the water-frame processes. In 1830, Richard Roberts invented the self-acting mule, which had many advantages over the hand mule. It was operated by steam power; it also spun longer lengths of yarn, wound an increased number of spindles, automatically operated drawing rollers and rove creels, and required fewer skilled workmen for its operation. The mule did the work of 1000 hand spinners.

39

Fig. 17.   Spinning Mule. Machine-spinning method. (Photograph courtesy of
A. & M. Karagheusian, Inc., Manufacturer of Gulistan Carpets.)

FLYER, CAP, AND RING SPINNING FRAMES

The United States contributed three new devices to the repertoire of spinning methods: (1) the flyer, a U-shaped arm which rotated above and around a stationary spindle and thus wound the yarn onto it; (2) the cap, a thimble-shaped stationary spindle cover which distributed the yarn evenly along a whirling and up-and-down moving spindle; and (3) the ring frame, a disc plate which contained a ring through which the yarn passed. This ring surrounded a revolving spindle, and, by moving up and down around it, distributed the yarn evenly. This principle of the ring frame was worked out by John Sharp in 1831. Today, ring frames are used for the spinning of coarse threads and yarns, and the mule spinning process is still used for the spinning of finer threads and yarns. (See Fig. 17.)

3. Yarns and Threads

As we have already remarked, primitive man discovered thousands of years ago that bast fibers could be twisted together into firm coarse strands which, when retwisted or braided, formed ropes or cordage.

Later, when the potential value of softer textile fibers was beginning to be realized, these last fibers were twisted and retwisted into plies, or what we know as yarn. It was also soon discovered that the strength of these softer plies, or yarns, could not be fully utilized unless they were combined into a fabric by weaving or some other structuring.

Finally, after improved spinning methods were adopted, cotton, linen, and silk fibers were twisted into fine, hard yarns known as thread.

YARN SINGLES AND PLIES

After the cleaned and properly prepared fibers have been pulled into roving or have been wound onto a distaff, they are ready for spinning. From the roving or from the distaff, the spinner pulls out long thin wisps or strands of fibers and twists them into a "singles" yarn. All yarn which results from the initial twisting is known as a singles yarn, as it has a single-direction twist. The direction may be either clockwise, known as an S-twist, or counterclockwise, known as a Z-twist. These terms have been adopted by the American Society for Testing Materials.

Loosely twisted yarns, those with a twist angle of 5°, are known as soft-spun yarns; yarns twisted with an angle of about 20° are said to be medium twisted; when tightly twisted, with a twist angle of 30° to 45°, they are known as hard-spun yarns. When very tightly twisted, at an angle of about

41

65°, yarn has a tendency to crinkle and is known as crêpe-spun yarn.[4] (See Fig. 18A.)

When two or more singles are combined to form a yarn, they make a ply—two singles combine to form a two-ply yarn, etc. (See Fig. 19.) Two singles of Z-twist structure are combined by twisting them together in an

Fig. 18A. S-Spun Yarn. Left, a soft twist. Center, a medium twist. Right, a hard twist.

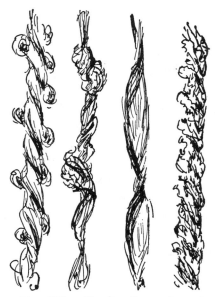

Fig. 18B. Novelty Yarns. Looped, slubbed, pulled, and crinkled yarns.

S-twist direction; similarly, two S-twisted singles are combined into a Z-twisted ply. This difference of direction in the twist of the singles and that of the combined singles or ply is necessary to keep the combined strands interlocked. This plying process can be tried out by making the twisted cord described on page 342.

Bird and Bellinger (70) use the following symbols to express the S- and Z-twists in yarns:

/ = a singles Z-spun yarn
// = two Z-spun singles, used together but not plied
\ = an S-spun singles
\\ = two S-spun singles, used together but not plied
∧ = a Z-spun, S-doubled yarn: two Z-spun singles doubled into a ply

[4] O'Neale (51) illustrates these twist-angles as taken from a book by A. F. Barker and E. Midgley, *Analysis of Woven Fabrics,* Van Nostrand, London, 1914.

V = an S-spun, Z-doubled yarn: two S-spun singles doubled into a ply

$\wedge$ = a Z-spun, S-tripled yarn: three Z-spun singles combined into a ply

N = two Z-spun, S-doubled plies retwisted into a compound ply, etc.

TYPES, SIZES, AND NAMES OF YARNS

Yarns possess various identifying characteristics. They vary according to (1) the fiber content; (2) the type of structure (see Fig. 18B), such as smooth, rough, fine, glossy, dull, slubbed, knotted, and swiveled; (3) the tightness of the twist; (4) the direction of the twist; and (5) the size of the yarn.

The size of the yarn is called its number; the larger the number, the smaller the diameter of the yarn. In this numbering system, a two-ply No. 20 (20/2) yarn is equal to a single No. 10 yarn (20 ÷ 2 = 10). The number of a yarn is set by comparing it with a length-weight standard. The standard for No. 1 cotton yarn is 840 yards to the pound; for No. 1 linen yarn it is 300 yards to a pound. Wool has no single standard; each manufacturer sets his own, and the weaver should request the manufacturer's specifications. The New England numbering system for wool is based on the number of 560-yard hanks to a pound for worsted, and of 1600-yard hanks to the pound for woolen yarns.

Several international numbering systems for wool have been suggested. The international metric system is based on the number of meters in one gram, the Grex system on the number of grams per 10,000 meters of yarn, and the Typp system on the number of thousand yards of yarn to one pound (except glass fiber yarn). The last two systems were proposed by A.S.T.M.[5]

Fig. 19. Plying Yarn. Machine method of making two-ply yarn. (Photograph courtesy of A. & M. Karagheusian, Inc., Manufacturer of Gulistan Carpets.)

The sizes and trade names of some of the best-known yarns are listed below:

Cotton Yarns

Cotton yarns are used more than any other type for hand weaving. Cotton weft yarns are usually too soft to be used as warp, but cotton warp can be

[5] American Society for Testing Materials.

used as weft.[6] Cotton warp yarns include the following types: Egyptian cotton (the best cotton)—sizes 16/3, 16/4, 24/3, etc.; Sea Island and Peeler cotton—sizes 5/2 to 30/2; mercerized cotton—sizes 16/4 to 30/2; and carpet warp—sizes 5/4 and 8/4.

Cotton sewing thread was once a three-ply yarn; now it is six-ply. A number 60 sewing thread signifies the number 60/3; this number is a carry-over of the three-ply numbering system. At the present time, a number 60 thread is actually a number 120/6 thread. Mercerized sewing thread is a three-ply yarn and about a number 50 in size.

Cotton yarns are often known by special descriptive names or by given trade names. Some of these are as follows:

GASSED. A fine mercerized yarn.
GRANDRILL. A yarn made from two colors of roving.
MERCERIZED. A yarn with luster, which has been treated with caustic soda under tension.
MOULINE. A two-ply yarn, each ply being a different color.
MULE. A loosely twisted yarn.
ONDÉ. A yarn with an uneven diameter.
PERLE. A highly mercerized, medium twisted, three- or four-ply yarn, sizes 3 to 20.
STRAND. A loosely twisted two-, three-, four-, or six-ply yarn which may or may not be mercerized.
TROSSEL. A single hard-twisted warp yarn.
WATER. A hard-twisted warp yarn.

Woolen Yarns

These come in both worsted and woolen qualities. Worsted warp yarns are made of the best quality combed or carded fibers, usually in tightly twisted plies. They are used for weaving serge, broadcloth, poplin, and twill fabrics. The name worsted comes from the town of Worsted, England, which specialized in making this type of yarn. Warp yarns of tightly twisted woolen quality are used for weaving tweeds. Both worsted and woolen warp yarns can be used for weft, but typical weft yarns cannot be used as warp, since they are often single-strand yarns and usually rather loosely twisted. Rug and carpet yarns are usually made of strong low-grade wools.

Every manufacturer has special trade names for the yarns produced by his company, some of which eventually become a standard of quality. Some yarns are named after the city where they were first made. The names of

[6] Warp yarns run the long way of the loom and of the fabric. Weft yarns are woven through and across the warp.

others are purely descriptive. Among the yarns which are especially popular with hand weavers are the following:

CHEVIOT. A long-staple, lowland, woolen yarn.
CORDONNET. A three-ply worsted and gassed yarn.
FABRI. A high-grade tightly twisted yarn.
GERMANTOWN. A soft fluffy worsted yarn.
HOMESPUN. A woolen singles yarn.
ICELAND. A loosely twisted worsted yarn.
MELANGE. A multicolored yarn.
ONDÉ. A yarn composed of a folded and hard-twisted worsted yarn.
PERLE. A two-ply hard-twisted yarn.
SHETLAND. A two-ply plain or mercerized worsted yarn.
SHODDY. A reconditioned once-used woolen yarn.
VIGOREAUX. A multicolored worsted yarn.
ZEPHYR. A three-ply slightly twisted yarn of merino wool.

Linen Yarns

These yarns are often used as warp for cotton or woolen rugs. Linen yarn can be very strong, depending upon the ply and the twist; it can also be very fine. Among the linen warp yarns are the following: *line linen*—in singles in sizes 10, 14, 18, and 20, and in plies in numbers 20/2, 30/2, 40/2, etc.; *round linen*—a hard-twisted yarn used for rug warp; and *tow linen*—used for warp for certain rug weaves. Linen weft is usually a singles yarn. It comes in fine and medium grades of line linen in sizes 10/1, 14/1, 20/1, etc. A singles tow linen or linen floss is sometimes used for weft; it is a loosely plied yarn with a flat finish.

4. Calculating Yarn Needs for Weaving

Before attempting to start a piece of weaving, it is wise to have enough yarn available to satisfactorily complete the project. Naturally, the design of the fabric must have been previously decided upon, and the texture, sizes, and colors of the yarns to be used must have been selected.

It is always wise to make a test sample if yardage is to be woven; small looms can be used for this purpose. A test sample serves several purposes. The interaction of the yarns upon one another and the total effect of their combination can be studied. The amount of shrinkage expected of the finished fabric can also be computed from a test sample—the dimensions of the sample before and after washing can be recorded and the percentage of shrinkage can be ascertained. Allowance for this shrinkage should be made when calculating the amount of yarn needed for the weaving project. Of course, not

45

all fabrics woven will be washed, but a test sample can serve as the basis of other tests.

A little experience usually enables a weaver to calculate the amount of yarn needed for a particular project. After once using a type of yarn, it is easier to estimate the coverage of that yarn; for example, an experienced weaver estimates quickly that a half-pound of woolen yarn will weave one yard of 36-inch tweed. A person less experienced in weaving may need help in figuring out the relationship between a particular type of yarn and its coverage. Sometimes the needed information can be found in weaving journals; sometimes the weaver must make his or her own calculations.

If mathematical calculations are to be undertaken, it is necessary to know the yarn number and the standard yardage to the pound. These figures have already been explained (see page 43). To calculate the weight of a particular yarn, multiply the yarn number by the standard yardage: for example, a 20/2 cotton yarn is multiplied by 840 yards, the standard for No. 1 cotton yarn. The answer is 8400 yards to the pound.

What we really need to know is the coverage of the yarn. In order to determine this, we must find the number of yarns to the inch; this is the yarn count. The number of yarns—or the number of diameters of yarn— to the inch is equal to the square root of the yards per pound, minus 10 percent for loss by friction. If we continue our calculations for 20/2 cotton, the problem would look like this:

$$\sqrt{(840 \times \tfrac{20}{2})} = 91.6$$
$$-10\% \text{ of } 91.6 = \underline{9.1}$$
$$82.5$$

However, yarns are never actually woven this close together, except perhaps in a warp-faced weave. In a 50–50 weave, for example, if a space were to be allowed between each yarn equal to the diameter of a yarn, there would result just 41 warps to the inch, or half as many as the above calculation shows. However, the space allowed for the weft is usually about 8 percent greater than the allowance made above. We could, therefore, use 40 warps of 20/2 cotton to the inch (two to a dent in a No. 20 reed) for a firm fabric, or 36 warps of this same cotton to the inch (two to a dent in a No. 18 reed) for an average hand-woven cloth.

With these problems solved, we can start to calculate the pounds of warp yarn needed. Suppose we want 10 yards of 30-inch material which has 36 warps to the inch in a No. 20/2 cotton yarn. The problem would be solved as follows: $36 \times 30 = 1080$, the number of warp threads across the fabric; $1080 \times 10 = 10,800$, the number of yards of yarn needed; $10,800 \div 8400$ (yards per pound for a No. 20/2 yarn) $= 1.29$, the number of pounds

needed without an allowance for waste. But we must allow for waste—
1 yard for up to 10 yards and 2 yards for more than 10 yards; calculated,
this would be .13 parts of a pound for 10 yards. Add this amount to 1.29
and we would have 1.42 pounds of warp needed.

Weft needs vary with different weaves. In a balanced weave (50–50),
there are as many weft as warp yarns; so the calculation would be 1.42 plus
1.29 = 2.71, the total pounds of yarn needed. However, if a colored pattern weft is to be used in addition to a tabby weft, then we could get along
if we ordered half as much tabby as we ordered warp, or 1.42 plus .65 =
2.07 pounds of yarn that must be purchased, plus about .65 pounds of colored pattern weft yarn.

5. Planning Patterns and Plotting Drafts

Designs for weaving can be secured from various sources. A pattern can
be copied directly from an attractive piece of material, selected from a weaving manual, varied from the established warp setup on the loom, or planned
and plotted by the weaver. The last method requires considerable knowledge
of weaving, but none of the methods are too difficult for the novice, providing that suitable instructions are available. All of the above methods are
described in detail on page 269. Additional information on textile designs
and their structure is to be found in the Introduction of this book. The
reader should also study the basic weaves described in Chapter VII before
selecting a design.

6. Preparation of the Warp Yarns for the Loom

A very important step prior to weaving, braiding, and mesh making is
the preparation of the warp yarns for the loom and their installation on
the working frame or loom. The warp yarns are the longitudinal yarns
through which the filler or weft yarns are interlaced in weaving. The early
weavers soon learned that it was much easier to install warp on the loom
if it had been first wound on a preliminary frame or set of pegs; the ready-
made warp could then be stretched with greater ease on the loom. (No preliminary warping is needed for modern foot-power looms. See page 212.)

Pegs have been used for warping for thousands of years. Clay and wooden
models found in ancient Egyptian tombs, *ca.* 2500 B.C., show weavers
winding their warp around three pegs placed in the wall. (See Fig. 20A.)
Warping pegs are still used by native weavers in various parts of the world.
Guatemalan women are seen sitting on the ground and winding their yarns

around pegs driven into the ground. (See Fig. 20B.) Experienced weavers still use warping pegs for preparing the short warps needed for sample making and belt weaving. Warping pegs can be installed in various types of frames. (See Fig. 21.) Warping frames are called either winding frames or warping boards. Before the invention of the sectional warp beam, now

Fig. 20A. Ancient Spinners and Weavers. A model from an Egyptian tomb showing workers spinning, warping, and weaving. (Courtesy of the Metropolitan Museum of Art.)

installed on all modern foot-power looms, warp yarns had to be prepared for the loom by first winding them upon a set of pegs.

WARPING BOARDS

Warping boards can be obtained which take care of definite lengths of warp; a typical board warps about 10 yards of yarn. Shorter lengths can be wound on the same boards which accommodate a long warp. These boards are about 6 feet long, 1 foot wide, and 1 inch thick, and contain 12 hardwood pegs about 6 inches long and 1 inch thick. The warping board can rest upon a table, but more often it is hung at a convenient height upon the wall. Some vertical warping boards are installed in movable frames. The first and last pegs of all warping boards must be removable, so that a cross, explained on page 51, can be formed in one or both ends of the warp. (See Fig. 21, No. 6.)

Various pieces of equipment can be converted into temporary warping boards. Inkle looms which are open on one side are often used for this purpose.

Fig. 20B. Guatemalan Weavers. Women in San Pedro de Aitlan preparing the warp and weaving. (Courtesy, J. L. LeGrand.)

WARPING REEL OR MILL

A warping reel is an open drumlike frame with four vertical treads which revolve around a vertical metal rod. The treads are about 4 1/2 feet long by 2 inches wide and are set 27 inches apart. The first three warping pegs are placed horizontally around the top of the reel; the last two are placed horizontally around the bottom of the reel; and all the others are placed vertically about 12 inches apart along the treads. The two warp crosses are formed on the first three and the last two pegs—the removable ones. (See Fig. 21.) One hand turns the reel while the other hand guides the yarn.

One complete turn around the reel is equal to 3 yards—27 inches between treads times four treads. The length of the warp is thus easily controlled.

49

Fig. 21. Warping Methods. (1) A warping reel. (2) Warping on pegs in the ground. (3) A warping board placed on a table. (4) A warping rack on the wall. (5) A warping rack resting on floor supports. (6) The cross and lease rods in place.

STRINGING THE WARP ON THE WARPING BOARD OR REEL

Before the yarn is strung on the warping board or reel, some preliminary planning is necessary. The type of yarn must be carefully selected—cotton and linen warp yarns are easiest to handle; the weave pattern must be chosen; the color arrangement must be decided upon; and the length and width of the warp must be known. About 1 yard for waste must be added for 10 yards of warp.

When all is ready, proceed as follows: attach the end of the warp to peg A; guide the yarn under peg B and over peg C—this forms the first cross. (The location of these pegs is illustrated in Fig. 21, No. 3.) If another cross is to be made at the other end of the warp, it is started when the yarn reaches peg D; carry it under peg D, around the back of peg E, and then over peg D as it returns toward the starting point. When it reaches peg C, it goes under it, over peg B, and around the back of peg A. Repeat this process until all the yarn is warped.

These crosses hold the yarns in their proper positions relative to each other, prevent tangling, and establish a shed at either end of the warp. Some weavers use but one cross, and others make two in case one is accidently "lost."

Some system should be devised to keep count of the warp ends as they are being strung on the warping device. Some weavers tie a colored yarn loosely around every 20 warps; others use safety pins to fasten groups of warps together.

WARPING MORE THAN ONE THREAD AT A TIME

To save time and to facilitate the handling of a long warp, two or more yarns can be carried around the warping board[7] simultaneously. When two warps are being wound at the same time, the cross is formed as for one yarn; but when four, six, or eight yarns are handled, a spool rack and a perforated paddle are needed. The yarns then pass from the spool rack (see Fig. 22, No. 1) to and through the holes of the paddle (see Fig. 22, No. 3). The paddle usually hangs in the warp midway between the spool rack and the individual doing the warping; when the pegs holding the cross are reached, the paddle is grasped in the left hand while the right forms

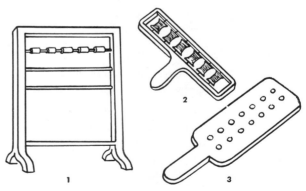

Fig. 22. Warping Aids. (1) A spool rack. (2) A spool frame. (3) A hole board.

[7] The reader should form the habit of using the Glossary at the back of this book to look up any textile terms which are not thoroughly understood.

51

the crosses in the yarns as follows. Starting with the yarns at the bottom of the paddle and working toward those at the top, the bottom yarn on the left is pulled under the forefinger and over the thumb of the right hand; the bottom yarn on the right is pulled under the thumb and over the forefinger. Working in this manner, all the yarns are crossed, and the cross is transferred directly to the warping board. Some weavers use a spool frame for putting multiple warp on the warping mechanism (see Fig. 22, No. 2).

REMOVING THE WARP FROM THE WARPING BOARD OR REEL

When the warping process is completed, the warp yarns must be carefully removed from the warping frame. First, the ends of the yarn and the cross or crosses are tied. To tie the cross, put one lease stick to the front and another to the back of the cross; tie the ends of the lease sticks together. Now remove an end peg, preferably peg E, and remove the warp from the warping board. Short warps can be folded in sheets of paper to store; long warps must be made into a chain. To make this chain, throw the warp over itself into a loop, pull it through this loop with the right hand and form it into a new loop. Continue this crocheting movement until all of the warp is chained to within a few inches of the second cross; then remove it carefully. The warp is now ready for the loom (see page 210). Specific methods for putting the warp on each type of loom are described as these different looms are considered in the following chapters.

Native peoples in various parts of the world stabilize the position of their warp yarns by using heading cords. Several methods of forming these cords are described in this book.

7. Knots Used in Weaving

The weaver has a whole array of knots which he uses to assist him in the handling of the warp yarns and in tying up the loom. Knots which are easily untied should be chosen to tie up the loom; a discussion of this subject is to be found on pages 216 and 218. On the other hand, firm, flat knots are needed to mend broken warp yarns; the weaver's knot is best to use for this purpose. Knots are never made in the weft. To join weft yarns, the end of a new strand of weft is laid in the shed so that it overlaps the end of the strand of weft formerly in use; this "joining" is made near the center of the warp. If it is found necessary to join the weft near the selvage, the end of the first weft is brought around into the next shed; sometimes it is twisted

52

THE TEXTILE ARTS

once around the outside selvage warp before being placed in the new shed, and the end of the new weft is placed so that it slightly overlaps that of the first.

Common knots used in weaving are: The *granny knot*, also known as the "common knot"; this knot is hard to untie, and is used for tying the ends of string heddles. The *square knot*, also known as the "reef" knot, consists of two double-hitch knots. This knot is quickly untied by pulling apart the two ends that are close together; it is, therefore, used for temporary knots, such as those used to join weft yarns on a shuttle. Knots in weft yarns must be un-

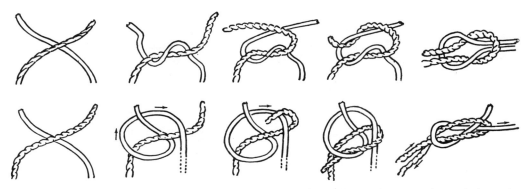

Fig. 23. Two Important Knots. The top knot is the square knot, which can be opened easily; the lower knot is the weaver's knot which forms a permanent knot. The latter is used for joining broken warp.

tied before the yarn is put into the shed. The *weaver's knot*, also known as the sailor's knot, is the most precious of the knots. It is used to join broken warp ends, because it is flat and secure. (See Fig. 23 for the last two knots.) The *half-hitch* and *hitch* are common knots; the half-hitch knot is sometimes called the buttonhole stitch. These two knots are described under "Half-Hitch Looping" and "Tatting" in Chapter VIII. A *slip knot*, also called a double-hitch knot or a lark's head knot, is used to tie string heddles to the heddle-bar of an inkle loom. (See Inkle Loom, Chapter IV.) The *snitch knot*, a slip knot combined with one half of a square knot, is used to tie up the treadles of the loom. (See Fig. 122B.) The *bow knot*, a knot which is easily untied, is employed to join the warp ends to the fly rod which is fastened to the cloth beam of the loom. The *loop knot*, a crocheted type of loop, is used to hold together temporarily the groups of warp yarns which have been threaded through the heddles and through the reeds during the threading of the loom.

53

8. Shuttles Used in Weaving

Although strands of weft yarns may be inserted into the warp on the loom either with the fingers or with a blunt sewing needle, the usual procedure is to use a bobbin or a shuttle upon which the weft yarn has been wound. Shuttles come in different sizes and types; each is best suited for a particular width of loom and a particular type of weaving. (See Fig. 24.) A description of the various types of shuttles follows.

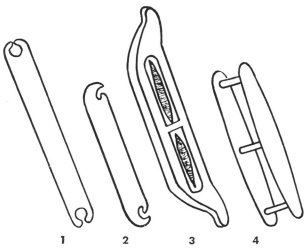

Fig. 24. Shuttles. (1) Stick shuttle. (2) Knife-edged shuttle. (3) One version of a boat shuttle. (4) A rug shuttle.

Stick Bobbins

Primitive weavers usually use a bobbin, often the one upon which the yarn was spun, as a shuttle. The stick bobbin may vary in length, but is usually the diameter and length of a standard knitting needle.

Argyle and Match-Folder Bobbins (Used as Shuttles)

For pattern work, especially when multicolored designs are inserted into a fabric being woven or knitted, tiny bobbins which hold the different colored yarns are needed. These bobbins are very useful in swivel weaving. Argyle bobbins may be purchased in any yarn shop; match-folders are, as their name suggests, simply the little folders or books that hold paper-stemmed matches.

Stick Shuttle (Shuttle)

This flat shuttle is about 20 inches long, 1 1/2 inches wide, and is really a stick which is knotched at both ends. This shuttle is used on narrow looms, such as on table and back-strap looms. The yarn is wound end over end around the shuttle. These shuttles are sometimes called poke shuttles; they are wider than the warp on the loom and are put in by hand.

Knife-Edged Shuttle

These shuttles are really stick shuttles, but they differ slightly in form. A knife-edged shuttle is usually about 10 inches long, is knotched at either end of one side, and has a smooth knifelike edge on the other side. This shuttle is used on very narrow looms, such as on inkle looms, and is especially adapted for use in warp pickup belt weaving.

Netting Needle (Shuttle)

This arrow-shaped shuttle, illustrated in Fig. 163, is used principally for constructing knotted nets.

Boat Shuttle

There are many types of boat-shaped shuttles: some are pointed at the center of both ends; some are pointed to the side of center, some have casters in the bottom; and some are shallow, while others are deep. All are provided to hold one or two bobbins. Boat shuttles are used on wide mechanical looms, such as on foot-power looms, and are designed to be thrown through and to move rapidly through the shed of the warp. (See Figs. 24, 90.)

Rug Shuttle

These are the largest of the shuttles. They are designed to hold heavy weft rug yarns. The shuttles are really long, large spools in which the top and bottom surfaces are connected with three or four 2-inch dowels. (See Fig. 24.)

Flying Shuttle

This shuttle, sometimes called a fly-shuttle, is boat-shaped and has metal tips on the points in the center of each end. It is used in connection with shuttle boxes.

CHAPTER III

Simple Looms and Their Uses

Most of the standard weaves may be woven on either simple or complex looms. Before discussing the different types of looms, it might be well to pause here and decide upon a fitting definition of loom. Sometimes a loom is defined as a frame for weaving, but more often it is defined as a frame equipped with heddle devices. While the last definition is considered more acceptable, it disqualifies many primitive looms. A simple stick loom, for example, is composed of but two sticks, between which the warp is stretched. Actually, the only real prerequisite to weaving is that the warp yarns be held in place by some type of support. A loom, then, may be considered to be any arrangement which supports the warp. In this book, therefore, all devices upon which fabrics are either woven, twined, or braided are called looms.

Native peoples in many parts of the world can be seen today weaving upon primitive looms similar to those used in very ancient times. Necessity has often forced the continuous use of this primitive equipment. Weaving on these simple looms, however, has not prevented patient native craftsmen from creating materials of rare beauty—the textiles of Guatemala are a witness to this.

In Europe, many people of rural areas, especially in northern countries, have continued to do hand weaving, sometimes on very simple looms, because they prefer the products of the hand loom to those of the machine.

The abundance of machine-woven fabrics in the United States has discouraged the use of hand looms, but recent trends indicate a renewed interest in hand-woven fabrics. By experimenting with various primitive looms, modern weavers have not only gained a better understanding of old weaving techniques, but have also acquired a keener appreciation of the accomplishments of textile artisans of the past.

1. Free-Warp Looms

Making fabric on a free-warp loom is perhaps the most primitive of all textile processes; no heddle device is used and no frame is needed. If the supports which hold up the warp can be called the frame of the free-warp loom, then it can be said that nature supplied the first loom, since ancient workers undoubtedly stretched the heading cords for their free-warp looms between two trees. These cords can, of course, be stretched between any two vertical supports, such as two poles stuck in the ground or two chair backs. Loom frames can also be constructed to take care of a free warp; two such frames are described below. (See Fig. 25.)

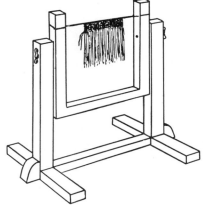

Fig. 25. A Free-Warp Loom. A special swivel support used for free-warp weaving and for braiding.

THE OJIBWAY LOOM

A very interesting handbag or shopping bag can be made in the free-warp twining technique on a simple, portable frame loom constructed for this purpose. It has become customary to call such a frame an Ojibway loom, after the Ojibway Indians, an Algonquin tribe living near the Great Lakes, who have long been skilled in using the twining technique. This simple loom is made as follows.

Two 3/4-inch dowel sticks, approximately 15 inches long, are inserted vertically and glued firmly into the broad side of a board which is about 12″ x 4″ x 2″. The distance between them is determined by the width wanted for the bag to be constructed. (See Fig. 26.) Both dowels and board should be smoothed with sandpaper.

Fig. 26. Ojibway Looms. Left, two regular Ojibway looms. Right, two box-frame looms.

WARPING THE LOOM

The warp for this loom is hung over a heading cord. This is formed by stretching a cord or several strands of yarn between and around the outside of the two dowel sticks near the top; **57** the cord does not encircle each dowel but passes around its far side. In other words, it runs continuously, in one large loop, entirely around the loom. The cord is then tightened and the two ends are tied together.

The warp yarns are all cut at the same time and the same length—about two and one-half times the length needed for the bag to be made. Cut one yarn first and test it on the loom for length. To facilitate cutting the yarns, use a cardboard template, which is cut to the right size. When the warp yarns are cut, attach them to the heading cord one at a time, starting from the left, by means of slip knots. (For an illustration of a slip knot, see the upper half of the treadle tie in Fig. 122B.) When this process is finished, the warp should hang in pairs entirely around the loom, as well as around the outside of the vertical supports.

PLANNING THE PATTERN AND TWINING IN THE WEFT

Various patterns can be made in free-warp twining (see page 64). The weft is twisted into the warp by means of the twining process described in the next section. The twining stitches pass continuously around the loom in a left-to-right direction; the loom is turned as needed. A bag made in this manner has no side seams. When it is finished and removed from the loom, it is sewed together at the bottom, on the wrong side, and lined. If desired, a zipper can be sewed across the top.

A BOX-FRAME FREE-WARP LOOM

The box-frame loom is also a bag loom, like the Ojibway. The origin of this particular loom is not known. It is really a simple open box frame, similar in shape to that of a honeycomb, held upright on a firm base or stand. Its size is determined by the size of the bag to be made. (See Fig. 26.)

The bag is twined in an upside-down position on this loom, the bottom being twined first. The warp for the bag is all cut at the same time; the warp that runs lengthwise over the top and down the sides is cut longer than the rest. The warp is put on the loom as follows. The longer lengths are put on the loom first; they are laid lengthwise on the top of the box or loom, so that they are centered and the ends hang down the full length of each side of the box frame. Thumbtacks and masking tape can be used to hold them in place. The warp yarns for the front and back of the bag are now twined one at a time, across the lengthwise yarns and at right angles to them so that half of the length of each yarn falls to the front and half to the back of the box frame. When the entire top of the frame has been covered with the twined yarns, the warp will be hanging from the top entirely around the box frame. Some weavers attach weights to the ends of this warp.

The sides and ends of the bag are now twined in as described in the next section. The weft yarn is carried entirely around the box frame, one row at a time, and is intertwined into the warp yarns. Interesting color patterns, such as stripes or checks, can be obtained by careful planning of the warp and weft yarns. When all the twining is finished, the bag is slipped from the loom, the top edge is finished by hemming or braiding, and a strip of heavy cardboard or lightweight wood, cut to fit, is slipped into the bottom. Handles of metal, wood, tortoise shell, or yarn can be attached; yarn loop handles can be covered with half-hitches.

2. Warp-Weighted Looms and Twining Techniques

A weighted warp can be used on both vertical and horizontal looms. It is generally thought that a vertical weighted warp is the older form, since early man would soon discover that twining on a vertical weighted warp is much easier than twining on a free warp, as just described.

Horizontal warp-weighted looms have been used for centuries in the Near East and North Africa. (See Fig. 104.) This is one of the table looms described in Chapter VI. An older form of inkle loom was also equipped with a weighted warp. (See the top left loom on Fig. 56.)

Vertical warp-weighted looms were used in ancient times on both the Eastern and Western Hemispheres. The looms used in pre-Dynastic Egypt, in early Greece, and in southwestern Asia seem to have been equipped with heddle rods which made possible various weaving techniques. The looms used in the Americas and in the Pacific Islands apparently lacked heddle devices; consequently the twining technique was of necessity depended upon to fill in the weft. The loom without heddles is undoubtedly the more ancient form. Both are described here.

VERTICAL WARP-WEIGHTED LOOMS WITHOUT HEDDLE DEVICES

Vertical warp-weighted looms without heddles were used in ancient times in widely separated areas. In the northwestern part of North America the Chilcat Indians, an Alaskan Tlingit tribe, still make twined woolen blankets on vertical warp-weighted looms. Using designs typical of the Indians of the Northwest, they twine weft yarns into the warp in isolated color areas, giving a pseudo-tapestry effect to their work. (See Fig. 27.) In South America the ancient Peruvians may also have used a warp-weighted or free-warp loom. Junius Bird (*11*) reported finding textiles in an excavation in northern Peru which he dated at about 2500 B.C. The majority of them were done in the twining technique. He classified them as among the earliest cotton fabrics in America. He said, "the emphasis on twining at that time suggests that heddling devices were not known in that region." Two of the twining techniques he found are illustrated on Fig. 29.

Fig. 27. Chilkat Loom. Warp-weighted loom showing a section of Chilkat twining. (Courtesy, Museum of the American Indian.)

The Maoris and other natives of the South Sea Islands have long used warp-weighted looms for twining mats, bags, and belts. The Maoris, especially, are noted for their interesting variations of the twining technique.

Small warp-weighted looms are said to have been found in the sites of ancient Swiss lake villages.

STRUCTURE OF THE LOOM

The warp-weighted loom may be identical in structure to the free-warp loom described in the preceding section, except that weights are added to the warp.

VERTICAL WARP-WEIGHTED LOOMS WITH HEDDLE DEVICES

From both legend and art we learn that vertical warp-weighted looms equipped with heddle rods were used in pre-Greek and early Greek cultures. Early Minoan and Grecian vase paintings show maidens weaving on very unusual vertical looms. (See Fig. 28.) The addition of the heddle rod to their looms made it possible to do weaving instead of twining. Weaving must have been tedious, however, since the weavers usually stood up to weave and the weft had to be pushed upward as in twining. Herodotus spoke of making cloth by "pushing the woof upwards." But even though weaving must have been difficult on these looms, elaborate patterns were apparently woven in the tapestry technique. Homer described "the Trojan wars she wove."

Fig. 28. Grecian Warp-Weighted Loom. Athenian vase painting of about 560 B.C., showing women preparing yarns, spinning, and weaving on a warp-weighted loom. (Courtesy of the Metropolitan Museum of Art.)

There is not too much evidence that this loom, with its heddle rod, was used in ancient times in other parts of the world, though it is said that the Egyptians used it at one time. In more recent times, however, it was popular in the Scandinavian countries; in fact, according to Thomson (62) the Scandinavian peoples have only recently discontinued using warp-weighted looms.

DESCRIPTION OF AN EARLY GRECIAN LOOM

The frame of the Grecian loom consisted of two vertical poles, set a little wider apart than the desired width of the fabric and connected to one another with three horizontal supports: the top castle, often very elaborately carved, the warp beam, and the brace at the bottom. The top castle often supported small upward projecting pegs, spaced about 6 inches apart, which held loose yarn, spools, and bobbins.

The warp yarns were attached to or rolled upon the horizontal warp beam at the top of the loom. The warp passed over and under a heddle sword and a heddle rod, respectively, and then fell loosely to the bottom of the loom, where it was gathered together in groups and weighted, a weight to each group.

The heddle sword and heddle rod were often attached to the top castle by cords, or they were supported by pegs projecting from the side of the loom frame. The sheds were formed by pulling the heddle sword and heddle rod forward. The weft, of course, was battened upward.

TWINING TECHNIQUES ON FREE-WARP AND WARP-WEIGHTED LOOMS

Clay impressions of twined work, found in very ancient sites in various parts of the world, indicate that twining was used for making basketry

61

long before becoming a textile technique. Likewise, according to Bennett and Bird (8), there is evidence that twining was used for fabric formation prior to the invention of weaving. Twining is, therefore, a very ancient textile art. (See Fig. 29.) It has also long been used by primitive peoples for building simple house shelters. Walls are formed by twining horizontal courses of vines or willows into perpendicular limbs or poles and this "wattle" is covered with a coating of mud, usually mixed with leaves and grass; the process is known as wattle-and-daub construction.

Described in the following paragraphs are various procedures which may be used to form a heading cord and to set up the warp for twining. Tapestrylike patterns that can be made by twining are then described in the next section.

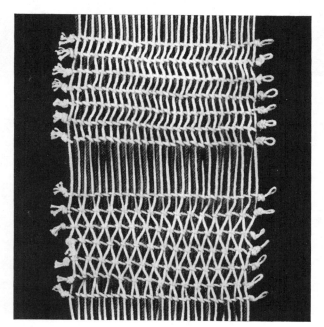

Fig. 29. Transposed Warp Twining. Two twining techniques found in an early Peruvian site. (Courtesy, Junius Bird and *American Fabrics Magazine*.)

WARPING THE LOOM FOR TWINING

After the color pattern and the length of the warp yarns have been decided upon, a heading cord —which supports the warp on the loom—is prepared. To prevent the sagging that would result when twining is made on a warp-weighted loom, the heading cord is bound temporarily to a strong horizontal rod. The manner of making the heading cord varies with different cultures, as shown by the following accounts.

The Ojibway method of warping was described at the beginning of this chapter, page 57.

The Maori Method of Warping

The Maoris use a twisted heading cord, formed of three lengths of heavy twine. These are knotted together at both ends and twisted between the thumb and forefinger of the left hand into a strand of many twists. This twisted strand is then stretched between two upright supports and tied to them.

The warp yarns are added to the twisted heading cord in this manner. Beginning at the left, open the first twist and insert two warp yarns cut a little more than twice the length needed. Open the second and third twists and insert a pair of warp yarns in each twist. Pull all these warp yarns so that half of the length is above and half below the twisted cord. From here on the warp pairs are added in an alternate fashion. Open the fourth twist, insert the ends of the upper half—that above the cord—of the *first* pair of warps and pull them down into place. Open the fifth twist and insert a new pair of warps—the fourth pair. Open the sixth twist, insert the ends of the *second* pair of warps, and pull these warps into place. Open the seventh twist and insert a new pair of warps. The system should now be apparent: the upper half of a pair of warps located three twists back alternates in the twists of the heading cord with a new pair of warps inserted near their centers.

Tongan or Pacific Island Method of Warping: Variation I

First make a braided heading cord, using several strands of yarn or cord for each strand of the three-strand braid. Stretch this heavy braid between two firm vertical supports and tie it to them. Cut the warp yarns a little more than twice the length needed. Pull these yarns, one at a time, through the loops along the bottom of the braid, letting one-half of the warp fall to the front and one-half to the back of the braid.

Variation II

This method of warping is often used by the natives of the various Pacific Islands as a base for knotted netting. The *warp yarns* are braided together to form the heading cord, as follows. Cut the warp yarns a little more than twice the length needed. Holding three of these yarns near their centers, braid them together for two or three loops. Then release one warp strand and take a new warp near its center; incorporate this into the braid for two or three turns; release it and add another warp yarn. Half the length of each warp yarn will fall from the braid at its point of entry, and the other half will fall from the braid at the point where the yarn is released. When this braided strand, with its trailing warp yarns, is completed and stretched between two vertical supports, it is ready for the insertion of the weft twining, described in the following section.

WEFT TWINING AND RELATED TECHNIQUES

Weaving and twining have one element in common: both are formed by yarns which interlace into one another at right angles. There the likeness ends. Regular weft twining has a double weft: one strand passes under and the other over the warp, crossing between each warp so that the strand which was below one warp is above the next. This continuous crossing of the weft yarns in the same direction forms a horizontal twisted weft column across the warp. This is known as the full-twist process. The weft yarns can enclose one, two, three, or four warp yarns; ordinarily they enclose pairs of warp yarns. After each row of weft twining is finished, the weft is pushed upward with the fingers or is battened upward with a comb. Bobbins, needles, hooks, and other textile tools are seldom used in twining.

Weft twining is a versatile textile medium, allowing for a variety of pattern expressions. Weft yarns can be twisted, looped into pile, braided, crocheted, or ornamented with beads, seeds, or sequins; they can be twined back and forth across limited areas in the warp to give a tapestry-like appearance; they can be twisted to give a herringbone effect. Many of these techniques which are described below[1] are also illustrated in Fig. 30.

ONE-STRAND WEFT TWINING

Type 1: The Crochet Method of Twining

In this method of twining the warp yarns are held in place by a series of crocheted weft loops made with a single yarn. A slip knot is made at one end of the weft yarn, and secured around the first pair of warp yarns. A loop of the weft is pulled through this slip knot and held below the warp yarns. Between each pair of warps, the strand of yarn is picked up and pulled through the loop above the warp; it then becomes the next loop. The weft yarn between the next pair of warp yarns is looped into it. A crochet hook can be used for this work if desired.

Type 2-A: Pseudo-Soumak Twining

The single-weft yarn passes *over* the top of a warp or pair of warps and then wraps around that warp or pair before passing onto the next warp or warps. The weft may pass over three warps and under one, or over four warps and under two, as in Soumak weaving.

Type 2-B

The weft passes *under* the warp yarns and then wraps back over and around one or more warps.

[1] The author is indebted to Mary Atwater, by personal communication, and to Albert Mohr and L. L. Sample (43), for information which finally led to the formulation of this classification.

TWO-STRAND WEFT TWINING

Type 3-A: Regular or Simple (Counterclockwise) Twining

This method is used far more than any of the others listed here. Two strands of yarn are twisted counterclockwise around one another between each warp, or more often between each pair of warp yarns. Either a weft yarn is doubled or two strands of weft are tied together, and one strand is placed above and one below the warp yarns. Between the first and second pairs of warp the weft is twisted so that the top yarn passes downward, crosses the bottom yarn, and goes under the second pair of warp yarns. The bottom weft is brought to the top and carried over the second pair of warps. The weft on the top of one pair will always go under the next pair. (See Fig. 30.) The twining is carried back and forth from right to left, working first on one side of the loom and then on the other. The weft is pushed upward into place.

Type 3-B

This is the same as 3-A, except that the yarns are carried clockwise.

Type 3-C

A row of counterclockwise

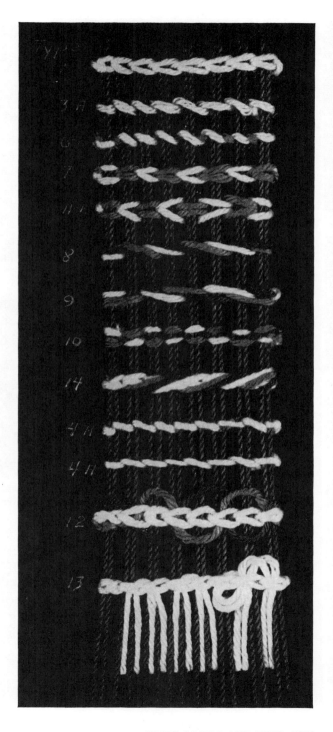

Fig. 30. Types of Weft Twining. These techniques are described in the text according to type number.

twists is combined with a row of clockwise twists to form a herringbone pattern.

Type 4-A: Open-Work Twining

The rows of weft are widely spaced; also a number of rows of weft, compactly spaced, may be alternated with areas of no weft.

Type 4-B

Sometimes areas of braided or twisted warp alternate with areas of compact weft. Both 4-A and 4-B make a lacy open fabric.

Type 5-A: Chilcat Method of Twining

A twining technique that closely resembles tapestry is made by the Alaskan Chilcat Indians. Regular simple twining is used, as in Type 3-A, but in-

Fig. 31. Taniko Twining. From New Zealand comes this interesting tapestrylike twining; the section shows the bottom edge of a tunic. (Courtesy, American Museum of Natural History.)

stead of carrying the weft entirely across the warp, it is carried back and forth in each pattern and background area. (See Fig. 27.) Between patterns, the wefts interloop, dovetail, or intermittently pass around an extra warp. Outlining each pattern is a three-strand twined border (see Type 8) which when turned vertically becomes warp twining and passes through loops of weft. (See G. T. Emmons, Am. Mus. Nat. Hist., III, Anthro. V. II, Part 4, 1907.)

Type 5-B

Similar to 5-A, except that the weft yarns of the different pattern areas meet and interlock around the same warp.

Type 6-A: The Taniko or Maori Method of Twining

One yarn is carried across the back of the warp and held in place by a second yarn carried across the front of the warp. The front yarn passes around the back yarn between each warp or pair of warps. The weft yarns must be closely set. This method produces a very firm fabric, the material often being used for upholstery purposes. Fig. 31 shows a typical design.

Type 6-B

Several colored weft yarns floated across the back of the warp are brought to the surface and used as needed to make a varicolored pattern.

Type 7: Two-Strand Crochet

This technique is accomplished in the same way as Type 1, except that two yarns of different colors are carried across the back of the warp and picked up alternately to form the surface chain loop. A two-tone chain results.

THREE-STRAND WEFT TWINING
Type 8-A: Three-Strand Diagonal Twining

In this method three weft yarns are used; each one is carried counter-clockwise under one warp, under two wefts, and then over two warps. Each weft passes beneath a different warp. The effect is similar to a twisted cord.

Type 8-B

A three-strand braid is arranged around the warp, each strand passing beneath a different warp. The effect is about the same as 8-A. It is made in about the same way, too, except that each strand passes over one weft and under the other weft, instead of under two wefts as in 8-A.

Type 9: Three-Strand Parallel Twining

Three weft yarns of different colors are used. Each weft passes over one weft, under one warp, over one weft, over two warps, under a weft, under a warp, under a weft, and then over two warps; repeat. (See Fig. 30.)

Type 10: Bird's-Eye Twining

This type of three-tone twining was originated by the author. Three weft yarns are used, all of different colors. One is carried on the back of the warp and two on the face. The bottom weft is pulled up to a loop between each pair of warps. Through this loop the two top yarns cross. All the yarns are then pulled tight again.

67

Type 10-B

This is the reverse of 10-A. Two yarns are carried under the warp and one on the face. In this case the two bottom yarns cross above the top weft between each pair of warps.

FOUR-STRAND WEFT TWINING

Type 11-A: Interlocking Four-Strand Twining

Four wefts are interlocked into a pseudo-crocheted chain, as follows. Two pairs of wefts, each pair of a different color, are tied together at one end. One pair is carried above the first pair of warps, the other is carried below this same pair of warps. Between the first and second pair of warps, the two pairs of wefts exchange positions in this way: the pair on the top is separated and the pair on the bottom is brought up between them; the two bottom wefts then pass over the top of the second pair of warps. The wefts that were on top of one pair of warps are beneath the next pair. The two weft pairs continue to exchange positions across the warp; the colors passing over the warp pairs thus alternate.

Type 11-B

The two weft pairs are twined, so that the bottom wefts separate and pass over the next pair of warps. Types 11-A and B are illustrated in Fig. 30.

ACCESSORY WEFTS USED IN WEFT TWINING

Type 12: Looped Accessory Weft

Accessory wefts can be interlooped into the regular weft to form an ornate pattern on the surface of the warp. These accessory wefts are usually pulled through loops of corcheted twining, since the crochet technique of twining makes a firmer stitch. (See Type 1.) Two accessory yarns can run parallel to the weft, one above and one below the regular weft, and cross through the weft at regular intervals, thus exchanging positions. Accessory wefts can also be laid down to form diagonal or zigzag patterns on the face of the warp.

Type 13-A: Tags, Fringe, and Looped Pile

Tags can be looped into twined stitches to form an ornamental fringe: short strands of yarn are pulled through two adjacent twining stitches, the free ends forming the fringe.

Type 13-B

In another version of 13-A a loop of yarn is pulled through one twining stitch and the ends of the loop are pulled through the next twining stitch. (See Fig. 30.)

Type 13-C

An accessory weft yarn can be looped so that a high loop is left between two twining stitches, and a close tight-fitting loop is made between the next two twining stitches.

Type 14: Raised Surface Cord

The regular weft yarn is formed into a slip knot and attached to the first pair of warp yarns. A three-tone twisted cord is then made. From accessory wefts, select three harmonious colors in a fairly heavy woolen yarn. Lay one strand of the colored wool on top of the second pair of warps and bind it to that pair with crocheted loops of the regular weft; this holds them firmly together. In like manner, lay two more strands of different colors above the next two pairs of warps and bind them. These colored yarns are laid on the warp so that the short ends are at the top and the long ends hang downward. The short ends should be turned back and locked into the preceding chain loop. (See Fig. 30.) The long ends of the colored yarns are always below the crocheted loop and the looped ends are always above.

To start the twisted cord, the first strand of colored yarn is carried over the top of the second and third colored strands—now bound to the third and fourth warp pairs, respectively; it is placed on top of the fifth pair of warp yarns, and is held in that position with a crocheted loop of the regular weft, pulled to the right tension. The second and third woolen strands are carried to the sixth and seventh warp pairs, respectively, in their turns, and are bound to these warps by the next two crocheted loops. This series of steps is repeated continuously across the warp.

WARP TREATMENTS COMBINED WITH WEFT TWINING

Warp yarns may play as dominant a part in the design of a weft-twined fabric as does the weft. They may be multicolored and form plaids and checks with the weft; they may be opened and closed to form diamond patterns; they themselves may be twined, braided, crocheted, knotted into net, or twisted into meshwork or gauze. Listed below are some of the special warp treatments which are often used to enhance a weft-twined fabric.

69

Type 15-A: Separated and Recombined Pairs of Warp

On one row, of twining, the warp yarns of each pair are separated from each other and combined with the adjacent yarn of the neighboring pair; on the next row of twining, the mates of the original pairs are reunited. (See Fig. 30, No. 4A.)

Type 15-B

The warp pairs are again split; one of the pair is moved to the left on one row of twining and to the right on the next, the other warp of the pair being left in its regular place. When all the pairs are thus treated, a herringbone or chevron pattern is made across the fabric.

Type 16-A: Two-Tone Warp Patterns

When two colors are arranged alternately in the warp, the yarns of one color may be shifted forward on one row of weft twining and backward on the next. This diagonal direction of the warp yarns again forms a herringbone or chevron pattern, this time a two-tone one. (See Fig. 29, top.)

Type 16-B

In another two-color combination, the warps of one color are separated and recombined to form diamond openings in the warp. To make the diamond shapes more pronounced, double twists of weft can be made between the warps. In both 16-A and 16-B, the warps of the second color never change positions. (See Fig. 29, bottom.)

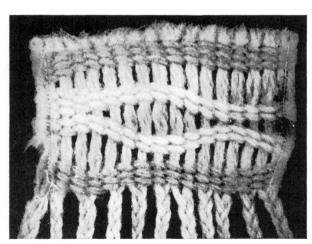

Fig. 32. Twining Treatments. The sample shows a wave pattern in the weft twining and a braided treatment of the warp.

Type 17: Accessory Warp Yarns

Extra warp yarns are carried diagonally over the surface of a weft-twined fabric and held in place by twining stitches. Various zigzag and other patterns can be added to the fabric in this way.

Type 18: Braided Warp

Strips of braided warp can be made in a weft-twined fabric to add interest. The warp yarns are grouped and braided in regular three-strand braids. (See Fig. 32.)

70

Type 19: Twisted Warp

The warp yarns are twisted in full or in half-twists around each other in the pair or around warps in neighboring pairs.

WARP TWINING AND RELATED TECHNIQUES

Warp twining is a process in which twisted warp yarns are held intact by courses of straight, regularly woven weft yarns. Pairs of warp yarns work together, twisting around one another; they thus form twisted columns in the warp of the fabric. These twisted columns not only identify warp twining, but they are also characteristic of another technique—tablet weaving, which is described in the next chapter. Warp twining and tablet weaving are both full-twist processes, since the warp yarns which form each column are completely twisted around one another.

Variation of pattern is accomplished in warp-twined fabrics by using different colored yarns or different combinations of the yarns, and by varying the direction of the twist of the warp yarns. Checks, plaids, stripes, and diamond patterns can be formed. A pseudo warp-twining technique used by the Amazon Indians to make beaded aprons is described later in this chapter, page 81.

While the author was reconstructing some ancient Peruvian textiles during the spring of 1956, she devised several new methods of warp twining. She found that two-holed cards, tubular beads, and hole-board heddles could be used to facilitate the twisting of the warp yarns. The use of these aids is described below, as well as the regular finger-weaving method of warp twining.

Type 20-A: Regular Warp Twining

The regular method of doing warp twining is a finger-weaving method. Pairs of warp yarns, usually stretched on either a horizontal or a vertical two-stick loom, are crossed by hand. The weft yarn can be carried from warp pair to warp pair as these pairs are crossed, but usually all of the pairs are crossed before the weft is put in. The weft is then carried entirely across the warp through the open shed which is formed by allowing the fingers of the left hand to remain between the warp pairs until all those on one row have been crossed. On wide fabrics it is advisable to slip a shed sword into the crosses as made. Turned on its edge, the shed sword opens the shed for the weft. This finger-weaving method of doing warp twining is described in greater detail in the next chapter, page 146. See also Fig. 33.

Fig. 33. Warp Twining. This belt pattern could have been made by finger weaving, card-heddle weaving, or with tubular beads. The design is copied from an ancient Peruvian belt. See Belt 14, page 146.

Type 21-A: Two-Holed Tablet Twining

Simple warp twining can be done with two-holed square cards, which are turned forward and backward in the warp as many times as needed, according to the requirements of the pattern. Pairs of warp yarns work together as in type 20–A. The holes are punched in the centers of opposite sides of the cards and the right-hand yarn of each pair is threaded through the top hole of each card, that is, through the A hole. (Tablet weaving is more fully described in the next chapter.)

Type 21-B

Diamond patterns can be made in warp twining by using these two-holed cards. In this case, cards which are slightly rectangular, about 1 1/4″ x 2″, are recommended. Half of each card, measuring lengthwise, should be painted or crayoned a different color from the other half. Certain cards must be twisted to the right and others to the left, and the color index quickly identifies them. The pattern illustrated in Fig. 33 can be made with these cards, providing that the yarns are arranged in the same order and are twisted in the same direction.

Type 22-A: Tubular Beads Used for Warp Twining

Tubular beads can be threaded with warp yarns in such a way that twisting the tubes forms a warp-twined fabric. Each bead controls a pair of warp yarns: one yarn enters one end, the other enters the other end, and they cross in the center of the bead. When the beads are turned, end over end, sideways, the yarns are twisted; when the beads are held up vertically, a shed is formed in the warp for the passage of the weft.

Type 22-B

Tubular beads can be used for warp-twined pattern weaving. Again, by properly arranging the warp yarns and turning the tubes to correct positions, the pattern in Fig. 33 is formed. The use of two-toned beads facilitates the work as two-toned cards do in 21-B.

Type 23-A: Warp-Twined Plaiting

The ancient Peruvians made a very intricately twined fabric which was a combination of twining and plaiting.[2] This type of work, which is also known as twined plaiting, could have been made on a frame like that sometimes used in meshwork, or it could have been made on a two-stick loom, or it is possible that bobbins similar to lace bobbins were used to make it. Some small sticks which may have served as bobbins were found by the author among the artifacts of the Columbia University 1952 Peruvian Expe-

[2] Raoul d'Harcourt (26) illustrates such a fabric on page 76 of his book.

dition. However made, the plait is dependent upon the interaction of warp yarns which work in pairs. Each time two pairs of warp yarns, going in opposite diagonal directions, cross each other, as they do in the regular plaiting process described in Chapter VIII, each pair makes a half-twist around itself and interlocks into the half-twist of the other pair.

Type 24: The Hole-Board Heddle Used for Warp Twining

The use of a hole-board heddle facilitates the process of warp twining. It stabilizes the position of the warp pairs which work together and provides one fixed shed. The use of this type of heddle is described later in this chapter, page 98.

3. Card and Frame Looms

A frame loom was probably first devised as long ago as 3500 B.C., when cotton and wool began to be used for weaving and a frame was needed to hold these fine fibers in place. Simple frame looms can be operated without heddles, the weft being interwoven into the warp with the fingers. The weft can also be darned in with a bone or tapestry needle, a cardboard needle (a strip of cardboard threaded with the weft thread), or with a long narrow bobbin stick shuttle.

Weaving on a cardboard or a box-frame loom is a slow process, but some very interesting small pieces can be made. These simple looms are often used in child recreation centers and veterans' rehabilitation hospitals. Various weaves can be made, depending on the type of loom and the kind of article to be made. Weaving done on a loom without heddles is properly classified as imitation weaving, mock weaving, darning, embroidery, or embroidery-tapestry, depending upon the resemblance of the weave to one of the known techniques.

THE CIRCULAR CARD LOOM USED IN BASKET WEAVING

STRUCTURE OF THE LOOM

The circular card loom is a circle of wood or cardboard. On it is made a circular medallion, similar in structure to the bottom weave on a basket. On the edge of a round piece of cardboard are cut an uneven number of evenly spaced notches. For a card 8 inches in diameter they are placed half an inch apart. A protractor can be used to mark off the sections of smaller or larger cards.

WARPING THE LOOM

To warp a circular card loom, the warp yarn is carried from one notch across the card to the opposite notch, from there around the back of the notch to the next adjacent notch, out of that one, and directly across the face of the card to the opposite notch. This threading is carried back and forth diagonally across the front of the card until all the notches are filled. Then the end of the yarn in the last notch is fastened to the end of the yarn of the first notch. (See Fig. 34.)

PLANNING THE DESIGN AND DIRECTIONS FOR WEAVING

This loom can be used for various types of weaving techniques, such as tapestry weaving, plain weaving, brocade weaving, and twill weaving. The pattern is planned according to the type

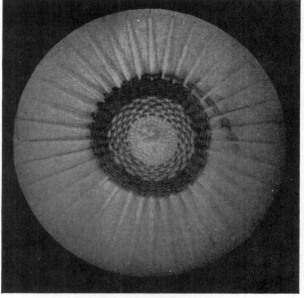

Fig. 34. Round Card Loom. Weft is put in with tapestry needle.

of weaving to be done. In plain weaving, variations of pattern are created by changing the colors of the weft yarns at intervals. (Only the weft yarns show when this weaving is finished.) In another variation, the weft yarns are carried entirely around each of the crisscross warp yarns; the warp yarns then show up as spokes or ribs. In another variation, one or two weft yarns are allowed to skip several warp yarns progressively on alternate rows of weaving; this forms a swirl-like design in the weaving.

DIRECTIONS FOR WEAVING ON A ROUND CARD LOOM

1. Use a tapestry needle for this work.
2. Weave the center first: divide the yarns which cross the center into two approximately equal parts; separate each of these again into two parts. Carry the weft yarn over and under the two parts of the top group for a distance of

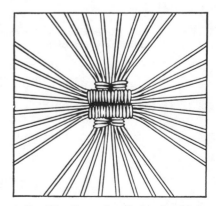

Fig. 35. Center Detail. Crossing of the yarns at the center of a round card loom.

about 1/4 to 1/3 of an inch; this binds them together. Repeat this process with the bottom group of yarns. (See Fig. 35.)

3. Using the darning technique, carry the weft yarn over and under the warp spokes continuously around the card, pushing the weft toward the center with a comb or the fingers to firm the fabric.

4. When the outside edge of the card is reached, secure the weft to one warp.

5. The round "medallion" is removed from the card by releasing the warp

Fig. 36. Hand-Woven Ensemble. The front and back of the bag are made on the round card loom; the sides of the bag and the belt are made on the inkle loom.

loops from the notches in the card. The piece can be blocked by pressing it with a damp cloth and a warm iron before or after it is taken from the card.

These medallions can be used for hot pads and ear muffs. Two medallions can be combined and made into a bag. (See Fig. 36.) Table mats for hot dishes can be made by sewing two medallions around an asbestos pad, etc.

A CARD LOOM FOR A FAN-SHAPED BAG

A very interesting fan-shaped bag can be woven on a piece of cardboard. When the size and shape of the bag are determined, an outline of it is

76

drawn on a suitable piece of cardboard. The warp yarn is then threaded on the card to conform to the pencil outline, as follows. First, the top edge of the bag is formed on both sides of the card by a continuous cord which is carried across and through the cardboard. A needle threaded with the warp yarn now loops over this cord, pierces the cardboard at a point on the bottom margin, and loops over the top cord on the other side of the card; the warp should pierce the cardboard in even segments, about 1/8 inch apart. This process is repeated until all the warp is on the card.

The weft yarn is now interwoven into the warp with the help of a tapestry needle or a strip of cardboard. (See Fig. 37.) Any plain or patterned weave can be "darned" into the warp. One side of the bag is finished before the other is started. When both sides are finished, the cardboard is removed

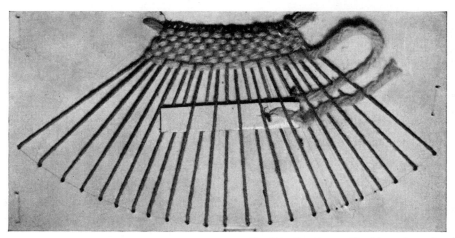

Fig. 37. Card Loom. Card loom for a fan-shaped bag.

and the side edges of the bag are sewed together. A zipper may be sewed in the top of the bag, if desired.

THE SIMPLE BOX-FRAME LOOM

Hot pads, pillow tops, knitting bags, and various small pieces of weaving can be made on a simple frame loom. This type of loom is often used for playground and recreation craft work for children.

STRUCTURE OF THE LOOM

The box-frame loom is an open rectangular or square frame of hardwood, bordered by finishing nails hammered part way into the wood, or by a row of grooves sawed at right angles to the frame. Nails and grooves can be placed all around the frame or only on the two ends. The size of the nails or the width of the grooves is determined according to the weight of the warp yarn to be used. (See Fig. 38.)

WARPING THE LOOM

The warp yarn is carried back and forth the length of the loom from nail to nail (or from groove to groove). In making the waffle mat described below, the warp yarn is also carried across the loom from nail to nail. When the yarns are carried only lengthwise, the loom can be equipped with a string heddle rod. (This is explained in the description of a strap-back loom, page 87.)

Fig. 38. Box Loom. Simple box-frame nail-head looms; the warp encircles the nails; the weft must be darned in by hand.

DIRECTIONS FOR WEAVING

Style I: Plain Weaving

The weft can be put into the warp with a tapestry needle in the simple over-and-under darning weave, or a patterned weave can be darned into it.

To prevent uneven edges, and also to give added interest to the piece woven, the weft yarns can be looped over the side nails at the end of each row. When the piece is removed from the loom at the end of the weaving, these side loops are then crocheted into one another to form a strong edge. They can also be cut to form a cut fringe or left uncut to form an uncut fringe. Machine stitching across the ends and down the sides of the finished piece will prevent fraying.

Style II: Waffle Pads or Mats

Hot pads, pillow tops, and small bags can be made on this loom with a special waffle weave technique. The yarn is carried crosswise as well as lengthwise of the frame and the "warping" is repeated in both directions until 5, 10, or 15 layers of yarn are around each nail. The thickness of the fabric will depend upon the number and size of the yarns used. For a fine fabric only a few layers of yarn are used.

After the amount of yarn needed is stretched on the frame, a tapestry needle threaded with yarn or with a firm fine cord connects and binds the intersections in the following manner: The yarn is carried parallel to the warp until an intersection is reached; it is then carried diagonally beneath the intersection and secured on the top with a half-hitch knot or blanket stitch. It is again carried under the intersection diagonally, but this time in an opposite direction to the first, and is again looped into place with a half-hitch knot. An extra slip knot, running under the two half-hitches further secures the intersection before passing on to the next intersection. When all of the intersections have been fastened, the mat is lifted off the frame.

A special pile finish can be given to the mat. After the mat is removed from the frame, cut a part of the warp layer in the center areas between the ties, on the side opposite that on which the binding work was done. These cut ends automatically bunch up and form little pompons over each intersection.

4. Bow Looms

The bow loom is a very primitive affair. There are three types: the apron, the mat, and the belt bow looms. These looms are described briefly below.

THE APRON BOW LOOM

This loom, used by the Indians in the northwest part of the Amazon basin, is very easily constructed—a young boy or girl could easily set it up. To make it, a green willow about an inch in diameter is cut and curved into a horseshoe bend. About 5 inches back from the open end, a short willow is thatched across the opening, and secured by a few shallow notches made in both willows at the points of intersection. (See Fig. 39A.) A tree-crotch loom which closely resembles an apron bow loom is shown in Fig. 65.

If at any time during weaving the warp yarns become too taut, a "release" can be improvised: a second willow is thatched across the frame, about 3 inches below the first crosspiece; a cord is then strung, in figure 8 fashion, around the two willows, and carried at intervals through the warp on the first willow; the cord is then tied to the side of the frame, and the first willow is released from the frame. By releasing the cord slightly, the tension of the warp on the first crossbar is eased. The cord, which should be long enough to allow for this release, is then tied firmly to the side of the bent willow frame.

Four methods of warping this loom are given here.

Method I

The Amazon jungle Indians make beadwork aprons upon the bow loom in the following fashion: First of all, three stout heading cords are tied across the bow, about 6 inches down from the top of the bend; the ends are left

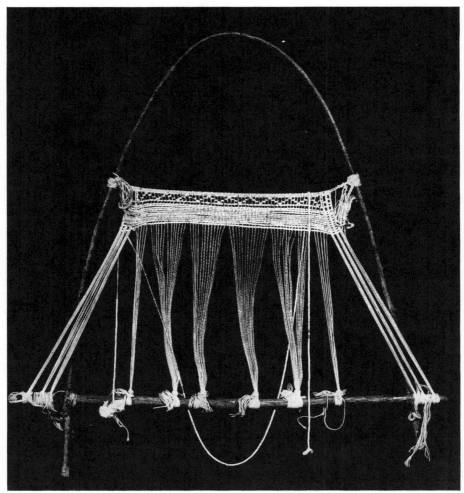

Fig. 39A. Bow Loom. Aprons are made in beadwork by the Kamarakoto Indians of Venezuela. (Courtesy, The American Museum of Natural History.)

hanging to serve as apron strings when the finished piece is taken off the loom. The warp yarns are then cut about three times the length needed. They are doubled and added one at a time to the heading cords, the doubled warp being woven into the heading cords so that the front and back strands pass over and under different cords. One-half of a doubled warp will now fall to the front and one-half to the back of these cords. These two strands are now twisted together in a series of rather small twists and tied together beneath the crossbar—the willow which crosses the open end of the bow. As many warps as are needed for the width of the article to be made are added to the loom in this way.

The weft is now strung across the warp, passing through the twists (see Fig. 39B). The Amazon Indians add the weft for their beaded aprons as follows. As the weft, threaded with beads, approaches a twisted column of the warp, the worker opens a twist and pulls the weft with its beads through, but leaves two beads imprisoned between the columns of the twisted warp. The beaded weft is carried back and forth in this way, through the twists in the warp, until the solid piece of beadwork is finished. When the fabric is finished, it has the appearance of a piece of warp twining. Other beadwork is described on p. 118.

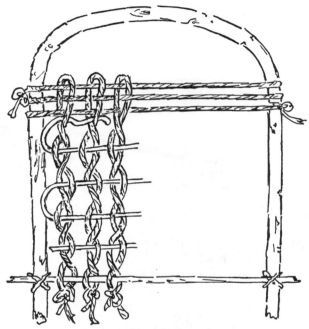

Fig. 39B. Detail Study, Showing the Twisted Warp and the Positions of the Heading Cords and the Weft.

Method II

In another method the three heading cords are braided together into a regular three-strand braid, which is tied across the bent end of the bow as above. A second identical braid is tied across the bottom crossbar on the loom and bound to it by a cord which wraps the braid to the bar, at about half-inch intervals. A continuous warp is threaded through the bottom loops of the top braid and carried through the top loops of the bottom braid. Any joints in the warp are made immediately adjacent to the braids. A tapestry needle is used to pull the warp through the braids. Plain weaving, tapestry, or other weaves can be darned into this warp. The braids form a finish to the ends of the warp.

Method III

The warp is either woven into three heading cords as in Method I, or pulled through a top braid as in Method II. It is then pulled tight and tied beneath the rod at the open end of the loom. Weaving is done as in Method II.

Method IV

In this method, a bar is thatched to the upper part of the loom, replacing the heading cords. The warp is rolled into a ball and carried over the top bar and under the bottom bar or willow. It can be used as either a continuous warp or a fixed warp. Weaving is done as in Method II above. When finished, the fabric is cut from the bars.

THE MAT BOW LOOM (NISSAN ISLAND)

The weaving area of this loom is around the center of a long narrow bow which looks exactly like the conventional bow used with arrows. In this

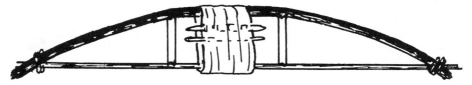

Fig. 40. Bow Loom. Nissan Island loom. After Roth (56).

case, however, the entire bow is of wood: that is, wood also replaces the thong of the regular bow. Two inner braces, one on either end, keep the two long parallel bow parts separated. A continuous warp is wound around

Fig. 41. Bow Loom. Loom used by Indians in Great Lakes area. After Roth (56).

and around the center of the bow. (See Fig. 40.) Continuous-warp looms are described later in this chapter. There are no heddles on this loom; the weft has to be put in by hand, using the darning method. Roth mentions that the Nissan Islanders use such a loom for mat making (56).

BELT BOW LOOMS

The Slave Indians weave quill belts on warp strung lengthwise on a long bow loom (see Fig. 41). This process is described in the next chapter, which is devoted to belt looms and belt weaves.

5. Back-Strap Looms

Back-strap looms were used by early peoples in various parts of the world; they were used in such widely separated areas as India, Tibet, China, Korea, Japan, the Philippine Islands, Santa Cruz Island, Peru, and Mexico. They are still used in Borneo, Indonesia, Formosa, Africa, the Philippine Islands, and by various tribes of Indians in Central and South America. Proof that the use of this type of loom has spanned many centuries is to be found in the Americas: ancient Peruvian vase paintings and Aztec pictographs show women working at the same type of back-strap loom as is used today by the Indians of Bolivia, Peru, Ecuador, Guatemala, and Mexico. (See Fig. 42.)

This loom gets its name from the strap support which passes around the back of the weaver. It is also called a body, thigh, strap, girdle-back, stick, and two-barred loom. The last two names come from the two sticks between which the warp is stretched. Other versions of the back-strap loom may be seen in Figs. 43 and 44A.

STRUCTURE OF THE LOOM

The back-strap loom is a very simple affair. It consists of six sticks, held together by the warp. They are placed in the warp in the following order, from front to back: the front cloth bar, the string heddle rod, the shed roll—also called a shed sword, the two lease sticks, which are tied together, and the back warp bar. (See Fig. 42.) In some cases of pattern weaving, pattern string heddle bars are placed in front of the regular string heddle rod.

The warp is stretched between the two end bars. The back warp bar is grooved at the ends and attached to an inverted Y support by a rope which fastens it to a tree or post. The ends of the front cloth bar are grooved and attached to the straps of the girdle, which may be of leather, of woven belting, or of metal mesh. The Ibanas of southern Borneo use a metal mesh girdle which passes around the waist of the weaver; the Indians of Guatemala use a woven girdle which passes around the hips; the Navahos use a fiber girdle which passes around the thighs.

Other loom equipment includes a secondary cloth bar, two temporary loom bars, bobbins, shuttles, picks, combs, and spathes. The secondary loom bar is placed on top of the woven cloth and above the cloth bar; as the cloth is rolled up on the cloth bar during weaving, this secondary loom bar prevents it from slipping around the cloth bar.

As the weaving proceeds and the cloth is continuously rolled upon the cloth bar, the weaver moves closer to the back loom bar.

PLANNING THE DESIGN AND WEAVING ON BACK-STRAP LOOMS

Nearly all types of weaves can be woven on back-strap looms; in fact, by substituting the expression "lift the heddle rod" for "lift the harness," the directions for the various weaves described in Chapter VII can be adapted to this loom.

The pattern weave possibilities of the back-strap loom are numerous. Upon this simple loom the Guatemalan Indians have been turning out some of the finest hand-woven fabrics on the Western Hemisphere. Some of the pattern weaves which can be made on the back-strap loom are double cloth, tapestry, inlay, leno, and gauze. (See Figs. 43, 45, 46.) All are discussed in later chapters. As described below, special string heddle rods are needed for most pattern weaves.

WARPING THE LOOM

The warp is put on a two-stick loom in several ways. The method given below is used by the Indians of Guatemala today; according to O'Neale (47), d'Harcourt (26), and Roth (56), it was also used in ancient Peru in the pre-conquest period.

The warp for a two-stick loom is usually prepared on either a warping board or around warping pegs which have been stuck in the ground. Sometimes these warping pegs also serve as the end bars of the loom, making the transfer of the warp unnecessary. Before removing the warp from the warping board or from the warping pegs, the leases or crosses must be secured with lease sticks, as described in Chapter II, page 51. A heading cord, sometimes called a loom string, is slipped into each end loop of the warp chain and tied loosely.

To put the warp on the loom, the heading cord is untied at one end of the length of warp chain, is stretched out parallel to a loom bar, and is tied to the ends of that bar. The warp yarns are now held between the heading cord and the loom bar. Another bar, a temporary loom bar, is slipped into the end loop of the warp, next to the heading cord. For convenience, the temporary and permanent loom bars can be tied together while the warp is being put on the loom. The two prongs of the Y rope support are attached to the two ends of the temporary loom bar; the rope is then tied to a tree, post, or other upright support. The warp is spread out evenly along the heading cord. The heading cord at the other end of the warp chain is attached to a loom bar, in this case the cloth bar; and the process is the same as that described above, except that the temporary loom bar is attached

Fig. 42. Back-Strap Looms. Some of the best weavers in Guatemala from the village of San Antonio Aguas Calientes. (Courtesy, United Fruit Company.)

to the girdle strap around the hips of the weaver. A few pulls backward on the warp will adjust the tension of the warp yarns.

The next step in setting up the loom is to bind the warp to the permanent loom bars. The several methods are given below.

Variation I

With the warp stretched tight in position, the front permanent loom bar —the cloth bar—is shifted to the top of the warp. If this bar has been fastened to the temporary loom bar, it must be untied at this time. A binding cord, or the end of the heading cord, if it is long enough, is fastened to one end of the cloth bar, winds through the warp at regular intervals of four to six warps and, passing over the heading cord and around the cloth bar, lashes the heading cord to that bar. When the wrapping is finished, the binding cord is pulled taut and fastened to the end of the cloth bar. A few pulls or jerks on this bar bring it to the end of the warp. The temporary loom bar is then removed, and the permanent cloth bar is attached to the girdle strap. The position of the temporary loom bars is shown in Fig. 86A.

The loom is now turned end to end and the heading cord at the opposite end of the warp is bound to its permanent loom bar—the warp bar—in the manner described above for binding the other heading cord to the cloth bar.

A similar method of warping, used on a Navaho two-stick loom, is described in Chapter V, in the discussion of tapestry.

Variation II

The binding cord picks up groups of warps from the top of the temporary bar and wraps them directly on the permanent bar.

Variation III

Two loom strings, running in alternate sheds, are bound to the permanent loom bar in the usual manner, with binding cords. Two loom strings woven into the warp in this manner are found on many ancient Peruvian looms. It is possible that extra crosses were made in the warp to take care of the sheds of these heading cords.

Variation IV

A twining process is used by the Navaho and Apache Indians to form the heading cords for the warp of their tapestry looms. (See Fig. 86.) This is described in the discussion of tapestry, in Chapter V.

Variation V

The end loom bars are wrapped with half-hitch knots made of string. The binding cord is now threaded through the eye of a tapestry needle; it whips the end loops of the warp—the ends of the warp chain—to the loops between the half-hitches.

Variation VI

Heading bars, which are small round metal bars, or heading canes, which are flat, narrow wooden spathes, are often substituted for heading cords. These can be placed in alternate sheds, as in Variation III, or they may be used singly, as in Variation I, and then bound to the loom bars with binding cords.

Variation VII

The permanent loom bars act dually as both heading canes and heading bars. They may be slipped directly into the end loops of the warp chain. A few rows of weaving, battened against these bars, hold the warp in place. This method is often used when a selvage is not needed on the ends of a piece of weaving or when a fringe is desired along the ends of a fabric.

REGULAR HEDDLE DEVICES FOR BACK-STRAP LOOMS

On back-strap looms sheds can be formed in the warp by a number of different types of heddle devices. The Indians in the region of Great Lakes use hole-and-slot heddles on their back-strap looms; those on the Yukon River use hole-board heddles. Both of these heddle devices are used on warp which has not been previously prepared on warping pegs. Since the Indians of Latin America prepare their warp on warping pegs prior to putting it on the loom, and since warp strung up in this manner is continuous and, therefore, cannot be threaded through such heddle devices as those just mentioned, other shed forming devices are obviously needed. These are described below.

The Shed Roll, the Shed Sword, and the String Heddle Rod

The sheds in the warp on back-strap looms are more often than not formed by alternately lifting a shed roll and a string heddle rod. Sometimes a shed sword is substituted for the shed roll. These two heddle devices are inserted into the front part of the warp in this manner: After the warp has been attached to the permanent loom bars as previously described, the weaver slips a shed roll in the shed behind the lease cords. In order to keep it in place, a cord is often carried across the warp and tied to each end of the shed roll; these ends are notched to prevent this cord from slipping. A shed sword is slipped into the shed in front of the lease cords. It may be temporarily tied in place; if this is done, the ties must run under the warp.

87

The lease cords are untied at this point, but are usually left slack in their respective sheds. It should be remembered that the lease cords were originally put in the warp to hold or protect the cross or crosses (see page 51). The warp must be kept taut during these operations.

The shed roll becomes part of the permanent loom equipment; when raised, it forms one of the tabby sheds. The shed sword is put in the warp to help with the installation of the second heddle device, the string heddle rod. After the string heddle rod is installed, the shed sword is removed. The string heddle rod is constructed in any of a number of ways, as described below. (See Fig. 44.)

DIRECTIONS FOR MAKING THE HEDDLES OF STRING HEDDLE RODS

Sheds are formed in the warp on back-strap looms by lifting a rod to which string loops are attached. O'Neale (46) calls these heddle devices "stick heddles with pendent loops."

The Figure 8 or Navaho Indian Method

The Navaho Indians use a simple, efficient method of preparing their string heddle rods. (It has been described by Washington Matthews [41] and again by Amsden [1].) Proceed as follows: place a ball of string in a round dish or jar on the right side of the loom; be sure there is enough string on the ball to make all the heddle loops. Open the front shed on the loom by turning the shed sword on its side; working from right to left, slip the end of the string entirely across this shed. Make a slip knot and slip it over the end of the heddle rod. (The heddle rod is usually a dowel stick; it must be somewhat wider than the width of the warp on the loom.)

Now holding the right end of the heddle rod against the left edge of the warp, push the first warp on the left, above the sword, toward the left, and pick up the string which runs through the shed. Twist the string into a loop in one complete turn clothwise and run the end of the heddle rod through this loop. (See Fig. 44A, No. 2.) Working from left to right across the loom, continue to pick up the heddle string between each warp, twist it, and loop it over the heddle rod. Tie the end of the string to the rod. A few jerks upward on the rod above a tightly stretched warp will quickly adjust the loops and make them all the same height.

Other Methods

Working from left to right, the warp yarns can also be enclosed in the string heddles by the following means:

Fig. 43. Cora Loom. A two-stick, back-strap loom with double-cloth weave, belonging to the Cora Indian culture of Mexico. (Courtesy, Museum of the American Indian.)

1. The No-Twist Method. This is the same as the Navaho method, except that the string is not twisted between warps before being placed over the heddle rod.
2. The Shuttle Method. A small shuttle, such as a tatting shuttle, can be used to carry the heddle string across the warp. Working from left to

89

right, as described above, slip this shuttle beneath each warp above the heddle sword in a reversed *right* to *left* direction. Bring the shuttle up at the back of the descending string and pass it over the rod from front to back.

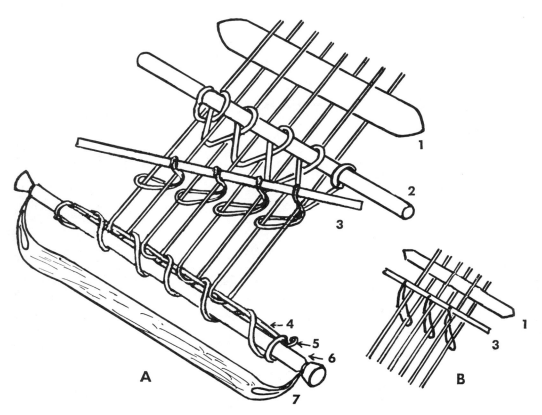

Fig. 44. Back-Strap Loom Details. A. (1) Heddle sword or shed roll. (2) String heddle rod. (3) Leno heddles (after O'Neale [47]). (4) Heading cord. (5) Wrapping or binding cord. (6) Breast beam. (7) Back-strap girdle. The loom is set up for gauze weaving if the heddle sword and the leno heddles are allowed to form alternate sheds. If the string heddle rod and the leno heddle rod alternate in weaving, leno weaving is formed. B. On the small section displayed, only leno weaving could be done.

3. The Double-Hitch Method. This is the method used for making the string heddles for Oriental knot rug looms. All of the heddle strings are cut about three times the length needed. Each string encircles a warp and is tied in a knot, using a template if necessary. A double-hitch knot (see Fig. 122B) made at the knotted end of the string is slipped over the rod.

4. The Sewing Method. The heddle rod is wrapped with half-hitch knots. A tapestry needle threaded with the heddle string is looped under a warp and through a loop of a half-hitch knot.

Some weavers like to loop a number of heddle strings over the forefinger of the left hand and to transfer these loops at intervals to the rod.

SPECIAL HEDDLE DEVICES FOR PATTERN WEAVING

For certain pattern weaves, a native weaver may use small sticks, called brocade sticks or warplifters, to pick up particular warp yarns. When the sticks are raised, with their respective warp yarns, they form pattern sheds in the warp. They can therefore be called special heddle devices. For some weaves, such as inlay, double cloth, and swivel weaving, special string heddle rods, placed in front of the regular string heddle rods, are used to form the needed pattern sheds. (See Fig. 43.)

Fig. 45. Gauze and Swivel Weaves. From Guatemala come lovely weaves as the combination pictured; the cloth, woven in Coban, was made on such a loom as pictured in Fig. 44A.

Both of these string heddle rods may be made in the same manner, except that the string loops on the special string heddle rods must be much longer, to allow the regular or tabby sheds to form through them. Ordinarily, groups of three or four warp yarns are carried through these large string heddles. If the pattern calls for two such special string heddle rods, alternate groups of three or four warp yarns are carried through the heddles on the alternate pattern harnesses.

Other methods of making pattern heddles for inlay weaving are described in Chapter VII, where inlay pattern weaving is discussed.

For gauze and leno weaving, the string heddles enclose the warp yarns on the loom in a special manner: the loops of the string heddles must pass below one warp and enclose the next warp. (See Fig. 44.) When the string heddle rod is raised, the enclosed warps are pulled under the free warps and raised to form the shed. Directions for making these half-twist weaves are

91

Fig. 46. Some Two-Stick Loom Weaves. Left, Guatemalan loom with inlay brocade weave. Center, tiny Navaho loom with tapestry weave. Right, modern adaptation with a modern tapestry.

given in Chapter VII, where leno and gauze weaves are discussed. Note the beautiful gauze weaves in Fig. 45.

6. Continuous-Warp Looms

Looms of the continuous-warp type were widely used in ancient times and are still very popular today. In Borneo, weavers use a continuous warp on their back-strap looms, though usually such a warp is hard to handle unless set up on a rigid frame loom. In Iquitos, Peru, Indian girls can be seen weaving fiber rugs on large vertical looms strung with continuous warp. In Ecuador, serapes are woven on horizontal continuous-warp looms stretched between ground stakes. (See Fig. 47.) On Nissan Island a continuous warp is used on the bow type of loom discussed earlier. The Navahos use a continuous warp on their belt looms. (See Fig. 65.) The continuous-warp loom is also called a tubular loom. A continuous warp is also called a ring warp.

STRUCTURE OF THE LOOM

Many different types of looms can be equipped with a continuous warp. Usually, looms used for this type of weaving are of the two-stick variety. Since the continuous warp runs around the outside of the two end bars or beams on the loom, some provision must be made to take care of the adjustment of the warp tension. Ordinarily, the bottom bar is made adjustable on a vertical loom, and the front bar on a horizontal loom. An adjustable bottom bar was described in connection with the apron bow loom, in this chapter; an adjustable top bar is described in the discussion of Navaho looms under tapestry in Chapter V.

The heddles are arranged and the sheds formed on a continuous-warp loom in the same manner as on strap-back, fixed-heddle, and trapestry looms.

92

PLANNING THE DESIGN

If the design is to be executed in plain weaving, the fabric is usually warp-faced. Methods of planning and weaving this type of design are discussed under inkle looms on pages 101–107.

WARPING THE LOOM

Method I

The warp yarns are carried around the loom to the outside of the cloth and warp beams, but not attached to either end beam. If a warp-stripe fab-

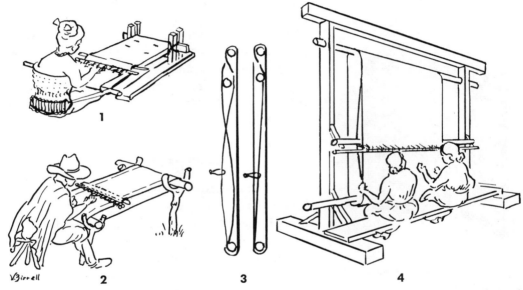

Fig. 47. Various Uses of a Ring Warp. A ring or continuous warp may be used on any type of loom. (1) Back-strap, continuous warp of the Ibans (Sea Dayaks) of southern Borneo (after a drawing by Hose and McDougall, 1912). (2) Ecuadorian weaver. (3) Shed formation of a ring warp. (4) A loom upon which fiber rugs are woven, from Iquitos, on the Amazon, Peru.

ric is planned, the different colored warp yarns must be joined or tied together across one horizontal strip of the warp, usually just in front of the front or cloth bar. This places all the knots across the same level of the warp, and the row of knots can then easily be cut off when the weaving is finished.

Whether the warp is strung directly on the loom or is arranged first upon a warping board, a cross must be provided in the warp, as described earlier. The heddles are formed as for the back-strap loom.

93

Method II

On many primitive continuous-warp looms, the warp is made continuous by a very ingenious device. When warping for this particular setup, pegs A and E on the warping board are one and the same. The warp yarn is carried around the A-E peg at both ends of each circuit on the warping board, reversing its path each time it reaches this peg. When the warping is complete, the peg is removed intact with the warp in place. Before removing the peg, however, the warp must be fixed: cords are carried through the sheds on either side of this peg and tied to the ends of the peg; other cords are carried over and under the warp and tied to either end of the peg. The warp is slipped over the two end beams on the loom with this A-E

Fig. 48. Swedish Heddle. An old Swedish hole-and-slot heddle. (Courtesy, Nordiska Museum, Stockholm.)

peg tied firmly in place. After the weaving is finished, the peg is slipped out of the warp, leaving a looped fringe at either end of the warp. This fringe should be stabilized by a row of hand sewing or by some other means. A number of Indian tribes on the Western Hemisphere use this system of warping.

7. Hole-and-Slot Heddle Looms

Also known as single-heddle harness looms, the hole-and-slot heddle looms have been called various other names: the Bronze Age loom, the hole-board loom, the T.D. (tongue depressor) loom, the Potawatami loom, the Zuni loom, the Balinese loom, the modern Peruvian craft loom, the European peasant loom, etc. Actually, there is no such thing as a "single-heddle harness loom," since a single-heddle harness can be installed on any type of loom. Certain primitive looms, however, are distinguished by this special type of heddle harness.

This loom was used anciently in both the Old and the New Worlds. It was known in India and on the island of Bali. According to Henschen (135), this type of loom is still used in northern Europe and in parts of Norway and Iceland. Some beautiful hole-and-slot heddles are still to be found among the weavers of India, Austria, Germany, Norway, and Finland. (See Fig. 48.)

Before North America was settled by the white man, the Zuni Indians were using a primitive loom with a single harness. The Potawatami Indians have been using such a loom for many years. (See Fig. 49.) Recently, the

94

loom has been "modernized" into two new forms: the T.D., or simple tongue-depressor loom, used in craft classes, and the Peruvian craft loom used in Peru to help revive an ·interest in weaving among the people.

STRUCTURE OF THE LOOM

The harness frame on a single-heddle harness loom is so constructed that alternate warps pass through the heddle eyelets and the slots between these eyelets. Although this arrangement limits the loom as to number of possible sheds—only two are possible—pick-up pattern weaves can be made by making additional sheds with the fingers or with pick-up sticks. The single-heddle frame can be equipped with heddles made of string, heavy wire, hard-wood strips, solid aluminum, or steel—regular commercial steel heddles can be slipped onto the single frame.

VARIANTS OF THE HOLE-AND-SLOT HEDDLE LOOM

The Zuni Loom

The heddles on the single-heddle harness of the Zuni loom are made of fine hard wooden strips, thorn spines, or drilled bird bones.

The T.D. or Tongue-Depressor Loom

A loom was devised some years ago by Sarah Patrick of Columbia University which had a hole-and-slot heddle made out of tongue depressors. A hole was burned or drilled in tongue depressors which were then stapled together, allowing a suitable space between each. (See Fig. 50.)

Old World Hole-and-Slot Loom

A solid hole-and-slot heddle harness, used in many areas of the Old World, is made from a thin piece of hard wood and is often crowned with a carved crest. (See Figs. 48, 51.)

Fig. 49. Hole-and-Slot Loom. Potawatami Indian weaving on a back-strap loom equipped with a hole-and-slot heddle harness.

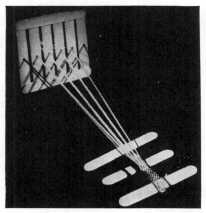

Fig. 50. T.D. Heddle. A T.D. (tongue-depressor) heddle for a loom.

Fig. 51. European Heddle. European hole-and-slot heddle.

The Peruvian Hole-and-Slot Loom

A loom is used in Peru which combines some of the principles of the foot-power loom with those of a hole-and-slot loom. The loom frame is

the height of a table, has a cloth beam and a warp beam, and is approximately 36 inches wide. The loom is equipped with a hole-and-slot heddle harness made of aluminum. The heddle frame must be raised by hand, since there are no foot treadles. Special supports on the sides of the loom frame hold the harness in the up position. (See Fig. 52.) The hole-and-slot harness could be automatically lifted and lowered on a foot-power loom equipped with one foot treadle.

The Swivel Slotted Heddle-Bar Loom

In parts of Europe and Asia, a round bar, known as a Ghandi web roller, which has alternately placed front and back notches, is used as the heddle for warp which is stretched along a board. (See Fig. 53.)

Fig. 52. *Above:* Peruvian Single-Heddle Harness Loom. The Peruvian weaver is using a loom with only one harness. *Below:* Detail of Peruvian Heddle. Detail of the heddle harness above; made of aluminum, encased in wooden frame.

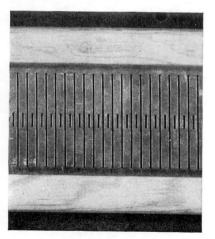

WARPING THE LOOM

The instructions below are for setting up a simple back-strap loom equipped with a hole-and-slot or a T.D. heddle harness.

The warp yarns are all cut at the same time, about 10 inches longer than the needed length. They are tied, one at a time, across a bar or dowel stick in the color arrangement desired. Working from left to right, the warp is now threaded alternately through the holes and slots of the harness; it can be threaded in pairs for a more solid fabric. The front bar of the loom, to which the yarns are tied, is now attached to a support, and the yarns are pulled through the heddle to an even tension. They are then pulled straight and tight and knotted together at the far end. If the warp is wide there may have to be several groups of these knots. Finally, a cord is tied around the warp in front of the knot; the warp is pulled taut, and the cord is fastened to a vertical support. The warp is now ready for weaving.

1. Before beginning to weave, attach a cord to the bar or cloth bar; carry it around the back of your waist, and attach it to the other end of the cloth bar. The bar should be notched to hold these girdle cords. The other end of the warp is attached to a vertical support.

2. Wind the weft yarn onto a shuttle stick which is wider than the warp.

3. Plain weaving or twill can be woven successfully on this warp. If any pick-up designs are to be made, a pick-up stick which is longer than the warp will be needed.

4. It is advisable to use a temple to keep the warp even during weaving.

5. Batten the warp with a spathe before and after each change of shed.

6. If a fringe is desired, insert a cardboard strip into the warp before starting to weave. After the weaving is finished, remove the cardboard; make a row of stitching along the top of the fringe to keep the fabric firm.

Fig. 53. Alternating Slot Heddle. A European version of the single heddle. (Courtesy, Rozina Skidmore.)

8. Fixed-Heddle Looms

Many natives in Africa and Madagascar weave on looms equipped with one set of permanently raised heddles. The heddle supports on these particular looms are similar in form to those used by the ancient Egyptians on their horizontal looms, except that their string heddle rod was only partly fixed; on alternate sheds, it could be lifted off the V-notched wooden supports and rested on the side bars of the loom. (See Fig. 54A.) Roth (56) illustrates the first three looms listed below.

There are a number of types of fixed-heddle looms, among them the following:

1. The Madagascar Loom. This fixed-heddle loom is structured much like the Egyptian loom described above (see Fig. 54B).

97

2. The A-Fipa Loom. The heddle strings of this loom are 2 or 3 feet long and are attached or fixed to the top superstructure of the loom.
3. The Nyasaland Loom. The fixed heddles on this loom are attached to a horizontal rod which is attached to ground stakes.
4. The Inkle Loom. These looms are discussed at the beginning of the next chapter.
5. The Hole-Board Heddle Loom. This loom is discussed in the next section of this chapter.

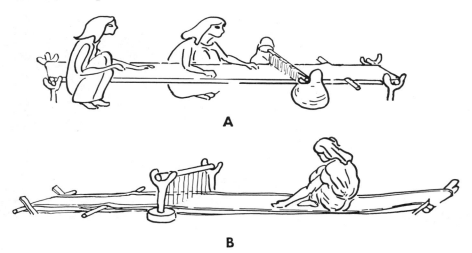

Fig. 54. Fixed-Heddle Looms. A. Sketch of early Egyptian weavers using a loom with a fixed heddle. B. Madagascar loom with what appears to be a fixed heddle. After Roth (56).

STRUCTURE OF THE LOOM

A fixed-heddle harness can be installed on any type of loom. It can be stationary, or it can be attached to a movable trestle which is pushed along the warp as the weaving proceeds.

In order to take care of the alternate sheds on the first three looms listed above, a shed roll or a wide spathe is placed behind the fixed heddles. No such arrangement is necessary on looms constructed on the principle of the inkle loom. On the hole-board heddle loom, a string heddle rod is placed in front of the fixed heddle to take care of the alternate shed. String heddle rods were explained earlier in this chapter; see page 90.

9. Hole-Board Heddle Looms

The Loucheux Indians, living on the Yukon River in Alaska, use a loom equipped with a hole-board heddle harness. This solid harness is unique in that it forms in the warp a permanently opened fixed shed (see Fig. 55).[3] The hole-board heddle is, therefore, classed as a fixed heddle.

STRUCTURE OF THE LOOM

A hole-board heddle can be used on many types of looms, but more often than not it is used on a simple loom such as a back-strap loom.

A hole-board heddle is made out of one solid piece of cardboard or plywood, usually about 15″ x 3″ x 1/4″ in size. It is perforated with two rows of holes, arranged so that pairs of holes are opposite each other. The rows are set about 1 inch apart, and

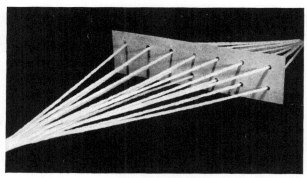

Fig. 55. Hole-Board Heddle. This heddle is used by the Indians on the Yukon River in Alaska. Only one shed can be formed with this heddle; the other must be picked up by hand.

the holes in each row about 1/4 inch apart. As many pairs of holes are needed as there are pairs of warp yarns on the loom.

Only one shed can be formed on a loom equipped with a hole-board heddle. The other shed must either be picked up by hand or formed by a string heddle rod installed in front of the hole-board heddle. The string heddle rod was described earlier.

DIRECTIONS FOR WARPING

The hole-board heddle is threaded as follows. Warp yarns are arranged in pairs, according to a planned color pattern. They are tied to a rod in the order arranged, and threaded in this same order through the holes in the hole-board heddle. One yarn is threaded through each hole; each pair of yarns are so threaded that they occupy opposite pairs of holes. (See Fig. 55.) When this procedure is finished, the tension is evened by pulling the yarns tight, and a knot is tied in the far end of the warp.

DIRECTIONS FOR WEAVING

Warp twining can be done on a loom which has no other heddle harness than the hole-board heddle described above, the alternate shed being picked up by hand. A belt made by warp twining is described in the next chapter, Belt 14, page 146.

If the loom is equipped with one or more string heddle rods installed in front of the hole-board heddle, most of the known weaves can be undertaken.

[3] Such a loom is on exhibit in The American Museum of Natural History, New York.

IV

Belt Looms and Belt Weaves

Prehistoric peoples found many uses for narrow strips of woven material. From them they made such things as tump-lines,[1] head bands, bag handles, straps, and belts. They frequently stitched together strips of woven belting to make underarm bags for holding quivers, coca, seeds, and sling stones.

Belt weaving has often been the means of preserving some of the ancient stylized designs of a people, since it sometimes remains as the sole remnant of the weaving expression of a native group. Such a condition exists in Ecuador.

Practically any loom can be employed for the weaving of belts. Many of the native Indian peoples of America still use the simple back-strap loom for their belt weaving. Some looms are, however, specially constructed for belt making, including the bow, inkle, and tablet looms.

Nearly all fabric weaves can be converted into belt weaves. In addition to this, some processes, such as tablet weaving and warp-faced pick-up pattern weaving, are especially adapted to belt weaving. Belts can also be made by processes other than weaving; many belts are made by braiding, meshwork, and knot work. These techniques are discussed on pages 278–325.

Anyone taking up weaving for the first time will find that belt weaving offers the greatest possible variety of experience.[2] Furthermore, the beginner can quickly see the results of his work and thus gains encouragement and

---

[1] A tump-line is a burden bearer's cord, used by the Indians of America, to support a burden carried on the back. The tump-line partially encloses the burden and passes around the forehead of the carrier.

[2] When belt making is taken up as a class project, a different belt weave should be selected by each student. This procedure will give the class a good overall view of the various weaves.

self-confidence. Since belt weaving offers great opportunities for creative design, even experienced weavers find this type of work very challenging. Some of the finest of the belt weaves are described in this chapter, with simple step-by-step instructions to help the novice and the expert alike.

1. Inkle Looms

The exact origin of the inkle loom is unknown. It is possible that this fixed-heddle continuous-warp loom may have evolved from a similar loom, such as the Madagascar loom described on page 97, which also has fixed heddles and a continuous warp. Inkle looms have been used in England and Scotland for approximately 300 years. Since woven belts were often called "inkles" (29) by the early American colonists, inkle looms may also have been used in America in the Colonial period.

The inkle loom is very simple; it is easy to set up and to weave on. For these reasons, weaving on inkle looms is now being used extensively for rehabilitation work in veterans' hospitals and for art-craft work in recreational programs. Inkle looms are frequently used in school to initiate students into weaving processes.

STRUCTURE OF THE LOOM

The inkle loom is usually used for belt weaving, but some versions of it are made to take care of the weaving of wider fabrics. The Jones loom is such a one.[3] The finest inkle belt loom on the market at the present time is the Gilmore inkle loom.[4] Fig. 56 illustrates all these looms. A description of a simple inkle loom which may be made at home is given below. This loom can either rest on a table during weaving, or it can be held between the knees of the weaver, with the feet resting upon the crossbar at the back of the loom.

This loom can be made any desirable length, but 40 inches is generally found to be the most satisfactory. Other dimensions are as follows: the height of upright arms is 9 inches; distance between front of loom and first upright arm is 12 inches; distance between the two upright arms is 8 inches; distance between the centers of the two pegs on each upright arm is 6 1/2 inches. The spaces between the holes along the bottom of the loom are about 1/2 inch.

Heddles are made by tying loops of string around a cardboard template; each loop is tied and cut separately. Although they are usually cut 5 1/2

---

[3] This loom was built by Hannah Jones, Langley, Washington.
[4] The Gilmore loom is manufactured by Mr. E. E. Gilmore, Stockton, California.

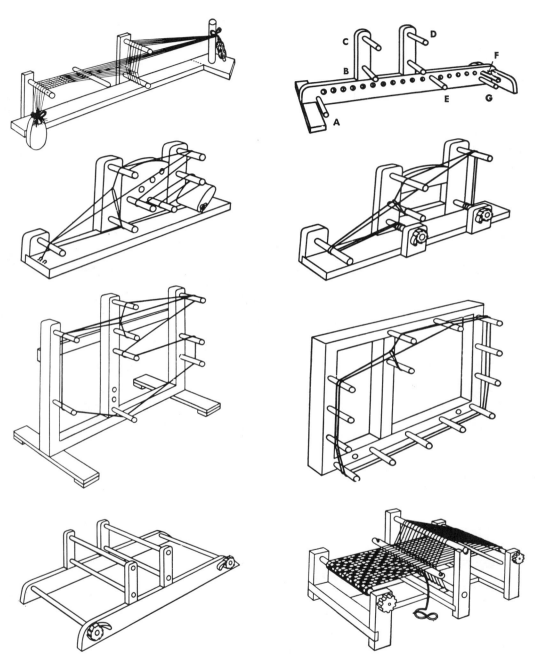

Fig. 56. Inkle Looms. Various types of inkle looms. These are fixed-heddle looms. Gilmore loom, second from top on left. Birrell loom, bottom left. Jones loom, bottom right.

inches long, their length will differ slightly for different inkle looms. Since half of the warp yarns are carried through the heddle loops and half through the slots, only half as many heddles are needed as there are warp yarns. (The spaces between the string heddle loops are called slots.) The string

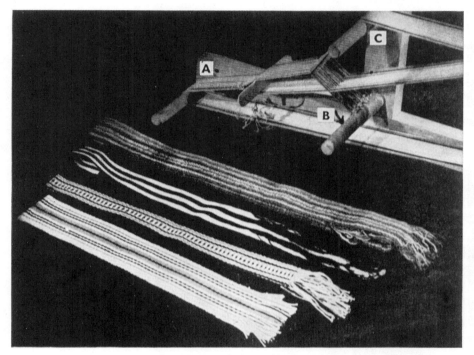

Fig. 57. Detail of an Inkle Loom. Close-up showing the fixed heddle in operation. Inkle belts are upon the table.

heddles are attached to the loom rod "B" by means of slip knots, keeping the knots of the heddle loops as close to the bar as possible. (See Fig. 56.)

PLANNING THE DESIGN

The pattern of an inkle belt is formed in the warp; that is, the surface of the fabric is formed by the warp yarns, the weft showing only at the selvage. Weaving made on the inkle loom is thus said to be warp-faced. An exception to this is described in 4, below. To determine the number of yarns needed to make an inkle belt of a given width, compare the size of the yarn selected with that of carpet warp: 110 strands of carpet warp make a belt about 2 inches wide.

Pattern possibilities for inkle weaves are almost unlimited. Some interesting design variations are listed below. (See Figs. 57 and 59.)

Fig. 58. Simple Pick-Up Weaving, Made on the Inkle Loom. There are two colors in the warp which alternate in positions.

1. Chain Designs

Single and double chain designs can be planned by special arrangement of the warp yarns. For a single chain, combine three warp yarns of the same color on a background of a contrasting color. For a double chain, divide two pairs of warp yarns of the same color by a yarn of a contrasting color: for example, arrange two black, one yellow, and two black yarns on a background of light blue. The yarn which separates the pairs may or may not be the same color as the background.

2. Stripe Designs

The warp can be, and often is, arranged in stripes. For vertical stripes, four or more yarns of the same color are arranged next to one another in the warp. For horizontal stripes, yarns of two contrasting colors alternate as warp, the yarns of one color being threaded through all the heddle loops, and those of the other color carried through all the slots. When warping the loom for such a pattern, the colored yarns do not need to be cut and knotted together at the end of each circuit; small balls of each color can be carried alternately around the loom, and thus used continuously for the entire warp.

3. Warp-Faced Pick-Up Designs

Many interesting warp pick-up designs can be made on the inkle loom. Some require a special threading of the warp, as in belt designs 8 and 10, pages 134 and 140. Others are made by placing light-colored warp through all heddle loops and dark-colored warp through all of the slots, as in Belt 7, page 134. The design is formed by picking up the dark warp and holding it above the light warp. (See Figs. 58 and 73.) Given below is a suggested threading plan for a design of this type.

4. Brocade Weaving

During the weaving process, brocade weft patterns can be set into an otherwise warp-faced inkle belt weave. To do this, colored weft is carried

104

above a group of lowered warp yarns. Belt 1-A, described on page 125, is such a belt.

5. Combined Pattern Techniques

Several of the above design methods can be combined into one belt. For example, warp can be set up so that a border of horizontal stripes is made on either side of a central area containing two lengthwise chain patterns.

SUGGESTED PATTERN FOR AN INKLE BELT

One inkle belt design is described here in detail to make clear the process of planning a pattern. This belt has a yellow border on each side, in the

Fig. 59. Inkle Belts. Three simple chains run along the belt on the left.

center of which a single black chain runs lengthwise. Between these borders, horizontal stripes of the black (B) and yellow (Y) form the center panel. To obtain this effect the warp yarns are put on the loom in this order:

Y.Y.Y.Y.Y.B.B.B.Y.Y.Y.Y.Y.B.Y.

The last B.Y. unit is repeated 18 times. This carries the warp to the center of the belt, or half of its width; for the other half, the warp yarns are placed on the loom in the reverse order. A belt—or any other strip of weaving, for that matter—has a better color balance when the center area is wider than the border area. Symmetrical designs need not be used, however. The above threading may be woven in a plain weave or may be picked up as described in 3, above. If a pick-up pattern is to be woven, an odd number of the black-yellow (B.Y.) units must be provided; for example, there should be 35, 37, or any odd number of units.

WARPING THE LOOM

Although inkle looms may differ in certain structural details, the warping process is about the same for all looms equipped with a continuous or ring warp. To keep all the knots in the same area so that they can be cut off together when the weaving is finished, the yarns of different colors are joined to the front of the front bar A. (See Fig. 57.) All warp yarns pass alternately through the heddle loops and the slots, unless the pattern calls for some other arrangement. (See Fig. 56, top, right.) The regular process of warping a simple inkle loom is as follows:

1. Tie the first warp yarn temporarily to the front bar A. Before beginning to weave, it must be untied from this bar and tied to the next adjacent warp yarn so that all of the warp can be easily rotated around the loom as weaving progresses.

2. Decide on the length of belt desired. Carry the warp yarns around the loom and over the pegs by whatever path is necessary to insure the proper length, allowing for 8 inches of waste. The adjustable peg must be used to control the warp tension during weaving—the warp must pass partially around it.

3. If the same color is used for all of the warp, a small ball of the yarn is carried continuously around the loom and through the heddles during warping.

4. Put the warp on the loom to form two alternate sheds: carry the first yarn and all odd-numbered yarns from bar A under bar C, over bar D, over the adjustable bar E, and back to the front bar A. Carry the second yarn and all even-numbered yarns from bar A through a heddle loop, over bar C, over bar D, over the adjustable bar, and back to the starting point, bar A. Continue this alternate threading until all the warp is on the loom, putting the yarn first through a slot and under bar C, and then through a heddle and over bar C. (Bars F and G can be used if an extra long strip of weaving is desired. In this case, the warp yarns are carried from bar D to F then to E, back to G, and finally back to A.)

5. Refer to a pattern plan, a pattern draft, or a sample belt constantly during warping.

6. When the necessary warp is on the loom, tie the last warp to the immediately preceding one, just in front of bar A.

7. Warp is put on a wide inkle loom—one equipped with a warp beam—in about the same manner as it is put on a table-model or a foot-power loom so equipped. The warp is rolled onto the warp beam, carried over the D and C bars from back to front, threaded through the heddles on the loom from the back, and is finally attached to the apron on the cloth beam. A sectional warp beam, a regular warp beam with an apron, or a hexagonal metal beam[5] can be installed on wide inkle looms.

DIRECTIONS FOR WEAVING

A knife-edged shuttle, a small stick shuttle, a tongue depressor, or a strip of cardboard can be used to carry the weft. Since it will show only at the selvage, it should be the same color as that of the warp yarns on the outside edge of the belt. If a fringe is desired, all of the warp must be pulled down and under the loom as far as is needed for the length of the fringe. To insure even edges, make a frequent check of the width of the belt with a ruler or a marker.

1. To start to weave, form a shed by drawing down on the warp yarns below bar C and between bars C and D, using the right hand to make this separation. This move forms a shed between bars A and B, usually called the down-shed. Wrap the end of the weft around the first warp yarn, near bar A, and stick the waste end into the shed. Slip the shuttle through the shed and batten down the weft. For a firm fabric, batten before and after changing each shed. A ruler, spathe, or tongue depressor can be used as a battening device.

2. Change the shed by pulling upward on the warp yarns which are below C and between C and D. This is the up-shed. Pass the shuttle through the shed.

3. Continue alternating sheds, weaving, and battening down the weft until the work is completed. The adjustable dowel stick, bar E, can be moved forward as needed to adjust the tensions during weaving.

4. To remove the belt from the loom, cut the warp yarns just to the rear of bar C. To prevent unraveling, stitch across the ends of the belt with a sewing machine. Finish the belt with a buckle or a fringe. Types of fringe are described on page 341.

Some very interesting pick-up weaves for the inkle loom are described later in this chapter, page 120. See especially Belts 1, 2, 7, 8, 9, and 10.

[5] Manufactured by Structo Manufacturing Company, Freeport, Illinois.

2. Card-Heddle Belt Looms—Tablet Weaving

Tablet weaving is a very old form of warp-twined weaving; it is also a form of ingrain weaving, and is sometimes called card, card-heddle, and Egyptian-card weaving. A revival of interest in this type of weaving is apparent in this country, probably due to recent publications of Mary M. Atwater and other contemporary weavers.

In certain parts of the world, such as northern Europe, tablet weaving has been in constant use since early historic times. Perforated tablets were

Fig. 60. Tablet Weaving. Makeshift supports for card-heddle weaving.

employed as heddles for belt weaving by the Norsemen and the Celts. In Denmark, tablet weaving seems to have been a Bronze Age art; at least tablets have been found associated with objects of that age (101). As the name Egyptian-card weaving implies, this art is thought to have been known in ancient Egypt. In the New World, tablet weaving was apparently unknown before the arrival of the Spanish, though weaves of identical structure have been found in ancient Peruvian graves (2, 11). These weaves, known as warp twinings, are described on page 146, Belt 14.

The card-heddle system of weaving has never been mechanized. Cards used on the Jacquard loom somewhat resemble the cards used in tablet weaving, but their operation is entirely different.

STRUCTURE OF THE LOOM

No loom frame is necessary for tablet weaving. The warp can be tied between any two vertical supports, such as a door knob and a low chair back; the weaver then sits straddling the chair and shifts its position to lessen the warp tension. The warp may be stretched between bars and handled as on a back-strap loom; now the weaver needs only to shift her position to change the tension of the warp.

An inkle loom can be used as a loom frame, with the warp stretched between its two outside pegs. A simple loom frame is made by fastening a vertical support on each end of a 1″ x 2″ x 40″ piece of lumber; the supports can be the same width and thickness as the base, or they can be dowel sticks or heavy metal spikes. If spikes are used, they should be hammered into additional blocks of wood set on each end of the base plank. (See Fig. 60.)

STRUCTURE OF THE TABLETS

Tablets for this type of weaving can be made of heavy cardboard, wood, metal, or plastic; they can be made out of a shoe box if nothing else is handy. Whatever material is used, they must have smooth edges and rounded corners to facilitate turning them in the warp. Three-inch square tablets are the most commonly recommended size and shape, but for certain patterns narrow rectangles, equilateral triangles, or pentagons can be used. Hexagon or octagon tablets are rarely used. (See Fig. 61.)

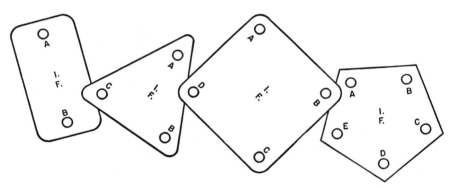

Fig. 61. Tablet Heddles. Tablet heddles may contain from two to eight holes. All the heddles for one loom should have the same number of holes and should be the same size and shape.

Punch holes in each corner of the cards, 1/4 to 1/2 inch from the edge. Mark each hole in black ink with a letter (A, B, C, D, etc.) running clockwise around the card, and print the letter F on the middle of the front of each card. Turn the card over and letter the holes on the back also, this time in red pencil. The letters must coincide in position with those on the front of the card, and hence will run counterclockwise. Print B in the center of the back of the card.

Number the cards, in black pencil on the front and red on the back. (Pencil is used so that the numbers can be changed for different patterns.) **109**

Place the numbers at the top of the card between the A and B holes. The cards are usually numbered consecutively from 1 to 16—or to 20 or 24, depending on the requirement—but some weavers prefer to number them in two halves: for example, from 1 to 8 and 8 to 1. In this case, a notation designating the right or left must be made on the front and back of each card. This method makes it easier for the weaver to find particular cards on either side of the center when weaving a difficult pattern.

Various means are used to help identify the position of the cards quickly; sometimes the A corner is cut on a diagonal so that it may quickly be recognized. The author prefers to paint the A-B edge of the card with red paint.

PLANNING THE DESIGN

A pattern must be planned before setting up the loom. Pattern drafts are usually plotted on squared graph paper, with each square representing one yarn, and each row of squares representing one card. There will be as many vertical columns as there are holes in the cards, and as many horizontal columns as there are total cards. Fig. 62 shows pattern drafts based upon 16 square cards with four holes to a card. The top row represents the four outside yarns on the right-hand side of the belt, which twist together to form a solid color margin.

There are other ways of writing the threading draft than the one pictured. For example, each card can be drawn with a color notation made for each hole, but this method consumes unnecessary time and is not recommended.

To get an idea of how a pattern will look in the finished weaving, turn the draft on its side; one-half of a reversible pattern will then be perfectly evident, representing four turns of the cards forward in the warp. It is customary to turn the cards four turns forward and four turns backward, continuously, to form the sheds for weaving and consequently to form the complete pattern.

The F and B which appear on the draft represent the direction in which the warp yarns enter the holes of the cards. Note that the manner of threading the cards is reversed for each group of eight cards: the yarns of the first set of eight are threaded through the holes from the front of the cards, those of the other eight through the holes from the back of the cards.

VARYING THE DESIGN AND THE WEAVE

Patterns are varied according to the color combinations selected, the order in which the holes are threaded, and the manner in which the cards are

Fig. 62. Tablet-Weave Patterns. Patterns are given for four belt weaves. The belt shown in the insert was made from pattern No. 2.

- 1 -

	A	B	C	D
1	W	W	W	W
2	W	W	W	W
3	W	W	W	W
4	R	W	R	W
5	R	W	R	W
6	B	B	B	B
7	Bl	Bl	Bl	Bl
8	B	B	B	B
9	R	W	R	W
10	R	W	R	W
11	W	W	W	W
12	W	W	W	B
13	W	W	W	B
14	W	W	R	R
15	W	R	R	R
16	R	R	B	B
16	Bl	Bl	B	B
15	W	Bl	Bl	Bl
14	W	W	Bl	Bl
13	W	W	W	B
12	W	W	W	B
11	W	W	W	W
10	R	W	R	W
9	R	W	R	W
8	B	B	B	B
7	Bl	Bl	Bl	Bl
6	B	B	B	B
5	R	W	R	W
4	R	W	R	W
3	W	W	W	W
2	W	W	W	W
1	W	W	W	W

- 2 -

	A	B	C	D
1	B	B	B	B
2	B	B	B	B
3	R	B	R	B
4	R	B	R	B
5	W	W	W	W
6	R	W	W	W
7	R	R	W	W
8	W	R	R	W
9	W	W	R	R
10	B	W	W	R
10	B	W	W	R
9	W	W	R	R
8	W	R	R	W
7	R	R	W	W
6	R	W	W	W
5	W	W	W	W
4	R	W	R	W
3	R	W	R	W
2	W	W	W	W
1	W	W	W	W

- 3 -

	A	B	C	D	
1	W	W	W	W	F'
2	W	W	B	B	B'
3	Bl	W	W	Bl	B'
4	R	R	W	W	B'
5	R	R	W	W	F'
6	Bl	W	W	Bl	F'
7	W	W	B	B	F'
8	B	B	B	B	F'
8	B	B	B	B	B'
7	W	W	B	B	B'
6	Bl	W	W	Bl	B'
5	R	R	W	W	B'
4	R	R	W	W	F'
3	Bk	W	W	Bl	F'
2	W	W	B	B	F'
1	W	W	W	W	B'

- 4 -

	A	B	C	D	
1	B	B	B	B	F'
2	B	B	B	B	F'
3	B	B	B	W	F'
4	B	B	B	W	F'
5	B	B	W	W	F'
6	B	W	W	B	F'
7	W	W	B	B	F'
8	W	B	B	W	F'
8	W	B	B	W	B'
7	W	W	B	B	B'
6	B	W	W	B	B'
5	B	B	W	W	B'
4	B	B	B	W	B'
3	B	B	B	W	B'
2	B	B	B	B	B'
1	B	B	B	B	B'

W = White   B = Black

R = Red   Bl = Blue

turned. Several methods of obtaining interesting patterns in card-heddle weaving are described briefly below:

1. Variation in Draft Notations

Many different color arrangements are possible, but the colors of the pattern proper and of the background should always be in sharp contrast. Bright pattern units on a very dark or a very light background are most feasible. The color combination selected is plotted on graph paper.

Diagonal stripes are made by threading the cards in successive progressive sequences, such as threading the A hole of the first card, the B hole of the second, the C hole of the third, and the D hole of the fourth with the same color, and treating the color sequences in all the holes and on all the cards in this manner. To get the full benefit of this arrangement, the cards are turned in one direction only; this necessitates occasionally straightening the warp yarns at the back of the loom.

2. Variation in Threading Methods

The pattern is affected by the manner in which the holes are threaded. Cards are threaded from front to back or from back to front. In either case it must be remembered that the cards on one side of the center are threaded in the same sequence but in reverse order to those on the other side of the center. Possibilities are (1) all cards are threaded from the front, (2) alternate cards are threaded in reverse, (3) half the cards are threaded one direction, half in the opposite direction, etc.

The purpose of threading the cards in two directions is to insure even squares, perfect diamonds, and other such figures, when they occur in a pattern. When stripes with smooth edges are wanted, it is best to thread all cards concerned in the same direction.

Remember that all the yarns for one card must enter the holes of that card from the same direction; otherwise it would not be possible to turn the cards during weaving.

3. Variation in Turning Arrangements

Many intriguing patterns result from turning groups of cards in opposite directions to one another. See, for example, Belt 14, page 146. The cards can be threaded as in 5 below, but rearranged so that the black and white yarns alternate, or so that the two blacks on one card alternate with the two whites on the other, etc. A chevron pattern is formed from design No. 2 on Fig. 62 if the cards are turned in one direction only; in this case the warp at the back of the cards will have to be straightened occasionally.

4. Variation in Shed Composition

The shed is usually formed between the two yarns from the top and the two from the bottom holes of a card when the card is in the proper position. If the cards are only partially turned (one-eighth turn instead of the regular one-quarter turn), two sheds are formed. The weft can be carried over and back, through both of these sheds, to form a very heavy belt.

5. Variation in Weaving Technique—Double-Cloth Weaving

When all the A and B holes are threaded with yarns of one color, such as white, and all of the C and D holes with yarns of another color, such as black, white patterns can be formed upon a black background, in the same type of designs as are woven for double cloth. (See Fig. 43.) This is done by controlling the position of the colors—that is, by turning the black down and bringing the white up when needed, and using only two turns to rotate the cards—two turns forward, two turns backward, repeat. The holes in all the cards which form the border may be threaded with the same color.

6. Variation in Weaving Technique—Split and Chain Belts

Split belts are made with two different sets of cards threaded with the same design. The two sets are placed side by side in the loom and woven as one belt. At intervals, the sets are separated slightly and woven as two belts; this arrangement makes a slit between the belts. If the separately woven pieces are now crossed—that is, if the set of cards on one side is transferred to a position on the opposite side of the warp—a cross or twist appears in the belt. When again woven together, the two belts then occupy opposite sides of the warp from those they first held.

Two narrow belts of one pattern can also be combined with two narrow belts of a second pattern: these are woven together as one belt, and then at intervals they are separated and woven as four separate belts. The four-belt strands can also be crossed in various combinations.

7. Twisted Warp Finger Weaving

A belt can be woven which looks as though made by tablet weaving; actually it is made by a pseudo-card weaving process, described under Belt 14 on page 146.

WARPING THE LOOM
Preparing the Warp Yarns for the Loom

In card weaving, warping the loom really means threading and arranging the cards. This is done as follows: First of all, it is necessary to calculate

113

the total number of yarns needed. This is ascertained by multiplying the number of cards to be used by the number of holes in each card; thus in a 16-card weave, such as those patterns illustrated in Fig. 62, the total yarns needed are 64. Now we will want to count how many yarns of each color are needed. The total number of yarns of all colors must, of course, equal 64.

The next item to be determined is the length to cut the yarns. In calculating this, allowance must be made for shrinkage and for waste. For shrinkage, add about one-fourth of the actual length needed for the belt; add an additional 20 inches for waste. If a fringe is desired, allowance must be made for this also.

When the number, color, and length of the yarns have been decided upon, the yarns are measured and cut. A warping board can be used to speed this process. If none is available, a measure marked on a table will help. The cut yarns, grouped according to color, are hung over and spread along the back of a chair.

Threading the Cards

To thread the cards, sit at a table with the chair which holds the cut yarns at your right. Place the 16 cards on the table at your right, stacked with front or F facing upward and arranged in numerical order—from 1 to 8 and 8 to 1. Card number 1 is on top and the A holes are arranged immediately under one another. Place the pattern draft on the table at your left. Each hole in each card is now threaded consecutively according to the pattern draft, as follows:

1. Pick up card No. 1; place it in front of you on the table with the front side up and the A hole at top left; select the yarns designated by the draft for the top card, No. 1. Thread the warp yarns through the holes from front to back as designated by F on the draft, pulling them through about 14 inches. Turn the card front face down and place it on the table about a foot in front of you. Even and straighten the yarns.
2. Thread the balance of the cards in the same manner, from the front or back as the draft designates, and place them all front face down on top of one another so that the A holes coincide. Remember that the direction of threading each card in the second half of the pile is exactly the reverse of that used for threading the matching card in the first half of the group.
3. When all the cards are threaded, tie them together across both ways. Divide the shorter lengths of yarn into four sections, each section being the yarns from one hole, and loop the ends of each section into a knot.

114

With a cord, tie all the knots together. Untie the cards, pull on the long ends until all the yarns are straight and the tension is even, and tie these into two knots. Tie a cord around these knots. Tie the cards together again.

The Tablet Loom

Stretch the warp between any two vertical supports, as previously described under "Structure of the Loom." The shorter end of the warp represents the front end of this loom; the weaving is begun by throwing the weft in sheds formed in this end of the warp.

DIRECTIONS FOR WEAVING

Fig. 63. Tablet-Woven Belt.

1. Select a weft the same color as the margin yarns. (See Fig. 63.) Use a knife-edged shuttle if one is available. Untie the cards.
2. By turning the cards one-quarter turns forward and backward, make a few rows of plain weaving to stabilize the warp and even the tension of the warp yarns. Use a very coarse weft for this and beat it into place by using a ruler, a tongue depressor, a spathe, or a knife-edged shuttle as a beater.
3. When ready to weave the pattern, check the cards and place the A holes in all the cards in the back top position. Form a shed and slip in the weft yarn. Tuck the loose end of the weft into the next formed shed, leaving it a little slack in the shed. Beat the weft into place and then pull it to correct tension, being careful to keep the edges of the belt even. Use a gauge.
4. Change sheds by turning the cards one-quarter turn forward. Place the weft in the shed and beat. The next two sheds are formed the same way, by two successive one-quarter turns forward. Then the turning must be reversed. Make four one-quarter turns toward the rear of the loom for the next four sheds. Continue four one-quarter turns forward and four one-quarter turns backward to form the sheds until the weaving is finished.
5. Keep the sheds clear. If a shed is not clear, pull the cards apart and let them fall back into place, or shift them backward and forward in the warp.

115

6. If the weft should break, any joining must be made by crossing the weft yarns inside a shed. No knots or loose yarns must show on the margins or elsewhere in the warp.

7. If it should be necessary to leave the loom, tie the cards together so that they will not slip out of place—leaving the A holes in position at the top and toward the back.

8. The ends of the belt may be finished in several ways: (1) Make a few rows of machine stitching on either end of the finished belt. (2) Make one end of the belt into a point, by folding the end double lengthwise and stitching the top edge of this fold. When the fold is reversed and flattened a pointed end appears. (3) Finish the belt with buckles or fringe.

3. Bow Belt Looms

The bow loom is, as its name suggests, a very simple loom built upon the same principle as the bow used with arrows. At the time of the arrival of the white man it was being used by the Slave Indians, the Iroquois, and other Indians of the northern and eastern parts of North America for weaving porcupine quill belts (*56*); later, they used it for weaving their wampum bead belts (*149*). (See Fig. 41.)

STRUCTURE OF THE LOOM

The warp of this particular loom is stretched between the two ends of a bent limb or bow, taking the position of the thong of a regular bow. The natural spring of the bow holds the warp at a tight tension. As weaving progresses and the warp tightens, the flexible bow bends slightly to adjust to this change in tension.

On the early primitive bow looms, pieces of heavy leather called warp spreaders, a little wider than the width of the warp, were fastened at the ends of the bow. The warp yarns were sewed through and stretched between them and were thus kept properly spaced for weaving. Sometimes two pieces of birch bark, drilled with as many holes as there were warp yarns, were used instead of the leather warp spreaders. Most of the early bow looms did not have heddles; the weft had to be darned into the warp with the fingers, a thorn, or a needle.

This simple loom is so easily made that it can be used for weaving projects in recreational programs. A modern version of it can also be easily constructed. The warp yarns are tied to and stretched between two small rods held parallel; when the warp needed has been tied on, these rods are attached to the loom so that they are crosswise and at right angles to the bow. The ends of the rods and the ends of the bow are notched, and cords tied in these notches attach the rods to the bow. If a cord loop is made between the notches at the ends of each rod, the rod can be attached to the bow by winding the center of the loop several times around the notch at the end of the bow. A continuous ring warp can be arranged by stringing the warp continuously over and between two such rods. In this case two temporary warp yarns are tied to the ends of the two rods and stretched between them. The rods are then attached to the bow as described above, and the regular warp, rolled in a ball, is carried around and around between the rods. When sufficient warp is on the loom, the temporary warp yarns are removed. When such a simple belt loom is equipped with the proper heddle devices, most of the common weaves can be woven on it. If only a string heddle rod and a heddle sword are added, pick-up work can be done as on the girdle-back, inkle, or single-heddle harness looms.

DESIGNS FOR BEADWORK

At the present time the bow belt loom and its modern counterpart (see Fig. 64) are used principally for beadwork. For this reason, beadwork is described below in connection with the use of this loom.

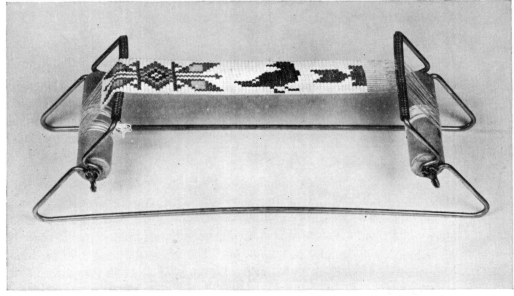

Fig. 64. Bead Loom. A craft loom which is used in schools and in recreational programs. (Courtesy, Walco Bead Company, New York City.)

Beadwork designs are generally worked out on graph paper, each square representing one bead. Some draft patterns originally made for weaving can

117

be converted into beadwork; simple pick-up design patterns planned for weaving are especially adaptable for beadwork.

DIRECTIONS FOR WEAVING BEADWORK

To weave upon this bow loom, the weaver either sits and holds the loom between her knees, or kneels and places it between her thighs. If a modern box bead loom is used, the box frame rests upon a table during weaving.

Four methods of doing beadwork are described below.

Method I

When using the belt bow loom or its modern frame adaptation, the beadwork is made as follows. A string of beads, loosely strung onto a strong fine thread, is laid across the warp. The beads are spread out so that a certain number fall in the spaces between the warp yarns. They are then attached to the warp by means of a needle and thread; the needle is carried in a half-hitch stitch, around a warp yarn and around the thread which holds the beads. At the same time the beads are properly distributed and spaced. The beads can also be threaded onto a yarn, a few at a time, and attached to the warp as the work proceeds. For example, two beads are threaded on to the weft, and the weft is then looped in a half-hitch around a warp; two more beads are treated and attached in this same way, etc.

Method II

Other simple looms, such as the single-heddle harness loom used by the North American Indians, can be used for beadwork weaving. The strand of beads is placed in the shed as weft and woven into the warp. Usually, the number of beads between each warp yarn is regulated before changing the shed.

Method III

Many museums in the United States display North American Indian belts, bags, and moccasins ornamented with beadwork. In the majority of these pieces, the beads appear to have been sewed directly onto buckskin. However, upon closer examination it is usually discovered that the beads were first threaded in strands; the strands were laid across the surface of the buckskin, and were couched down on the leather with a needle and thread. This type of beadwork is closely associated with embroidery.

Method IV

The description of a method of doing beadwork, used by certain South American Indians, was given in the preceding chapter, page 81.

4. Miscellaneous Belt Looms

NAVAHO BELT LOOMS

The Navahos use three different belt looms: a regular back-strap loom, a long narrow rectangular frame loom, and a tree-fork loom, described here. This loom is made from a section of a sapling which has been cut below the juncture of a limb and a trunk, or below the fork of two limbs. The two limbs are usually drawn together at the open end to narrow the loom. (See Fig. 65.) One bar is braced across the forked area, and a second bar is secured across the open end. The warp is strung over these two bars or secured to two other bars attached to them. Pick-up design weaving, similar to that of Belt 9, described on page 137, is used by the Navahos for their belts.

CROSSED-STICK LOOMS

The Kamarakoto Indians of Venezuela have a special frame loom on which they make braided belts. (See Fig. 66.) This loom, which is easily constructed, consists of four sticks: two are crossed and secured at their centers; two others are tied across opposite open ends, serving as braces for the frame. The warp is strung continuously around these top and bottom sticks or braces. Sometimes a two-stick loom with adjustable tension ropes is stretched inside between the two braces.

SARAWAK TWO-STICK BELT LOOMS

The Sarawaks of Borneo use a regular two-stick loom supported in a rectangular frame. After the desired warp has been stretched between the two sticks, the loom is set inside a rectangular frame and stretched between its end bars. The frame is made up of two pairs of sticks, short ones for the ends and

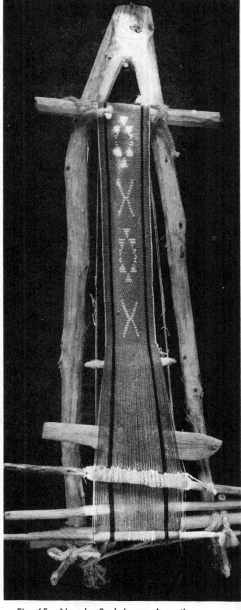

Fig. 65. Navaho Sash Loom. A continuous-warp loom; made on a tree crotch. (Courtesy, The American Museum of Natural History.)

119

long ones for the sides. The two pairs are set at right angles to one another so that their ends cross; the frame is made by lashing them together at their points of intersection.

GUATEMALAN SIMPLE FOOT-POWER BELT LOOMS

Some of the Indians of Guatemala make belts on narrow back-strap looms operated with foot-pedal-controlled harnesses. The weaver sits upon a low stool to work. His warp, which is stretched horizontally out in front of him, is attached to a girdle at his waist. It runs through a little frame which supports two small counterbalanced heddle harnesses, connected by means of cords to the two foot pedals. These simple looms are used in San Pedro and in other small villages near Qualtzaltenango. Very ornate tapestry head bands and belts are woven on them.

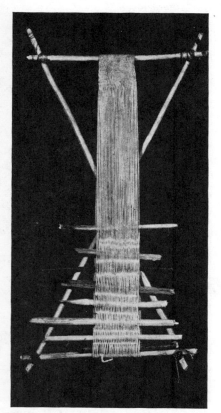

Fig. 66. Crossed-Stick Loom. A continuous warp held on a loom frame made of crossed sticks, used by the Kamarakoto Indians of Venezuela. A braid is partially made on the loom; notice the shed sticks in place. (Courtesy, The American Museum of Natural History.)

TWO-STICK BELT LOOMS

Small two-stick looms are used all over the world by native peoples for belt weaving and for constructing narrow strips of braided, meshed, or twisted warp fabrics. These small looms, which are really identical in form to the regular back-strap looms, are generally stretched between two vertical supports. They may, however, be supported in the same manner as those of the larger back-strap looms.

5. Pick-Up Pattern Weaves for Belt Looms

Many warp-faced pattern weaves are made by lifting and holding certain warp yarns above the shed during several throws of weft. Similarly, many weft-faced pattern weaves are formed by opening up the warp—that is, by lifting a limited number of the warp yarns above the shed. Both types of such pick-up work can be done on mechanical looms as well as on hand looms. When warp-faced pick-up work is done by hand, it is generally better adapted to narrow looms and to belt weaves.

120

Since remote times, weavers in many parts of the Old World, as widely separated as Africa, Syria, Norway, and Sweden, have been skilled in pick-up weaving, making beautiful belts, bags, and other articles.

In the New World, many beautiful belts, ornamented with hand pick-up patterns, are now being woven by the Indians of Mexico, Central America, and South America. Some of the patterns and the methods used to weave them undoubtedly have their origins in the distant past. Warp-faced belt weaves containing pick-up patterns which resemble some of the work of the Peruvian Indians of today, have been found in ancient Peruvian sites which may date from 2500 to 1200 B.C. (11). When we consider that pick-up pattern weaving represents a definite technical advance over such textile processes as plaiting and twining, we are able to visualize the extent of the background of weaving on the Western Hemisphere.

The majority of the weaves described in the following pages are taken from actual Indian belts from Central and South America in the collection of the author. Counterparts of many of these pick-up pattern weaves can also be found in the work of skilled weavers in other parts of the world.

GENERAL INSTRUCTIONS FOR WARPING BELT LOOMS

As already stated, pick-up pattern weaves can be made on nearly all types of looms. Mechanical table and foot-power looms are especially recommended for weaves which require three or more heddle harnesses. Before setting up any loom for weaving, the novice should review the directions for using that loom.

After the type of loom to be used and the type of weave to be made have been decided upon, a suitable heddle-threading draft should be selected. The beginner should start her weaving experience by selecting a two-harness loom and a heddle-threading draft for such a loom. A draft can be chosen from a weaving manual or plotted by the weaver. Directions for plotting drafts are given on page 269. Heddle-threading drafts for most of the belts described in this section are shown in Fig. 67.

Warp-faced designs are most effective when the pattern yarns contrast sharply in color and value with the yarns of the background. Usually, too, the pattern yarns are heavier than those of the background. Unless otherwise specified, black and white yarns are used for the warp in the belt weaves described in the following pages, in order to simplify the instructions presented. The weaver will, of course, select other colors as desired.

The warp yarns for a simple belt loom are usually prepared on a warping board before they are strung upon the loom, though there are certain exceptions: (1) on some looms, such as the inkle loom, the warp has to be

121

Belt No.4

4
3
2
1

End | Repeat | Border

4-Harness
Sinking Shed
Tie-Up

| | 1 | 2 | 3 | 4 | a | b |

Belt No.8 — Heddles: W W G G G G G W B B B B
Slots: W W G G G G G W W

Border | Repeat

Belt No.9

4
3
2
1

End | Repeat | Border

| 1 | 2 | a | b | 1 | 2 | 3 | 4 | a | b |

4-Harness
Sinking Shed
Tie-Up

4-Harness
Sinking Shed
Tie-Up

Belt No.10 — Heddles / Slots (Inkle)

2
1

Border | Repeats | End | End | Repeat | Border

Belt No.11

6
5
4
3
2
1

End | Repeat
4-Harness Loom

End | Repeat
6-Harness Loom

Border

| 1 | 2 | 3 | 4 |

4-Harness
Sinking Shed
Tie-Up

Belt No.12

4
3
2
1

End | Repeat | Border

| 1 2 3 4 | a | b | 1 | 2 | 3 | 4 |
(a) (b)

Rising Shed
Tie-Up
Method II

Rising Shed
Tie-Up
Method I

End | Repeat | Border | End | Repeat

Belt No.13

4
3
2
1

| 1 | 2 | 3 | 4 | 5 | 6 |

Type No.1 | Type No.2

Belt No.15

4
3
2
1

End | Repeat | Suggested Border
(No Border is Necessary)

| 1 | 2 | 3 | 4 | 5 | 6 |

Rising Shed
Tie-Up

put directly onto the loom; (2) when a large loom equipped with a sectional warp beam is used for belt weaving, the warp yarns can also be wound directly onto the loom. For many of the belts described here, black and white yarns are placed alternately in the warp. When winding these yarns onto the warping board, a white and a black yarn can be carried together around the warping board; they can also be wound onto the sectional warp beam of a loom equipped with such a beam.

GENERAL INSTRUCTIONS FOR PICK-UP WEAVING

Patterns for pick-up weaving are generally plotted on graph paper, as described on page 270. The blacked-in areas of the draft indicate to the weaver the location of pattern warp or weft yarns. Each square on the graph paper represents one pair of warp or one throw of patterned weft; when the yarns used are very fine, one square may represent several yarns. A selection of patterns suitable for belt weaving is shown on Fig. 68. The pattern draft selected should be referred to constantly during weaving.

In hand pick-up work, the warp yarns are picked up with the fingers, with knitting needles, or with slender, smooth pick-up sticks, sometimes called brocade sticks. The sheds formed beneath the picked-up yarns are usually held open with shed swords turned sidewise in the warp.

Many of the weaves described mention pattern weft and tabby weft. These terms should be well understood. The pattern weft is often a loosely held weft; that is, it engages only a part of the warp. A tabby weft is, therefore, needed to strengthen the structure of the fabric. One throw of tabby is made between each throw of pattern weft. Alternating rows of tabby must mesh to form a plain weave.

After the weaver has woven a trial stretch of any of the pick-up weaves, she should systematize her weaving procedure. For example, it might be found better always to make the pick-up from right to left, etc.

So that the directions given will fit all types of looms, the shed formation is designated by specifying either the harness or harnesses to be raised or the color of the warp to be raised. Whenever the instructions direct the weaver to raise a harness, it should be understood that the previous harness used is simultaneously lowered. When instructions read, "raise harnesses 1 and 3," these harnesses are raised together.

The width of the belt must be kept uniform during weaving, and the outside edges kept straight. To maintain uniformity, the width of the weaving should be checked frequently with a gauge made out of cardboard.

Fig. 67. Belt Weaves. Heddle-threading drafts for pick-up weaving for belts described in this chapter.

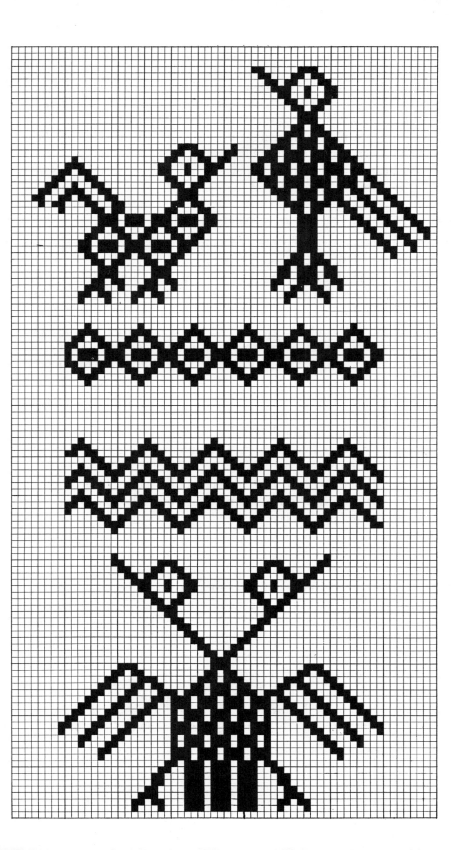

BELT WEAVES CONTAINING WEFT-FACED DESIGNS

BELT 1-A. BROCADE WEAVING FROM PERU AND MEXICO (A TWO-HARNESS WEAVE)

The pattern of this belt is formed of certain weft inserts. These pattern wefts are usually of bright colors and are floated on the basic background tabby weave which is either balanced or warp-faced. An inkle loom or any other two-harness loom can be used for this weave. Of course, looms with four or more harnesses facilitate the weaving of intricate patterns. When such patterns are woven in brocade on wide fabrics, either a draw loom or a Jacquard loom is needed for the work. This work is discussed in a later chapter.

WARPING THE LOOM

The warp is usually coarse and of one color, generally white cotton. It is threaded alternately through the heddles of two harnesses. The warp is spaced about 50 to the inch. The general directions for warping the loom, given earlier (page 121), should be followed. See also the discussion of inkle looms (page 101).

DIRECTIONS FOR WEAVING

In this type of brocade weaving, the pattern weft is hidden in the shed except where exposed in open or pattern areas. It is common practice in this weave to carry the pattern weft completely across the width of the warp, or entirely through the shed. However, a better selvage or smoother border will be formed if the pattern weft is carried only as far as, but not into, the warp yarns of the selvage.

In this weave, the pattern weft often floats over large numbers of warp yarns. The warp is opened for these floats by either picking up certain warp yarns to form a shed or dropping certain ones to a position beneath a shed. Although the pick-up for the belt weaves is generally made by hand, a loom can be provided with special heddles for this work. See pages 88 and 237.

The stabilizing or tabby weft is usually finer than the warp but of the same color, whereas the pattern weft yarns are heavier than the warp and are generally of colored wool. Two strands of fine woolen yarn can be used in place of one strand of coarse. The contrast of weight and color gives the colored yarn the advantage, but the real pattern is dependent upon the openings in the warp, through which the colored weft yarn passes.

It is a good idea to work out some system of inserting the weft: it may save time always to make the pick-up from right to left, always to throw the tabby weft in the same direction as the pattern weft in their respective

Fig. 68.   Designs for Pick-Up Weaving.

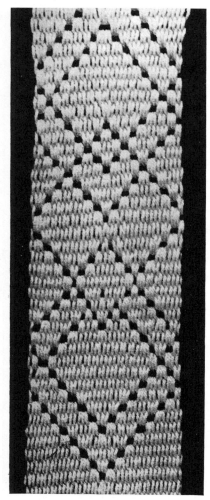

Fig. 69. A Pick-Up Pattern. Woven on an inkle loom with regular threading and with one color warp.

sheds, and always to throw tabby and pattern yarns in the same order; usually the tabby is thrown in first. In some weft pattern weaves, two single warp yarns, called tie warps, are floated across the ends of a weft pattern area; they hold the long weft floats in place.

If the warp is close-set, as it is on the inkle loom, the design motif stands out in sharp contrast to the one-color background. (See Fig. 69.) On looms where the warp is carried through a reed or in cases where it is not close-set, the colored weft yarns show faintly through the warp.

To make a belt in this weave, follow these steps:

1. Select a pattern draft. Review general instructions for pick-up weaving given on page 123.
2. To begin the weave, raise harness 1, put tabby weft into the shed, and batten down.
3. While the harness is still raised, use a pick-up stick and pick up the background warp yarns—those yarns which will not be lowered for the pattern. Now lower harness 1, place a shed sword on edge in the same shed with the pick-up stick, and remove the pick-up stick. Throw the colored weft yarn through this shed. Remove the shed sword and batten. Remember that the weft is battened firmly into place before and after each change in shed.
4. Repeat this process for the second shed, which is formed with the second heddle harness. Referring constantly to the pattern draft, continue weaving in this manner until the belt is finished.

BELT 1-B. SWIVEL WEAVING FROM GUATEMALA AND PERU (A FOUR-HARNESS WEAVE)

Swivel weave patterns closely resemble those used in the brocade weave just described. There is, however, a slight difference in structure between them. In the swivel weave, the colored pattern weft is carried back and forth in the immediate area of a unit pattern, but it is not carried entirely through any shed. The tabby weft is the basic weft, forming most of the structure of the fabric. Looms equipped with three or more harnesses, with string heddle rods, or with other accessory harness devices are generally selected for this type of weaving. Swivel weaving is more fully described in Chapter VII.

BELT 2. TWO-TONE PATTERN WEAVING FROM PERU (A TWO-HARNESS WEAVE)

An attractive Peruvian belt is made without a special tabby weft thread. Two weft yarns of different colors serve alternately on the same row of weaving as tabby and pattern weft. The design has a half-and-half effect; that is, one half of a row of weaving is in one color and the other half is the other color. This two-tone effect can be staggered to produce zigzag, step, and meander patterns.

WARPING THE LOOM

The general directions for warping given earlier (page 121) apply to the warping for this belt. The warp for this weave is usually coarse white cotton. The warp yarns are threaded in singles or in pairs through the heddles of a two-harness loom. If they are threaded in pairs, the sequence is as follows: on harness 1, thread heddles 1 and 2; on harness 1, thread heddles 1 and 2; repeat this order of threading the yarns across the two harnesses.

DIRECTIONS FOR WEAVING

This Peruvian weave can be accomplished by two methods: (1) The pattern wefts are thrown in the shed one at a time and carried across the entire width of the warp, each serving part of the way as pattern and part of the way as tabby. (2) The two yarns are carried through the first part of the warp, one serving as tabby, the other as pattern weft; the two then exchange positions for the remainder of the distance across the warp, the first now serving as pattern weft, and the other as tabby weft. The first of these methods is described below.

In this weave, a few tie warps are usually floated above the pattern weft, crossing the weft pattern about 1/8 inch from either end of the exposed weft and serving to anchor the weft down. These ties also enhance the weft design. Notice how they are spaced above the weft on Fig. 70.

1. Make or consult a pattern draft. Black and yellow yarns are used for the pattern described below. Before beginning to weave, review the general directions for pick-up weaving, page 123.
2. Raise harness 1. Allowing for the ties described above, start at the right and with a pick-up stick pick up the pattern on the right side of the warp; then with a second pick-up stick, pick up the pattern on the left side of the warp.

3. While harness 1 is still up, start from the right and throw the black weft
   yarn into the regular tabby shed, carrying it across the warp to the
   place where the left pick-up stick engages the warp. Now lower the
   harness, form a shed under the left pick-up stick, and carry the black
   weft the balance of the distance across the warp through this shed.
   Then carry the yellow yarn into the warp from right to left. It
   passes first into the pattern shed—that is, beneath the warp held up by

Fig. 70. Peruvian Double-Weft Weaving. A novel belt weave; see Belt 2. (From
Mary M. Atwater, *The Shuttle-Craft Book of American Hand-Weaving,* Macmillan,
1951. Used with permission of The Macmillan Company.)

the right pick-up stick. When the yellow yarn reaches the left pick-up
stick, raise harness 1 again and carry the yellow yarn into the regular
tabby shed. A shed sword can be used to hold the pattern sheds open.
Batten down both wefts. Both weft shuttles should now be on the left
side of the loom. (From the standpoint of selvage structure, weaving
the two colors from opposite directions instead of from the same direction has some advantage.)

4. Raise harness 2. Use two more pick-up sticks to hold up the pattern
   warp in the second row of weaving; they are slipped into their positions
   before the first two sticks are removed. The two colored weft yarns are

Fig. 71. Belt Weaves from Latin America. Top, left, ingrain weave (Belt 12)
from Peru. Center, black and white, tapestry weave from Guatemala. Three lower
belts, weaves from Ecuador, described under Belt 13.

THE TEXTILE ARTS

now carried into the warp from left to right, one at a time, reversing the order in which they formerly passed through the tabby and pattern sheds, respectively, but forming the pattern weave and the tabby weave on the same side of the warp as on the previous row of weaving. Continue the use of alternate yarns of black and yellow and alternate pattern and tabby sheds until the belt is finished.

BELT 3. TAPESTRY WEAVING FROM PERU AND GUATEMALA (A TWO-HARNESS WEAVE)

Belts with very intricate designs are often woven in tapestry. (See Fig. 71.) The tapestry weave is an ancient one on the Western Hemisphere; the Indians of Peru used this technique long ago for weaving belts and mantles. Today many of the Indians of Guatemala use the tapestry weave for making belts and headbands. Various tapestry techniques are described in a later chapter.

WARP-FACED BELT WEAVES CONTAINING WEFT-FACED ACCENTS

BELT 4. A TOTONICAPAN BELT WEAVE FROM GUATEMALA (A FOUR-HARNESS WEAVE)

The design for this belt silhouettes a dark unit pattern against a light background. Neither pattern nor background warps form solid areas; both are made up of interlocking warp yarns and are open-meshed. In other words, pairs of black warps interlock to form the pattern, and pairs of white warps interlock to form the background. (See Fig. 72.) The design can be planned on graph paper, with each square representing a pair of warp yarns. The design of this weave is not reversible.

The pattern weft is coarse and shows color slightly through the warp, except in areas where it rides above sections of the warp—a treatment often used to add color interest to the design. (See Belt 6.) In some belts, different colored weft yarns are laid down in 1-inch horizontal strips.

WARPING THE LOOM

The general directions for warping the loom, page 121, again apply to this belt. A loom equipped with four heddle harnesses is needed for this weave, but one with six harnesses is better, because the border yarns can then be threaded alternately on harnesses 5 and 6.

The yarn for the white warp should be about a No. 20 and that for the black warp about a No. 10, both cotton. Although the white is finer than the black, a strand of each color can be warped and beamed together. Sixteen to 20 yarns of No. 20 cotton are used for the border.

130

This unique belt weave is dependent upon the manner in which the warp

Fig. 72.   Totonicapan Belt. From Guatemala comes this beautiful belt weave;
see Belts 4, 5, and 6 in text. (Courtesy, Mary M. Atwater.)

yarns are threaded on the loom. Study the heddle-threading draft in Fig. 67. Note that all of the black warp is threaded on harnesses 1 and 3 and all the white on harnesses 2 and 4. The border is threaded alternately on harnesses 1 and 2, unless a six-harness loom is used; then it is threaded alternately on harnesses 5 and 6. The belt is often edged with a wide border containing several lengthwise stripes of a harmonizing color.

Thread the warp into the heddles after the border, starting from the right side of the loom, as follows: harness 3, heddle 1, black; harness 4, heddle 1, white; harness 3, heddle 2, black; harness 4, heddle 2, white. This threading forms one set of yarns, one pair of black and one pair of white. For the second set, thread as follows, after the border: harness 1, heddle 1, black; harness 2, heddle 1, white; harness 1, heddle 2, black; harness 2, heddle 2, white. Thread the sets in this order until the left border is reached. There must be an uneven number of white and black warp pairs on the loom. The yarns of the left border pattern are threaded in reverse order to those of the right border.

DIRECTIONS FOR WEAVING

The general directions for pick-up weaving, given earlier (page 123) apply here. If the belt is to have a fringe, slip a cardboard strip into the warp before beginning to weave to allow for it.

1. Begin the belt with six or more rows of plain tabby weaving, made by raising harnesses 1 and 3 together, alternating with harnesses 2 and 4 raised together. The tabby weaving forms alternating black and white rows in the warp. The tabby weft is usually of the same color as the outside border warps and slightly heavier, but not as heavy as the pattern weft. The tabby weft is always carried through the border; the pattern weft is never carried through it. After six rows of tabby weaving, begin the pattern weaving.

2. Several different colors of yarn can be used for the pattern weft. They are often laid down in horizontal strips about an inch wide. The pattern weft must be heavier than the warp.

3. To begin the pattern weave, raise harness 1 and pick up the black pattern warps in pairs on a pick-up stick. Lift harness 2 and pick up the white background warps in pairs, running the second pick-up stick through the sheds of the first pick-up stick. The first pick-up stick may then be removed. Care must be taken to see that for every pair of warps picked up in one color, a corresponding pair of warps is left down in the other color.

4. Raise harnesses 1 and 3. Weave a row of tabby, holding the pick-up

stick above the shed. Raise harnesses 2 and 4, and, still holding the pick-up stick above the shed, weave a second row of tabby. The stick shuttle can be left in the shed to assist in battening.

5. Lower all harnesses; form a shed beneath the picked-up warps and insert a shed sword. Turn the shed sword on its side and remove the pick-up stick. Throw the colored pattern weft through this shed, keeping in mind that it does not go through the border warps. Remove the shed sword and batten well.

6. Raise harness 3 and pick up the black pattern warps. Lower this harness, raise harness 4, and pick up the white background warps. Again let the second pick-up stick run through the shed of the first pick-up stick. Raise harnesses 1 and 3 and weave tabby, holding the picked-up warp above the shed. Raise harnesses 2 and 4 and weave tabby, still holding the pick-up stick above the shed.

7. Lower all harnesses. Form a shed beneath the warp on the pick-up stick, slip in a shed sword, turn the shed stick on its side, and remove the pick-up stick. Throw the colored pattern weft through the shed, remembering that it does not go through the border warp.

8. Repeat steps 3 through 7 until the weaving is finished. End the belt with six rows of plain weaving.

BELT 5. A TOTONICAPAN BELT WEAVE (A FOUR-HARNESS WEAVE)

The design of this belt depends upon the manner in which the pattern weft yarns are floated at intervals over lowered warp yarns. The loom is threaded in black and white as for Belt 4; if desired, the entire warp can be of either black or white. In this case any two-harness loom, such as an inkle loom, can be used.

When the loom is threaded with black and white, the white is caught up only in the tabby weave and is always carried below and covered entirely by the colored weft. The pattern therefore appears on a black background.

This belt is woven the same as Belt 4, except that the white warp yarns are never picked up. Certain of the black warp yarns—those in the pattern areas—are also not picked up; this leaves open areas in the black warp and exposes sections of colored weft. When these openings are staggered in definite sequence, a pattern results.

BELT 6. A TOTONICAPAN BELT WEAVE (A FOUR-HARNESS WEAVE)

This is a combination of Belts 4 and 5. The pattern is made up of a black warp background, but colored weft yarns are floated over areas of the black warp. (See Fig. 72.) The yarn is put on the loom as for Belt 4 and

133

the manner of weaving is the same. The pattern, however, is formed by weft floats as in Belt 5.

WARP-FACED BELT WEAVES

BELT 7. AN INKLE LOOM PICK-UP WEAVE (A TWO-HARNESS WEAVE)

The warp-faced designs described below can be woven on an inkle loom or on any two-harness loom strung with closely set warp.

WARPING THE LOOM

Before setting up an inkle loom for this belt weave, review the discussion of inkle looms, page 101, and the general directions for warping, page 106.

The inkle loom is set up for this pick-up weave as follows: for the left border, thread six white warp yarns followed by ten red; for the pattern area, thread white and black yarns alternately, white in all the heddle loops, and black in all the slots between the loops, ending with an uneven number of both. Then thread the right border, ten red followed by six white yarns. The white and black yarns can be of the same weight, but a black yarn a little heavier than the white makes a more definite pattern in the weave.

DIRECTIONS FOR WEAVING

Although this belt is not illustrated here, the method of weaving it is similar to that of Belt 10. (See Fig. 76.)

1. Using white carpet warp for the weft, weave six rows of plain weaving, ending with a row of white warp raised.
2. Form a shed with black on top—the up-shed—and weave. While the black is still raised, start the pattern, picking up the black warps with a pick-up stick. Count the yarns carefully and center the pattern. Still holding up the black pick-up yarns, form a shed with white—the down-shed—and weave.
3. From a shed with the black warp up and weave. With the first pick-up stick still in the warp, take a second pick-up stick and pick up the second row of black pattern warps. Remove the first pick-up stick.
4. Repeat steps 2 and 3 until the design is completed. Separate each completed design unit with several rows of plain weaving, ending with the white warp raised. End the belt with six rows of tabby weaving.

BELT 8. A WEAVE FROM BOLIVIA AND FROM MOMOSTENANGO, GUATEMALA (A TWO-HARNESS WEAVE)

This weave is one of the easiest of the pick-up belt weaves. (See Fig. 73.) The design is nonreversible; that is, it appears on the right side of the belt

only. The instructions given below are for the inkle loom, but
any other two-harness loom could
be used.

WARPING THE LOOM

Before beginning to set up the
loom for this weave, reread the
discussion of inkle looms, page
101, and the general instructions
for warping, page 106.

The heddle-threading draft for
this weave is given on Fig. 67. On
that draft, white (W), green
(G), and black (B), yarns are indicated. Use a yarn similar to
Lily soft-twist cotton for the
black pattern warp and 24/3 cotton for the white warp. The Lily
twist is twice the diameter of the 24/3 cotton.

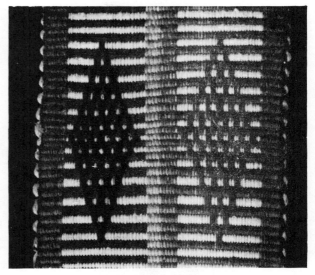

Fig. 73. Momostenango Belt. A Guatemalan belt weave; see Belt 8 in text. This
belt is set up in the same way as that in
Fig. 58.

To thread the loom, first thread the left border, then the white, two-
black (W-2B) unit 21 times, and then the right border. Always thread an
uneven number of the white, two-black units. A belt about 1 1/4 inches
wide is formed by this setup.

GENERAL DIRECTIONS FOR WEAVING

In this weave, the pick-up is always made when the white shed is up and
is always made through it. *No white warp yarns are ever dropped.* The
pattern widens or narrows by one white yarn only. Two white yarns
separate each pair of black yarns picked up, unless the pattern calls for more
than two. White carpet warp yarn is used for the weft.

Before continuing reread the general directions for pick-up weaving, page
123.

DIRECTIONS FOR WEAVING A DOUBLE-DIAMOND PATTERN

1. Weave six or more rows of plain weaving, starting and ending with the
   white warp up. (See Fig. 74A.)
2. Start the design by reaching through the white warp and picking up
   the center pair of black warps—the pair in the center of the belt. Always
   start in the center to pick up the design. Weave under the white and this
   black pair. Change sheds and weave under the black warp.

135

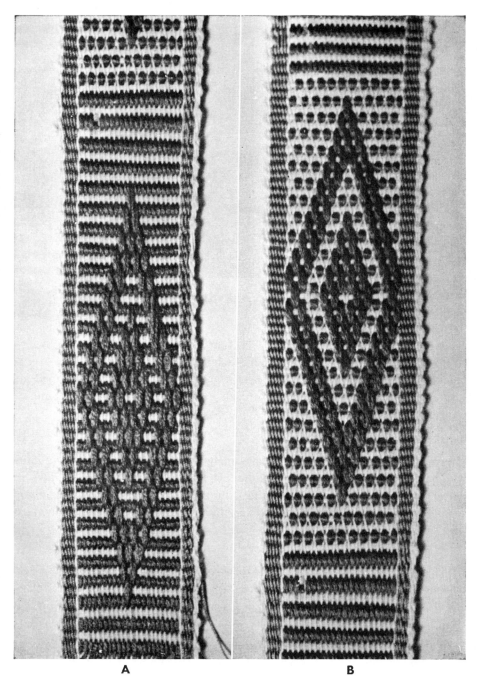

A   **B**

Fig. 74. A Two-Weave Warp Plan. Two different and distinctive belts may be woven from the threading of Belt 8: A. The belt resembles the Momostenango belt of Fig. 73, but is set up differently. B. The weave is the Navaho and Oaxaca weave; see Belt 9, and Fig. 75.

3. Change sheds. Through the white warp, now up, pick up two black pairs, one pair on either side of the first pair picked up. Always do the pick-up *one white warp* to the outside at right and left of the last black pair or pairs of warp picked up. Weave. Change sheds and weave under black.

4. Change sheds. Again pick up the black through the white. Using the same system as above pass one white and pick up two pairs, one on either side of the last two picked up; this time again pick up the center pair of black. Weave. Change sheds and weave under black.

5. On the following rows, weave the following series: Change sheds and pick up four pairs of black; these four increase the width of the pattern and alternate positions with the three pairs of the preceding row. Change sheds, weave under black. Change sheds. On this row the double diamond begins to open. Make the following pick-up: 2 black, 2 white, 2 black, 4 white, 2 black, 2 white, 2 black. Weave. Note the four white in the center; the next row of pick-up will have six white in the center; and the pick-up which follows will start the small inside diamond by raising the center black pair again. (See Fig. 74A.) Remember to pass only one white when increasing or decreasing the diamond pattern.

6. Continue to weave, reversing the direction when the diamonds are of the desired width, gradually picking up fewer black pairs until the apex of the diamond is reached. Then weave six rows of plain weaving.

BELT 9. A NAVAHO AND OAXACA BELT WEAVE (TWO OR FOUR HARNESSES)

The Navaho Indians in the southwestern part of the United States weave interesting belts on primitive bow looms. (See Fig. 65.) The same weave, but with different native patterns, is used by certain Zapotec Indians near Oaxaca, Mexico. A belt from this part of Mexico is illustrated on Fig. 75. The design for this belt is reversible—that is, it appears in opposite colors on the back. The distinguishing feature of this belt is the crisscross diamond effect formed by the white warp of the background. This background weave resembles that of the Summer and Winter weave described on page 245. The background and pattern areas are of different weaves, and are explained below. The plain weave on this belt is always *under* the white warp.

Review the general directions for warping and weaving given earlier in the chapter, pages 121 and 123.

WARPING THE LOOM

This belt can be set up for a two-harness loom from the heddle-threading draft for Belt 8. For a four-harness loom weave, see the draft given in

137

Fig. 67. In Mexico, black, orange, and red yarns are used for the border, fine white cotton for the background, and coarse red cotton for the pattern. The weaver can select any colors desired.

DIRECTIONS FOR WEAVING

Three different weaves can be made on a loom set up for this particular belt weave, and all three can be used on the same belt. They are described below.

To Weave Solid Black

1. Raise the black warp and weave. Change the shed. Through the white, which is now up, pick up every other black pair in the following manner: pick up a black pair, pass two white, pick up a black pair, pass two white, etc. *The white is never dropped.* Weave under the shed formed.
2. Change the shed and weave under black all the way across. Change the shed. Through the white warp, now raised, pick up every other black warp pair—the pairs left down on the preceding pick-up.
3. Continue to alternate the sheds, picking up the black pairs through the white.

To Weave the Crisscross Background Effect

1. Raise the white shed and weave. Raise the black shed. Pick up the first black pair and drop the second black pair; continue across the warp picking up a pair and dropping a pair. Lower all the black warps except those held up in the pick-up. Weave through the shed formed.
2. Change the shed and weave under white. Change the shed—the black is now up—and again pick up the black pairs. This time, drop the first black pair, pick up the second black pair and continue across the warp, dropping alternate black pairs. Note that the black pairs picked up on one row of weaving are dropped on the next. Weave under the picked-up warp yarns.
3. Continue to alternate the sheds in this manner until the weaving is finished.

To Weave a Diamond Pattern on a Crisscross Background

When part of the warp is to be woven in the pattern weave and part in the crisscross or background weave, both sheds are manipulated. In this case there are no plain-woven sheds. When the black warp is up, alternating black pairs are dropped, except in the pattern area; in the pattern area, *all* the black pairs are left up. When the white warp is up, alternating black pairs are picked up only in the pattern area; that is, the black pairs, picked

138

up through the white warp, alternate on every other white shed formed. *The white warp is never dropped.* Step-by-step instructions for making a diamond pattern in this weave (see right belt in Fig. 74) are as follows:

1. Begin the belt by alternating six rows of solid black weave with six rows of the crisscross background weave, as described above. End with six rows of the crisscross background weave.

2. Raise the black warp, find the center, and pick up the center black pair. Drop the two black pairs on either side of the center pair, and then drop alternate black pairs across the warp. Weave under the shed made.

3. Change the shed. Now the white warp is up. Pick up, through the white shed, the same pair of black as in the last pick-up. Hold up all the white, plus the one center pair of black, and weave.

4. Change sheds. Black is now up. Pick up the three center pairs of black, push down or drop the pair on either side, and then pick up and drop alternate black pairs across the warp. Weave under the shed thus made.

5. Change the shed; the white is now up. Of the three pairs in the previous black pick-up, pick up, through the white, the two outside black warp pairs. Weave.

6. Change the shed; the black is now up. Pick up the five center black pairs, etc. Continue weaving in the manner described in steps 4 and 5 until the pattern is completed. The number of pairs picked up after the center of the diamond has been reached is gradually decreased, row by row, until the pattern is finished.

Fig. 75. Oaxaca Belt. This interesting weave from Mexico is also used by the Navaho Indians to weave their sashes; see Fig. 65. It closely resembles the Summer and Winter weave of Fig. 133. This belt is described under Belt 9 in the text.

Fig. 76. Pebble Weave. This two-harness weave was made on an inkle loom; see Belt 10.

7. Weave six rows of the crisscross background between each pattern unit, and the pattern weaving is ended with six rows of this crisscross weave. Finally, the belt is finished by alternating rows of the solid black and the crisscross background weaves as in step 1.

BELT 10. A PERUVIAN PEBBLE WEAVE (A TWO-HARNESS WEAVE)

Any two-harness loom, such as an inkle loom, can be used for this weave, but it is more easily made on a loom equipped with four or six harnesses, like Belt 11. Belt 10 is illustrated in Fig. 76. General directions for warping and weaving should be checked before setting up a loom for this weave.

WARPING THE LOOM

Figure 67 shows the heddle-threading draft for this belt. (The inkle-loom draft is read from left to right, and the harness-loom draft from right to left.) Two colors of coarse yarn of equal weight are used for the warp.

DIRECTIONS FOR WEAVING

In the two methods of weaving given for this belt, no specific pattern is described; instead, the general system of manipulating the warp for any pattern is presented. A coarse colored weft should be selected. If the belt is woven on an inkle loom, substitute the word "shed" for the word "harness" in the directions given below.

Pebble Weaving. Method I

1. Weave six rows of plain weave, alternating harnesses 1 and 2.
2. To start the pattern, raise harness 1 and weave. While this harness is up, use a pick-up stick and pick up the white warp in the pattern areas. Count the yarns and center the pattern.
3. Leaving the pick-up stick in the warp, raise harness 2 and weave. Still leaving the first pick-up stick in place, pick up the alternate white warps in the pattern area and place them on a second pick-up stick. Remove the first pick-up stick.

140

4. Leaving the second pick-up stick in the warp, raise harness 1 and weave. Using the first pick-up stick, again pick up the alternate white warps in the pattern area. Remove the second pick-up stick.

5. Repeat steps 3 and 4 alternately until the belt is finished. End with six rows of plain weaving.

Pebble Weaving. Method II

1. Weave six rows of plain weaving, alternating harnesses 1 and 2.

2. Raise harness 1 and weave. Pick up the white warps of the pattern area with the first pick-up stick, and the black warps in the background area and the border with the second pick-up stick. As the black warp is being picked up, slip the second pick-up stick under the white yarns —those picked up on the first pick-up stick. Since all the picked up yarns are now on the same stick, the first pick-up stick can be removed.

3. Raise harness 2 and weave. The second pick-up stick can be removed at this point, but more often it is left in the warp until the new pick-up is made. Use the first pick-up stick to pick up the alternate white warps of the pattern, and a third one to pick up the alternate black warp of the background; again include the white pick-up on the stick which picks up the black warp. Remove the first and second sticks. Repeat steps 2 and 3.

Fig. 77. Peruvian Pebble Weave. A four-harness loom is needed for this weave; see Belt 11.

4. Repeat the above process, alternating harnesses 1 and 2, until the belt is finished. Finish with six rows of plain weaving.

BELT 11. A PERUVIAN PEBBLE WEAVE (A FOUR-HARNESS WEAVE)

A weave used by the Peruvian Indians of the high Andes for making coca bags has a pebblelike two-tone effect. This weave is described below. (See also Fig. 77.)

WARPING THE LOOM

Although any selection of colors can be chosen for this weave, a combination of very dark and very light yarns gives the most effective contrast. **141**

In the following directions black and white yarns are used for the warp. The warp is set close: No. 3 perle cotton, set 40 ends to the inch—in a 10 dent reed, 4 threads to the dent. Remember to review general instructions for warping on page 121.

Four heddle harnesses are needed for this weave. They are strung according to the heddle-threading draft shown in Fig. 67, with a sufficient number of repeats to make the desired width of the belt. Some weavers thread the first four warps as shown on the draft, but change the threading order for harnesses 2 and 4 to white, black, white, black, alternating the white and black yarns entirely across the warp.

Unless a six-harness loom is used, this belt is best made without a border. On a six-harness loom the border is threaded on harnesses 5 and 6. Harness 5 is raised with harnesses 2 and 3, and harness 6 with harnesses 1 and 4, following each pattern weave.

DIRECTIONS FOR WEAVING

The weft yarn can be black or white. If a six-harness loom is used, the weft should match the outside warps of the border. Double weft can also be used. The weaving can be modified to give a variety of effects.

An All-White Effect

Raise the harnesses in pairs in the following combinations: 1 and 2; 1 and 4; 1 and 2; 2 and 3; repeat this series. Always end with the 1 and 2 combination.

An All-Black Effect

Raise the harnesses in pairs in the following combinations: 3 and 4; 1 and 4; 3 and 4; 2 and 3; repeat the series, ending with the 3 and 4 combination.

Stripes

The plain weave automatically forms black and white stripes. The sheds are formed by raising harnesses 1 and 2 together alternately with 3 and 4 raised together.

A Pebbled Background Effect

To secure a pebbled effect in the background, raise harnesses 2 and 3 together alternately with harnesses 1 and 4 raised together.

To Weave a Pattern

The following directions are for weaving a white pattern against a black-and-white pebbled background.

142

1. Weave several rows of the pebbled background weave as described just above.
2. Raise harnesses 1 and 2 together. Pick up the white pattern warps on a pick-up stick. Lower harnesses 1 and 2 and raise harnesses 3 and 4 together. The black warp is now up. Push the first pick-up stick back on the warp, place the second pick-up stick in front of the first, and pick up the black background warps. This stick may also incorporate the pick-up of the first stick as it is being carried through the warp. The first stick is then removed. Leave only one warp down before each contrasting group: for example, leave one white warp down before and after picking up a black group, and one black warp down before and after picking up a white group. Take care to leave down the same number of black yarns as the number of white yarns picked up on the first pick-up stick, and leave down the same number of white yarns as the number of black yarns picked up on the second pick-up stick. Lower all harnesses and weave beneath the pick-up, using a shed sword to help form the special shed. Take out the second pick-up stick.
3. Raise harnesses 1 and 4 together and weave.
4. Repeat step 2, above. Then raise harnesses 2 and 3 together and weave.
5. Repeat steps 2, 3, and 4 until the design area has been completed. End the belt with several rows of pebbled background weave.

BELT 12. A PERUVIAN INGRAIN WEAVE (A FOUR-HARNESS WEAVE)

The Peruvian Indians weave a belt which is spectacular in both color arrangement and design. One popular color combination is brilliant green and purple vertical stripes on a bright yellow background. Two complete sets of warp are necessary for this weave. Unlike the double-cloth weave described under Belt 15, the warp here intermeshes to form a single fabric, but like the double-cloth weave, the belt design is reversible. (See Fig. 71.)

WARPING THE LOOM

The warp for this weave should be of a fine, tightly twisted, strong yarn, set very close. Number 9 quilting cotton has been used satisfactorily. Fig. 67 shows the heddle-threading draft.

In the following arrangement, black is used for one set of warp yarns and white for the other. If desired, however, harnesses 1 and 3 can be threaded in one color, and harnesses 2 and 4 in one-fourth-inch stripes of several colors. Thread the heddles as follows: the right border; harness 1, heddle 1, black; harness 2, heddle 1, white; harness 3, heddle 1, black; harness 4, heddle 1, white. Repeat this system of threading for the other heddles until the desired width of the belt has been achieved; then thread the left border. The border yarns may be of one color or two, one for each set of warp.

DIRECTIONS FOR WEAVING

Any type of design, plotted first on graph paper, can be used as a pattern for this belt weave. Figure 68 illustrates several designs.

Since the weft will show only at the edge of the belt, it should be the same color as the outside warp yarns. It should be coarse—either twice as heavy as the warp, or made of two strands. In the latter case, the bobbin can be threaded with double weft, or, better, two bobbins can be used.

The pattern on this belt can be woven in two ways, both described below. Some weavers prefer the second method because they feel it is the easier. Actually it requires more manipulation than does the first. The pattern areas are often separated by strips of solid color. A solid color area is obtained by the following methods.

To Weave Solid Black

Lift the harnesses in pairs in the following combinations: 1 and 3, 1 and 2, 1 and 3, 3 and 4; repeat the series, always ending with the 1 and 3 combination.

To Weave Solid White

Lift the harnesses in pairs in the following combinations: 2 and 4, 1 and 2, 2 and 4, 3 and 4; repeat the series, always ending with the 2 and 4 combination.

To Weave a Pattern. Method I

1. To begin the belt, weave a half-inch strip of solid black, followed by a half-inch strip of solid white, as described above.
2. Raise harnesses 2 and 4. Starting from the right, pick up the white yarns in the pattern area on a pick-up stick. Lower these harnesses and raise harnesses 1 and 3. Pick up the black background warp, running this second pick-up stick under the white yarns picked up by the first stick. Remove the first pick-up stick. In this weave, the same number of black warps are left down as there are white warps picked up and vice versa. Place a shed sword in the special shed made by the second pick-up stick and remove the stick. Turn the shed sword on its side and weave. Remove the shed sword.

3. Raise harnesses 1 and 2 and weave.
4. Repeat step 2 above. Raise harnesses 3 and 4 and weave.
5. Repeat steps 2, 3 and 4 until the belt is finished. Weave areas of solid black between the pattern areas.
6. End the belt with a half-inch strip of solid white and the same of solid black, as in step 1 above.

Reversing the sets of warp raised will reverse the color patterns, but always remember to end the weaving by raising harnesses 1 and 2 together before reversing the color patterns.

To Weave a Pattern. Method II

In the following method the harnesses are raised in consecutive order. Choose two pick-up sticks which can be readily distinguished from one another.
1. Weave a strip of plain black and then one of plain white; end with white harness 2 up.
2. While harness 2 is still up, pick up the white pattern warps with the first pick-up stick. Lower harness 2, raise harness 3 and weave. While harness 3 is still raised, push the first pick-up stick toward the back of the loom and, with the second pick-up stick, pick up the black background warps to the front of the previous pick-up. Lower harness 3, raise harness 4, and weave.
3. While harness 4 is still raised, remove the first pick-up stick from the back of the warp and push the second stick to the back of the loom. now placing the first stick in front of the second, pick up the alternate white pattern warps. Lower harness 4, raise harness 1, and weave.
4. While harness 1 is still raised, remove the second pick-up stick from the back of the warp, place it in front of the first stick, and pick up the alternate black background warps. Lower harness 1, raise harness 2, and weave.
5. Repeat steps 2 through 4 until the design unit is complete. Weave an area of all black before beginning each new pattern unit. Notice from the above description that one pick-up stick always picks up white yarns, and the other always picks up black yarns.

BELT 13. AN ECUADORIAN BELT WEAVE (A FOUR-HARNESS WEAVE)

The Ecuadorian Indians weave very beautiful belts, achieving intricate warp-faced designs by several different methods. Two common threadings are shown at the bottom of Fig. 67. In threading up their looms, these people alternate single or double strands of fine white cotton yarns with single

145

strands of coarse hand-spun woolen yarns. A common threading used is a three-harness twill, in which the first two harnesses are threaded with fine white cotton yarn for the tabby weave, and the third with the pattern yarn, a colored heavy woolen yarn. Twill is discussed at greater length in Chapter VII. The Ecuadorian belts illustrated in Fig. 71 are set up from the threading draft given for Belt 13, Type 2, Fig. 67. The loom can also be threaded as for Belt 12 in Fig. 67. In this case coarse woolen yarns are alternated with fine cotton yarns.

Ecuadorian belts are not difficult to weave. Although no special instructions are given for these belts, the weaver should be able to copy the patterns in Fig. 71, using a weaving technique similar to that for Belts 7 and 10. All the patterns are formed, of course, by pick-up weaving.

TWISTED- AND CROSSED-WARP BELT WEAVES

BELT 14. AN ANCIENT PERUVIAN WARP-TWINED WEAVE (NO HARNESSES NEEDED)

A very rare and unusual warp-faced weave is formed by a twisted-warp technique. A belt woven in this technique resembles, in both appearance and structure, one which has been woven on an Egyptian-card or tablet loom. The weave may therefore be called a pseudo-tablet weave. Technically, the weave of this belt, if made by the finger-weaving process, is properly classified as warp twining. Both tablet weaving and warp twining were described earlier in this chapter (also see Fig. 33). The structure of the weave is formed by repeated crossing of the yarns; this results in vertical columns made up of pairs of twisted warp.

Other textile techniques, somewhat related to the one we are discussing, can be used for making belts. Such related processes as warp-twined plaiting, braiding, and meshwork are all constructed without the use of true weft. Also related to warp twining are gauze weaving, tablet weaving, and certain cord weaves, all of which have a true weft.

WARPING THE LOOM

Heavy yarns are generally used for warping. In the belt described here black (B) and white (W) woolen yarns are used. Working from left to right, the yarns are tied to and stretched between two 10-inch rods in this order: 1W, 2B-2W (the last unit of four is repeated 11 times); then add 2B, 1W. There should be 48 yarns altogether. The warp yarns are stretched between the two rods in a horizontal position and held taut during weaving. The rods are tied to two supports as for a back-strap loom, or they may be fastened to only one rod and allowed to hang down in a vertical position.

146

In this case they must be held taut with weights as in any warp-weighted loom.

When the warp stretched between the two rods is to be woven from one end only, a hole-board heddle can be installed to assist the weaver with shed formation. The use of tubular beads for warp twining, described on page 73, also facilitates the formation of the sheds.

DIRECTIONS FOR WEAVING

When the warp is stretched between two rods as described above, both ends can be woven simultaneously. This is accomplished by opening the shed the length of the warp and putting weft in both ends. This technique is similar to that used when braiding with shed sticks.

The weft is usually the same type of yarn as the warp. When black and white yarns are used for the warp, either black or white yarn is chosen for the weft. Black weft forms a better defined pattern, and white a more continuous pattern. The ancient Peruvians used both black and white weft yarns, alternating them on alternate rows of weaving; this enabled them to form a twisted selvage which matched the technique of the rest of the belt. Alternating weft makes a better pattern if used on a belt half as wide as the one described here.

In the directions given here, diamond patterns are formed in the warp. To weave them, the yarns are twisted first away from and then toward the centers of the two diamonds. (See Fig. 33.)

To weave one row across the belt, start at the left and lift the second black warp yarn toward the left, over the first white warp yarn. Pick up the white yarn, hold it over the fingers of the left hand, and drop the black yarn under the fingers of that hand. Continue across the row crossing black over white, then white over black, until six yarns are above the fingers. The center of the first diamond has now been reached and the crossing process must be reversed. To do this, carry the next white yarn toward the right over the adjacent black yarn. Drop the white and pick up the black. Continue across the warp until six more yarns are above the fingers. Half of the yarns are now above the fingers of the left hand, and the center of the warp has been reached. The second half of this row of weaving is twisted in the same manner as the first half. When all of the yarns have been picked up across one row, the weft is thrown through the open shed.

Note that this crossing process divides a row of weaving into four sections. Counting from left to right, the yarns in the first and third sections are crossed in one direction, those in the second and fourth sections are crossed in the opposite direction. On the first row of weaving the white

147

and black yarns that are held above the fingers of the left hand appear in the following order: W, B, W, B, W, *B, B,* W, B, W, B, *W, W,* B, W, B, W, *B, B,* W, B, W, B, W; the doubles are centers. The yarns held below the fingers of the left hand are in the reverse color to those held above these fingers.

Firm the fabric by pulling the warp yarns on either side of the shed in opposite directions; this pushes together the weft of the previous rows of weaving. Then pull the last weft yarn to the proper tension. Use a gauge to control the width of the belt.

This method of crossing the yarns is repeated for five consecutive rows of weaving; then the direction of crossing the yarns is reversed, and the yarns are crossed in the opposite directions for five rows. The ten rows of weaving thus made form the two diamond patterns across the warp. Repeat this procedure for the other sets of diamonds along the length of the belt.

BALANCED WARP AND WEFT BELT WEAVES

BELT 15. A DOUBLE-CLOTH BELT WEAVE (A FOUR-HARNESS WEAVE)

The double-cloth weave described below is a balanced weave; i.e., it is both warp- and weft-faced. It could also be called a 50/50 weave. A set of black and a set of white yarns are used for the warp. Since two complete sets of warp are used, a four-harness loom is needed.

WARPING THE LOOM

The warp yarn used for the pattern illustrated in Fig. 134 is No. 10 cotton set 40 to the inch, 2 to a dent, in a No. 20 dent reed, white pairs alternating with black pairs, as shown in Fig. 67. After the selvage, the four harnesses are threaded in this order: harness 1, heddle 1, black; harness 2, heddle 1, black; harness 3, heddle 1, white; harness 4, heddle 1, white; repeat this order for the other heddles, threading the loom to the width desired for the belt.

This weave is easier to make on a jack-type of loom equipped with six treadles. The harnesses should be tied to the six treadles as follows: 1 and 2, 3 and 4, 1, 2, 3, 4.

DIRECTIONS FOR WEAVING

The double-cloth weave is very versatile. Some of its variations are given below; for other possibilities see the description of double-cloth weaves in Chapter VII and Figs. 43, 134A and B.

To Weave Solid Black

Raise harness 1 and weave. Lower harness 1, raise harness 2, and weave. Raise harnesses 1, 2, 3, and weave. Raise harnesses 1, 2, 4, and weave. Repeat this process until the desired amount of black has been woven.

To Weave Solid White

The above system is also used for weaving solid white, only this time start with harness 3. Raise the harnesses in the following order and weave: 3, 4, 1–3–4, 2–3–4.

To Weave a Pick-Up Pattern

A pick-up pattern in a double-cloth weave is reversible. Because it is easier to weave a black pattern on a white background than vice versa, this is the arrangement described below.

Two shuttles are needed for double-cloth weaving, one for the black weft and one for the white. Keep in mind that when black warp is picked up on the pick-up stick, white yarn is used for the weft; and when white warp is picked up on the pick-up stick, black yarn is used for the weft. The picked-up warp design binds the white fabric sections to the black.

1. To weave, raise harnesses 1 and 2, black, and pick up the pattern warps, allowing two black warps for each square in the pattern draft. (See Fig 68.) Lower harnesses 1 and 2 and all warp except that above the pick-up stick. Raise harness 3 and weave with white. Batten well after each throw of weft while the shuttle—usually a stick shuttle—is in the shed. Raise harness 4, and weave with white. Remove the shuttle stick and the pick-up stick, and batten again.

2. Raise harnesses 3 and 4, white, and pick up the background warps on a pick-up stick. As many white warps must be left down—not picked up —as black warps were picked up on the previous pick-up, and these warps *must be in the same location.* Care must be taken when picking up white warp, to lift up only one white from each pair *immediately before and after the design pick-up.* For example, if four black pairs, eight warps in all, were picked up for the design, then eight white warps above that design would have to be skipped—not picked up—in this order: 1 white, 2 white, 2 white, 2 white, 1 white—eight warps in all. The two end yarns in the above combination are one-half of the end pairs bordering the black warp design.

3. Now lower harnesses 3 and 4, and all the warp except that above the pick-up stick. Raise harness 1 and weave, using the shuttle stick threaded in black. Batten. Lower harness 1, raise harness 2, and weave, again using

149

the black shuttle. Remove the pick-up stick and the shuttle stick and batten down again.

4. Repeat steps 1 through 3 until the pattern has been completed. A solid black or white strip, or stripes of black and white, can be woven between the design units and at both ends of the belt.

ECCENTRIC PICK-UP BELT WEAVES

Ancient weavers of Peru and creative weavers of other lands have experimented with pick-up weaving and discovered some unusual variations of this art. The ancient Peruvians, for example, carried extra warp yarns along the back of a piece of warp-faced weaving, picking up these warp yarns at intervals as needed and incorporating them into the design. They also combined many techniques in one belt. With the same warp yarns in operation, they would combine one or more of such techniques as braiding, meshwork, warp twining, eccentric gauzes, warp-faced weaving, and tapestry.

CHAPTER V

Rug Looms and Rug-Making Techniques

On the floors of his rude shelters ancient man used sand, grass, pine needles, and other materials, both to freshen up his abode and to ease foot strain. Later he tamped and fire-hardened the earth of his dwelling. Finally he covered his floors with interwoven mats made from plant fibers. After the art of weaving was developed, he indulged in the luxury of using blankets and rugs for floor coverings.

The lands of southeast Asia, especially Turkistan, Turkey, and Persia, have long been famous for their knotted-pile rugs, as well as for their Soumak, Kilim, and other tapestry rugs. On the foothills of the Himalaya Mountains and on the southern slopes of the Steppes, cashmere and angora goats, camels, and sheep graze in some of the best pasture lands in the world. Fleeces that come from the mountain towns of Persia—especially Shiraz, Kirman, and Khorassan—are among the world's finest; it is possible to spin very fine yarns from these fleeces, since the fibers contain so many serrations to the inch.

Perhaps the Babylonians were the earliest weavers of carpets; early historians often lauded the beauties of the rare carpets from Babylon (*88*). The Persians acquired this art when they conquered Babylon, and they then became the foremost producers of elaborate carpets. Herodotus, in the fifth century B.C., wrote of the Persians' silver and gold rugs.

Rug making gradually spread westward. The Romans, the Moslems, and the Crusaders, in turn, were instrumental in its expansion. In the last part of the Middle Ages and in the early Renaissance, small rug-making establishments were set up in Europe. Although hand-loomed rugs are still produced

151

in many parts of the Old and New Worlds, power looms have now taken over most of their production.

1. Flat-Surfaced, Nonpile Carpet Weaves and Their Looms

The earliest woven carpets, made many centuries before the Christian era, were flat-surfaced weaves. *Tapestry* is possibly the oldest type of flat-surfaced, patterned carpet weaves. The rugs which the Queen of Sheba spread before Solomon were undoubtedly tapestries. The Soumak weave (*87*) has also been traced to an early beginning in the Near East. Other flat-surfaced rugs are ingrain rugs, warp-faced hemp fiber rugs, and rugs woven of heavy woolen or bast fiber yarns, reinforced with stuffer yarns, and woven in several standard weaves. Woven and braided rag rugs could also be considered flat-surfaced rugs.

Flat-surfaced rug weaves are either weft-faced or warp-faced; woven rag rugs are an exception. Tapestry, Soumak, the saddle blanket, and the Summer and Winter weaves are weft-faced. Of these, the Soumak and the Summer and Winter weaves need a supporting tabby weft. Ingrain and warp-striped hemp fiber rug weaves are warp-faced.

Fig. 78. Chinese Tapestry. Slit (Kilim) tapestry of the Ming Dynasty, fifteenth century. (Courtesy, Cooper Union Museum.)

TAPESTRY LOOMS AND WEAVES

Tapestry weaving represents a technical advance over the many other early methods of weaving. Since early historical times, the pattern possibilities of tapestry have made it especially precious to weavers.

The art of tapestry weaving was known in ancient times in both the Old and the New Worlds. The record of tapestry weaving in the Far East goes back at least to the Han Dynasty of China, 220 B.C. to 206 A.D., when tapestries were being woven of silk. (See Fig. 78.)

Fig. 79. Bolivian Tapestry. Poncho from Island of Titicaca, found in a stone chest near Muro-Kato, Bolivia, possibly Incan. (Courtesy, The American Museum of Natural History.)

Tapestry was woven in the New World long before the arrival of the Spanish. (See Figs. 2, 79, and 81.) Beautiful tapestry bags, belts, and mantles have been found in ancient burial sites on the southern coast of Peru—at Paracas, Nazca, and other places—and in the highlands of Bolivia. Today the Indians of Guatemala are considered the best native weavers of tapestry on the Western Hemisphere. One wonders if they learned this art in prehistoric times from South American sources. A second center of native tapestry weaving is the southwestern part of the United States, where the famous Navaho rugs and blankets are made. (See Figs. 13 and 46, center.) It is commonly understood that the Navahos learned tapestry weaving from the more ancient peoples of the Southwest, the Hopi.

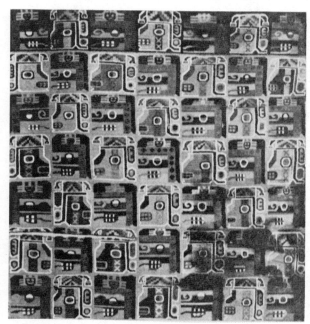

Fig. 80. Peruvian Tapestry. Very fine (coastal) Tiahuanacoid tapestry of about 500 A.D. (Courtesy, Brooklyn Museum Collection.)

In the Near East, tapestry was produced in many areas. As already noted, Babylon appears to have been the site of the first rug industries in the ancient world. A fragment of tapestry, estimated to be the oldest piece now in existence, was found by Dr. M. A. Stein in an archaeological excavation in some old ruins near Khotan in Eastern Turkestan; the weave used was practically identical to that of modern Kilim tapestry (89). Another piece of tapestry, estimated to have been made about 400 B.C., was found in the Crimea and is now in the museum of Leningrad. A piece of tapestry dated about 300 B.C. was found in a former Greek settlement on the north shore of the Black Sea.

Many statements found in ancient writings may have referred to tapestry. The Bible actually mentions tapestry: "I have decked my bed with coverings of tapestry." (Proverbs vii.) The *Iliad* mentions fabrics that must have been tapestry: "The Trojan wars she weaves." The famous embroideries of the ancient Phoenicians may have included tapestry. It is also possible that many of the famous picture-designed fabrics of the early Greek and Roman periods, referred to by many historians and poets, were of tapestry con-

THE TEXTILE ARTS

struction. According to M. De Ronchaud, tapestries were hung in the Parthenon. The awning or velarium made for Nero, which showed Apollo driving his chariot across the skies, may also have been a tapestry fabric.

Egypt has had a long record of tapestry weaving. Exactly when the Egyptians began to weave in tapestry is not known, but it is thought by some that it was introduced there by the ancient Syrians. An illustration of a loom similar to a tapestry loom in the hypogeum at Beni Hasan came from the period of 3000 B.C.; a similar painting, dated *ca.* 1600 B.C., came from Thebes and is now in the museum in Cairo. In 1903, T. M. Davies found in the Valley of the Kings one of the oldest pieces of tapestry known, estimated to be dated at 1448 to 1420 B.C. The tapestry is skillfully woven of linen, finished on both sides, and decorated with the titles of Amenhotep II and with lotus and disc designs. The designs, which are all outlined in black, are woven in blue, red, brown, yellow, and green. Three small pieces of tapestry containing hieroglyphic,

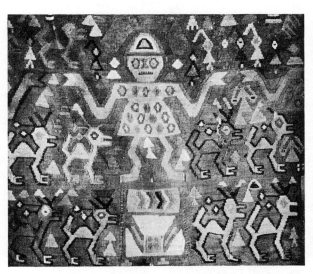

Fig. 81. Nasca Tapestry. Detail of ancient Nasca (Peru) poncho. (Courtesy, The American Museum of Natural History.)

scarab, and lotus designs and belonging to about the same period are in the Metropolitan Museum in New York.

Vast quantities of tapestries have come from the graves of the Copts, the early Egyptian Christians. Most of them were made between the second and eighth centuries. The Copts used Grecian geometric motifs, curvilinear leaves and vines, and isolated pattern units, and were especially fond of weaving portraits. (See Fig. 3.) They ornamented their shirts with tapestry borders and medallions. Eventually the designs of Persia—fantastic bird, animal, and floral patterns—influenced the subject matter of Coptic tapestries. Between 600 and 1000 A.D., most of the Egyptian weavers were engaged in making ornate tapestries for the Mohammedans.

The Romans sent Coptic weavers to Gaul to teach the people to weave the tapestry bands used to ornament Roman clothing, thus starting the tapestry industry in southern France. Much later, about the year 1000, a group of Moors from Spain settled in the Creuse Valley in southern France and

Fig. 82. German Tapestry. Seventeenth-century wool and silk cushion top.
(Courtesy, Cooper Union Museum.)

initiated the weaving of tapestry rugs. Gradually the tapestry art spread from these southern centers toward the north and there was a general revival of interest in it. About this time the Low Countries began to weave tapestry, and some of the finest tapestries woven in Europe eventually came from this area. Indeed, the Flemish tapestries from Brussels and other centers are considered the best of those in the early Renaissance. During the late Middle Ages and early Renaissance it became the style to hang tapestries on the walls of the great audience halls of the courts and castles of

Europe, some of them enormous. They illustrated mythological, historical, and Biblical subjects. A similar design can be seen in Fig. 82.

Naturally, very large looms were needed for weaving such fabrics. In 1313, high looms were established in Arras, France, an old Coptic weaving center. In Paris the Gobelin Factory became famous for its tapestry rugs and wall hangings; Louis XIV was its special sponsor. (See Fig. 83.) In England, James I established a tapestry rug industry at Mortlake, and similar industries were then established in other towns, staffed principally by French and Flemish refugee weavers.

Fig. 83. French Tapestry. Aubusson carpet of the early nineteenth century. (Courtesy of the Metropolitan Museum of Art.)

It can be seen even from this brief account that large sums of money must have been spent for tapestries during the Renaissance period. The inventory of the effects of Henry VIII of England, taken at the time of his death, shows that he left 2000 pieces of tapestry to friends and relatives.

There has been a recent revival of interest in tapestry weaving in Europe and America, and a number of modern artists have turned to this art as a medium of expression. Modern and eccentric designs are being "painted" with the needle—in other words, designs suitable for modern paintings are being woven into tapestry. This use of tapestry apparently started in Sweden; Swedish modern tapestry rugs and wall hangings have enlivened many museum exhibits. (See Figs. 84 and 85.)

STRUCTURE OF THE TAPESTRY LOOM

European tapestry looms are built on durable vertical frames equipped with side arms which hold one of the heddle bars. (See Fig. 85B.) The simple Navaho tapestry rug loom is likewise an upright loom, but it is a crude affair when compared with its European counterpart. It consists of two large forked limbs or the forked trunks of two small trees placed vertically in the ground; a stout pole laid horizontally across and through the forks supports the two-barred loom; ropes wound around this pole and the top bar of the loom are used to adjust the height of the loom. The cloth

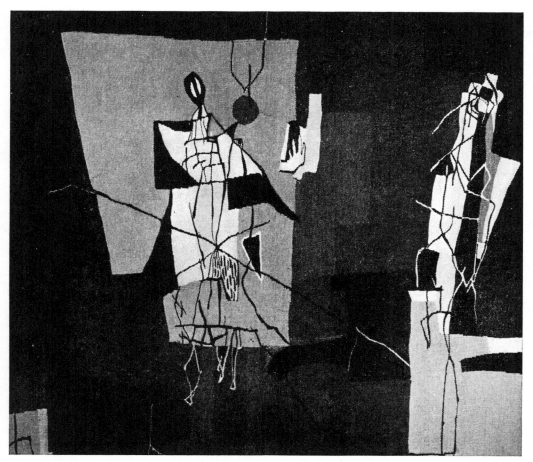

Fig. 84. Detail of a Modern Tapestry. By Johanna Schidlo, Frankfurt, Germany. (Courtesy, Bertha Schaefer Gallery, N.Y.)

beam—the bottom loom bar—is held taut by rope stretchers attached to stakes in the ground. (See Figs. 13 and 86.) The heddle devices are described later in the discussion of warping the loom.

Tapestry can be woven on practically every type of loom. The Indians of Guatemala make narrow tapestry head bands on horizontal looms. (See Fig. 71.)

THE TEXTILE ARTS

PLANNING THE DESIGN FOR TAPESTRY WEAVING

Designs for tapestry weaving are plotted on squared paper, each horizontal row of squares representing one weft thread in the shed. There are, of course, as many different weft yarns in the same shed as there are breaks on one row of weaving or interruptions in the pattern.

Any subject can serve as the theme for a tapestry design. The

Fig. 85A.   Detail of a Modern Tapestry. Detail of a large tapestry by Jan Yoors.

Fig. 85B.   A Modern Tapestry in the Making. Mr. Yoors and weavers in his New York studio. Note the high-warp loom and the position of the shed roll and string heddle rod.

Navaho Indians use the typical symbolic designs common to the Indians of North America—crosses, diamonds, zigzags, and step patterns.

WARPING THE LOOM

The loom should be strung with a strong, firm yarn, preferably linen. The Navahos use a coarse bast fiber for their warp. The warp is usually prepared upon some type of warping frame before it is strung upon the tapestry loom. When a very wide warp is needed, it should be made up in sections and one section at a time prepared on the warping board. When an extra long warp is needed, it must be looped or crocheted into a chain as it is being removed from the warping board to prevent the yarns from tangling.

The method of setting up a tapestry loom used by the Navaho Indians (1) is as follows: After the warp has been wound upon the warping frame but before it is removed from it, they twine two heavy wefts, known as heading cords, into the two end loops at opposite ends of the warp. Depending upon the spacing desired, one to three twists of twining are made in this heading cord between each warp yarn. The crosses in the warp are secured with lease sticks before the warp is removed from the frame. (Warping frames, twining, and crosses are all described in earlier chapters.)

When all is ready, the warp is carefully removed from the frame and a temporary loom bar is slipped into each end of the warp. The warp is then stretched horizontally on the ground between these bars. Working first at one end of the warp and then at the other, the warp is bound to the permanent loom beams in the following manner: The end strands of the heading cord are tied to the ends of a permanent loom beam; a length of strong string is tied to the left end of this same beam. Working from left to right, the string is wrapped through the warp; it is carried over the heading cord and around the permanent loom beam at even intervals across the entire warp. (See Fig. 86A.) After both ends of the warp have been tightly secured to these permanent beams, the temporary loom bars are removed, and the loom is stretched between the horizontal bars of the vertical loom frame. (See Fig. 86B.) Note that a similar method can be used to put the warp on the bars of a strap-back loom; see Variation 1, page 86.

Many tapestries are woven on looms equipped with a continuous warp; in this case, the warp yarns are carried directly around the end beams of the loom (see Fig. 47).

The string heddle rod and the heddle sword, which form the alternate sheds in the warp during weaving, are now inserted in the warp. For directions for preparing these two heddle devices, see Fig. 44 and page 90.

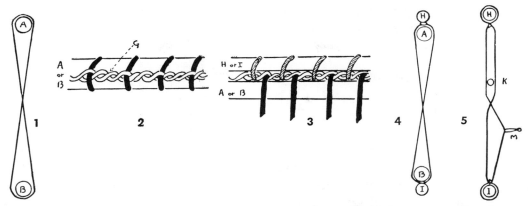

Fig. 86A. Navaho Loom Parts. (1) Warp stretched on temporary loom beams. (2) Detail showing twined ends of warp. (3) Detail showing binding cord joining warp to permanent loom beams. (4) Position of permanent loom beams (I and H). (5) Insertion of shed roll or heddle sword (K), and string heddle rod (M); two sheds may now be formed. (Courtesy, Denver Art Museum.)

Fig. 86B. Navaho Loom. Note the ties at top which allow for lowering the warp as the weaving proceeds. The rug is rolled gradually onto the bottom beam as it is finished.

The warp for tapestry weaving is usually threaded for a plain weave, but it may be set up for a twill weave. The Guatemalan belt in Fig. 71 was woven on a four-harness plain twill threading.

GENERAL DIRECTIONS FOR TAPESTRY WEAVING

The weft for tapestry weaving can be of any fiber content. The Chinese used silk for tapestry weaving long before the Christian era; the early Peruvians used cotton and wool; linen was used by the Egyptians during the Dynastic periods; and linen, cotton, and wool were used by Coptic weavers. During the Renaissance, cotton, wool, and silk were used by tapestry weavers. Since the Spanish introduced sheep into the New World, coarse wools have been used by the Navahos for their rugs and blankets.

In tapestry weaving, the weft can be drawn through the warp with the help of small sticks or with the fingers; it can be carried through the warp on a small shuttle; or it can be darned into the warp with a tapestry needle. When the weft is added to the warp during weaving, tapestry is considered a weaving technique, but when the weft is darned into an area of open warp in a woven fabric, the technique is considered a type of drawnwork embroidery, even though the stitches are identical in both cases.

Before beginning to weave tapestry, 1/2 inch of plain weaving is made with heavy, loosely spun yarn. This preliminary weaving, which evens the tension of the warp, is followed by 1/4 inch of plain weaving with fine cotton, which, battened down firmly, stabilizes the warp.

The tapestry weave is usually considered a variation of the plain weave. The weft is allowed to fit rather loosely around the warp to prevent constriction of the warp and is then battened in place, starting with the side of the loom opposite the shuttle. In this way the shuttle can supply more weft without drawing in the outside edges of the warp. A wooden comb is usually used for battening the weft in place; such a comb is illustrated in Fig. 12, No. 4. In simple tapestry weaving, however, a battening sword is often used. When it is necessary to splice weft yarns, the ends are overlapped in the center of a pattern area.

The tapestry weave is made up of isolated areas of pattern. Since each pattern area consists of a different color or value, there are as many insertions of yarn across one row of weaving as there are pattern areas across that row. When a shed is opened, each pattern weft is carried across only the particular area concerned. On horizontal foot-power looms, it is customary to weave one row of each pattern unit in regular sequence across the warp with each opening of the shed. On vertical high-warp looms, it is customary to weave independently of the entire warp; the worker weaves in small areas, opening the shed in these areas as needed by reaching up and pulling on the particular strings of the string heddle rod which are concerned. In some very unique tapestries each pattern unit is woven without relation to the customary direction of the weft. No tabby wefts support the pattern yarns in tapestry weaving; this is a distinguishing feature of this weave.

The manner in which the weft yarns of different pattern areas meet or are joined often determines the character of the tapestry. A variety of methods, sometimes classified as types, are used to make this transition. Although the list below does not exhaust the range of possibilities of making these transitions between patterns, the types most frequently used are described here.

TAPESTRY TYPES AND RELATED WEAVES

Type 1-A: Single-Warp Interlocked Tapestry

Two weft yarns, coming together from opposite directions, partly encircle the same warp yarn before returning, again in opposite directions, in the next shed.

Type 1-B

Weft yarns, coming together from opposite directions, alternately pass around the warp in singles as in Type 1-A; or alternate groups composed of two or three rows of wefts interlock around the same warp yarn. This method forms zigzag or serrated edges along the pattern areas.

Type 2-A: Multiple-Warp Interlocked Tapestry

The weft yarns, coming together from opposite directions, enclose two adjacent warp yarns. The weft from the right encloses the left warp, and the one from the left encloses the right warp of a pair of yarns located at the margins of two pattern areas. (See Fig. 87.)

Type 2-B

The interlocking extends the distance of three warps.

Type 3-A: Diagonal Multiple-Warp Interlocked Tapestry

This process is fundamentally the same as 2-A, except that the interlocking is carried progressively forward—one warp to the right or the left—on each row of pattern weaving.

Type 3-B

The diagonal interlocking extends the distance of three warps.

163

Fig. 87. Tapestry Techniques. These techniques are described in the text under the following headings. The types in the left column, arranged from top to bottom are 1a, 2a, 6c, 6b, 16 (top), and 11b (bottom). In the right column, top to bottom, are 4a, 5b, 9a, 11a, 14 (center column), and 15 (background).

Type 4-A: Single-Weft Interlooped Tapestry

Two weft yarns, coming together from opposite directions, interloop around each other before starting their paths in opposite directions back across the warp in the next shed.

Type 4-B

The two weft yarns interloop above or below a warp which is left free.

Type 5-A: Diagonal Single-Weft Interlooped Tapestry

The weft yarns, interlooping as in 4-A progress in position, one warp to the right or left on each row of weaving. This makes diagonal edges on the pattern areas.

Type 5-B

The same as 4-B, except that the interlooping progresses forward by one warp, in a right or left direction on each row of weaving.

Type 6-A: Multiple-Weft Interlooped Tapestry

One weft coming from one direction loops into the end loops of two wefts coming from the opposite direction.

Type 6-B

A weft coming from the left interloops into two wefts coming from the right.

Likewise, each weft coming from the right interloops into two wefts coming from the left. Each weft is therefore interlooped twice. (See Fig. 87.)

Type 6-C

The interlooping is made by yarns of various colors in dovetailed arrangements. Two wefts of different colors are alternately thrown in alternate sheds, each in turn interlooping with alternate pairs of weft yarns coming from the opposite direction. (See Fig. 87.)

Type 7: Single-Warp Interlocked and Weft-Interlooped Tapestry

Two weft yarns, coming together from opposite directions, interlock around the same warp yarn and at the same time interloop around each other, before returning across the warp.

165

Type 8-A: Multiple-Warp Interlocked and Weft-Interlooped Tapestry

This method is similar to Type 7, except that one weft, after interlocking a warp and interlooping a weft, interloops into a second weft before retracing its course across the warp.

Type 8-B

One weft interloops into the two wefts coming from the opposite direction and also interlocks into the last two warps encountered by the same two wefts.

Type 9-A: Diagonal-Warp Interlocked and Weft-Interlooped Tapestry

The interlocking-interlooping process described in Type 7 can be continued around warps and through wefts diagonally, progressing forward by one warp on each row of weaving.

Type 9-B

The interlocking-interlooping described in 8-A can also be made to progress forward in the warp. (See Fig. 87.)

Type 10: Kilim or Slit-Warp Tapestry

The Kilim is considered the oldest rug weave of the Near East. The finest rugs of this type are the Sehna Chileens, which have 100 cross yarns to the perpendicular inch. Some types, such as the Verne, are famous for their bird and animal patterns. This weave is also variously called Killim, Khilim, Kelim, Gilim, Gileem, Ghileem, and Chileen.

Two wefts, coming from opposite directions, turn back in the next or alternate shed without interlocking a warp or interlooping into another weft, leaving a slit between them. Several rows of such weaving leave a long narrow slit in the fabric. To avoid weakening the structure of the fabric these slits are usually arranged in a progressive manner or in stair-step patterns. (See Figs. 81 and 87.)

Type 11-A: Diagonal Open-Warp Tapestry Weaving, a Version of Kilim Tapestry

The two wefts, coming together from opposite directions, turn back without interlocking or interlooping as in Type 10; but in this weave they progress forward one warp on each successive row of weaving. This makes a diagonal edge to the pattern area and does not weaken the structure of the fabric. Yarns of contrasting colors can be threaded through these openings to provide additional pattern elements.

166

Type 11-B

This method is the same as 11-A, except that one free warp floats between the two opposing wefts. Sometimes a pattern weft interweaves diagonally through this opened warp. The openings can be arranged in zigzags, diamond patterns, and rhomboids. (See Fig. 87.)

Type 12-A: Patchwork Tapestry

This unusual type of tapestry, called patchwork by archaeologists and tipoy by the Indians, was woven in ancient Peru.[1] Warp yarns interloop with warp yarns and weft yarns interloop with weft yarns, the interlooping being so arranged that the warp and weft patterns coincide to produce clear-cut areas of single colors.

The easiest way to set up a loom for this weave is to use a skeleton loom in which temporary or skeleton weft heading cords are stretched crosswise between firm upright supports. In one method the warp is stretched between and around these temporary weft cords and is interlooped, end to end, into the warp strung in the preceding pattern area. When the warping is completed, the temporary weft heading cords are removed.

Type 12-B

There are other methods of joining the yarns of the warp sections: In some cases, the warp yarns do not interloop into one another but are alternately carried over the heading cord. This is the same treatment for the warp as 1-A was for the weft. Similarly, other methods of joining the weft yarns of adjacent pattern areas in the tapestry weave can be used to join the warp yarns of patchwork. In tie and dye work (see Fig. 190), the ancient Indians of Peru disjoined their patchwork and then recombined it after dyeing.

Type 13: Darned-In or "Eccentric" Tapestry

Weft yarns are sometimes darned into the warp, usually with the help of a tapestry needle, to form curvilinear eccentric patterns. Both ancient Peruvians and contemporary Guatemalans have produced beautiful examples of this technique. The belt shown in Fig. 71 was woven on a four-harness loom threaded for a regular twill weave; it shows areas of eccentric tapestry.

Type 14-A: Wrapped-Warp Tapestry

A very unusual slit-warp tapestry was made in ancient Peru. Groups of warp yarns, often pairs of coarse warp, were wrapped with colored yarns.

[1] Illustrations of this weave are to be found in the Paracas studies of O'Neale (48) and d'Harcourt (26).

Regroupings of the warp and progressive wrapping made a very lacy open-work tapestry.

Type 14-B

Individual warp yarns are encircled once by weft yarns which then pass diagonally from warp to warp. This is also a form of eccentric tapestry weaving.

Type 15: Fagoting-Stitch Embroidered Tapestry

If the weft wraps the warp in a figure 8 or fagoting stitch, slits can be left between pattern areas or the fagoting stitches dovetail between the different pattern areas. A tapestry needle or a small stick shuttle is used for this work. This is illustrated by the stem of the plant shown in Fig. 71, the right bottom unit in Fig. 87, and in Fig. 183, top. (See also page 369.)

Type 16: "Spanish Lace" Tapestry

In this special tapestry weave only one weft yarn is used. It progresses from pattern to pattern entirely across the warp, carried by a small shuttle or a tapestry needle. Starting from the right, the weft is taken three times over and under the first ten warp yarns, or back and forth, over and under any chosen number of warp yarns. It is then carried forward toward the left and interwoven in the same manner into the next set of ten warp yarns, and so on until the left-hand selvage is reached. Then the weft yarn is returned from left to right, interweaving three times in the same set of ten warp yarns, immediately above the previous group of three. Several rows of plain weaving are usually woven between these rows of pattern weaving. The movement always starts from the bottom and works up, making a "wing" pattern between sections of solid weaving. (See Fig. 87, left column, near the bottom.)

Type 17: Open-Lace or Spot Tapestry Weaving

Upon a rather coarse but smooth warp an openwork fabric is made by grouping and regrouping the warp yarns and weaving an area of tapestry at the place the groups meet. For example, twelve pairs of warp are divided; six pairs are carried right and six left. About 1/2 inch below the point of separation, the six left pairs join with the six right pairs of the next adjacent 12-pair group. Tapestry weaving joins the six pairs together below and above the point of contact and joins the 12 pairs together at the point of contact. On the next row, the warp yarns recombine in their original

168

groupings and are held in place with another spot of tapestry. This arrangement makes open diamond patterns in the fabric.

SOUMAK WEAVING

The Soumak or Soumaki weave, used for carpet weaving in the Near East some centuries before the Christian era, is thought to have been first made in Soumaki, a province west of Shirvan and near Shemakha, Baku District, Transcaucasia. The ancient Peruvians used a sort of Soumak stitch as an embroidery stitch; when used upon a previously woven fabric, this is called the stem stitch (26).

The Soumak is a flat-surfaced weave, and is often classed as a form of tapestry weaving. It is also often classed as an embroidery technique. In it each pattern weft is carried forward over four warp yarns and then backward under two warp· yarns. This over-four-under-two movement makes a diagonal stitch on the face of the fabric and a wrapped stitch on the other side. The stitches on the face are arranged so that those in each two rows face, or are woven toward, one another; the resulting weave has a herringbone effect. Unlike regular tapestry, a row of tabby weaving is thrown between the rows of Soumak stitches. Like tapestry, the Soumak weave is made up of a number of unit pattern areas. A tapestry needle or a small shuttle is used to carry the pattern wefts over and under the warp. Many yarn ends appear on the under side of Soumak rugs. This weave is illustrated in Fig. 88.

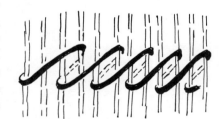

Fig. 88. Soumak Stitch. The stitch is carried over 4, under 2 warps. If done on a woven fabric, the stitch is called the stem stitch.

Soumak rugs are solid, heavy, and often coarse in texture. The yarns are usually of loose spongy wool. Modern Soumak rugs have about seven rows of stitches to the inch, whereas the old Soumaks had 10 to 12 rows to the inch. (See Fig. 89.)

TWO-HARNESS WARP-FACED FIBER RUG WEAVES

Flat-surfaced, warp-faced, bast-fiber rugs are woven in many areas of the world. In Central and South America, native peoples are seen sitting before tall vertical looms weaving coarse but colorful warp-striped fiber rugs. These rugs are customarily woven in a warp-faced plain weave, from yarns made of tightly twisted cordage of sisal. One center of such weaving is Iquitos on the Amazon River.

Fig. 89. Soumak Rug. Late eighteenth-century Caucasian rug of wool. (Courtesy of the Metropolitan Museum of Art.)

When a vertical loom is used the warp is usually a ring or continuous warp. The heddle devices used are similar to those installed on tapestry and knotted-pile rug looms. (Continuous-warp looms are discussed on page 92.) When a horizontal loom is used, the loom can be equipped with a fixed heddle, a hole-and-slot heddle, or a string heddle rod.

FOUR-HARNESS FLAT-SURFACED RUG WEAVES

Some heavy woolen rugs are woven on foot-power looms of heavy spongy woolen yarns. Many of the weaves are strengthened with stuffer yarns.

The Navaho Saddle-Blanket Weave

The best of these weaves is the Navaho saddle-blanket weave, which is really a version of bird's-eye twill. (See Fig. 132B. Note that the warp is threaded in doubles.) The loom is tied up in such a way that each harness can be raised separately.

Usually three different colors or three values of one color are used for the weft. They are put into the warp as follows: With the lightest colored yarn, treadle and raise the harnesses in the order of 1, 2, 3, and 4; do the same with the medium-colored yarn and then with the dark yarn. If this treadling is continued a chevron pattern occurs. For a bird's-eye diamond pattern, make the three throws of weft just described and then reverse both the order of treadling and the order of putting in the colored weft: that is, treadle 4, 3, 2, and 1 for each dark, medium, and light value of the weft. For lengthwise stripes omit one treadle; for example, weave over and over treadles 1, 2, and 3.

Summer and Winter Rug Weaves

When the Summer and Winter weave is used for rug weaving, the pattern blocks should be made in long sequences. (Summer and Winter weaving is described on page 245.) The basic warp for this rug weave is carried on the first two harnesses. The stuffer wefts are thrown in the sheds formed by the pattern harnesses. Almost twice as much weave warp is needed as stuffer warp. Because of the difference in tension which results from such a treatment, two warp beams are needed on the loom. Mrs. Atwater recommends that the warp be set in a 12-dent reed so that one of the weave-warp yarns is in the first dent and four of the stuffer-warp yarns in the second dent; repeat this order across the reed (4).

The more harnesses a loom has, the more elaborate the pattern can be. Two block patterns are possible on a four-harness loom, four are possible on a six-harness loom, and six on an eight-harness loom.

A number of other weaves which can be woven on foot-power looms can also be adapted for rugs. They are outlined on page 184.

MULTIPLE-HARNESS, WARP-FACED, INGRAIN CARPET AND FABRIC WEAVES

Ingrain carpets are made of two or three sets of warp yarns which mesh to form a two- or three-ply fabric. The pattern is reversible but in opposite color arrangements on the two faces of the fabric. The hand method of doing the ingrain weave is described in Belt 12 on page 143. Tablet weaving is also a form of ingrain weaving.

So much ingrain carpeting was once made in Scotland that it is often called Scotch carpeting. In England it was first made in 1736 at Kidderminster on hand looms in the homes of the people (87). At Medway, in Norfolk County, Massachusetts, a small ingrain carpet factory was started in 1825 by Henry S. Burdette, who commissioned Alexander Wright, a Scotsman, to manage and supervise the factory. Wright brought hand looms from Scotland. Before long, ingrain carpeting was being made in several centers. In Philadelphia the Jacquard mechanism was employed in weaving patterned ingrain carpets (87). The first steam-power loom for ingrain carpet weaving was invented by Erastus B. Bigelow in 1839. Ingrain carpeting is no longer woven in the United States (86).

2. Pile-Surfaced Rug and Fabric Weaves and Their Looms

Some of our most beautiful fabrics have a soft furlike surface known as pile. Velvet, plush, simulated fur, and pile carpeting belong in this category. In a pile weave, loops or tufts of yarn are raised above the surface of a fabric during the process of weaving. They may or may not be cut; the uncut is usually called looped pile. A pile weave can be either warp-faced or weft-faced, depending upon whether the pile is formed by extra warp or extra weft yarns. The warp-pile weaves and most of the weft-pile weaves are woven on horizontal looms; knotted pile, which is a weft-pile weave, is usually woven on a vertical loom. Various types of pile weaves are classified and briefly described below.

CLASSIFICATION OF PILE WEAVES

WARP-FACED PILE WEAVES

1. Raised Warp-Pile Weaving

Warp for the pile in this weave is carried on an extra warp beam at the back of the loom, which is so threaded that the pile warp forms a separate shed. When it is raised, a rod placed in the shed holds it up above the basic fabric. After several rows of plain weaving are made to stabilize the pile, the rod is removed and the pile loops remain. If the pile is to be cut, this is done with a special rod equipped with a small sharp blade at one end; as this rod is pulled out of the warp it cuts the loops. This has been the basic weave of the carpet industry for over 100 years. (See page 185.)

Although velvet and plush were at first woven by this raised-warp pile process, they are now generally woven by the double-cloth weave, described in the next paragraph. Brocade velvets, however, are still made by the original method. It is generally believed that velvet was first woven in the Near East, possibly in Persia. A Coptic linen velvet is the earliest surviving example of a cut-pile fabric (37). The Italians, however, claim that this weave was invented in Florence during the early Renaissance by members of the Velluti family.

2. Double-Cloth Warp-Pile Weaving

As just noted, most velvet and plush are woven today by the double-cloth method, which requires at least three sets of warp and two bobbins of weft. Two separate fabrics are woven simultaneously, usually in a plain weave, and bound together with an additional set of warp yarns which cross back and forth between the two fabrics. When the double cloth is finished, the two layers are cut apart, making two strips of pile fabric.

3. Terry Cloth, a Warp-Looped Pile Weave

This fabric is woven with two sets of warp, one taut and one slack. When several rows of filling yarns are beaten back at the same time, they push the slack yarns before them. The loops thus formed appear on both faces of the fabric, making an uncut or looped pile.

WEFT-FACED PILE WEAVES

Most handmade pile weaves, including both cut and looped pile, are weft-faced.

1. Looped Weft-Faced Pile

Both the ancient Egyptians and the ancient Peruvians knew how to weave a looped weft-faced pile fabric. An example of an ancient Egyptian piece is shown in Fig. 3. Similar blouses were made in ancient Peru. The weave is made as follows: Working from the side of the warp opposite the position of the shuttle, a pointed stick is used to pick up loops of coarse weft through the warp shed at regular intervals across the loom. These loops are held above

173

the stick and above the warp shed until several rows of tabby have been thrown in. (See Fig. 90). The ancient Peruvians wove a decorative cut and uncut pile fabric by lifting a double weft above the warp at about 1/4 inch intervals across the loom on every six to ten rows of weaving. Small throw rugs can be woven on a foot-power loom using this weft-pile weave. The pick-up of the weft can be spaced so that the loops are arranged and varied on alternate rows to form patterns.

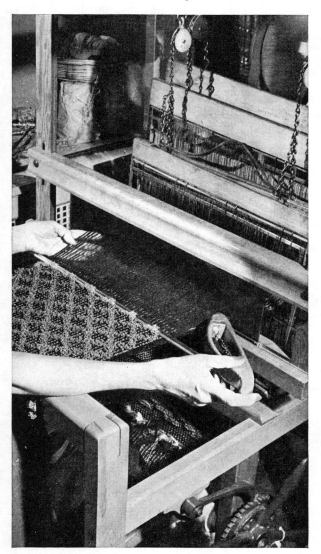

Fig. 90. Weft Pile. By Dorothy Liebes, famous designer of textiles. Mrs. Liebes demonstrates here the use of pick-up sticks to lift the weft-pile pattern. (Courtesy, Dorothy Liebes Textiles, Inc., N.Y.)

2. Hand-Knotted Pile Weaves

The ancient weavers of the Near East used three types of knots for cut-pile carpet weaving: Sehna, Ghiordes, and "Spanish" knots. (See Fig. 91.) These knots are constructed as follows.

The Sehna knot is made by carrying a yarn over and crossing it beneath a warp; one end of the yarn is brought to the surface and the other is passed to the right or left below the next warp before being brought to the surface. The Sehna knot thus has either a right-hand or a left-hand tie. The close pile on Persian carpets results from the use of this knot. The Chinese use the same knot for their knotted-pile carpets. Such rugs have more knots to the inch than those made with the Ghiordes knot.

The Ghiordes knot is sometimes called the Turkish knot because it has been for centuries the favorite knot of Turkish weavers. The French also used it in weaving their beautiful Savonnerie rugs.

174

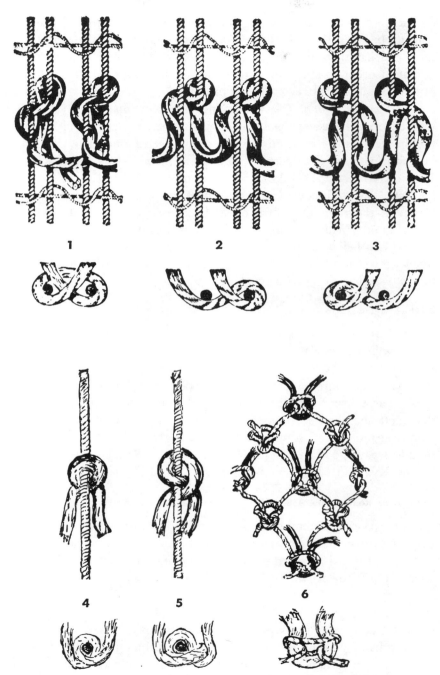

Fig. 91. Pile Knots. (1) Turkish or Ghiordes knot. (2) Persian or Sehna knot, left-hand tie. (3) Persian or Sehna knot, right-hand tie. (4) Spanish knot. (5) Old French knot of Middle Ages. (6) Pile locked in knot work, used in prehistoric Peru. (Nos. 1, 2, and 3, courtesy, The Hoover Co., No. Canton, Ohio.)

The knot is made by carrying the yarn over two warps and bringing the ends up between the two. This knot is much easier to make than the Sehna knot and has therefore almost supplanted it. The obvious reason for this is that in order to speed up production of hand-knotted rugs, quantity of output is placed above quality of product.

The Spanish knot is one which encircles only one warp. The name is derived from the use of this knot in Spain, where intact samples dating from the thirteenth and fourteenth centuries have been found. The knot was used in Cairo in the twelfth century, as rugs in New York's Metropolitan Museum of Art testify. The knot was known in the Near East at a much earlier date; LeCoq discovered a fragment of this type of knotted-pile in Turkestan in the ruins of a fifth- or sixth-century culture strata (*88*).

The knot is made as follows: The yarn is passed over the top of one warp and crossed below it; the two ends of the yarn come up on either side of the warp to form the pile. This is the least desirable of the three knots used in the weaving of Oriental pile carpets.

3. The Rya and Flossa Weaves

Soft throw rugs are often made by the peoples of northern Europe in a weave which is similar to the knotted-pile weaves of the Near East. This Rya weave closely resembles the Ghiordes knot technique just described; in the Rya weave, however, the yarn is carried on a shuttle and is not cut between warps. Yarns for the pile are looped around the warps as in the Ghiordes knot, and then are looped over a rod; when the rod is removed the loops remain. Several rows of tabby weaving are placed between the rows of pile weaving. If the loops are cut the weave is known as the Flossa weave. Rya and Flossa are Scandinavian words.

4. Peruvian Knotted-Pile, Bound-Pile, Cut-Pile, and Twined-Pile Weaves

On the Western Hemisphere before the Spanish Conquest the ancient Peruvians used at least five methods of obtaining a pile-surface on fabrics: (1) They formed a looped pile by interlocking loops of yarn into a twined weave. (2) They wove a weft-looped pile (see page 173). (3) They wove a weft-cut pile. (4) They made a pile fabric by looping short yarn strands into a needle-made looped-knotted netting (*26*); (5) They made an ornamental cord with a pile surface by using a needle and thread to wrap cut lengths of yarn on the warp. In this last technique the pile was formed by carrying a spiraling weft around a circular strand of taut warp; as the weft approached each warp, it encircled that warp and at the same time enclosed a short strand of cut pile yarn. The last two techniques were apparently unique to Peru, though d'Harcourt calls the first one the Chinese fillet stitch (26). The fourth is illustrated in Fig. 91, No. 6 and described on page 318, Type 20.

5. Machine-Woven Weft-Faced Pile Weaves—Corduroy, etc.

A twill weave made with long floats is cut to form corduroy and velveteen. For corduroy the twill floats are arranged in columns and held up by guides; when they are cut the pile appears in ribs. For velveteen the twill floats are evenly spaced so that a smooth material results when they are cut.

6. Chenille Pile Weaving

A ready-made pile is slipped into a shed in the warp and woven into a fabric. This technique is described on page 189.

7. Tufted and Hooked Pile

No discussion of pile weaves would be complete without mentioning tufted and hooked pile fabrics. The pile in these fabrics is added to an already woven heavy canvas or burlap. In tufted fabrics the pile is added with a needle or needles; in hooked pile fabrics, it is added by manipulating special hooks. The tufting process is sometimes called candlewicking. Many rugs are now made by these processes. See pages 189 and 190 for further discussion of them.

ORIENTAL KNOTTED-PILE RUG LOOMS AND WEAVES

For more than two millenniums the rare and beautiful rugs of the Persians have been coveted by king and layman alike. These costly rugs, often woven on crude looms in the simple homes of shepherd peoples, came chiefly from the northern provinces of Persia, now called Iran. Persian weavers have traditionally used the Sehna knot for their rug weaving and peoples to the north and west use the Ghiordes knot. More anciently the Spanish knot is thought to have been used over a wide area of the Near East (88).

It is rather difficult to trace the historic background of Oriental knotted-pile carpet weaves. It is entirely possible that they originated with the nomad shepherds of the Near East, since that area is the source of so many of the textile arts (88). The earliest known specimens of knotted-pile carpeting found by Sir Aurel Stein in excavations in Turkistan are said not to antedate the Christian era (84). The earliest rug specimens with tufted or pile surfaces, the dates of which are actually known, are those of the Ro-

Fig. 92. Persian Rug. Sixteenth-century Sehna-knotted rug of silk. (Courtesy of the Metropolitan Museum of Art.)

man-Egyptian period a few centuries after the time of Christ (*85*). The knowledge of this art spread from Persia and other countries of the Near East to distant lands in the east and west, the Moslems being the principal carriers.

The quality of an Oriental rug is judged by the type of knot used, depth of the pile, closeness of the weave, fineness of yarn, richness of color, fastness of dyes, and subtleness of pattern. Oriental carpets are truly works of art. They have long been famous for their beautiful coloring, which results from the use of rare natural dyes. Since natural dyes are often costly and difficult to procure, aniline dyes are now frequently substituted. These dyes often produce harsh colors, and the color quality of oriental rugs has suffered tremendously from this substitution.

There are many, many types of Oriental rugs, most of them classified according to the name of either the province or the town in which they were made. Each locality manufactures a particular quality, size, color, weave, or pattern. Some of the well-known Oriental rugs from Persia are the Sehna, Kirman, Tabriz, and Saruk rugs; woven in the Sehna knot, they have about 160 knots to the inch. From Turkey come the Ghiordes and Gulistan rugs; woven in the Ghiordes knot, they have about 75 knots to the inch. From Caucasia come the Daghestan rugs; woven in the Ghiordes knot, they have from 64 to 144 knots to the inch. Figs. 92 and 93 show illustrations of these rugs.

One of the most famous of the Persian rugs, known as the Ardebil, is now in the British South Kensington Museum. It has a jewel-like design of rich colors scattered over a deep blue ground. It is 34 feet long by 17 feet wide and took ten weavers 3 1/2 years to make. It is now valued at a half-million dollars.

Some historians suspect that knotted-pile rug making in China may date back as early as 600 A.D. (*88*). The Sehna knot was used there during the Ming Dynasty (1368–1644). Chinese rugs are woven in a deep lustrous pile, of beautiful jade greens, subtle pinks, and other colors typical of China. Silk is often used in them. Usually their backgrounds are of one color with a design appearing in border and corner motifs. The designs include the well-known dragon, fret, and floral patterns. (See Fig. 94.)

Persian weavers brought to India by Emperor Akbar in the middle of the sixteenth century founded the rug-making industry there. A rug from India woven in silk, and now on exhibit in the Metropolitan Museum, is said to have 2500 knots to the square inch. The most important rug-making center in India today is Mirpur.

In France the Ghiordes knot, introduced during the reign of Henry IV,

Fig. 93.   Turkish Rug. Prayer rug woven in Ghiordes knot, about 1600 A.D.
(Courtesy of the Metropolitan Museum of Art.)

was used to weave the beautiful Savonnerie rugs. (See Fig. 95.) Their chief characteristic was their soft pastel colors and the floral patterns of the French Renaissance. During the reign of Louis XIV two of these rugs were sold to the King of Siam for $90,000. The name Savonnerie was given to them because they were first made in an abandoned soap factory. In 1825 the Savonnerie industry was incorporated into the workshops of the Gobelin factory.

England became interested in knotted-pile weaving in 1575, after Morgan Habblethorne visited the Near East and returned to England with a knowledge of this technique. Carpets, bags, pillows, etc., woven in knotted pile became known in England as Turkey work.

In the Scandinavian countries a type of weft-pile weaving is used for making scarves, pillow covers, and rugs. As previously noted, the cut and uncut versions of the pile weave are known in these northern lands as the Rya and Flossa weaves.

In Spain the Spanish knot was used during the thirteenth century to make knotted-pile rugs.

During the second World War immigrants from Europe started several hand-knotted rug industries in South America. In Cusco, Peru, beautiful knotted and sculptured rugs were made from the natural-colored fibers of sheep, llamas, alpacas, and vicuñas. There was established in Quito, Ecuador, a small factory called Folklore, where Indian girls were employed to weave and sculpture rugs. In both of these areas ancient Quechua designs were sculptured into the deep pile of the rugs.

In New York City several small factories now produce hand-knotted rugs, employing weavers coming to this country from Poland, Rumania, Turkey, and Iran. Immigrants from these districts often set up looms in their own homes and weave knotted rugs, thus continuing a practice learned as children.

TYPE OF LOOM USED FOR KNOTTED-PILE WEAVING

A regular vertical tapestry two-shed loom is generally used for making hand-knotted pile rugs. The string-heddle rod is attached to a support which hangs from the top of the frame, or to an arm which pivots from the side of the frame. (See Fig. 85B.) The method generally used to construct the heddles is described on page 90, No. 3.

PLANNING THE DESIGN FOR A KNOTTED-PILE FABRIC

Any type of design can be woven in the knotted-pile weave, since the technique allows for great pattern flexibility. Patterns are usually worked out in sections on graph paper.

Fig. 94. Chinese Rug. Nineteenth-century rug woven in Sehna knot. (Courtesy of the Metropolitan Museum of Art.)

Fig. 95. French Rug. Section of seventeenth-century woolen Savonnerie rug woven in Ghiordes knot. (Courtesy of the Metropolitan Museum of Art.)

DIRECTIONS FOR WEAVING KNOTTED PILE

When the loom is warped and ready for weaving, the weaver pins the section of the pattern to be woven first to the warp in front of her, slightly above her eye level. She also hangs hanks of yarn of the needed colors where she can reach them, often attaching them to a pole which hangs horizontally above her head. Studying the pattern, she adds the knots one at a time to the warp. All knots of one color are made across a row of weaving before those of another color are added. When one row of knotting is finished one or more rows of tabby are woven into the warp. As the rug is woven, it may be rolled onto the lower cloth beam; more often, since a

183

fixed vertical warp is customarily used, the weaver sits on a scaffold which is raised continuously higher as weaving progresses.

Working at maximum capacity, a weaver can make about 900 knots an hour. The Sehna and Ghiordes knots are used most frequently in rug making; the Spanish knot is seldom used. (See Fig. 91.)

3. Vertical Rug Looms

When we investigate the origin of rug weaving, it is only natural that we turn to the lands of the Fertile Crescent where so many weaving techniques have been developed. Both before and after the Christian era the looms used for rug making in Egypt and the Near East were chiefly of the vertical type. Some, like those on which the royal hand-knotted carpets were woven, were tremendous affairs, at which six or more weavers, stationed along the face of the warp, worked on the same rug at the same time.

In the Western Hemisphere the Navaho Indians still use a crude vertical loom for weaving their rugs and blankets. The warp-faced hemp fiber carpets of Mexico and Central America are also customarily woven on vertical looms, the warp for which is usually set up as a continuous or ring warp. Vertical looms are illustrated in Figs. 13, 47, and 85B. Additional information about them is given under the treatment of tapestry and pile weaves in this chapter.

4. Rugs Made on Regular Foot-Power Looms

Simple flat-surfaced rug weaves, as well as some pile rug weaves, can be woven on regular foot-power looms, which are described in the next chapter. The types of rugs that can be woven on foot-power looms are outlined below.

RUG WEAVES FOR FOOT-POWER LOOMS EQUIPPED WITH ONE WARP BEAM
Rag Rugs

Strips of woolen or cotton cloth are used as weft and woven into a heavy cotton or linen warp. The plain weave is generally used.

Fiber Rugs

Using the plain weave, hemp cordage, split bamboo, and other coarse plant fibers are used as weft and woven into a heavy cotton, hemp, or jute warp.

Wool or Cotton Rugs

Heavy yarns of homespun wool or cotton are woven into a tightly twisted wool or cotton warp. A plain weave can be used, but bird's-eye twill, Summer and Winter, or other pattern weaves make a more attractive surface.

Weft-Looped Pile

This interesting weave is described on page 173.

RUG WEAVES FOR FOOT-POWER LOOMS EQUIPPED WITH TWO WARP BEAMS
Heavy Flat-Surfaced Rugs

Stuffer yarns, wound on a separate warp beam and fed into the warp for both patterned and plain rug weaves, add weight and padding to a rug; they cannot be seen from either back or front surfaces, but run through the center of the rug fabric.

Looped and Cut Warp-Pile Rugs

Looped and cut-pile warp-faced weaves can be woven on foot-power looms that are equipped with a second or auxiliary warp beam to hold the special warp for the pile.

5. Mechanically Powered Rug Looms

During the late Renaissance rug looms with mechanical devices began to appear in Europe. Flat-surfaced ingrain carpets were among the earliest rugs attempted by machine methods. Ingrain weaving may have been invented in Scotland, for Scottish weavers seem to have taken the lead in setting up this weave. In 1736 ingrain carpet weaving was undertaken in Kidderminster, England. In 1825, ingrain looms were brought to America from Scotland and a rug factory was established in Medway, Massachusetts.

The Brussels loom, on which a rug with a pile surface could be woven, was invented in Brussels some time prior to 1740, for in that year Antoine Dufossy carried to England the knowledge of its operation. Legend says that he was smuggled into England in a sugar cask in which he almost suffocated. At Wilton, where he was taken by the Earl of Pembroke, he helped to set up a rug factory (*92*). Other Brussels rug factories were eventually established at Moorfields, Axminster, and Kidderminster. By 1838, in Kidderminster alone, nearly 2000 looms were turning out Brussels carpeting. In 1825, the principles of the Jacquard loom, which had been perfected in France about the year 1804, were combined with those of the Wilton loom.

RUG LOOMS AND RUG-MAKING TECHNIQUES

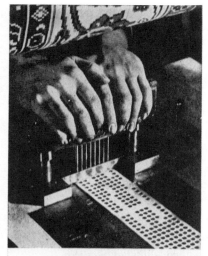

The process of applying the pattern to rug yarns before weaving, by dyeing the yarn over a drum, was developed by Richard Whytock of Edinburgh in 1831. This process made possible the weaving of tapestry and velvet rugs, two versions of the same weave. The loom was later (1843) improved by John Johnson. In 1839, James Templeton and William Quigley invented the "chenille" method of rug weaving in Glasgow (87).

In the United States, rug factories were established in several localities soon after the War of Independence, carpet weaving having been initiated in 1774 by William Calverly in Philadelphia. In 1791, W. P. Sprague of Quakertown made the first Axminster rug in this country. Erastus Bigelow of Lowell built the first rug power loom in 1839, perfecting it in 1848. The Axminster weave was not popular until 1876, when the spool type of weave, known as moquette, was invented by Halcyon Skinner at Yonkers, New York. It was later improved by his sons, Charles and A. L. Skinner. In 1878, the Shuttleworth brothers brought from England 14 Wilton looms with Jacquard attachments and established a small factory at Amsterdam, New York. These first looms were operated by water power. Eventually all rug looms were run by electricity.

Because of the narrow looms used, the first machine-made carpeting was only 27 inches wide. The weaving of wider widths on "broadlooms" was not undertaken until the early 1920's. A rug book (87) published in 1925 does not mention the word "broadloom" in either text or glossary,

Fig. 96.   Top, Cutting Jacquard Cards. (Courtesy, Bigelow-Sanford Carpet Co., Inc.)

Fig. 97.   Center, Jacquard Loom. Wilton carpet being woven. (Courtesy, Bigelow-Sanford Carpet Co., Inc.)

Fig. 98.   Bottom, Spool Frames for Jacquard Loom. (Photograph courtesy of A. & M. Karagheusian, Inc., Manufacturer of Gulistan Carpets.)

though it states that Jacquard mechanisms were then being used on Axminster looms to produce wide seamless carpeting. The first Axminster broadlooms were 9 feet wide. Wider widths of carpeting in other carpet weaves soon followed. By 1935, the word broadloom no longer referred to Axminster carpeting alone, but was a general term for all carpets woven in wide widths. In the 1930's 12-foot carpeting was being woven in Wilton, velvet, and Axminster weaves; in the 1940's, 15-foot carpeting was being woven.

A few identifying characteristics of machine woven pile-surfaced rugs are listed below. After being woven, all of the rugs described below go through a finishing process in which they are sheared, brushed, steamed, etc.

WILTON AND BRUSSELS WEAVES

A Jacquard type of loom is used to weave both Wilton and Brussels carpets (see Figs. 96, 97, 98, and 99), which differ only in that Wilton has a

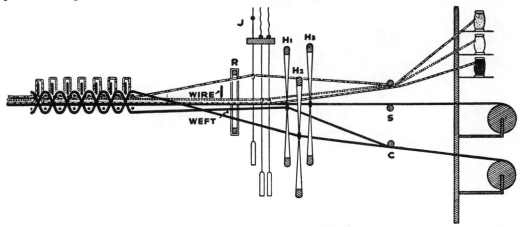

Fig. 99. Jacquard Pile Weave. Detail of the mechanics of the Jacquard loom weaving of a Wilton rug: S-stuffer warp; C-chain warp; yarn fed from back lifted by heddles. (Courtesy, Hoover Co., No. Canton, Ohio.)

cut pile and Brussels an uncut pile. The many spools of colored warp yarn needed for the pile are held on large spool racks at the back of the loom. These yarns are carried in the backing of these rugs between the colored patterns; they are raised to the surface of the rug only when needed for the pile pattern. The warp yarns for the pattern pile are raised over special wires during weaving. After several rows of plain weaving have been made to stabilize a row of pile weaving, the wires are pulled out of the warp, thus making a looped-pile Brussels. If the wires are equipped with a small blade hook at one end, they automatically cut the pile as they are pulled out, and a cut-pile Wilton results. (See top sketch, Fig. 100.)

VELVET AND TAPESTRY WEAVES

Velvet and tapestry rugs are cut and uncut pile versions of the same rug. (Tapestry rug is a trade name, not real tapestry.) The pile warp yarns for these rugs are carried over a wire on the surface of the rug as described for Wilton rugs, but they are never carried along in the back of the rug. Most velvet rugs are of one color; in patterned rugs, the pile yarns must be printed before weaving by being drum-dyed. Only one beam is needed to hold the warp during weaving. The operation of this loom is the simplest of the carpet looms. Where the strands of cut pile once stood up individually in a V-shaped loop which could be easily plucked from the body of the rug, a coating of latex now binds the base of the loops permanently to the backing. (See bottom sketch, Fig. 100.)

Fig. 100. Machine-Made Pile Weaves. Top, structure of Wilton rug. Bottom, structure of the pile of a velvet rug weave. (Courtesy, Hoover Co., No. Canton, Ohio.)

AXMINSTER WEAVING[2]

The Axminster weave was invented to replace the hand-knotted rug weaves. The cut pile of the Axminster rug is made in a unique way; it is inserted into the warp mechanically by finger-like projectors.

The many spools of colored warp needed for each row of pile are arranged on individual tables, and yarns from them are wound onto a large master warp beam. This beam is the width of the rug being woven, and there is one for each crosswise row of pile. The colored yarns are wound onto the beam in the exact order they appear in one row of weaving, the principle being about the same as that used for the winding of a sectional warp beam. (See Fig. 118.) Each yarn is pulled forward through a flat metal tube or finger-like projectors about 10 inches long; these tubes are placed side by side, seven to the inch. The warp beams are placed on a long chain in the order of their use. As the beam passes over the loom, it is selected by a sprocket-chain mechanism which lifts it into position; the fingerlike projectors are then lowered into the backing warps on the loom. The weft is carried into the sheds by

[2] The information concerning the method of weaving Axminster carpets and concerning the origin of tapestry and velvet carpets was supplied by the Mohawk Carpet Mills, Inc., Amsterdam, New York.

thrusts of loom needles which operate from the right; it is held to the left selvage by the action of a small shuttle running in a circular race at the left. This is a three-shot motion: two yarns are inserted with each motion; the needle leaves a yarn as it passes across and another as it returns. Two wefts bind the tufts into the warp, two act as filling wefts between the rows, and two form the backing construction—the backing of an Axminster is identified by heavy crosswise ridges. After the pile is bound into place, a comb pushes the tufts upward and two knives meet to cut them. The beam is then lifted back into place in the chain.

SEAMLOC BROADLOOM

This carpet is woven in the plush or velvet double-cloth weave described on page 173. After the two layers have been cut apart, the back of the carpet is coated with a layer of plasticized wax cement which binds the loosely attached pile to the backing and prevents shedding and fraying.

CHENILLE WEAVING

The chenille rug is more expensive to weave than other machine-made rugs, because two weaving processes, on two different looms, are involved. The first loom weaves an open-warp and compact-weft "blanket" fabric. The warp yarns are set in the loom in groups of six, arranged about an inch apart. After this fabric is woven, it is cut warpwise into strips which become the "fur" or weft pile for the second loom. The carpet loom usually has three warp beams: one for the binding yarn which holds the chenille in place, one for the regular warp, and one for the stuffer warp. Four rows of plain weaving are thrown in between each row of chenille weaving. The chenille pile is beaten into place with a wooden comb; the regular reed is used to batten down the tabby weft.

6. Nonwoven Rug-Making Techniques

A description of rug-making techniques would be incomplete without a brief discussion of rugs made by processes other than weaving. Rugs can be made by tufting, hooking, and felting processes, by braiding, by crocheting, and by knitting. All but the last two processes are discussed below.

TUFTED FABRICS AND RUGS

The hand tufting of heavy cotton fabrics, principally used for bedspreads and known as candlewick work, was an activity of early colonial housewives. Interest in this type of work was revived in the 1930's, especially in the southeastern part of the United States, where it became a craft of the mountain people. Bedspreads, bath mats, and throw rugs were soon being manufactured commercially by a special tufting process. About 1948, one of the leading manufacturers of tufted bedspreads and throw rugs, the Cabin Craft Company, of Dalton, Georgia, a division of the West Point Manufacturing Company, experimented with the process for carpet making. By adding more needles and widening the frame they were able to produce tufted broadloom carpets.

The tufting process is a combination of sewing and hooking techniques: a piece of yarn is pushed through a fabric, caught by a latch, and drawn up through the fabric. A tufting machine resembles an oversized sewing machine with hundreds of needles operating at one time. Tufting machines run from 36 inches to 15 feet in width and operate at a speed of 550 rows of stitches per minute. The yarns are fed through copper tubes into the machine. Although tufted carpets are usually piece-dyed after the yarn is tufted into the fabric, some are made of yarn which has already been dyed. After the carpets are tufted and dyed, they are put through a series of finishing processes, the last of which is the latex-backing process which cements the tufts to the backing cloth. This backing cloth is usually a canvas woven of jute; some cotton duck is used, however.

The first tufted rugs were all of cotton. Today the pile of tufted carpets is also made of viscose rayon, nylon, nylon blends, and low-grade wool. Most better grade woolen pile-surfaced rugs are still woven on rug looms, but each year a better quality of tufted rugs appears on the market. Machine-tufted rugs are gradually replacing machine-woven rugs in sales. They can hardly be distinguished from woven rugs, but are considerably less costly to produce. A tufting machine can produce some 20 times as much carpet per hour as traditional power rug looms.

Since the potential qualities of the tufting machine were recognized, an amazing growth in tufted-rug production has taken place. Twenty million square yards of cotton tufted carpeting were produced in 1949, 33 million in 1950, and 42 million square yards in 1951 (87). Approximately 42 percent of the carpets made in America in 1955 were made by the machine-tufting process. Census reports show that 278.2 million dollars worth of these rugs were shipped during that year. Since that time the output has gradually continued to increase.

HOOKED RUGS

Pile fabrics constructed by hooking loops of yarn into a woven fabric are thought to have been made by the Copts, Chinese, Moors, and Arabs rather early in the Christian era. Most of the fabric so made was used for clothing. Hooked fabrics were later made in Europe, the Scandinavian countries, England, and the United States. Colonial housewives in America often dyed and used strips of old cloth in place of yarn to create interesting and durable hooked rugs.

EQUIPMENT NEEDED

A hand-hooked rug is made on heavy backing cloth, such as burlap, buckram, cotton canvas, etc., which is stretched on a frame quite similar to the embroidery frames used during the early Renaissance. This frame rests on a floor support or stand usually 33 inches high, but both the stand and the angle of slant of the frame should be adjustable. When not in use the frame can be stored in a vertical position.

The burlap backing cloth must be securely attached to the frame. If a loom is used as a frame, the backing cloth can be fastened to the loom beams in various ways: (1) It may be attached to the loom beams which have previously been wrapped with cord; (2) it may be attached to the aprons on the loom beams; or (3) it may be thumbtacked directly onto these beams. Whichever system is used, the burlap should be stretched taut in the frame and the side edges must also be stretched and

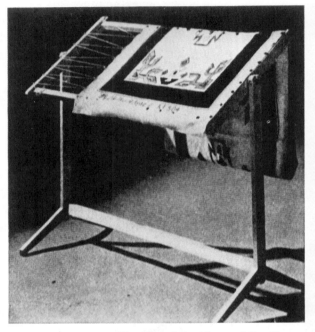

Fig. 101. Embroidery and Rug Frame. Frame used in making hand-hooked rugs. (Courtesy, James Lees and Sons Co., Bridgeport, Pa.)

fastened. This is done with cords which interlace the burlap to the sides of the frame. (See Fig. 101.)

Other equipment needed includes either a medium-fine crochet hook set in a wooden round-ended handle, a rug needle or lachet hook, depending on the method used; a cutting machine for sculptured rugs; a pair of hooking scissors with blades set at about a 135° angle; and colored yarns as needed. Strips of fabric about 1/8 inch wide are sometimes used in place of yarn for hooked rugs; they should be torn or cut on the straight of the goods.

191

Any type of design can be used for hooked rugs. Realistic floral designs are usually selected, but "modern" and geometric designs can also be used. The design is either drawn or stamped on the burlap backing cloth. Burlap can be purchased already printed with a pattern ready for hooking; such designs are often colored to assist the worker.

METHOD I. DIRECTIONS FOR HOOKING A RUG USING A CROCHET HOOK (UNCUT PILE)

1. Hold the wooden handle of the crochet hook in the palm of the hand. *The pressure of the hand sends the hook through the burlap.* One hand holds the hook above, the other holds the yarn below the surface of the burlap. The hook opening is held *away* from the worker.
2. For the first loop hold the yarn over the index finger; for subsequent loops it is held between the thumb and the index finger; it then crosses the palm and passes between the fourth and fifth fingers.
3. Pull all starting and finishing ends through to the right side and clip them even with the height of the loops. The loops themselves are not clipped. They should be between 1/8 and 1/4 of an inch high.
4. Place the loops in nearly every hole in the burlap, in irregular and fan-shaped paths—never in straight lines except along the border.

METHOD II. DIRECTIONS FOR HOOKING A RUG USING DE LUXE RUG NEEDLE (CUT PILE)

1. The De Luxe Needle (see Fig. 102) is a special needle that automatically controls the height of the pile. Instructions for using it come with the needle.[3]
2. Warp rug cloth can be used in place of burlap. Warp cloth stamped with patterns can also be purchased.[4]
3. Mount the warp cloth or burlap and stretch it on the frame.
4. If a fringe is to be put on the ends of the rug, make buttonhole stitching next to the pattern on the ends to be fringed.
5. Adjust the needle for the height of pile desired and thread it. The thread passes through an eyelet in the top of the handle, through a groove in the body of the handle, and then through the eye of the needle. Hold the needle in a vertical position when working, letting the yarn cross the back of the hand.
6. Always work from right to left. Starting in the lower right-hand corner of the rug pattern, plunge the needle through the fabric and, with the left hand held underneath the rug frame, pull the yarn through with that hand.

[3] This needle is made by James Lees and Sons Rug Company, Bridgeport, Pennsylvania.
[4] Ready-stamped burlap can also be purchased from James Lees and Sons Rug Company.

THE TEXTILE ARTS

7. Without lifting the needle above the surface of the warp cloth, slide the needle point along the surface over two threads and then plunge it in again as far as it will go. Do this for each stitch. Keep the left hand below on the pile side of the rug, holding the pile flat as the work progresses in order to prevent matting or interlocking.

8. Before filling in the designs, outline them all with one row of the same color as the body of the design. Before filling in the background, outline the design again with a row of the background color. Never work out into an open area— *work only next to an area which has already been completed.*

9. In this method the entire rug is hooked in straight rows except around the outlines.

10. Immediately after hooking a row of loops, clip the loops with scissors, inserting the tip of the scissors into the loops.

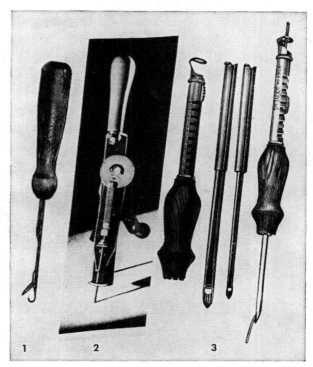

Fig. 102. Tools for Hooked Rugs. (1) Latch hook. (2) Robot needle. (3) De Luxe needle and parts. (Courtesy, James Lees and Sons Co., Bridgeport, Pa.)

11. After the rug is completed it can be sculptured with a cutting machine if desired. A raised pattern is achieved by making higher loops in the areas concerned.

METHOD III.

DIRECTIONS FOR HOOKING A RUG USING A ROBOT RUG NEEDLE (UNCUT PILE)

1. The Robot needle works by means of a small hand crank.[5] When this handle is turned the needle goes forward, passes through the cloth, and leaves a loop on the opposite side. When the crank handle is turned clockwise, the needle moves forward; when it is turned counterclockwise, it moves backward. (See Fig. 102.)

[5] This needle is distributed by James Lees and Sons Rug Company, Bridgeport, Pennsylvania.

2. The method of work is the same as for Method II except that the needle automatically spaces and does the work and the pile is not cut. All areas are outlined before filling in.

METHOD IV. DIRECTIONS FOR HOOKING A RUG USING A LATCH HOOK (CUT PILE)

1. A special hook with an automatic closing latch is used for the knotted-pile rug. (See Figs. 102 and 103.)
2. Heavy Smyrna Rug Canvas or heavy cotton is used for the backing.
3. The tufts of yarn are all precut. To cut the pile, wind the yarn evenly on a rug ruler or any grooved ruler, never allowing it to overlap. Cut it with scissors or a razor blade along the groove of the ruler.

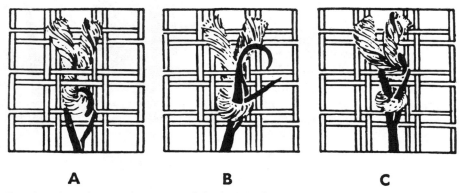

A   **B**   **C**

Fig. 103. Use of Latch Hook. Steps showing use of the latch hook. (Courtesy, James Lees and Sons Co., Bridgeport, Pa.)

4. Push the latch hook down into an opening in the porous rug canvas at a point where a knot is wanted, and up again into the next opening in the canvas. Always thrust it into the canvas deep enough—that is, past the length of the latch on the hook.
5. Take one loop of cut yarn, double it, and place the loop in the projecting latch hook. Holding the ends of the loop in the left hand, let the latch hook pull the loop under and up into the first opening in the canvas. Always work on the right side of the canvas.
6. Still holding the ends of the yarn in the left hand, pass the entire hook through the loop and, with the latch open, catch hold of the ends which are being held up. Pull the latch hook; this motion automatically pulls the ends of the yarn into and through the loop and makes a slip knot.
7. Check to see that the knot is firm by giving it an extra pull with the fingers before making the next knot.
8. After all the knotting work is finished, hem the rug.

194

MISCELLANEOUS RUG-MAKING TECHNIQUES

SHAG RUGS

Any throw rug which has a long-cut pile made into or sewed on a canvas backing can be called a shag rug. The pile of such rugs is usually made from heavy cotton rug yarns. The rugs can be made by weaving techniques, by various hooking processes, by sewing or couching methods, and by machine-tufting processes.

CROCHETED RUGS

Heavy cotton or wool yarns are used in making crocheted rugs. A large crochet hook is used for this work. The rugs are round or oblong. Dyed or undyed strips of cotton or wool fabric may also be crocheted into a rag rug.

GROS POINT RUGS

A heavy wool cross-stitch rug can be made upon a specially prepared canvas or heavy open mesh hemp or jute buckram. This rug may be of one color or it may be multicolored. The design may be of one color, for example, and the background of another.

WRAPPED-CORD RUGS

Wrapped cords sewed together in oval or round shapes make interesting rugs. To make them, two cords are placed side by side and wrapped together by a yarn which passes over and under them in a figure 8, covering the cords completely. At intervals different colored yarns can be used in the wrapping to provide variation and add pattern to the rug. The cords are usually heavy cotton and the yarns medium-weight cotton or wool.

To keep the rug flat, the rug making and cord twisting are carried on together: that is, a little of the cord is wrapped and this section is then sewed to the embryo rug. The curvature of the cording is controlled in this way.

BRAIDED RUGS

Narrow strips of cotton and woolen fabrics can be braided into strands which are then sewed together, edge to edge, around and around, starting from the center and working out into circular or oblong shapes. The fabric strips often give a more attractive appearance if they are dyed before being braided. Grasses, hemp, and other fibers can also be braided and sewed together for rugs.

195

FELTED RUGS

In India, goat's hair and wool are felted together in large thick sheets, which are then embroidered with beautiful colorful patterns, using woolen yarns. Known as Numdah rugs, they are ornamented with a tree of life design, which has heavy pods and flowers hanging from a slender tree form. For a discussion of felting see page 2.

CHAPTER VI

Mechanically Operated Looms

Mechanical improvements to weaving equipment have developed very slowly in the history of mankind. In both the Old and the New Worlds primitive methods of weaving continued to be used long after marked advancements occurred in the other arts and sciences. Even today, Guatemalan Indian women use the same type of stick loom as that pictured on ancient Peruvian vases. It is difficult to explain this extremely conservative attitude toward the textile arts. Perhaps man has ever been wary of changing the tools which satisfy his basic needs.

In the Old World simple hand looms were used for thousands of years before foot-power looms were adopted, and it took another 2000 years to operate them by water power. The ancient draw loom in use at the time of Christ or shortly thereafter was not converted to a mechanically powered loom until nearly 2000 years later, when the Jacquard loom appeared, in 1804. As soon as water power began to be utilized for operating spinning and weaving equipment, improvements quickly followed. It is interesting to note that today, when large electrically operated looms produce hundreds of yards of cloth in a matter of minutes, the basic principles of weaving and the basic weave structures remain unchanged.

Even though large factory power looms now turn out enough cloth to supply our actual needs, more and more foot-power looms are finding their way into American homes. The current vogue for the use of textured fabrics in clothing and interior decoration has helped to turn our thoughts again toward hand weaving, because this handicraft serves to satisfy the creative needs of many individuals. In fact, it appears that we are again approaching a Renaissance in the hand-weaving arts; some of the new fabrics being produced are breathtaking in both color and texture arrangements.

197

1. Table Looms

The loom which we call the table-model loom can be traced back to the Near East. In the early historical periods of Syria and Egypt weavers sat on the ground and wove on small upright horizontal looms. The loom

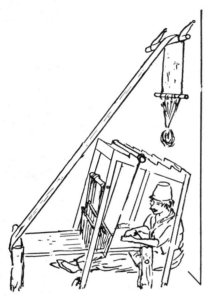

Fig. 104. Near Eastern Loom. Loom used in Syria, Egypt, and other countries of the eastern Mediterranean. Notice weighted warp and counterbalanced heddles. The loom has no foot treadles.

used was of the counterbalanced type and was equipped with two hand-operated harnesses, which were supported between the upright capes on either side of the loom. The warp was weighted and suspended over rods placed high above the heads of the weavers. (See Fig. 104.)

There are many types of table looms. Some of them have fixed-heddle harnesses similar to the inkle loom; some have single-heddle harnesses which operate like hole-and-slot heddle harnesses; some have counterbalanced heddle harnesses (see Fig. 105) which can be equipped with heddle horses; some have heddle harnesses which operate with draw strings similar to those on the draw loom; finally, some have jack-operated heddle harnesses with side or front levers. (See Fig. 106.)

Apparently the table-model loom operated with draw strings was one of the first types used in the United States. It was known as the Wonder Weaver and was manufactured in Mishawaka, Indiana. Small acorns were attached to the ends of the draw cords. When an acorn was pulled down and set into a socket arranged for it on the side of the loom, a harness was automatically hoisted. Some weavers believe that the principle of this loom originated in one of the Scandinavian countries. The use of acorns may have been a Scandinavian invention, but the principle of the draw loom is thought to have been developed in the Near East.

STRUCTURE OF THE LOOM

The table loom has the same basic structure as the foot-power loom, except that it has no legs, floor supports, or foot treadles. The operation of the harnesses differs only in that those on the table-model loom are operated by hand levers, while those on the foot-power loom are operated by foot treadles. Since it takes longer to operate hand levers, the table-model loom is not satisfactory for weaving long lengths of fabric.

DIRECTIONS FOR WEAVING ON A TABLE LOOM

The table loom is warped and strung up like the foot-power loom. Ready-warped spools can be purchased for both looms,[1] but they are more frequently used on the table-model looms. For directions for warping, see the discussion of foot-power looms, page 210.

The same types of weaves are woven on table-model looms as on foot-power looms. However, it should be remembered that table-model looms are either jack or counterbalanced and hence a weave should be selected which is set up for the type of loom at hand. Since most table looms are of the jack type, the weaves described here have special operating instructions for a jack loom. By reversing the operation of the lever plan, these weaves could be woven on a counterbalanced loom.

The two weaves described are known as overshot weaves. The pattern yarns should be heavy and colored; the tabby yarns are usually of the same weight and color as the warp. The tabby sheds alternate: harnesses 1 and 3 for tabby A and harnesses 2 and 4 for tabby B. A row of tabby

Fig. 105. Table Loom. Loom equipped with counterbalanced heddle harnesses. (Courtesy, Lily Mills Co., Shelby, N.C.)

Fig. 106. Table Loom. Loom equipped with jack-hoisted heddle harnesses. (Courtesy, Structo Mfg. Co., Freeport, Ill.)

precedes a row of pattern weaving: for example, weave tabby A, weave pattern, weave tabby B, weave pattern, weave tabby A, etc.

[1] The Structo Manufacturing Company, Freeport, Illinois, supplies these ready-warped spools.

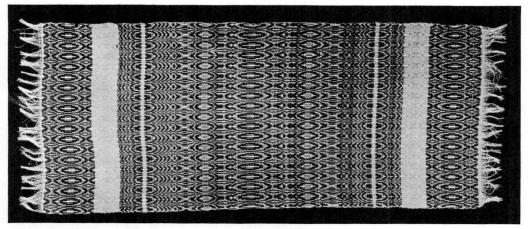

Fig. 107. Honeysuckle Pattern. A piece of weaving showing the versatility of this weave.

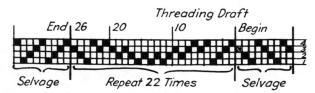

Threading Draft

End 26   20   10   Begin

4
3
2
1

Selvage   Repeat 22 Times   Selvage

Fig. 108. Draft for the Honeysuckle Weave. Use standard tie-up with this draft; see Fig. 132. Usually used on a rising-shed table loom. (Courtesy, Mary M. Atwater and Structo Mfg. Co., Freeport, Ill.)

HONEYSUCKLE PATTERN

The Honeysuckle pattern is one of the most popular of the coverlet designs. (See Fig. 107.) So many different designs can be made from this one threading! (See Fig. 108.) Colored yarn is usually selected for the pattern weft. The number of heddles needed are as follows: harness 1, 114; harness 2, 180; harness 3, 181; harness 4, 115.

PATTERN A. TREADLE PLAN

Tabby—harnesses 1 and 3, alternate with harnesses 2 and 4.
Pattern—the pattern sheds are raised in the following order:

3 and 4	once	
1 and 4	once	
1 and 2	twice	
1 and 4	once	

3 and 4	once	
2 and 3	once	
1 and 2	three times	

1 and 4	three times	
3 and 4	six times	
1 and 4	three times	
1 and 2	three times	
2 and 3	once	

Repeat entire pattern, and then repeat again as far as the line.

PATTERN B. TREADLE PLAN

Tabby—same as above.
Pattern—the following pattern sheds are raised in order:

200

3 and 4	once		1 and 2	twice	
1 and 4	once		1 and 4	once	
1 and 2	twice		3 and 4	once	
2 and 3	twice		2 and 3	once	

---

3 and 4 three times   1 and 2 three times

1 and 4 six times   2 and 3 once

3 and 4 three times

2 and 3 twice

Repeat entire pattern, and then repeat again as far as the line.

QUEEN'S DELIGHT PATTERN

The Queen's Delight is another pattern that most weavers like. (See Fig. 109.) Interest is added to the weaving if the outside warp pattern units are threaded in a different color from the rest of the warp. For example, two chocolate brown stripes could be warped on either side of a dusty pink background. (See Fig. 111.) Use the threading draft in Fig. 110 as follows: thread right-hand edge; thread A to C twice; thread A to B once; thread left hand edge. For weaving the design according to the pattern sheds given below, weave edge A; weave B through C twice; weave B once; end by weaving D. The repeats of the pattern should be planned according to the width of the loom. (See Fig. 111.) Treadle plan:

Tabby—harnesses 1 and 3, alternating with harnesses 2 and 4.
Pattern—raise the following pattern sheds in this order:

A (THE EDGE)

1 and 2 once ⎤
2 and 3 once ⎟ twice
3 and 4 once ⎟
1 and 4 once ⎦

1 and 2 once
2 and 3 once
3 and 4 three times
1 and 4 three times

B

1 and 2 three times
2 and 3 three times
3 and 4 five times
1 and 4 six times
3 and 4 twice
1 and 4 six times
3 and 4 five times
2 and 3 five times
1 and 2 four times ⎫ seven times
2 and 3 four times ⎭

1 and 2 four times
2 and 3 five times
3 and 4 five times
1 and 4 six times
3 and 4 twice
1 and 4 six times
3 and 4 five times
2 and 3 three times

Fig. 109. Queen's Delight Pattern. (Courtesy, Mary M. Atwater and Structo Mfg. Co., Freeport, Ill.)

Fig. 111. Queen's Delight Pattern Applied. Two bags made of this interesting weave.

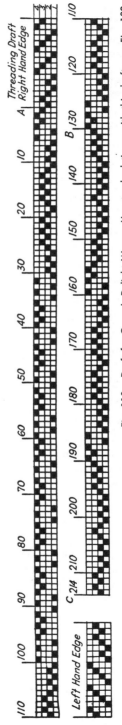

Fig. 110. Draft for Queen's Delight Weave. Use standard tie-up with this draft; see Fig. 132. Usually used on a rising-shed table loom. (Courtesy, Mary M. Atwater and Structo Mfg. Co., Freeport, Ill.)

C

1 and 2	three times		3 and 4	twice	
1 and 4	five times		1 and 4	six times	
3 and 4	six times		3 and 4	five times	
1 and 4	twice		2 and 3	three times	
3 and 4	six times		1 and 2	three times	
1 and 4	five times		1 and 4	five times	
1 and 2	three times		3 and 4	six times	
2 and 3	three times		1 and 4	twice	
3 and 4	five times		3 and 4	six times	
1 and 4	six times		1 and 4	five times	

D

1 and 4	three times	1 and 4	once	
3 and 4	three times	3 and 4	once	twice
2 and 3	once	2 and 3	once	
1 and 2	once	1 and 2	once	

2. Foot-Power Looms

"The origin of the treadle loom remains a matter of some doubt. As the European never made use of his feet to facilitate his work to the extent which the peoples of Asia especially [those] of the Far East, did, it seems probable that Asia was the original home of treadle weaving."[2]

Since there are two basic types of foot-power looms, jack-hoisted and counterbalanced, there may have been separate origins for each type. For example, the earliest jack-hoisted loom may have come from China, where old drawings show such a loom in use for weaving silk. This Chinese loom had a bow or C-spring attached to the top of a heddle harness; when one treadle was lowered, the bow arched backward, lifting the harness. (See Fig. 112.) The earliest counterbalanced loom may have been invented in India. A simple foot-operated horizontal loom with a counterbalanced heddle harness has been in use in India for an unknown time. This early loom was called a pit loom, since the weaver sat on the edge of a small pit, his feet hanging down in it. Cords fastened to each of the harnesses ended in loops which slipped over his big toes. When he pressed one foot downward and lifted the other, one harness was lowered and the other was raised. (See Fig. 113.)

It is possible that the foot-treadle counterbalanced loom was introduced into southern Europe by the Romans when they installed weaving centers there. These looms may have been used later to weave the "burre," that

[2] G. Schaefer, *Ciba Review*, No. 16, Ciba Company, New York, December, 1938, p. 544.

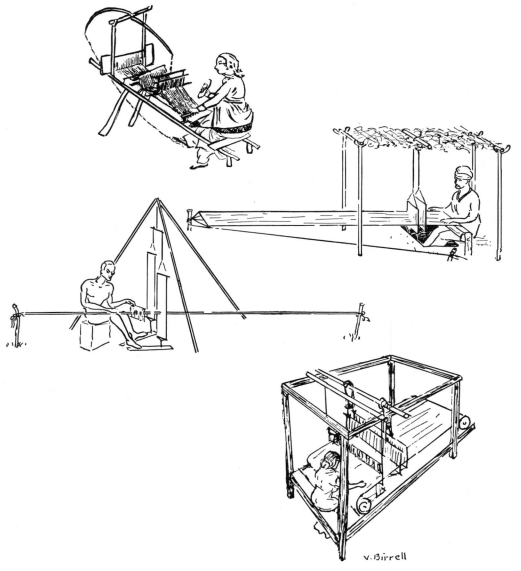

v. Birrell

Fig. 112.   Left Top, Korean Bow Loom. Early foot-treadle loom. (From drawing by H. M. Becher, 1950, British Museum Collection.)

Fig. 113.   Center, Versions of Foot-Power Looms. Above, pit loom from India. Below, African belt loom. After Roth (56), who shows a similar loom with only one foot on treadle.

Fig. 114.   Right Bottom, Early Renaissance Loom. Early fifteenth-century French loom.

plain brown cloth used by the common folk of the Middle Ages. Another loom trait that appears to have diffused from the Near East, and which may have been carried to Europe simultaneously with the foot-power loom, was the location on the loom of the lay, to be described shortly.

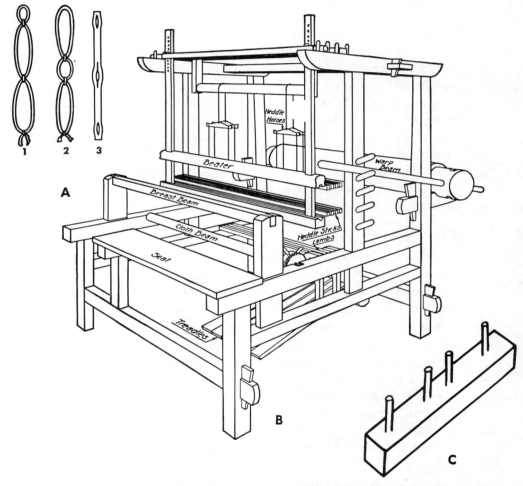

Fig. 115. A. Heddles. (1) Brocade heddle. (2) Standard heddle made of linen cord. (3) Steel heddle. B. Counterbalanced foot-power loom. Swedish counterbalanced type, with parts named (from Edward F. Worst, *Foot-Power Loom Weaving*, Bruce Publishing Co., 1924). C. Template for making string heddles.

The earliest European foot-power looms seem to have been equipped with a lay which swung from the top of the superstructure—a principle used on the still earlier horizontal ground looms of Egypt and the Near East. (See Fig. 114.) However, all of these suppositions have to be based upon hearsay. Very little actual information is available on the subject of loom structure; to base our judgment we have only Egyptian and Greek drawings on vases and on murals, tomb artifacts, and the crude drawings of the Middle Ages. By the time of the late Middle Ages, the treadle loom was a perfected invention in Europe, but we are at a loss to know its origin. In fact, there is some evidence that foot-power looms were being operated in England and Ireland as early as 1000 A.D.

In America weaving became synonymous with patriotism. Every home had its foot-power loom and was its own cloth producer. Itinerant weavers traveled about the countryside to help women with their weaving. The first looms used by the early American colonists were patterned after those of northern Europe. (See Fig. 115B.) The lay swung from the top of the loom; in fact, the lay which swung from the bottom of the loom frame was not used until the second quarter of the twentieth century. After the War of Independence, weaving inventions gradually led to factory-operated looms and replaced home industries. In recent years, interest in hand weaving has been revived, as already noted.

STRUCTURE OF THE LOOM

Various styles of foot-power counterbalanced and jack looms are illustrated in Figs. 90, 115A, and 116. The average foot-power loom rises approximately 33 inches from the floor, but can vary in width. They can be purchased in widths of 27, 32, 36, 42, and 46, inches.

The loom is supported by a frame of four upright posts held together by cross supports. The height of the uprights varies: on old European looms, they completely boxed in the loom and rose to a height of about 5 1/2 feet all around; on the northern European (Scandinavian) looms, these high supports boxed in only the back half of the loom, the two front supports being only about waist high; on most current American looms the four vertical supports are only waist high on both the back and front of the loom, while the center capes rise high enough to support the heddle harnesses.

Some looms are equipped with two shuttle boxes placed opposite one another at the opposite ends of the open shed. By a sudden jerk of a cord, which hangs in front of the weaver, the shuttle is thrown through the shed, along the shuttle race, and into the box on the opposite side. Weavers who weave fabrics for the market often use shuttle boxes and flying shuttles.

The reed is set in a frame, the lay, which is fastened to the superstructure or to the base of the loom and which rocks back and forth in the front

Fig. 116. Jack Looms. Above, heddle harnesses hoisted on the principle of jacks. (Courtesy, L. W. Macomber, Saugus, Mass.) Below, jack loom built with a minimum of superstructure. (Courtesy, E. E. Gilmore, Stockton, Calif.)

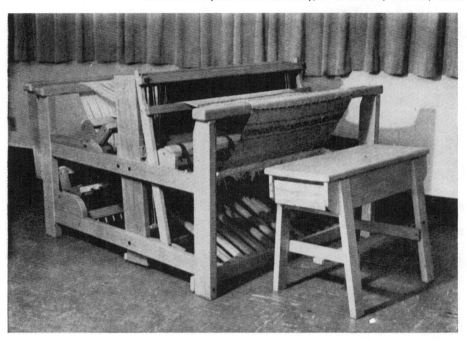

half of the loom. When the reed is pressed forward against the weft it battens down and firms the fabric. The reed proper consists of a wooden or metal frame in which a number of metal strips or teeth are closely set. The spaces or slits between the teeth are known as dents; the warp yarns pass through them. In warp-faced weaves a number of warp yarns are threaded into each dent of a coarse reed—a number six, eight, or nine. In weft-faced weaves the warp is often threaded in alternate dents. The denting or spacing of the warp often determines the appearance of the fabric: close-set warp becomes warp-faced and wide-set warp weft-faced. Reeds come in many sizes, ranging from No. 5 to No. 100, and in different lengths to fit different widths of looms. The standard width of reeds is 4 inches. The sizes most popular with hand weavers are, in order: 15, 12, 10, 18, 16, 9, 8, and 20.

Behind the reed and the lay are the heddles. On most modern foot-power looms these are made of steel, and most commercial looms come already equipped with steel heddles. However, many weavers still prefer heddles made of linen string. Some weavers have suggested that the string heddles on each heddle harness should be dyed a different color, to facilitate the identification of each harness and to save time when threading the heddles. The heddles are arranged in their harnesses so that they are held at right angles to the warp. As many heddles are needed as there are warp yarns on the loom, each warp passing through an eye of a heddle.

The heddle harnesses, together with their lever and hoist mechanisms, are held in place in the capes or superstructure which is raised in the center on either side of the loom. The operation of the harnesses differs on the two types of foot-power looms. On the counterbalanced or sinking-shed loom, the harnesses are attached to pulleys formed by cords carried over and around rollers suspended from the top superstructure; the harnesses are lowered by a down tread on the foot pedals. On the jack-hoist or rising-shed loom, the harnesses are pushed up—in some cases, pulled up—by means of jack levers attached to the foot pedals.

Some looms have a sectional warp beam which has a circumference of 1 yard; one complete turn winds 1 yard of warp on the beam. The sectional warp beam is divided into four to six horizontal sections or cogs; it is further sectioned with quarter-inch hardwood dowels 2 1/2 inches long, placed in rows around the beam and set along the cogs 2 inches apart from peg center to peg center. Other smaller sectional beams are 1/2 yard around; they are divided into four or six horizontal cogs, and are sectioned with 3/16-inch steel pegs. These pegs are 2 1/2 inches high and are placed along the cogs 1 inch apart from peg center to peg center. It is important that a short tape with an eyelet at its end be attached to and wrapped around each section of the beam; this replaces the fly rod attached to the regular nonsectional type of warp beam.

The weaver sits on a bench which is often constructed as part of the loom, and raises and lowers the heddle harnesses by pressing down on the foot pedal levers, which are near the floor immediately in front of him.

POINTS TO CHECK WHEN PURCHASING A FOOT-POWER LOOM

1. *Decide upon the type of loom wanted.* A counterbalanced loom is cheaper than a jack loom and is good for ordinary weaving. A jack loom is more versatile and better for intricate pattern weaving.

2. *Decide upon the size of the loom,* that is, upon the width and the number of harnesses. Looms come in different widths, as described above. The wider the loom, the farther the weaver will have to reach to throw in the shuttle and the more tiring weaving will be. In deciding the number of heddle harnesses wanted, remember that for ordinary weaving two heddle harnesses are sufficient, but for pattern weaving four, eight, or ten might be needed. The standard loom has four harnesses; a loom with eight harnesses is more costly but is a good investment. For an experienced and creative weaver, ten harnesses offer more variation in pattern weaving and should be ordered if possible. A four-harness loom should have six treadles, and an eight-harness loom should have at least fourteen.

3. *Choose a loom with a sectional warp beam.* This saves both time and energy. The beam should be well constructed. Beams less than 1/2 yard in circumference are impractical.

4. *Select the correct size of reed.* Looms usually come equipped with a No. 15 dent reed. Additional reeds in various sizes can be ordered.

5. *Check the lay carefully.* Select one in which the reed is removable. The lay should be equipped with a shuttle race in front at the base of the reed. A lay that pivots from the bottom of the loom is easier to operate than one that pivots from the top.

6. *Check the number and kind of heddles.* Steel heddles are to be preferred to linen heddles. They slip more easily along the harness, do not stretch, do not wear out or fray, and do not restrict passage of the warp. (See Fig. 115B.) The heddle frame should be detachable from the loom, and the heddles detachable from the frame.

7. *Check the balance of the shed.* The angle of the warp at the bottom of the shed should be equal to that at the top. This arrangement maintains an even tension in the warp.

209

MECHANICALLY OPERATED LOOMS

8. *Check the distance between breast beam and heddle harness.* The minimum distance should be 18 inches.
9. *Check the rachet wheel releases.* Hand or foot brakes or pulls should be located on the front of the loom, within easy reach. These brakes release the dogs on the rachet wheels of the warp and cloth beams.
10. *Check the wood and finish of the loom.* It should be made of good close-grained hardwood, with a surface finish of several coats of satin-finish varnish, well sanded and rubbed down with pumice between coats. To make heddle threading easier, the breast and back beams should be collapsible, folding toward the capes of the loom. The two people threading the loom can then sit close to the heddle harnesses.

SELECTION OF THE WEAVE

Before any preliminary preparations are made for weaving, the weave structure to be used must be decided upon and an appropriate pattern selected if one is to be used. The various basic weaves are classified and described in Chapter VII.

GENERAL DIRECTIONS FOR WARPING THE LOOM

Thousands of years ago, the Egyptians used warping pegs in preparing their warp. Warping pegs and boards are still used for preparing warp for special pattern weaving or sample making. (This process is described on page 47.) However, the sectional warp beam, and other devices used with it, can now take care of all pattern needs. The use of the sectional warp beam greatly lessens the tedious process of warping, and makes it possible for one person to warp the loom easily without help.

Many looms are now equipped with special hexagonal warp beams which hold special warp spools.[3] These come already wound with warp, 60 ends to the spool. Their use saves warping the beam, but limits the plotting of creative designs.

WARPING THE LOOM FROM THE WARPING BOARD

It is taken for granted at this point that the warp has been correctly prepared on a warping board and carefully removed from it as described on page 52. It usually takes two people to handle the following method of warping: The lease rods and chained warp are held by one person, who stands about 4 feet back of the loom; the second person handles the warp entering the loom. If an accessory frame is attached to the back of the

[3] These beams and spools are sold by Structo Manufacturing Company, Freeport, Illinois.

loom, one person can handle this job. Wide lease rods can be substituted for the regular lease rods, slipped into the warp, and fastened to the frame. The raddle (see Fig. 117) can then be placed a foot or so in front of the lease rods on this accessory frame; if no accessory frame is available it can be fastened to the back of the loom.

1. Now carry the end loops of the warp through the dents of the raddle; put the center loops through the center of the raddle and evenly space the balance of the warp on each side of the center. When all the loops of warp are set through the raddle, slip the fly rod from the warp beam through them, put the cap on the raddle, and tie the fly rod to the warp beam.

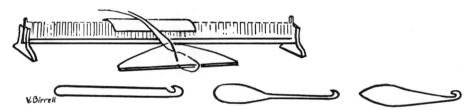

Fig. 117. Warping Equipment. Top, a raddle. Bottom, three styles of hooks used for threading the warp yarns through the eyes of the heddles and the dents of the reed.

2. One of the workers now slowly winds the warp onto the warp beam. Strips of paper wrapped in it as it is being rolled on the warp beam prevent the matting and tangling of the warp. To maintain an even tension in the warp the paper should reach entirely across it. Allow the warp to pass gently through the lease rods, maintaining an even tension by pulling it taut back of the lease rods. A comb can be used to straighten the warp, should it tangle.

3. When the far end of the warp is reached—the place where the first crocheted loops were made—remove the raddle and attach the lease rods to the back crossbar of the loom frame. About 3 feet of warp, the far ends, are left hanging; in other words, this warp is not drawn through the raddle.

4. Now thread the heddles with these warp ends, cutting the ends, loop by loop, as threading progresses. The stretch of warp now in front of the cross must be long enough to pass through the heddles of the reed with about a foot to spare; the warp is then long enough to be attached to the fly rod on the cloth beam.

There are other methods of putting a chain of warp on the loom, but they are not described here, since they not only take longer, but they also   **211** cause more wear on the warp as well as on the nerves of the people doing the warping.

WARPING THE LOOM EQUIPPED WITH A SECTIONAL WARP BEAM

There is no question but that it is much easier to put the warp on a loom equipped with a sectional warp beam. (See Fig. 118.) Furthermore,

Fig. 118. Warping the Sectional Warp Beam. Note the position of the bobbins, the spool board holding the bobbins, the tension box, the sectional warp beam, and the crank.

such a loom minimizes tangling of threads and handling long chains of warp, and one person can easily put the warp on such a loom.

Preparing Bobbins for Warping

When a sectional warp beam is used, the spools or bobbins which supply the warp are held on a spool rack or board placed at the back of the loom. If bobbins are used instead of spools, they are wound as follows:

A cone or cap of heavy paper is wrapped around the spindle shaft of a bobbin winder—an electric bobbin winder with a foot-pedal control, if possible. (See Fig. 119.) A spool of yarn is placed on a spool rack, and an end of a yarn from it is slipped under the flap of the paper-cone bobbin. The yarn is then wound from the spool onto the paper cone, taking care to distribute the yarn evenly along the cone, to come no closer to the edges of the cone than half an inch, and to narrow the span of yarn gradually toward the ends of the cone. When sufficient yarn is on the cone, it is released from the shaft and another cone is arranged in its place. A meter to record the number of revolutions made by the shaft is a helpful appliance, for then the amount of yarn can be kept uniform on all the bobbins used. If the yarn is to be warped 30 ends to the inch, 30 bobbins will be needed for a sectional warp beam equipped with pegs set 1 inch apart, and 60 will be needed for a beam with pegs 2 inches apart.

Fig. 119. Bobbin Winder. Electric bobbin winder used for winding bobbins for shuttles and for use on the spool board.

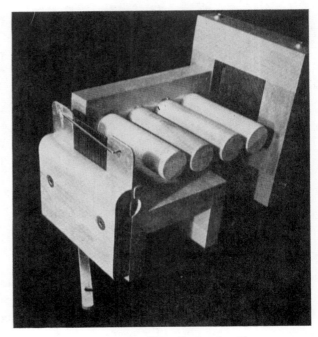

Fig. 120. Tension Box. The warp yarns pass through this box prior to being wound on the sectional warp beam; this keeps all yarns at the same tension.

Winding Warp on Sectional Warp Beams

The warp is put on a sectional warp beam as follows: First thread the tension box. (See Fig. 120.) This box regulates the tension of the warp yarns being wound onto the sectional beam, and distributes the yarns evenly in one section of that beam. The box is clamped onto the back bar of the loom immediately above the section on the beam which is to be wound; it is moved along the bar from section to section as the winding on each section

213

is completed. The yarns from spools or bobbins are carried from the spool rack or board through the dents in the tension box. After being threaded through the tension box they are tied onto the end of the tape in one section of the sectional warp beam and are then wound onto that beam by turning the handle of the crank attached to it. (See Figs. 118 and 121.) To make sure that the same amount of warp is wound onto each section, the revolutions of the beam must be counted. After each section is wound, fold wide cellophane tape over and under the warp yarns before cutting them from the tension box; the cut is made in the center of the tape. To prevent accidental unwinding of the warp from a sectional warp beam, secure the ends temporarily to the warp with masking tape until all sections are wound.

Fig. 121. Rachet Wheel and Dog. These two parts prevent the loom beams from unwinding during warping and weaving.

THREADING THE HEDDLES AND THE REED

After all of the warp has been wound onto the warp beam, it is then ready to be threaded through the heddles.

1. Choose a heddle-threading draft which will furnish the weave pattern wanted. (These drafts are discussed in Chapter VII.) If part of the heddle-threading draft is to be omitted because the loom is too narrow or for any other reason, one complete repeat of a unit block must be eliminated so that the pattern will not be affected. For example, most heddle-threading drafts come with a sequence of unit blocks to be threaded in a number of repeats. Several repeats can be omitted without affecting the pattern.

2. The heddle draft is read from right to left. The threading of the heddles also takes place from right to left.

3. The front heddle harness—harness 1—is nearest the front of the loom. The others behind the first are in order 2, 3, 4, etc.

4. The weaver usually threads the heddles from the back of the loom, as the source of the warp is there. Threading the heddles is facilitated if

214

two people do the work: one chooses a warp yarn and starts it through a heddle eye, the other draws it through the heddle. A heddle hook is used to assist in the threading by pulling the yarn through the heddles. (See Fig. 117.)

If only one person does the threading, the loom is threaded from the side front. A strand of warp is laid over the top of the harness. The weaver selects one warp yarn at a time from this strand and threads it through a particular heddle eye.

5. A selvage must be allowed for all patterns, even though the draft does not show a selvage.

6. Before starting to thread the heddles, push all heddles to the left side of the heddle harnesses. Select the heddles from their respective harnesses according to the heddle-threading draft. Move the heddles from the left side of the loom as needed, thread them, and push them to the right side of the loom.

7. After a section of the warp has been heddled, tie it together loosely into a loop knot in front of the heddles to prevent the yarns from sliding out and tangling. The heddles, too, can be tied together in groups in unit design blocks as they are threaded; this helps the weaver check the threading in case it needs to be reëxamined. When the warp has all been threaded through the heddles, it is ready to be threaded through the dents of the reed.

8. The reed is threaded one dent at a time. Push a loop of the yarn through a dent; a heddle hook will help pull the yarn through. After a group of warp yarns has been dented, knot it together loosely in front of the reed. Tie the reed to the loom frame to keep it stationary while denting.

The distribution of warp yarns in the dents of the reed is determined by the type of design chosen. In pattern coverlet weaving, 24/3 Egyptian cotton is dented 30 warp yarns to the inch, 2 to a dent in a No. 15 reed. Too little attention is usually paid to the distribution of yarns in the dents and the size of openings of dents. Most of the instructions which follow supply this information, but it would be well to review the matter in the discussion of the structure of the loom, page 208.

9. After the dents in the reed have been threaded, draw one section of the warp at a time to an even tension and attach it by means of a bow knot to the fly rod, having first brought this rod to the front of and over the top of the breast beam. To make the knot, divide a section of about 30 warps into two parts and take both over and partially

around the fly rod; bring one part up on the left side and the other up on the right side. Cross them over and under the section, bring them up again to the top, and tie them in a bow knot. Sometimes this crossing over and under is omitted and the bow is tied directly above the warp.

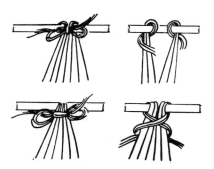

Fig. 122A. Bow Knots. Method of tying the knot that holds the warp to the apron of the breast beam of the loom.

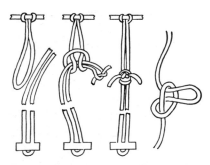

Fig. 122B. Snitch Knot and Loop Knot. The first three drawings show the steps in making a snitch knot; note that the upper center part is a double-hitch knot. On the right is a loop knot. The snitch knot is used in tying up a loom. The loop knot is used to temporarily hold together warp yarns during warping.

TYING UP THE LOOM

The next step is to check the tie-up of treadles and lams to the heddle harnesses and retie any that may be slack. A strong, heavy, woven cord—linen if possible—is always used for these tie cords. If a loom is being tied up for pattern weaving a tie-up draft may be furnished with the pattern. A snitch knot is used to make the tie-ups. The structure of this knot is shown in Fig. 122B. Many looms come from the manufacturer already tied up. All tie-ups should be checked, however, before commencing any weave. (When purchasing or selecting a loom, it should be remembered that the jack loom is considerably more versatile than the counterbalanced loom. The jack loom is not limited to any standard tie-up; each treadle may be independently tied to a lam, or the treadles may be tied in any combination which will facilitate the weaving of the pattern selected.)

The tie-up draft is symbolized on graph paper with crosses (x) for sinking-shed counterbalanced looms, and with circles (o) for rising-shed jack-type looms. (See Fig. 132.) Tie-up drafts are also known as peg plans, pegging plans, and lifting plans. Special tie-up systems alter the structure and design of a weave. (See Fig. 123.)

On the loom the tabby treadles are placed on the right side of the treadles, on the left side or in the center. On a two-harness loom each harness is tied to a separate foot pedal. On a four-harness counterbalanced loom they are usually tied up in pairs to six treadles as follows, starting from left: 1–2, 2–3, 3–4, 1–4, 2–4 and 1–3. For a rising-shed jack loom the opposite combinations are made: 3–4, 1–4, 1–2, 2–3, 1–3, 2–4. Diagrams are shown in Fig. 132.

216 The tie cords should be of equal lengths and should be set straight up

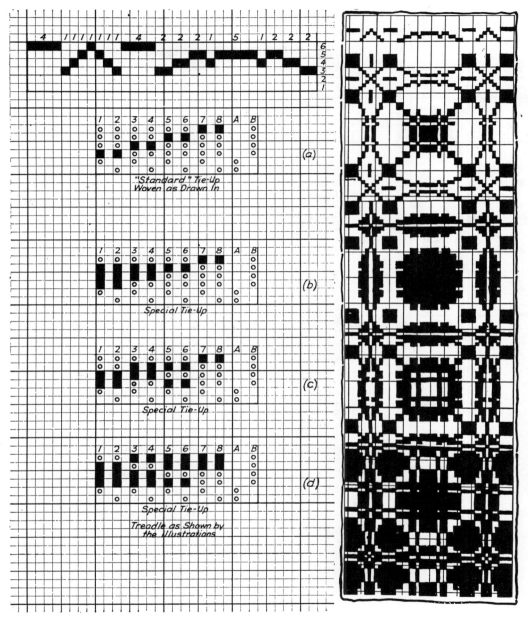

Fig. 123. Tie-Up Variations. Effect of changes of tie-up of the treadles on a six-harness colonial pattern. (Courtesy, Mary M. Atwater.)

and down. They should hold the pedals up at a slant. When a treadle is pressed down, a proper opening or shed should be made in the warp. The center treadles are tied first and the tension of the warp checked before tying the rest of the treadles. The correct knots for tying up loom are explained in Fig. 122B.

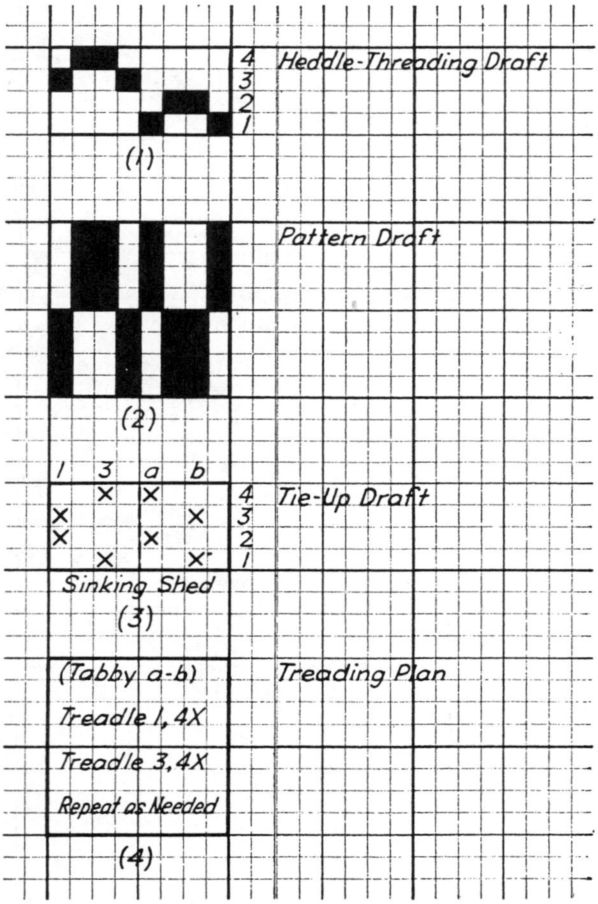

DRESSING THE WARP

Both woolen and singles linen yarns must be dressed before or after being warped on the loom. This is done by sponging or dipping the warp into a light flaxseed starch. Combed cotton or Egyptian cotton needs no dressing, but soft-carded cotton yarns are often dressed. The Indians of Guatemala often dress the cotton warp on their various hand looms. Dressing is made by boiling 1/2 cup of flaxseed in 3 cups of water to consistency of starch. It is applied to warp with a sponge. In addition to this dressing, woolen and linen warp should always be kept slightly damp during weaving.

THE TREADING PLAN

The treading plan is not itself a draft, but rather the end product of all the drafts made for weaving. (The tie-up draft has been described above; the other drafts are described on page 269.) It lists the order in which the treadles are lowered to bring about the formation of a given weave. (See Fig. 124.)

The experienced weaver may be able to weave without a treadle plan, because she is able to follow the pattern draft and treadle accordingly, or she may be able to "weave as drawn in." This last expression means that she is able to tell by the position of the warp in the shed which treadle she needs to use. Weaving as drawn in is described on page 273. The circular plan in

Fig. 124. Drafts Used in Weaving.

THE TEXTILE ARTS

Fig. 132 is a treading plan. Treading plans are also listed on pages 200 and 201 in connection with the weaving of two overshot weaves.

GENERAL DIRECTIONS FOR WEAVING ON A FOOT-POWER LOOM

1. Check the loom carefully to see that all is in order. Choose the correct yarn. (See pages 45 and 269.) Put the warp on the loom. (See page 210.)
2. Thread heddles correctly. If a yarn skips a heddle, make a heddle out of string for that yarn. However, if a heddle is forgotten during the threading processes, the entire warp may have to be rethreaded.
3. Dent the warp correctly for the yarn count desired.
4. Lift the harnesses and see that the warp forms uniform sheds. Also check the sheds to see that the proper tie-up has been provided for the pattern chosen and that the treadle tie cords are of the proper length.
5. Dress the warp if necessary.
6. Start weaving at least 8 inches above the fly rod. Put in a few rows of plain weaving, using a coarse yarn. These coarse wefts will even the tension of the warp and when beaten back will pull uneven warp yarns smooth. The warp should be maintained at an even tension during weaving.
7. The selvage edges should be kept even. On warp-faced weaves, the weft can be pulled firmly across the shed. However, in weft-faced or balanced weaves, an arch or open angle must be left in the new throw of weft on the end nearest the shuttle; when it is battened into place, the angle allows enough leeway to prevent the weft from pulling in the selvages. Use the same angle on every throw of weft to keep the selvages uniform. A warp stretcher (see Fig. 125) is used to help keep the selvages even.
8. Maintain an even rhythm in weaving. For example, pick up the shuttle, throw, beat, put down the shuttle, change sheds; repeat.
9. Formulate a systematic approach to weaving. For example, always throw the tabby from right to left with the tabby treadle tied up on the right side, and return the tabby from left to right when the left tabby treadle is pressed down. The pattern throws of weft should follow the tabby throws. The weft can be battened in place before and after each throw of weft or after each two throws, depending upon how firm a fabric is desired. Whichever method of battening is used, the same system should be maintained for the entire piece of fabric to make for uniformity of structure. After a shuttle is used, put it back of those yet to be used.

10. Keep the flat side of the shuttle to the back. The shuttle glides across the shuttle race.
11. Keep the sheds clear (see Fig. 90), making any adjustments necessary to clear a shed: retie a treadle, correct a broken or crossed yarn, etc. Keep the hands clean. Keep the cloth clean. Use a loom cover if necessary. Do not acquire lazy habits.

Fig. 125. Temple. Temple or "warp stretcher" in place. This tool assists in maintaining an even width on the fabric being woven.

12. Release the warp tension by releasing the rachet wheel whenever you leave the loom. (See Fig. 121.) Do not leave shuttles in warp.
13. Tie no knots in the weft yarn. Do not leave weft yarns hanging from the selvage. Make all joinings on the inside of a shed by twisting the end of a broken weft around an outside warp and then turning this end back into shed. Before changing the shed, lay the end of a new weft across the end of the last weft, then carry the new weft across the remainder of the shed.

220

14. Wool as well as singles or round linen warp should be kept damp while weaving. Place a damp turkish towel over the warp at the back of the loom. Do not beam a very long woolen warp on the loom, as wool sometimes loses its life.
15. After taking a woolen fabric from the loom, wash it thoroughly with mild soap and lukewarm water. Wool should be handled carefully, but linen should be soaked and washed vigorously.
16. So that heddles will not have to be rethreaded when the weaving is finished, leave the ends of the old warp on the loom. When putting on a new warp, either tie the new warp to the old with weaver's knots or thread the heddles one at a time as the old warp is drawn out.

3. Multiple-Harness and Mechanical Looms

Intricate pattern weaves such as brocade and matelassé can be woven on regular hand looms, but with great difficulty. Actually, such weaves as these require special looms equipped with devices for forming many sheds. A few such looms are briefly described here.

THE DRAW LOOM

The draw loom is thought to have been the first one equipped with multiple harnesses. Its exact origin is not known, but most historians are inclined to give China credit for its invention; Han Dynasty silks have been found by Sir Aurel Stein.[4] Persia is known to have been weaving intricate patterned silk fabrics about 320 B.C.; since the silk yarns used in these fabrics came from China, and the design influences were mostly of Chinese origin, it is possible that Persia began to use the draw loom at about this time. When Damascus first started to use the draw loom is not known, but it was being used both there and in Egypt at the beginning of the Christian era. Damascus is one of the oldest weaving centers in the world; some say that the art of weaving there extends back 5000 years.

The draw loom is said to have been introduced into Europe by the Crusaders, who learned about it while sojourning in Damascus and the Near East. In Europe in the seventeenth century the loom was improved and comber boards, described below, replaced the many harnesses. Even-

[4] Miss Edith A. Standen of the textile study room of New York's Metropolitan Museum recommends the following as good references for information on the draw loom. "L'historique du métier pour la fabrication des étoffes façonnées," by C. Rodon y Font, translated by Adolphe Hullebroeck, Paris, 1934, discusses the Stein findings; "Etude analytique des petits modèles de métiers exposés au Musée historique des tissus," by C. Razy, Lyon, 1913; "The loom and the spindle: past, present, and future," by Luther Hooper, in the Annual Report of the Smithsonian Institution, 1914, pp. 629–678.

tually the Jacquard loom took its place, but the draw loom is still used in certain rural areas, such as in certain Guatemalan villages.

In addition to the many pattern harnesses on a draw loom, there are usually two and sometimes four counterbalanced harnesses operated with foot pedals, which form the tabby and other basic weaves. The pattern weave harnesses, each controlling a certain group of warp yarns, are attached to cords called simples, which are drawn up and over the superstructure of the loom; when they are pulled down by the draw boy— a boy at the side of the loom—the harnesses affected are raised. Sometimes the simples hang down in front of the weaver and are operated by him. Some Guatemalan looms have as many as 56 simples. They are arranged in numerical order (1, 2, 3, etc.), which makes it easier for the draw boy to pull the exact cord needed. In Europe in the seventeenth century the individual heddles for the pattern weave on draw looms were individually weighted and strung through comber boards—boards perforated with the necessary holes. This improvement dispensed with the numerous pattern heddle harnesses. A simple could now lift a group of heddles; it often ran over pulleys to facilitate raising the heddles.

JACQUARD LOOM

The Jacquard loom, invented in France about 1804, was the final result of the cumulative effort of a number of men. In 1727, Basile Bouchon substituted a band of perforated paper for the bunches of looped string which had been used to select the simples for the sheds of the draw loom. In 1728, M. Falcon invented perforated cards to simplify the use of the simples, but a draw boy was still needed to manipulate the simples. In 1745, Jacques de Vaucanson united in one machine Bouchon's band of perforated paper and Falcon's cards, and designed a mechanism for operating this loom from one center. Around the turn of the nineteenth century, Joseph Marie Jacquard in about 1804, with Vaucanson's invention as a guide, perfected his own version of the perforated card loom, now known as the Jacquard. (See Figs. 96, 97, and 98 and pages 20 and 187.) The Jacquard loom operates as follows:

When an intricate pattern, calling for individual warp end control, is to be woven into a fabric, a Jacquard loom is employed. A Jacquard loom consists of any one of several types of basic looms—cotton, woolen, carpet, etc.—coupled to a Jacquard machine. It is the Jacquard machine which selects the ends [warp yarns] to be woven in accordance with the designer's pattern. The operation of the Jacquard loom is described below; because of the many types of techniques of Jacquard weaving, only the basic principles are outlined:

222

1. The designer draws a pattern on gridded paper, each square of which represents an end [a warp yarn] to be selected in weaving.
2. Pattern cards are cut to select the ends called for by the design. In the newer type of Jacquards, a hole is cut only for those ends to be raised to the upper shed. [Each row of holes across a card represents a warp shed and, consequently, a throw of weft.] The holes are round and the number of rows of holes and the number of holes per row on each card depend upon the index [spacing] of the Jacquard: however, there must be a space for each warp end which the Jacquard controls. (See Fig. 96.)
3. The pattern cards are laced together in their proper sequence to form a series of cards, called sections. The number of cards laced together to make a section depends upon the number of picks [rows of weft yarn] needed in the fabric. In other words, the cards in each section represent one complete lengthwise strip of the fabric to be woven; the strip contains a series of repeats of a horizontal unit of the design. The number of sections which are placed side by side across the loom depends upon the width of the fabric to be woven and upon the type of Jacquard employed. (See Fig. 97.)
4. The sections of pattern cards are mounted on the loom and are carried over a multisided cylinder which presents them to the needles of the Jacquard. The Jacquard needles are mounted in a horizontal position; there is a needle for each hole cut in a card. Each needle controls the position of a hook with respect to a lifting member [called a knife or a griff]. Wherever there is a hole in the pattern card, the needle passes through the card, in turn allowing the hook to be raised by the knife.
5. A harness cord is attached to the bottom of the hook and to the top of a lingo heddle. The lingo heddle consists of a wire, having an eyelet through which a warp end is threaded, and provision for attaching a weight at the bottom end. When a hook is engaged by a knife and lifted, it in turn lifts the harness cord and the lingo heddle, carrying the warp end into its top position, allowing the weft [or pile wire in rug making] to pass under the warp end.
6. After each lash [throw of weft], the Jacquard returns to its selecting position and another card is pressed against the needles.[5]

THE CAM-CONTROLLED LOOM

The first mechanical step made to convert the foot-power loom into a machine-operated loom was the addition of the cam apparatus. Cams, which are heart-shaped levers, are mounted on a revolving cylinder set below the harnesses. They are set to take care of the design to be woven. When the cylinder revolves, the cams revolve, and as one comes into contact with a heddle harness, it pushes the harness up. This system is somewhat limited in design planning, but is still used for some forms of weaving today.

[5] The description of the Jacquard loom was written by a member of the staff of the James Lees and Sons Company, manufacturers of carpets and yarns, and is presented here with their permission.

MECHANICALLY OPERATED LOOMS

THE DOBBY LOOM

The dobby loom contains a series of pieces of wood, called a chain, containing projecting pegs. When this chain revolves, the pegs come in contact with the levers which control the harnesses. The projecting pegs arranged on each piece of wood control one pick or weft throw on the loom. Patterns can be altered by changing the position of these pegs in the pieces of wood; this can be done without changing the threading of the heddles.

Dobby attachments, called head-motion attachments, can be purchased for hand looms. A circular peg attachment which has some characteristics of both the dobby and the cam looms can now be purchased for table looms.[6]

Small allover patterns, such as diaper, bird's-eye, and nail-head patterns, are usually woven on dobby looms.

OTHER POWER LOOMS

The great power looms of today are capable of making every known weave except perhaps the hand type of tapestry weaving.

The tremendous output of the textile mills is difficult to comprehend. Some idea of the performance of a power loom may be had from the following figures: A Draper X-2 Automatic loom is capable of weaving 200 picks or weft throws a minute. One man is needed for each 100 looms. One establishment of 300 looms, operating at 180 picks a minute, will produce 180,000 yards in 5 days. It requires 3300 pounds of yarn at an approximate cost of $18,000 to do this job.

In addition to fabric weaving, many other textile processes, such as lace making, tricot knitting, etc., are now carried on by machine methods. They are described in a later chapter.

[6] Nadeau Loom, Eiphege Nadeau Co., Woonsocket, Rhode Island.

CHAPTER VII

Basic Weaves

The difference in structure between a simple plain weave and an intricate one depends upon the manner in which warp and weft yarns interlace. Through the ages, man has added to his repertoire of weave structures and has varied those already developed by others. Certain cultures have been considerably more creative than others. Peru in the pre-Columbian period and Guatemala in the present period are examples of versatility on the Western Hemisphere; while China, the Near East, Egypt, and at a later period Italy are examples of excellence in the Old World. These areas are mentioned many times in this book in connection with their weaving crafts.

Although the great number of weaves, each with a specific name, may confuse and worry the beginner, the whole story of weave structure is truly not as complicated as it first appears. Weaves can be classified and grouped according to their basic structure. Since there are not many basic structuring techniques, this simplifies the problem. This chapter groups the weaves into related treatments and describes the processes of each basic weave in each category. The glossary at the back of the book describes numerous variations of the basic weaves.

The beginner should select a simple plain two-harness weave for his first attempt at weaving. As experience and confidence are gained, more complicated pattern weaves can be undertaken. It is a very stimulating experience for a beginner to graduate from a two-harness loom to one equipped with three, four, six, or eight harnesses.

CLASSIFICATION OF WEAVES

In this chapter all of the weaves discussed are grouped under the following structure headings: plain, twill, extra warp and weft pattern weaves,

225

double-cloth weaves, open lacelike weaves, uneven tension weaves, rough and uneven-surfaced weaves, and combination weaves. The various weaves may be grouped in other classifications, which may be described as follows:

1. A woven or nonwoven fabric
2. A flat-surfaced, uneven-surfaced, or pile-surfaced weave
3. A compact, average, or loose weave
4. An undulating warp, a crossed warp, or warp-pile weave
5. A weave composed of a single set of warp yarns or two or more sets of warp yarns
6. A two-stick, a regular, a dobby, or a Jacquard loom weave
7. A plain, twill, satin or sateen, tapestry, inlay, ingrain, wrapped, pile, open-lace, leno or gauze, double-cloth, embossed, or combined weave
8. A single or combined fiber-content weave
9. Design inherent in the weave or applied to it
10. A warp-faced, weft-faced, mixed, or balanced weave

With the exception of item 10, the various techniques included in the above list are all described elsewhere in this book. No. 10, which is really a phase of yarn count, is discussed in the following section.

YARN COUNT

The yarn count is the number of warp and weft yarns in 1 square inch of fabric. Depending upon whether warp or weft yarns are in the majority, weaves are called warp-faced, weft-faced, mixed, or balanced. The size of the yarns used in a weave must also be considered, since the yarn count alone does not always accurately describe the appearance of a fabric. For example, a high yarn count of very fine weft yarns against a low count of coarse warp yarns may still represent a rather open-weave fabric.

A warp-faced weave is one in which only the warp yarns show on the surface of the finished fabric. Warp-faced patterns include lengthwise stripes formed by color or texture; horizontally ribbed rep, formed by fine close-set warp with coarse weft; imitation rep, formed by two warp beams of different tensions; pick-up pattern weaving, accomplished by using two or more sets of warp of contrasting colors; warp loop and pile weaves, formed by extra warp yarns raised above the surface of the fabric; and warp-faced twill and satin weaves, formed by irregular warp floats in a twill weave.

A weft-faced weave is one in which only the weft yarns show on the surface of a fabric. Weft-faced patterns include crosswise stripes, formed by yarns of different colors, different textures, and/or different fiber content; vertically ribbed rep, formed by coarse, wide-spaced warp and fine close-set weft; tapestry, when woven by hand in a standard tapestry weave; weft loop and cut pile weaves, formed by extra weft yarns raised above the surface of the fabric; and weft-faced twill and sateen, formed by irregular weft floats in a twill weave.

A combined warp-faced and weft-faced weave, usually called a mixed weave, is one in which both warp and weft yarns can be seen either singly or in groups. Weaves in this category include extra warp and extra weft weaves, leno and other open lacelike weaves, overshot and colonial pattern weaves, certain twills, certain uneven tension weaves, certain double cloth weaves, and damask. All of these are discussed in this chapter.

A balanced weave, also called a fifty-fifty (50–50) or tabby weave, is one in which the yarn count per square inch contains the same number and size of both weft and warp yarns. These weaves include balanced plain weaves; balanced twills; double cloth, if formed by a balanced yarn count; rep or faille, formed by alternating coarse and fine warp with coarse and fine weft; crêpes, formed by combining yarns of different twists; and open weaves, formed by an equally wide spacing of both warp and weft—leno, gauze, and twining weaves are not included in this classification. Checks and plaids, formed by yarns of different colors, textures, and weights, are considered balanced if these elements are arranged in balancing positions.

PATTERN IN WEAVING

Much of the value of a fabric depends upon its color and figure arrangement. From the standpoint of the weaver, patterned fabrics are not only more challenging to produce, but they are also more interesting to weave. The tedious jobs of threading the loom and weaving are both made more worth while if an attractive pattern has been selected for the work.

Since every weave except a single, balanced, plain weave has some indication of pattern, the weaver soon finds himself confronted with the question of the selection of a suitable design for his work. A truly creative weaver will soon tire of copying patterns from weaving manuals and will eventually desire to construct his own designs. To meet this need, not only are instructions given in this chapter for each of the basic weaves, but suggestions are also made for altering them. Other suggestions for altering weave patterns are given on pages 217 and 273.

Since the pattern in a weave is an intrinsic part of the structure of the cloth, it is said to be structural. If colored yarns are used in weaving, the color is also a structural part of the fabric. (See pages 6 and 269.)

Since the average weaver uses a foot-power loom, instructions given in this chapter definitely point toward the use of this loom. However, it should be remembered that, with only a few exceptions, most of the weaves described in this book can be woven on other types of looms. Even the most complicated weaves can be woven, though sometimes with difficulty, on very primitive looms; numerous examples of this have been given. Like-

Fig. 126A. Plain Weave. (Courtesy, Ida Heywood, University of Utah.)

Fig. 126B. Basket-Cloth Weave. (Courtesy, Ida Heywood, University of Utah.)

wise, most of the weaves described in connection with simple looms can be converted for use on foot-power and mechanical looms.

1. Plain Weaves

Plain weaves, resulting from the simple interlacing of weft and warp yarns, are classified as either single or double and either regular or irregular. (See Figs. 126A and 126B.)

SINGLE PLAIN WEAVES

In a *regular* single plain weave, the weft yarn passes into the warp yarns in a sequence of over one, under one, reversing its over-and-under positions on each adjacent row of weaving. When such a weave is balanced, the yarn count of the fabric formed has the same number of warp and weft yarns to the square inch. A balanced weave is also known as a tabby weave.

In an *irregular* single plain weave, the yarn count of warp and weft yarns differs considerably, because the warp and weft yarns may be of

228

different weights, of contrasting textures, and/or may be spaced in irregular groupings.

Variation of texture and pattern in plain weaves are brought about by the following treatments: (1) *Stripes* can be formed in either the warp or the weft by the use of different colors, weights, and/or textures of yarn. (2) *Checks* and *plaids* can be formed if the yarns of both the warp and the weft are arranged in identical color and texture patterns. (3) *Crêpe* is formed by combining warp and weft yarns of different twists. (4) *Rep* or ridge weaves are formed as follows: poplin is formed by the use of coarse weft with fine warp, causing crosswise ridges to appear in the fabric; limbric and Bedford cord are formed by the use of coarse warp and fine weft, causing vertical ridges to appear in the fabric; and faille is formed by the use of both coarse and fine warp and coarse and fine weft, the coarse weft always passing beneath the coarse warp, and fine weft beneath fine warp, causing definite ribs to appear in the fabric. When the loom is equipped with two warp beams, an imitation rep can be formed by using different tensions in the warp. Hand-woven *tapestry*, discussed on page 162, is another version of the plain weave.

Threading the Loom for a Single Plain Weave

Two-harness looms can be used for plain weaves. The warp yarns are threaded alternately through the heddles of the harnesses. The harnesses are raised alternately to form the sheds.

Plain weaves can also be set up on four-harness looms. There are two plain-weave threadings for a four-harness loom. (1) The heddles are threaded as a twill: 1, 2, 3, 4; 1, 2, 3, 4; repeat. In this case they are tied up to form two sheds, harnesses 1 and 3 being tied to one treadle and harnesses 2 and 4 to the other. (2) The heddles can also be threaded for a plain weave by using an irregular threading arrangement: 1, 3, 2, 4; 1, 3, 2, 4; repeat. The treadles for this last arrangement are tied up to form the two sheds by tying harnesses 1 and 2 to one treadle and harnesses 3 and 4 to the other. The last threading makes for clearer sheds.

One or two warps can be put through the dents of the reed, depending upon how compact a weave is desired. Allowance must be made for compact selvages.

DOUBLE PLAIN WEAVES

A regular double plain weave known as basket cloth is made by interlacing two weft yarns into—that is, over and under—two warp yarns. (See Fig. 126B.) An irregular double weave called Oxford cloth is formed when one thick weft replaces the two regular weft yarns of the double plain weave.

Threading the Loom and Weaving a Double Plain (Basket) Weave

Two warp yarns are threaded through each heddle eye on the two alternating harnesses on a two-harness loom. Only one yarn is threaded through each dent in the reed, however. When weaving, two wefts must be thrown through each shed; therefore two shuttles of weft are needed. Each weft is battened down separately.

Fig. 127A. Even Twill. (Courtesy, Ida Heywood, University of Utah.)

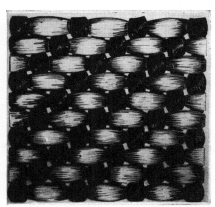

Fig. 127B. Uneven Twill. (Courtesy, Ida Heywood, University of Utah.)

2. Twill Weaves

In twill weaving one set of yarns skips at even intervals over and under another set of yarns. The skips, or floats, progress forward one or more yarns in each succeeding row, thus forming diagonal ribs, wales, or stair steps in the fabric. The ribs in twill may be steep, diagonal, or reclining. Depending upon the direction and the length of the floats, the twill is warp-faced, weft-faced, or balanced.

Twills are classified as regular or irregular. A regular twill is one in which the floats pass over and under the same number of yarns. (See Fig. 127A.) In an irregular twill the floats pass over and under a different number of yarns; depending upon the structure, broken, reversed, corkscrew, or interlocking twills result. Irregular twill patterns include zigzags, chevrons, diamonds, and herringbone designs. Satin and sateen weaves are usually classified as irregular rearranged twills. (See Figs. 128A, 128B.) Irregular warp floats of satin dovetail with one another to form a smooth lus-

230

trous surface; in sateen, irregular weft floats dovetail to form the smooth glossy surface. Damask, a mixed, warp-faced, weft-faced fabric, is also generally classed as a rearranged twill.

THREADING THE LOOM FOR A TWILL WEAVE

Twill is perhaps the easiest of the four-harness patterns to weave. For directions for threading the heddles for a simple four-harness twill weave, see the border design on Belt 13, Fig. 67. To thread the heddles for this weave, carry a warp yarn through the first heddle on each harness in the regular

Fig. 128A. Satin—Irregular Twill. (Courtesy, Ida Heywood, University of Utah.)

Fig. 128B. Sateen—Irregular Twill. (Courtesy, Ida Heywood, University of Utah.)

1, 2, 3, 4 order, starting with harness 1; repeat the same sequence for the second heddles on all the harnesses, and so on across the loom. Usually the selvage is formed by threading two warps into each heddle eye, threading the harnesses in the above order. In weaving, the heddle harnesses are raised in the order of 1, 2, 3, 4, or 4, 3, 2, 1. In uneven twill weaves the harnesses are raised in such sequences as 1, 2, 4, 3, etc.

Twill can be woven on a three-harness loom, using one harness up and two down for a weft-faced twill and two harnesses up and one down for a warp-faced twill. Twill can also be woven on four-, six-, and eight-harness looms. The more harnesses a loom has, the more variations of the twill weave are possible—at least 16 twill combinations are possible on an eight-harness loom.

One simple but interesting pattern weave in twill is the bird's-eye design, which forms a diamond pattern in the fabric. The harnesses are threaded for it in the following order: 1, 2, 3, 4, 1, 4, 3, 2; repeat.

231

3. Extra Warp and Weft Pattern Weaves

Some of the most beautiful pattern weaves are formed by the addition of extra warp or extra weft yarns to the fabric during weaving. Sometimes these weaves are called embroidery, but they cannot be true embroidery, which is needlework applied to a finished fabric; this subject is discussed further in a later chapter.

EXTRA WARP PATTERN WEAVES

Pattern weaves formed by the addition of extra warp yarns are usually woven on mechanical looms equipped with extra warp beams. Since these beams hold the pattern yarns, the tension of the warp on the beams can be varied as needed. Extra warp pattern weaves include regular warp-pile weaves; double-cloth warp-pile weaves; warp-faced pick-up weaves, when extra warps are incorporated at intervals in the weaving; and lappet weaving. When done by hand, using small bobbins, the latter is similar to swivel weaving. Lappet weaving is described below; the other weaves are discussed elsewhere in this book. (See pages 172 and 173.)

In lappet weaving the pattern yarns are threaded through the eyes of lappet needles which are held at right angles to the warp in a frame or needle bar in front of the reed. When this bar is lowered, the needles are automatically lowered into the bottom of the shed so that the lappet warp is placed below the throw of weft. After a throw of weft the needles are again raised and shifted horizontally a short distance to the right or left, according to the pattern. They are then lowered into the next shed formed. This shifting back and forth over the warp allows these extra warp yarns to float horizontally across the fabric to form a unit pattern. Opposite ends of one horizontal stretch of lappet yarn pass under alternate throws of weft. The pattern units of the lappet yarn appear on the upper side of the fabric; the floats between unit patterns also appear on the right side of the fabric. After the weaving is finished the floats between patterns are generally cut out.

Lappet weaving is done commercially on a power loom which has a chain attachment to control the action of the needle bar. The lappet yarns are fed into the loom from an extra warp beam at the back of the loom and are carried through the loom in a skeleton harness. There are often six ground and two lappet harnesses on this type of loom. According to the textile expert George Linton, who helped the author with this description, lappet weaving is now practically extinct in the United States.

EXTRA WEFT PATTERN WEAVES

Patterns can be set into a fabric during weaving by the help of extra weft yarns, in addition to the regular weft of the basic fabric. This class of weaves includes weft-pile weaving and inlay weaving. The latter includes such techniques as brocade, swivel, and overshot weaving. Summer and Winter weaves, seldom thought of as inlay weaves, technically are inlay.

Brocade and swivel patterns can be set into the warp of very simple hand looms by hand manipulation, as proved by the beautiful pattern weaves made by Guatemalan Indians. When these ornate weaves are made for commercial distribution, they must be made on looms which have Jacquard attachments.

INLAY PATTERN WEAVING

Inlay pattern weaving appears to vie with tapestry in its antiquity. From early in history, the peoples of the Near East have received recognition for their skillfully woven fabrics ornamented with inlay weaving. Much has been written of the beautiful silk brocade, often in silver and gold, from Damascus and Persia, which so intrigued the interest of the Crusaders that trade routes were established between Europe and the Near East. (See Figs. 4, 5, and 129.)

From ancient Egypt have come many pieces of dark blue fabric decorated with white inlayed swivel patterns, samples of which are in many museums in the United States and Europe as well as in Egypt.

From China, farther to the East, have come many of the world's finest fabrics. In fact, it has often been suggested that brocade weaving was invented in China, some time after the discovery of the use of silk for weaving. Even before the Christian era, precious cargoes of rich Chinese silks found their way to Persia over the old trade routes. There is evidence that the peoples of ancient India also added inlay patterns to their warp, using slender bamboo sticks to help them.

On the Western Hemisphere, a study of ancient Peruvian textiles shows that these people had acquired great skill in brocade, swivel, and embroidered warp weaving. The Indians of Guatemala, especially those of San Juan Sacatepequez and San Antonio Aguas Calientes, excel in brocade and swivel weaving today. (See Figs. 42 and 130.)

The Renaissance weavers of Europe attained great skill in the weaving of brocaded velvets and brocaded silks and satins. Examples of their work are shown in Figs. 6, 9, 10, and 11.

Fig. 129. Inlay Weave. Nineteenth-century swivel weave on twill base from either Persia or India; known as Persian paisley or Indian pine design.

CLASSIFICATION OF INLAY WEAVES

Practically all inlay weaves could be given the name of brocade, though there actually are various methods of weaving inlaid patterns. These methods are listed here and an effort is made to classify them accurately. There are five types of inlay weaving: standard brocade, overshot brocade, sectional brocade, swivel weaving, and laid-in work. In addition there is one which could be called an embroidered warp inlay weave.

In *standard brocade weaving*, the pattern weft is carried entirely across the warp, showing at intervals on the face of the fabric in the pattern areas and floating on the back of the fabric between the pattern areas. The fabric is woven face down. Accessory harnesses and brocade heddles are needed on a loom on which this weave is made. A mirror is placed beneath the warp to help the weaver study the pattern as it is woven. (See Fig. 130A.) Brocade fabrics produced for commercial distribution are woven on Jacquard looms. (See Fig. 11 for an early weave.)

In *overshot brocade weaving*, the yarn is carried entirely across the warp as in regular brocade, but the pattern is woven face up, the pattern yarn being hidden in the shed between pattern units. In regular overshot brocade weaving, hand looms are equipped with accessory harnesses carrying brocade heddles. Jacquard looms are used for commercial brocade weaving. The beautiful brocades of Japan are now woven in silk in this manner; the patterns are arranged on a satin or warp-faced twill ground.

Another group of common weaves that are closely related to brocade are the colonial overshot weaves. For these, the loom is not equipped with accessory harnesses and brocade heddles, but is set up so that all harnesses working together form the pattern units. The colonial coverlet and Summer and Winter weaves are of this type.

In *sectional brocade weaving*,

Fig. 130A. Brocade Weave. From Guatemala; made on a foot-power loom.

Fig. 130B. Swivel Weave. From Guatemala; made on a back-strap loom.

sometimes called *polymita*, the weft yarns which form the various pattern areas are thrown only partially across the shed and are carried forward or backward in the same position in subsequent sheds. This weave is related to both laid-in work and overshot brocade.

In *swivel weaving*, small pattern units are woven at intervals in the warp; the colored yarns of these patterns are not connected with one another. Webster calls this method true brocade; it is also called "dukagang" in northern Europe. Small shuttles carry the pattern yarns back and forth in each pattern area, a shuttle of colored pattern yarn being needed for each pattern unit. When there are many pattern units across the warp, many small shuttles are needed. The swivel weaving process is explained in detail in the following pages. (See Fig. 130B.)

In *laid-in weaving*, short lengths of yarn in contrasting colors are placed at irregular intervals across the warp in the regular shed and alongside the regular throw of weft. The ends of these detached strands are often allowed to hang out, thus giving a fringelike effect over the face of the fabric. Swivel weaving is sometimes called "laid-in" weaving.

Embroidered-Warp Weaves

Inlay weaving often closely resembles embroidery. Some writers have been so amazed at the beautiful patterns found in this type of work that they have classified the weave as embroidery, though true embroidery is needlework applied to a finished fabric. Some weaves, however, stand halfway between embroidery and weaving, and some embroidery techniques are closely related to weaving. There are, therefore, weaves which could easily be given an entirely new textile classification—embroidered warp weaves. Into this classification could be placed such weaves as Soumak, eccentric and some of the other tapestry weaves, some of the wrapped weaves, and the embroidered warp brocade weave discussed in the next paragraph.

While carefully examining some ancient Peruvian patterned fabrics, the author found some pieces in which the colored pattern yarns appeared to be embroidered into the warp during weaving using a needle. Rows of tabby weaving alternated with these rows of needle-inserted pattern weft, just as the tabby alternates in regular brocade weaving. The contours were not as accurate as those made on heddle-controlled warp, but the work was very effective. The chief advantage of making brocade in this way is that no intricate brocade accessory heddles and no extra harnesses are needed on the loom.

236

PLANNING THE PATTERN FOR BROCADE AND SWIVEL WEAVING

The patterns for brocade and swivel weaving are generally either conventional or geometric. The designs are plotted on graph paper, each darkened square on the paper representing an exposed area of pattern weft in the fabric. (See Fig. 68.)

When either standard or overshot brocade is woven on a Jacquard loom, there is no limitation on the color arrangement. Many colors may be used, and they may be arranged in any location demanded by the pattern.

When brocade and swivel patterns are woven on regular hand looms, the number of colors used in the pattern inserts is limited. In swivel weaving, the little isolated patterns are often woven in single-color units; seldom are more than three colors used in one little figure. When more than one color is used for one figure in the pattern, the colors are grouped in rows, which form horizontal stripes in the figure. Usually each of these separate unit patterns has its own unique color arrangement and so differs from the others in the same row. Ancient Peruvian and con-

Fig. 131A. One-Skip and Two-Skip Swivel Weave. From Guatemala.

temporary Guatemalan swivel weaves show a color repeat in every sixth pattern unit. Other pattern suggestions for swivel weaving are given below.

SETTING UP THE LOOM FOR INLAY WEAVING

A loom prepared for inlay weaving is usually equipped with one or two brocade or pattern weave heddle harnesses, in addition to the two regular tabby weave harnesses. The brocade harnesses are always set to the front of the tabby weave harnesses. One-skip patterns can be woven on looms equipped with one brocade harness, and two-skip weaves on looms equipped with two brocade harnesses. (See Fig. 131A.)

Three methods of setting up a loom for swivel or brocade inlay weaving are described here:

Method I

For inlay weaving on a simple loom such as the back-strap loom, an additional string heddle rod, which lifts alternate groups of warp for inlay weaving, is installed in front of the two regular heddle devices. (The method of making and installing a string heddle rod is described on page 91.)

Method II

When brocade or swivel is to be woven on foot-power and table-model looms, these looms must be equipped with one or two harnesses which hold special brocade heddles, which have very large eyes through which the tabby sheds are able to operate. They are made of string, and, except for the size of the eyes, are made in the same manner as regular string heddles. (See Fig. 115A, No. 1.)

To thread a loom for inlay weaving, the tabby harnesses are first strung in the regular manner; then the warp yarns in alternate groups of three or more are carried through brocade harnesses. If the loom is equipped with only one brocade harness, alternate groups of warp, usually three to a group, are carried through the heddles of that harness. Sometimes two yarns are carried through the heddles of the tabby harnesses and four yarns through the brocade heddles.

Fig. 131B. Brocade and Swivel Weave. The zigzag borders are in brocade; the figures are in swivel weaving. From Guatemala. (All inlay weaves from the author's collection.) The Guatemalan swivel weaves were made on back-strap looms.

Method III

No brocade harnesses are needed to weave swivel and brocade on four-harness table-model or foot-power looms which have been set up for a regular four-harness twill weave and which have pairs of warp yarns threaded

238

through the heddles. For the twill weave, the first heddle on each harness is threaded, starting with harness 1 and working in the order of 1, 2, 3, 4. This process is repeated when threading the second heddles, the third heddles, etc. The border on Belt 13, Fig. 67, is drawn in a twill threading.

The treadles are tied up so that both the two tabby sheds and the two pattern sheds alternate. To tie up the tabby harnesses, tie harnesses 1 and 3 to treadle 1 and harnesses 2 and 4 to treadle 2. To tie up the pattern harnesses, tie harnesses 1, 2, and 4 to treadle 3 and harnesses 2, 3, and 4 to treadle 4. Sometimes harnesses 1 and 2 are tied up to alternate with harnesses 3 and 4 to form the pattern sheds.

Method IV

A two-skip brocade or swivel weave can be made on a loom set up for the crackle overshot weave. (See Fig. 132B.)

GENERAL DIRECTIONS FOR INLAY WEAVING

In inlay weaving, the pattern weft should be coarser than the warp and of a contrasting color and value. The tabby weft is usually identical to the warp in weight and color.

The patterns for brocade and swivel weaving can be woven either face up or face down. If brocade is to be woven right side up (face up), the pattern weft yarns must be carried in the shed between pattern units; if swivel is to be woven right side up, the ends of the pattern weft yarns must be pushed through the warp at the beginning and end of the insertion of each pattern unit. When brocade is woven wrong side up, the pattern weft floats across the back of the fabric between pattern units; and when swivel is woven wrong side up, the ends of the pattern weft are already on the back of the fabric and so do not have to be specially handled. As noted previously, when swivel and brocade are woven wrong side up, a mirror is placed face up beneath the warp to help the weaver.

As noted earlier, swivel and overshot brocade can be woven in a one-skip or a two-skip weave. Only one pattern shed is needed for a one-skip weave, and a second and alternating pattern shed is needed for a two-skip weave. In a one-skip weave, the pattern weft appears in vertical columns; in a two-skip weave, the pattern weft takes alternating positions on two adjacent rows of weaving. Both treatments are shown in Fig. 131A. Patterns are easier to weave in a two-skip weave, since more variation in the contour of the pattern is possible. Detailed instructions for weaving a two-skip swivel pattern are given below, together with a list of pattern treatments for one-skip and two-skip weaves.

DIRECTIONS FOR MAKING A SWIVEL WEAVE

Before beginning to weave, review the general directions for inlay weaving, page 239. Remember that during weaving the two pattern sheds alternate with one another, and the two tabby sheds are formed alternately. In the instructions given below, the tabby sheds are designated as A and B and the pattern sheds as 1 and 2. A row of tabby weaving always precedes a row of pattern weaving. The weft is battened down before and after each change of shed. The pattern described here is woven face up.

1. To begin this weave, make a few inches of tabby weaving, alternating sheds A and B and ending with shed B.
2. To begin the swivel pattern weave, lift pattern harness 1 and insert a colored weft yarn, counting off the correct number of warp yarns to be used according to the pattern draft. A stick or hook will assist in pulling the pattern weft through the shed. Remember that in swivel weaving there may be many separate insertions of different colored weft yarns across one row of pattern weaving. Separate pieces of yarn can be used as weft, but usually the pattern weft is wound onto small shuttles—little matchbooks serve satisfactorily as such shuttles. When all the pattern weft insertions have been made across the warp, change the sheds and weave tabby A.
3. Lift the pattern harness 2 and return the pattern weft in the areas concerned. Change sheds and weave tabby B.
4. Continue to alternate the pattern harnesses and the tabby harnesses until the pattern is completed. Always tuck the ends of the pattern weft—those left free before and after weaving a pattern unit—into the next opened tabby shed, or push them through to the other side of the fabric.
5. A few rows of tabby weaving should separate the unit patterns. End the weaving with a few inches of tabby weaving.

PATTERN WEAVE VARIATIONS FOR SWIVEL WEAVING

Although some of the weave variations given below could be used in the brocade treatment of inlay weaving—that is, the weft on some of the patterns could be carried entirely across the warp—most of those listed are for swivel unit patterns.

The weaves listed here are grouped into one-skip, two-skip, and four-skip weaves. The basic treatment of the first two has already been discussed.

Style 1: One-Skip Weaves

Conventional birds and animals are generally used for this weave. The colored pattern weft is exposed in vertical columns. In Fig. 131A, the legs on the figure are in a one-skip weave.

Style 2

Small allover patterns can be woven in rectangles with diagonal ends (isosceles trapezoids). The right side is woven face up. The weft is not cut between units, but floats diagonally up to the next unit pattern, which is placed diagonally above the last. When the pattern weft reaches the margin of a pattern unit, it passes above the next formed tabby weft and loops back of the same single warp that held it on the preceding row, before returning in the next pattern shed.

Style 3

The pattern in this weave is only one long skip wide. Little unit blocks combine to form geometric patterns. As the pattern yarn reaches the edge of the pattern block, it passes back of the same warp as in Style 2.

Style 4

The pattern weft is sewed into the warp using the Soumak stitch. The method of making this stitch is described on page 169.

Style 5

Long floats of yarn can be made on a loom set up for a two-skip weave. The patterns for this weave are all based upon diagonal lines: diamonds, chevrons, zigzags, crosses, isosceles trapezoids, etc. The colored pattern yarn float or skips above the fabric from one border of the design to the other; the loops formed at the end of each row pass behind a single warp as in Style 2.

Style 6

For this weave, long single skips are made on a loom set up for a two-skip weave, as in Style 5. Uncolored squares of the background are left silhouetted within the colored patterns.

Style 7: Two-Skip Weaves

This uses a regular four-harness twill threading tied up for inlay weaving as described on page 231. The colored weft alternates positions on alternate rows of weaving. This weave is described on page 240.

Style 8

Inlay weaving can be combined with, or inserted into, a warp-faced fabric. Several belt weaves described earlier show variations of inlay weaving (belts 1, 2, 5, 6, and 7, pages 125–134).

Style 9: Four-Skip Weaves

On a loom threaded for the Summer and Winter weave, an inlay pattern can be woven based on solid blocks arranged in alternating combinations. Summer and Winter weaves are described on page 245.

Style 10

Two heavy weft yarns, which are carried through each pattern shed, enter the shed from opposite directions. After an uneven number of tabby wefts have been woven into the warp, the pattern shed is formed again and the two heavy yarns are carried over the face of the fabric and into the this pattern shed. The heavy weft yarns form loops on the face of the fabric between the pattern sheds.

OVERSHOT PATTERN WEAVES

Overshot weaves are closely related to brocade and in this book they are treated as a type of brocade. Many interesting overshot patterns have come down to us from the early settlers of New England. Probably most of these patterns were brought from England, but many were created by the colonists after they arrived in America. They are often called colonial pattern weaves. Three types of pattern weaving were popular with these early weavers: overshot, Summer and Winter, and Bronson lace. The first two weaves are described below; the Bronson weave is discussed later.

There are many overshot patterns, as glancing through any weaving manual will show. The Trellis is described below; two others, the Queen's Delight and the Honeysuckle, were presented in the last chapter. The Trellis weave as described is for a counterbalanced loom; the other two weaves are set up for a jack loom, but can be converted for use on a counterbalanced loom by reversing the tie-up plan. Similarly, the Trellis weave can be woven on a jack loom by reversing the tie-up plan. The drafts for the two other overshot weaves are illustrated in Figs. 108 and 110. Two additional weaves especially dear to the hearts of weavers are the M and O and the Crackle patterns. Drafts for these weaves are illustrated in Fig. 140A.

Overshot weaving can be distinguished from other pattern weaves by the overlap of pattern block units: that is, the last warp of one block acts as the first warp of the next. See page 273 for a discussion of block sequences. See also the encircled groups on the threading draft illustrated in Fig. 132. Anyone interested in weaving an overshot pattern will find that the general directions for the Trellis are applicable to other overshot weaves.

242

THE TRELLIS, AN OVERSHOT WEAVE

PREPARING THE LOOM FOR OVERSHOT WEAVING

The heddle-threading draft for the Trellis[1] weave and the treadle tie-up for it are diagrammed in Fig. 132. It should be remembered that harness 1 is the front harness on the loom. The pattern presented on the draft is repeated as many times as needed for the desired width of the fabric. If a narrow loom is used it may be necessary to plan some slight change in the pattern. If any part has to be left out, equal units should be omitted on either side of the center of the warp so that the pattern will remain symmetrical.

Rather fine cotton yarn is usually used for the warp of overshot weaves. The warp yarns and their set may be selected from the following combinations: 24/3 cotton, dented 30 to the inch or 2 to a dent in a No. 15 reed; 20/2 cotton, dented 36 to the inch or 2 to a dent in a No. 18 reed; 20/2 cotton, dented 34 to the inch or 2 to a dent in a No. 17 reed; or 20/2 cotton, dented 30 to the inch or 2 to a dent in a No. 15 reed. The closer the warp is set in the reed, the firmer will be the fabric. The manner of putting the warp on a loom was described on page 210.

DIRECTIONS FOR WEAVING THE TRELLIS AS DRAWN IN

In standard overshot weaving, the same weight and type of yarn is used for both tabby weft and warp. A heavier yarn should be selected for the pattern weft. The pattern yarn can be crochet cotton, strand cotton, carpet cotton, wool of the homespun variety, worsted such as two-ply Shetland, etc.

Overshot weaving can be woven as drawn in, in rose pattern, threaded and woven on opposites, or woven with accidents (these terms are discussed on page 273). Before beginning this weave, study the instructions given in the preceding chapter for weaving on a foot-power loom.

1. First, weave about half an inch of tabby. The tabby weft sheds are formed by alternately raising harnesses 1 and 3 together and harnesses 2 and 4 together.
2. To weave the Trellis figure as drawn in, find the treadle that opens up the first pattern block closest to the right margin. This shed can also be determined from the heddle-threading draft, since the harnesses containing the first block of the blacked-in squares on the draft are the ones to be lowered below the shed for the first block of the pattern. Weave this block with the pattern weft until it forms a square. Alternate each throw

[1] This weave was given the name of The Trellis by Mrs. Atwater, who adapted it from a weave in John Landes' book.

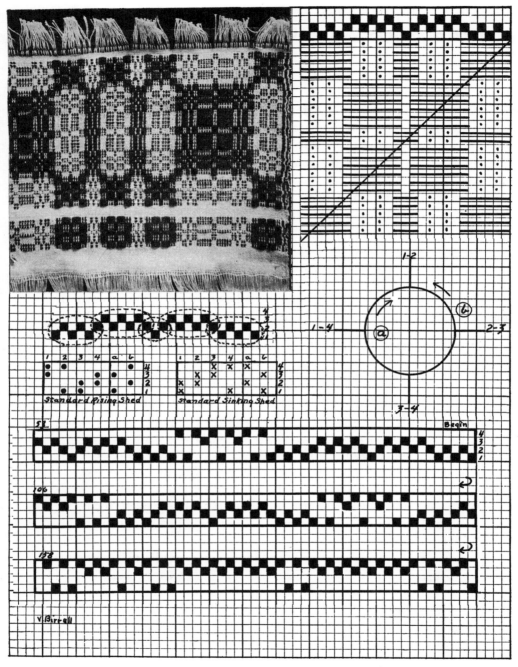

Fig. 132. The Trellis Pattern. This colonial overshot weave is shown in detail.
Top, left, section of cloth woven in regular weave as drawn in. Narrow border
woven in rose pattern, or in reverse treading. Top right, plotting a pattern draft
from a heddle-threading draft (or vice versa). Circle, order of using treadles on
standard loom tie-up. Upper center, unit block patterns encircled. Standard rising-
shed (jack loom) and sinking-shed (counterbalanced loom) tie-ups. Heddle-threading
draft for the Trellis weave.

of pattern weft with a throw of tabby weft. The tabby weft is always thrown across the warp in the tabby shed *before* the throw of pattern weft and in the same direction. For a firm fabric, batten down before and after each throw of weft.

3. Now find the treadle that opens up the second block and weave this block until square, alternating tabby and pattern weft. The second block will be located diagonally above and to the left of the first block. The last warp of the first block will be the first warp of the second block. Continue weaving the pattern, block by block, until the fabric is finished. End with about half an inch of tabby weaving.

DIRECTIONS FOR WEAVING THE TRELLIS IN A ROSE PATTERN

Review the general directions for weaving on a foot-power loom. Study Fig. 132 and note the illustration for weaving a rose pattern from the Trellis weave. Then begin to weave as follows:

1. Weave about half an inch of tabby.
2. To weave a rose pattern, reverse the treading from that used for weaving as drawn in. For example, if the regular drawn-in treading requires that harnesses 1 and 2 be lowered for the first block and harnesses 2 and 3 for the second block, then for a rose pattern harnesses 2 and 3 would be lowered for the first block and harnesses 1 and 2 for the second block.

SUMMER AND WINTER WEAVE

The Summer and Winter weave has been used by both the Navaho Indians and the Indians of southern Mexico for many years. How long these Indians have used this weave is not known; nor is its origin known. (See Figs. 65 and 75.) The Summer and Winter weave is also an old American colonial coverlet weave which is thought by many to have originated among the Dutch weavers of Pennsylvania (4). Although it is called a coverlet weave, it is used for bags, jackets, and other articles. Combined with stuffer yarns it can also be used for making rugs.

The Summer and Winter weave has certain advantages over the related overshot weaves: the skips are shorter and the fabric is more durable. In the pattern areas, the pattern weft skips over three and passes under one; in the background areas the opposite takes place.

The fabric is reversible: if a light pattern appears on one side, a dark one appears on the other. The name Summer and Winter stands for the dark pattern on a light background. If the pattern is woven in pairs, the background has a bird's-eye texture. (See Fig. 133.)

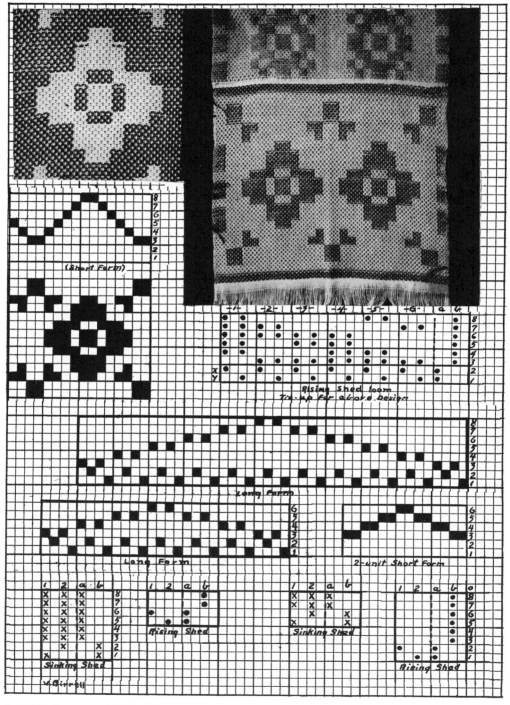

Fig. 133. Summer and Winter Weave.

There are many pattern variations for the Summer and Winter threading. Patterns can be altered by changing the tie-up or the treading plan. Asymmetric "modern" nonobjective designs can also be woven in this weave; it can also be used for hand pick-up designs. The designs can be woven in singles or in pairs.

Summer and Winter heddle-threading drafts are easily identified by their pyramid structure. The drafts appear somewhat as follows: 4 times 1–3–2–3; 4 times 1–4–2–4; 4 times 1–5–2–5; reverse the directions; repeat the sequence.

Because the threading has this regular sequence, a long black bar can be used to mark the squares of the pattern draft which represent the unit block of the weave. For example, if the bar is drawn through four spaces on the third harness, this would represent 4 times the 1, 3, 2, 3 unit threading. The substitution of this bar for the regular method of drawing a threading draft is known as the "short form." (See Fig. 133.)

The more harnesses there are on a loom, the more pattern blocks are possible, and the more intricate the pattern may be. Although interesting designs are made of two blocks on a four-harness loom, better ones are made with four blocks on a six-harness loom, and still better with six blocks on an eight-harness loom. Two harnesses are needed for the tabby yarns. The Indians of Guatemala usually weave aprons using a two-block design which they combine with pick-up weaving.

WARPING THE LOOM FOR THE SUMMER AND WINTER WEAVE

A jack loom should be used for the Summer and Winter weave, especially if more than four harnesses are to be used. Extra treadles are an advantage in weaving intricate patterns. To use an eight-harness loom to the best advantage it should be equipped with 14 treadles. The tie-up below is for a jack loom.

The warp and weft yarns are selected as follows: 24/3 cotton for the warp, dented 30 to the inch, 2 to a dent in a No. 15 reed; 20/2 cotton for the tabby weft, and 15/2 wool or worsted for the pattern weft. Another combination for coarser work could be 10/2 cotton for the warp, dented 24 to the inch, 2 to a dent in a No. 12 reed; 24/3 cotton for the tabby weft, and Shetland two-ply worsted or homespun for the pattern weft.

There are a few other points to keep in mind:

1. The heddles are threaded according to the threading draft in regular blocks—1, 3, 2, 3; 1, 4, 2, 4; 1, 5, 2, 5; etc. (See Fig. 133.)
2. The tabby sheds are tied up so that tabby A treadle raises harnesses 1 and 2, and tabby B treadle raises all other harnesses.

247

3. Each pattern harness needs two treadles and each pattern treadle includes either harness 1 or harness 2. Example: 1–8, 2–8.

GENERAL DIRECTIONS FOR WEAVING

If the design is woven in singles, a clear-cut pattern results; if woven in pairs the background has an interesting bird's-eye texture.

To form one pattern block, each pattern harness makes two sheds: one includes harness 1 and the other includes harness 2, for example: 1–8, 2–8. Tabby is woven between each throw of pattern weft. The throws of pattern and tabby weft should be systematized. When the Summer and Winter weave is woven in pairs special attention must be directed to the tabby insertions. Tabby B is woven *between* one pair and the next pair. Always throw tabby B from the left before starting to weave a pattern pair, and always start the pattern weft pairs from the left. Tabby A is woven between the two pattern wefts which make up a pair. Since the throw of pattern weft which ends one unit is half of a pair and the next throw of pattern weft, which starts the next unit, is also half of a pair, tabby A also precedes and follows each pattern unit. The two pattern blocks for a four-harness loom are woven with the harnesses raised together in the following groups:

One Unit of Block I	One Unit of Block II
Harnesses 2 and 4, once	Harnesses 2 and 3, once
Harnesses 1 and 4, twice	Harnesses 1 and 3, twice
Harnesses 2 and 4, once	Harnesses 2 and 3, once

The sequence in a unit is always the same. If it is necessary to make one block longer in order to complete a pattern, the unit may have to be repeated one or more times, always ending with a single.

The following instructions are for weaving a solid pattern on a bird's-eye background; the weaving is done in pairs.

To Weave the Pattern Texture

Raise harnesses and weave; note that tabby A is between pairs, in the following order starting from the left:

1. Tabby B; harness 1; tabby A; harness 1; tabby B; harness 2; tabby A; harness 2. Repeat the above until a sufficient area has been woven.
2. End the weaving with a single row of pattern weft—that is, the first half of a pair.

To Weave the Background Texture

Raise harnesses and weave in the following order, starting from the left:

1. Tabby B; all harnesses except 1; tabby A; all harnesses except 1; tabby B; all harnesses except 2; tabby A; all harnesses except 2. Repeat until a sufficient area has been woven.
2. End the weaving with a single row of pattern weft—that is, the first half of a pair.

To Weave Combined Pattern and Background in a Summer and Winter Design

Choose a pattern draft. A beginner should choose a pattern that is plotted immediately below the threading draft if such is available, as this will aid in treading. If an eight-harness loom is being used, the center of the design may be on either the 1, 3, 2, 3 or the 1, 8, 2, 8 block. Let us select the 8 block as the center of the figure and the 3 block to separate this figure from the other figures. (See Fig. 133.) Weave in pairs as follows:
1. Read the general directions for weaving on a foot-power loom, page 219.
2. Weave a few rows of the background texture as just described.
3. Starting from the right, weave tabby A, raise harnesses 1 and 8 and weave pattern weft, also starting from the right. Then weave tabby and pattern wefts in the following order: tabby B; harnesses 2 and 8; tabby A; harnesses 2 and 8; tabby B; harnesses 1 and 8. Repeat until one square block of pattern has been woven.
4. Now starting with tabby A, weave the 1, 7, 2, 7 block followed by the other blocks until the complete design is finished. End the weaving with a few rows of background.

PICK-UP DESIGNS IN SUMMER AND WINTER WEAVES

Dates, names, titles, etc., can be woven in the Summer and Winter weave. The background for the design is picked up from the tabby. The weave used is based on the throws of pattern weft, as just described. Choose any squared paper pattern draft. Weave as follows:
1. Weave several inches of tabby, ending in tabby A.
2. Open tabby B shed and pick up the background warp for the design. Slip in a pick-up stick. Working from right to left, insert the pick-up stick as the warps are picked up. Allow two warps for each square in the draft.
3. When all are picked up, leave the stick in the warp, raise harness 1, and weave pattern weft; raise harness 2, and weave pattern weft; weave tabby A; weave tabby B. It is not possible to batten down the pattern wefts, but it is sufficient to batten the tabby well.

249

BASIC WEAVES

Fig. 134A. Double-Cloth Pick-Up Weaving. Three of the possible weaves which can be made on a double-cloth threading. Top and bottom, pick-up pattern weaving. Center, quilted weaving. Lower center, tweed double-width double cloth.

Fig. 134B. Reverse Face of Fig. 134A.

4. Repeat steps 2 and 3 until the design is finished. End with several inches of tabby weaving.

4. Double-Cloth Weaves

Double-cloth weaving produces a fabric which is not only heavy and durable, but which may be very ornamental as well. Some attractive patterns can be woven in double cloth, even on simple looms, if pick-up pattern weaving is undertaken. The ancient Peruvians were skillful weavers of patterned double cloths; beautiful pieces of their work can be seen in a number of museums. Another native group able to create beautiful patterns in double cloth are the Cora Indians, who live in northwestern Mexico. (See Fig. 43.)

Depending upon the manner in which the weft is added to a warp set up for double-cloth weaving, fabrics of different shapes result—for example, one can weave two separate pieces of cloth or one piece twice the width of the warp on the loom, one piece of tubing, or a single strip of fabric of double thickness. A strip of fabric containing samples of all these types is shown in Fig. 134. Some of these methods are described below and other methods are described on pages 148 and 149.

When patterned double cloths are woven for commercial use, a

Jacquard loom is used. One or more extra warp beams are usually needed on the loom set up for any of the complicated double-cloth weaves, such as backed cloths, ingrain weaves, matelassés, and warp-faced pile weaves.

THREADING THE LOOM FOR DOUBLE-CLOTH WEAVING

The double-cloth weaves described below have only two sets of warp and, therefore, need no extra warp beam. The two sets of warp can be of contrasting or of the same color, but must be of the same weight of yarn. The warp yarns are threaded into the heddle harnesses according to a regular four-harness twill: 1, 2, 3, 4 repeat.

For a reversible fabric, one which is white on one side and black on the other, most weavers prefer to thread their harnesses with 1 and 3 in white and 2 and 4 in black, because this threading makes clearer sheds. Others prefer to thread the yarns for the top face of the fabric in the first two shafts—those nearest the reed—or 1 and 2 in white, and 3 and 4 in black. When woven on a foot-power loom, the six treadles on the loom are tied up so that two of them take care of the two double harnesses—1 and 3 together and 2 and 4 together, or 1 and 2 together and 3 and 4 together. The double-width double cloth and the tubular double-cloth weaves described below are based on the 1–3, 2–4 combination, and the quilted double-cloth weave is based on the 1–2, 3–4 combination. Each of the other four treadles is tied up separately to take care of one harness (1, 2, 3, 4). Double-cloth weaving is much easier to do if a jack-type foot-power loom is used; the weaves described below are planned for the jack loom.

PICK-UP PATTERN DOUBLE-CLOTH WEAVING

This very interesting technique is described on page 148.

DOUBLE-WIDTH DOUBLE-CLOTH WEAVE

A double-cloth fabric can be woven so that the top and bottom fabrics are connected on one side; when it is opened, there is one piece of fabric, twice as wide as it appeared on the loom. In this weave, the shuttle passes over and back forming the top layer of cloth; it then drops down and passes over and back to form the bottom layer. It always makes the transition on the same side of the fabric; hence the two pieces of fabric are joined on that side. When taken off the loom the fabric opens into one solid piece. The tweed effect shown in Fig. 134A was woven in this manner.

This weave is made as follows:

1. Thread all four harnesses with the same colored warp; or, if a tweed effect is wanted, thread harnesses 1 and 2 with black and 3 and 4 with

251

white, or use any color combination desired. The loom is threaded for the regular four-harness twill. Harnesses 2 and 4 work together to form one layer of cloth and 1 and 3 work together to form the other layer.

2. Determine which edge of the cloth is to hold the fold. This is usually that selvage edge which the weaver forms better than the other. Start to weave on that side of the loom. Use only one weft shuttle.

3. To weave, raise harness 1 and throw the weft in the shed formed. Lower harness 1, raise harness 3, and weave. Lower this harness and raise together harnesses 1, 2, 3, and weave. Lower these harnesses and raise harnesses 1, 3, 4, and weave. Repeat this series until the weaving is completed. Batten down after each throw of the shuttle.

TUBULAR DOUBLE-CLOTH WEAVING

A tubular fabric is fastened at both sides. The fastening is done during the weaving—the top and bottom layers being woven alternately. This means the shuttle must pass from the top to the bottom layer on one row of weaving, and from the bottom to the top layer on the next row. In making this transition, the weft automatically binds the two layers of cloth together at both side selvages. Bags, pillow cases, and various holders can be made from such tubing.

1. First, see step 1 of the directions given for the double-width weave. Use the same threading. Only one shuttle is used.

2. To weave, raise harness 1 and throw in shuttle. Lower harness 1, raise harnesses 1, 2, 3, and weave. Lower these harnesses, raise harness 3, and weave. Lower this harness, raise harnesses 1, 3, 4, and weave. Repeat the above sequence until the weaving is finished.

QUILTED DOUBLE-CLOTH WEAVING

Table pads, hot pads, baby quilts, and other quilted and padded fabrics can be made in this weave. For padding, use wool roving or cotton batting cut into strips.

To prepare the loom for this weave, thread harnesses 1 and 2 with white and harnesses 3 and 4 with black, in this order: 1, 2, 3, 4; repeat. If the fabric is to have a white and a black face, as the above threading indicates, two shuttles or shuttle sticks are needed, one for the white weft and one for the black. In the weave described below, the upper face is in white, the pick-up for the quilting in black.

1. For a plain double-cloth weave, raise the harnesses and weave in this order: raise harness 1 and weave with white. Raise harness 2 and weave

with white. Raise harnesses 1, 2, 3 and weave with black. Raise harnesses 1, 2, 4 and weave with black.

2. To quilt a pattern into the fabric, raise harnesses 1 and 2 and put in the padding. Lower the harnesses. Raise harness 3 and, using a pick-up stick, pick up the sewing stitch—the warp which is to bind the fabric together. Various designs, such as diamonds, zigzags, etc., can be made by planning the order in which the yarns are picked up. (See Fig. 134A.) Now lower harness 3 and push the pick-up stick back toward the reed. Raise harness 1 and weave with white. Remove the pick-up stick and lower the harness. Raise harness 2 and weave with white. Raise harnesses 1, 2, 3 and weave with black. Lower these harnesses, raise harnesses 1, 2, 4, and weave with black. If you should want a reversible pattern in the pick-up, drop one white warp below the shed for every black warp picked up. This is seldom done, however, as a slight pattern will automatically show on the under face of the fabric. If the stick shuttle is used, leave it in the shed to assist in battening down the fabric.

3. Repeat the sequence given in step 1 above until six threads are on the top face of the fabric; then repeat the sewing stitch sequence in 2. Repeat both of these sequences until the fabric is finished.

5. Open, Lacelike Weaves

There are a number of open weaves which tend to form lacelike fabrics. Open effects in fabrics can be obtained by a number of treatments: the warp yarns can be twisted into half-twists to form leno and gauze weaves; strands of weft can be wrapped tightly around groups of warp yarns as in hemstitching; the fabric can be loosely woven, as in plain weave medical gauze; it may consist of alternate groupings of loosely and closely woven warp and weft yarns, as in the Bronson weaves, which are discussed at the end of this chapter. The most important of the openwork weaves are described briefly below.

GAUZE, LENO, AND RELATED CROSSED-WARP WEAVES

Attractive openwork fabrics can be made by crossing warp yarns during the course of weaving. If such crossing is in the form of a half-twist, the process is known as gauze weaving, or in some cases as leno weaving. A loom set up for these weaves is often called a leno loom. (It should be remembered that when warp or weft yarns are completely twisted around one another in a full twist, twining results; this is described on page 71.)

The terms gauze and leno are often used interchangeably; actually the structures of the two weaves differ slightly. In both, pairs or groups of warp yarns work together, crossing and recrossing one another. There is a difference, however, in the manner in which they cross for these two weaves. In gauze weaving, the same warp yarns maintain the same position in relation to the weft: that is, one yarn in a pair is always below and the other always above the weft. (See Fig. 135.) In leno weaving, on the other hand, the warp yarns alternate in position on successive rows of weaving; those below the weft on one row are above it on the next row. The differences between gauze and leno structures will be more fully understood if the

string heddles illustrated in Figs. 44A and 44B are compared. When only the heddle sword and the leno heddle rod are used to make the weave, alternating to form the sheds, gauze is woven if the leno heddles are attached to the yarns which run *above* the heddle sword, and leno is woven if they are attached to or encircle the yarns which run *below* the heddle sword. In either case, each leno heddle must run under the yarn next to the one encircled. Other methods of weaving gauze and leno are described in the following pages.

Fig. 135. Gauze Weave Detail.

Although gauze and leno weaves are very similar in structure, the gauze weave seems to be preferred by most weavers, perhaps because gauze appears to have a better balance. Gauze weaves range from simple to complex, depending upon the number and arrangement of warp yarns engaged in each crossing at warp and weft junctures. Gauzes were woven anciently in both the Old and the New Worlds; two important centers were the ancient Far East and ancient Peru (49). One of the ornate gauze weaves of ancient Peru, which O'Neale named Peruvian and which the Guatemalan Indians currently weave, is shown in Fig. 136, No. 1, and Fig. 137. The Guatemalan Indians often weave simple gauze by the method just discussed (see Fig. 45). It is not known whether the ancient Peruvians used leno heddles or other mechanical aids in their gauze weaving.

HAND PICK-UP GAUZE WEAVES

If the weaver has the time and patience, gauze weaves can be formed in almost every warp setup and on almost every type of loom. No mechanical pattern harnesses are necessary, as the warp yarns are picked up and crossed by hand and an auxiliary shed sword holds the picked-up shed open for the weft.

THE TEXTILE ARTS

Gauze Weaving on a Two-Harness Tabby Loom Setup, a Simple Gauze

Simple gauze weaves can be woven on any regular two-harness loom which has been threaded for plain weaving, as follows: Weave a few rows of plain weaving and finish with the outside right warp yarn in the down position. Form a new shed, thus raising this outside warp above the shed. Push it toward the left and pull up the first warp on the bottom of the shed—this is the second warp on the loom, counting from the right. Insert a shed sword under this lifted warp, between it and the first warp. Continue across the loom, pulling the even-numbered warps under the adjacent odd-numbered warps and placing them above the point of the shed sword. When all of the even-numbered warps have been picked up, turn the shed sword on its side and throw the weft through the shed. Remove the shed sword, change sheds, and throw the shuttle of weft through the new shed. Change sheds, and repeat the pick-up process. The warp yarns which are above the weft in one shed must be above it in the next shed also. Instead of using single warp yarns to do this crossing, groups of two, three, or four yarns may be used. After every inch or so of gauze weaving, six or eight rows of plain weaving should be made to set off the gauze pattern.

Gauze Weaving on a Two-Harness Loom, an Ornate Peruvian Gauze

On a loom which has two harnesses threaded for plain weaving an ornate gauze called the Peruvian weave can also be woven. Groups of warps working together as a unit divide and combine with other groups, and then divide from those groups and recombine with their own original group. On the first row of weaving, the warps are divided into groups of four: counting from the right, the groups would include warps 1, 2, 3, 4; warps 5, 6, 7, 8; etc. On the second row of weaving, the warps involved in the group-

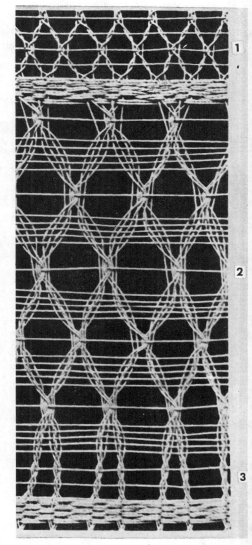

Fig. 136. Gauze Weave from Ancient Peru. Reconstructed weave from late period. (From O'Neale and Clark, "Textile Periods in Ancient Peru III: The Gauze Weaves," Am. Arch. and Ethn., vol. 40, 1948. Courtesy, University of California Press.)

255

ings are warps 3, 4, 5, 6; warps 7, 8, 9, 10; etc. The groups in the third and fourth rows are the same as in the first and second rows, and this grouping is repeated (47). (See Fig. 136, No. 1.)

There are only four steps in the complete process: Raise the heddle sword of a simple loom or the harness on a mechanical loom, which lifts the outside right warp. Push warps 1 and 3 to the left and pick up warps 2 and 4, slipping them over the point of a shed sword; this puts warps 1 and 3 beneath the sword. Then push warps 5 and 7 to the left and pick up warps 6 and 8, and continue across the warp in this manner, placing the even-numbered warps above the shed sword and the odd-numbered ones below it. When the warps on one row have been picked up, turn the shed sword on its side and insert the weft. Now the loom harnesses are shifted and the new shed has all the even-numbered warps in the up position. This shift automatically forms single gauze crossings between warps 1 and 2, 3 and 4, 5 and 6, etc. Throw the weft shuttle through the shed thus formed.

Fig. 137. Swivel and Gauze Weave. From Guatemala comes this beautiful fabric. The gauze is woven identically as No. 1 of Fig. 136.

The third step is similar to the first, except that different yarns are crossed. The harnesses are shifted and all of the odd-numbered yarns are brought to the up position in the shed. Now push warps 3 and 5 to the left, and pick up warps 4 and 6; push warps 7 and 9 to the left and pick up 8 and 10; etc. Again place the even-numbered warps above and the odd-numbered ones below the shed sword. When all of the even-numbered warps on this row have been picked up, turn the sword on its side and throw the weft through the shed. Step four is a repetition of the second step; that is, the weaver shifts harnesses, brings all of the even-numbered yarns to their regular up position, and throws the weft through the shed thus formed.

256

The four steps described above are repeated in the order given until an inch or so of gauze has been woven; then a strip of plain weaving is made. Strips of plain weaving and gauze are alternated until the weaving is finished.

Gauze Weaving on a Three- or Four-Harness Loom Set Up for Brocade Weaving

When a loom has been equipped with one or two inlay heddle harnesses (see Fig. 115), the groups of warp yarns which alternate for brocade weaving can be crossed to form a gauze weave. These groups are held in place by the weft in the same manner as when single warps are crossed.

Gauze Weaving on a Four-Harness Loom Set Up for Overshot Weaving

When a table-model or foot-powered loom has been threaded in any sequence of small even units similar to those in many of the overshot or colonial weaves, a gauze can be made by crossing these groups of warp. The same applies to a loom threaded in opposites. (See page 273.) These groups of warp can be crossed and woven into gauze in a manner similar to that of a simple gauze.

MECHANICAL METHODS OF WEAVING GAUZE

Both ancient and modern weavers devised tricks to help them overcome some of the handicaps of gauze weaving. For example, looms can be equipped with special heddles, sometimes called leno heddles, half-heddles, or doups; when lifted above the surface of the warp, these heddles pull certain warp yarns under other warp yarns. A number of special leno heddle devices for simple and mechanical looms are discussed below.

Gauze Weaving Using Two-Holed Tablets

Two-holed cards about 3 inches square can be used as heddles both for weaving gauze and for plain weaving. The holes in these cards are centered; they are placed opposite one another, and are punched about 1/4 of an inch from the edge of the card. Strands of the same or different colored yarns are threaded through the holes; the two yarns threaded in each card work together as a pair. Square cards can be turned forward and backward as in regular tablet weaving (see page 72); but if narrow rectangular tablets are used, with a hole pierced at either end, they are twisted to the right and left to form the necessary sheds. A very compact gauze can be woven by the tablet method.

To weave gauze, turn the cards forward in the warp one complete revolution or four one-quarter turns; throw the weft through the shed formed; then reverse the procedure, turning the cards one complete revolution backward, again throwing the weft through the shed. For plain weaving, the cards are turned only half of a complete revolution, that is, two one-quarter turns forward and backward, and the weft is thrown in the sheds thus made.

Gauze Weaving Using Tubular Beads

The author discovered, in 1956, while working with the two-holed tablets described above, that gauze and plain weaving could be done on a stretched warp with tubular beads used as heddles. Two warp yarns, working as pairs, are threaded through opposite ends of tubular beads. To weave gauze, the beads are turned individually one complete revolution toward the left and then one complete revolution toward the right, and the weft is thrown in the two sheds made. One half-turn to the left and one half-turn to the right would weave the plain weave.

Gauze Weaving Using a Two-Harness Leno Loom

The simplest arrangement for gauze weaving is that used by some of the Guatemalan Indians in the Coban district (47). They substitute a special leno heddle rod for the regular string heddle rod on their back-strap stick looms. The heddle sword and this leno heddle rod, pictured as rods 1 and 3 in Fig. 44A, alternate to form the two sheds necessary for gauze weaving. The same yarns are always above the sheds. Leno weaving can be done with a similar setup. (See Fig. 44B.)

If plain weaving is done on such a loom setup, the even-numbered warps must be picked up individually by hand and placed above the point of the shed sword, or another heddle rod must be made for the loom. The shed thus formed alternates with the regular heddle sword.

Gauze Weaving Using a Three-Harness Stick Loom

A leno heddle rod can be added to and set in front of the heddle sword and string heddle rod, the regular heddle devices of a stick loom. Unlike the diagram in Fig. 44A, the leno heddles in this instance usually encircle the even-numbered warps and pull them under the adjacent odd-numbered warps. To form the required sheds for gauze weaving, the leno heddle rod alternates with the string heddle rod. On the loom shown in Fig. 44A, gauze is formed by alternating rods 1 and 3; leno is formed by alternating rods 2 and 3; plain weave is formed by alternating rods 1 and 2.

Gauze Weaving on Mechanical Looms Using Special Doups[2]

Special heddles, usually called doups, can be attached to the jack-type of table-model and foot-power looms to facilitate the weaving of gauze. Doups are actually loops of fine, strong string which are attached to the

[2] The author is indebted to Mary M. Atwater for much of the information concerning the use of doups and beads for gauze weaving on foot-power looms.

bottom of harness 2 (this harness serves only as a skeleton harness for these doups). The doups are then carried through the heddle eyes of harness 1; each one encircles a warp yarn and pulls it under its neighbor to form the cross needed for gauze weaving. Naturally the length of the doups must be accurate. A sample doup is usually tested on the loom; it must be long enough so that it will not resist the formation of the tabby or other normal sheds, and it must not be so tight that it will be pulled back out of the heddle when harness 1 is raised. When the correct size of doup has been determined, a cardboard template is cut and is used as a pattern for making all the other doups, since they must be cut and tied the same length. Each doup consists of a doubled length of yarn with a loop at one end and a surgeon's knot at the other end. (A surgeon's knot is a square knot which has two turns in the first bend in place of one. It is described on page 53.) A strong hard-twisted round linen yarn is best for doups.

The doups are installed on the loom as follows: The second harness is raised, and the doups are attached to the bottom of it by slip knots. The looped ends of the doups are next threaded through the heddle eyes of harness 1. To prevent them from slipping out of the heddle eyes, pins are put through the ends of the loops; some weavers thread the doups through the heddle eyes, one at a time, as the warp yarns are being threaded through the doups.

When the weaver is ready to thread the warp into the heddles on the loom, she first threads the yarns alternately through the heddles of harnesses 3 and 4, working in a right to left direction. She then threads the leno heddles; starting with the first right warp from harness 3, she brings this yarn to the left of the first doup heddle of harness 1 and lets it hang over the reed while she handles a few more yarns. She then draws the looped end of the doup under this first yarn and threads the first right yarn on harness 4 through the loop; this yarn is also brought forward and hung over the reed. She continues across the loom, carrying the warp yarns from harness 3 to the left of the heddles on harness 1 and over the top of the doup loops, and carrying the yarns from harness 4 through the loops of the doups. As the threading continues, the warps which are hung over the reed are grouped and tied into bow knots. When the doups are all threaded, the yarns are carried through the dents in the reed. The two yarns affected by the same doup are carried through the same dent in the reed. Alternate dents may be skipped for a less compact fabric. For a variation of design for gauze weaving on a four-harness loom, pairs of warp yarns can be brought alternately to the left and then to the right of the leno heddles across the loom. This arrangement forms a herringbone effect.

The harnesses are tied up to three treadles: harness 3 to treadle 1, harnesses 2 and 4 to treadle 2, and harness 1 to treadle 3. When weaving gauze on this loom setup, the treadles are used as follows: first, alternate treadles 1 and 2, and weave about an inch of plain weaving; then alternate treadles 2 and 3 and weave gauze. Treadle 2 is always used between treadles 1 and 3 when starting or ending a piece of plain weaving. A strip of plain weaving should be woven to finish off the fabric.

To take care of the different tensions in the warp which result from the fact that one yarn of a pair does all the crossing, a foot-power loom which has two warp beams is recommended. The even-numbered warps are then wound on one warp beam and the odd-numbered ones on the other. Remember, however, that the Indians of Central and South America have been weaving gauze for centuries on stick looms which have a fixed warp!

Gauze and leno weaves can be set up on an eight-harness loom. In this case, four harnesses (5, 6; 7, 8) are threaded for a two-block pattern weave and four (1, 2; 3, 4) are equipped with doups; two of the leno harnesses will then serve one block of the pattern and the other two the other block of the pattern.

Gauze Weaving on Mechanical Looms Using Beads

Tubular beads about half an inch long can be used in place of doups for gauze weaving. They are placed in front of the harnesses on either jack or counterbalanced looms, and a release, which must be installed when beads are used, is placed in the rear of the harnesses. The release is a light frame consisting of two narrow wooden slats held about 2 inches apart by crossbars at either end.

When beads are used, the loom is strung or threaded in four-yarn units; the threading of each unit is in this order: 4, 1, 2, 3; repeat. Working from right to left, the warp is strung on the loom as follows: Carry the first yarn under the rear bar and over the front bar of the release, through the first heddle of harness 4, and through the bead. Carry the second yarn through the first heddle of harness 1 and the third yarn through the first heddle of harness 2. Carry the fourth yarn over the rear bar and under the front bar of the release, through the first heddle of harness 3, under yarns two and three, and through the same bead as the first yarn. The rest of the yarns on the loom are threaded through the heddles in this same order. The two yarns in the outside position (4, 3) act as a pair, and are carried through the release and through a bead; those on the inside position (1, 2) also act as a pair and are free, running above both the release and the bead.

When beads are used the tie-up is as follows: The harnesses of a jack loom are tied up to three treadles: harness 4 to treadle 1, harnesses 1 and 2 to treadle 2, and harness 3 to treadle 3. The harnesses of a counterbalanced loom are also tied up to three treadles, but in this order: harnesses 1, 2, and 3 are tied to treadle 1; harnesses 3 and 4 are tied to treadle 2; and harnesses 1, 2, and 4 are tied to treadle 3.

Since the yarns set up with beads act in pairs, a coarser fabric is woven than when doups are used. It is well to select a basket weave for the solid weave, in which case the gauze is formed by the crossing of two warp pairs. To weave the basket weave, treadle 1 alternately with treadle 2, throwing two strands of weft into each shed formed. To weave gauze, treadle 1 alternately with treadle 3, throwing a single weft into each shed formed. Note that when harness 4 is raised, the back bar of the release is lifted; this slackens the yarns on harness 3 and allows these yarns to come up with those on harness 4 and to the right side of the free yarns, on harnesses 1 and 2. When harness 3 is raised, the reverse action takes place: the yarns on harnesses 3 and 4 are brought up to the left of those on harnesses 1 and 2.

Gauze Weaving on Industrial Power Looms

Special steel heddles are used in industry for gauze weaving. These are described in books which deal with commercial weaving (*65*).

WRAPPED WEAVES

Some open weaves are formed by a semi-embroidery technique, a needle and thread or a small shuttle being used to cover or to constrict groups of warp or weft yarns. Some of these weaves, such as the Soumak weaves of the Near East and the allover wrapped-warp weaves of Peru, have a long historic past. (See Fig. 87, bottom right.)

Some of the wrapped-weave techniques are used to constrict groups of both warp and weft at regular intervals across the fabric. (See Fig. 138.) The methods most commonly used for this treatment are the double-wrapped and lock-stitched wrapped techniques described below.

WRAPPED-WARP WEAVES
The Soumak Weave

The Soumak stitch can be pulled tighter than in regular Soumak weaving and hence can be used to open up the warp across a fabric. Soumak weaving is described on page 169.

BASIC WEAVES

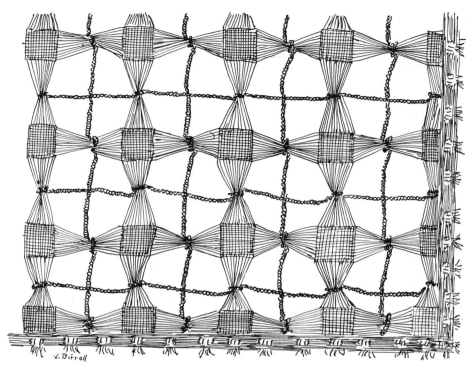

Fig. 138. Wrapped Weave. An "ancient" modern! This type of weave which is an important technique of contemporary weavers was woven in Peru long before the conquest. The illustration was copied from an ancient Peruvian fabric. See d'Harcourt (26).

Allover Wrapped-Warp Weaves

An ancient Peruvian cotton cloth in the Brooklyn Museum contains patterns made by wrapping each warp in certain areas with colored wool before weaving.

Wrapped Warp Tapestry and "Spot" Tapestry Weaves

These open weaves are described on pages 167, 168, Types 14, 17.

Hemstitching

The hemstitching technique can be used to open up areas in a fabric. Hemstitching is described on page 370.

Double Wrapped-Warp Weave

When a weft yarn, carried by a small shuttle or a tapestry needle, is passed twice around groups of warp yarns at regular intervals across the warp, a double wrapped-warp weave results. If the weft is passed three times around the groups of warp yarns, a triple wrapped-warp weave is produced.

Lock Stitch Wrapped-Warp Weave

This technique could also be called the loop stitch method of wrapping warp, or the warp treatment of the Danish medallion weave. It is made as follows: A small shuttle, wound with accessory weft, is carried from right to left under a given number of warp yarns, and then brought to the surface. At the specified interval to the right of the shuttle, a crochet hook is used to pull the accessory weft to the surface and into a loop. The small shuttle is slipped into this loop, the accessory weft is pulled taut, and the warp yarns are constricted into a tight bunch. This accessory weft yarn is then carried horizontally across the warp, connecting other groups of warp yarns. (If desired, the loop lifted by the crochet hook can be twisted a half turn to form a more secure crochet stitch.)

Chain Stitch Wrapped-Warp Weave

The chain or crewel stitch can be used to constrict groups of warp. Crewel embroidery is described on page 361.

Crocheted Wrapped-Warp Weave

The loops of a single crocheted chain can be used to constrict the warp yarns into groups. Crocheting is described on page 309.

Pile Wrapped-Warp Weave

This is not an open weave, but it is listed here because it is a wrapped warp weave. It is described on page 176.

WRAPPED-WEFT WEAVES

Many of the techniques described above for wrapping the warp can also be used for wrapping the weft.

Accessory weft yarns can also be wrapped around or otherwise constrict rows of previously woven weft, usually three to five rows at a time immediately in front of the open shed, at regular intervals across the warp. The accessory weft is usually carried through the open shed between the points of contact with the woven weft; however, it may be carried across the surface or across the back of the fabric. It may be a different color than the regular weft.

Double Wrapped-Weft Weaves

A tapestry needle carries the accessory weft, which is wrapped twice around sections of previously woven weft.

263

Lock Stitch Wrapper-Weft Weave, the Danish Medallion Weave

This technique is the same as the lock stitch wrapped-warp weave just described, except that the small shuttle is carried through the open shed instead of back of the warp. A crochet hook pierces through the weft four or five rows to the front of the open shed, and pulls the accessory weft into a loop through which a small shuttle is drawn. The wefts enclosed are then pulled tightly together.

Chain Stitch Wrapped-Weft Weave

The chain stitch is used to constrict sections of previously woven weft at regular intervals across the fabric.

Crocheted Wrapped-Weft Weave

A crochet hook pierces between rows of weft at regular intervals and, by means of single crochet, constricts groups of weft yarns.

THE BRONSON WEAVE, A GROUPED-WARP AND GROUPED-WEFT WEAVE

This weave is not a true gauze or leno weave. In old English weaving books it was called the "spot weave." It is also called pseudo-leno, mock leno, spot lace, spot Bronson, open lace, and fancy linen weave. The name Bronson was given to it by Mary M. Atwater.[3] (See Fig. 139.)

The weave can be set up on a loom with four or more harnesses. One identifying characteristic of nearly all variations of the weave, irrespective of the number of harnesses, is that half of all the warp yarns are threaded through the heddles on the first harness. A unit in the weave usually consists of four warp yarns arranged in two identical pairs. These units can be arranged in a pyramid form in a regular progressive sequence or in various other groupings.

The open pattern in a Bronson weave results from short skips of weft on one side of the fabric and short skips of warp on the reverse side. In spite of these open sections, it is considered a 50–50 weave.

Three Bronson weaves are described briefly here.

Plain Bronson

The threading of the warp yarns in the harnesses is as follows: 1, 2, 1, 2; 1, 3, 1, 3; 1, 4, 1, 4; repeat units in reverse order; repeat complete sequence. On a jack loom, the harnesses are tied so that 3 and 4 are attached

[3] Mrs. Atwater found several drafts of this weave in an old book, *Domestic Manufacturer's Assistant*, by J. Bronson and R. Bronson (1817).

to treadle 1; 2 and 4 to treadle 2; 2 and 3 to treadle 3; 2, 3, and 4 to treadle A; and 1 to treadle B. To weave the pattern, treadle each treadle twice in the sequence of 1, 2, 3, 2; always use treadle B between treadles—for example, treadle 1, treadle B, treadle 1, treadle B, treadle 2, etc.

Segmented Bronson

The units in this weave are separated with a 1–2 threading as follows: 1, 3, 1, 3; 1, 2; 1, 3, 1, 3; 1, 2; 1, 4, 1, 4; 1, 2; 1, 4, 1, 4; etc. On a jack loom, tie harnesses 2 and 4 to treadle 1; harness 2 to treadle 2; harnesses 2, 3, and 4 to treadle A; and harness 1 to treadle B. To weave the pattern, treadle 1, B, 1, B, A, B; repeat four times; 2, B, 2, B, A, B; repeat two times; repeat these two sequences as many times as are needed.

Irregular Bronson

A variant Bronson or Bronson-like weave is threaded as follows: 1, 4—repeat eight times; 3, 4, 3, 4; 1, 4; 3, 4, 3, 4; 1, 4; 3, 4, 3, 4; repeat the entire sequence twice. Thread 1, 4—repeat eight times; 1, 2, 1, 2; 1, 4; 1, 2, 1, 2; 1, 4; 1, 2, 1, 2; repeat this sequence twice also. Repeat the first and second sequences as many times as needed; end with 1, 4 repeated eight times. Tie harness 1 to treadle 1; harness

Fig. 139. Bronson Weave. Also known as the "fancy linen weave," an open weave.

4 to treadle 2; harnesses 2 and 4 to treadle 3; and harnesses 1 and 3 to treadle 4. To weave the pattern, use the treadles in this order for the first sequence: 4, 3—weave series eight times; 4, 2, 4, 2, 4, 3—weave series twice; 4, 2, 4, 2—weave series once. Repeat this entire sequence twice. End with treadle 4 before going to second sequence. Then treadle in this order for second sequence: 3, 4—weave series eight times; 3, 1, 3; 1, 3, 4—weave series twice, 3, 1, 3, 1—weave series once. Repeat this second sequence twice. End with treadle 3 before going to first sequence. Continue weaving, alternating these two sequences. End the weaving with the

265

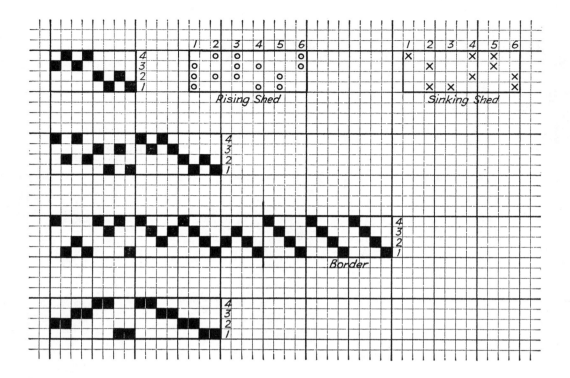

first sequence and end this sequence by treading 4, 3—weave eight times.

6. Tension and Texture-treated Weaves

An uneven tension in either warp or weft yarns will result in an uneven surface on the face of the fabric. Tension may be caused by feeding into the loom two sets of warp yarns held at different tensions; each set must be held on a different warp beam. Weaves, like brocatelle, which combine floated yarns with compactly woven yarns, usually result in an uneven surface tension. Weaves made up of yarns of different twists result in a crêped surface. Irregular battening will cause an irregular thickness in the weft. Irregular reeds, which can be purchased, will cause an irregular thickness in the warp. Fabrics can be woven of different yarns which, when heat-treated, shrink in varying degrees and cause an uneven surface.

Texture can also be achieved by a combination of unusual yarns and fibers and by various built-up structuring of certain weaves. Some weaves,

HUCK WEAVE	Heddle-threading draft—repeat as needed. Tie-up—special tie-up given above. Treadle plan—2, 1, 2, 1, 2, 4, 3, 4, 4, 4; repeat. Tabby—2 and 4; alternate with pattern weft. Pattern—many variations possible.

M and O WEAVE	Heddle-threading draft—repeat as needed.
	Tie-up—use standard tie-up; see Fig. 132.
	Treadle plan—treadle 1 and 3 alternately for 4 times
	              treadle 5 and 6 alternately for 4 times
	              (treadles 2 and 4 make a flat simple weave)
	Tabby—no tabby.
	Pattern—many variations possible.

CRACKLE WEAVE	Heddle-threading draft—repeat design area as needed reverse border on left of
	         warp.
	Tie-up—use standard tie-up; see Fig. 132.
	Treadle plan—1, 2. 3, 4; repeat.
	Tabby—2 and 4; alternate with pattern weft.
	Pattern—in the threading of the loom, the units may be repeated a given number
	        of times to obtain pattern variation.

INDIAN SADDLE-BLANKET WEAVE	Heddle-threading draft—repeat as needed. Tie-up—use standard tie-up; see Fig. 132. Treadle plan—1, 2, 3, 4; repeat. Tabby—no tabby. Pattern—Soft heavy wool should be used for the weft. Alternate dark, medium, and light colored weft yarns in weaving. Use hard-twisted linen warp.

Fig. 140A. Miscellaneous Weaves. Huck, M and O, Crackle, and Indian saddle-blanket weaves.

such as piqué, bird's-eye twill, huck, and modified Bronson weaves make interesting modern textured fabrics when they are done in coarse heavy or slubbed yarns. Texture is often acquired by combining uneven slubbed or rough yarns with rough weaves, such as those which contain sets of yarns arranged in unusual groupings. A few drafts illustrated in Fig. 140A can be used for rough-surface effects; combined with striking colors and unusual yarns, they can be used for weaving modern types of textiles. No specific directions are given here for methods of acquiring texture effects in textiles, but weave combinations too numerous to mention can be employed. For example, the addition of split bamboo, raffia, metallic or other unusual yarns to any weave may result in what could be called a "modern" textile. A creative weaver can invent many novel effects by experimentation.

7. Combination Weaves

Many of the weaves described earlier in this chapter can be combined in a single fabric. Most backed cloths and double cloths are combined

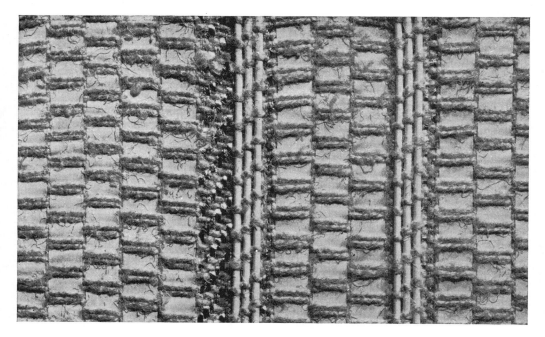

Fig. 140B. Modern Textured Weaves. Above, woven of leather, lurex, raw silk, and nylon. Below, woven of bamboo, silk, nylon, and lurex. (Courtesy, Dorothy Liebes Textiles, Inc., N.Y.)

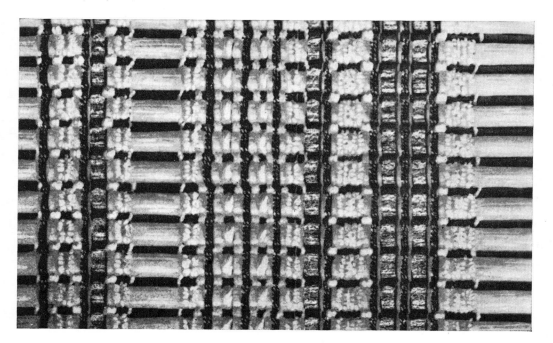

weaves. When brocade and double-cloth weaves are combined, matelassé results. Often the name of the fabric suggests the combination of its structure: for example, brocaded velvet, satin brocade, and satin-striped rep.

Many combined weaves are listed and described in the glossary at the back of this book. The reader will find it profitable to become acquainted with this glossary.

8. Planning Patterns and Plotting Drafts for Weaving

Designs for weaving are obtained from various sources: they may be copied directly from attractive pieces of fabric, selected from weaving manuals, varied from the warp setup already established on the loom, or planned and plotted by the weaver. All of these approaches to design are discussed in the next few pages.

Current interest in woven textiles revolves around unusual combinations of color, texture, and quality in the yarns. (See Fig. 140B.) A good practice for the novice is to make a test assortment of yarns in various color and texture combinations by arranging them over the index finger of the left hand, or attaching them temporarily in a series across a strip of masking tape. After studying the effect of the yarns upon one another and upon the total group, rearrangements can be made until a satisfactory combination has been achieved.

Before the weaver attempts to create a pattern which involves a difficult weave structure, she should study the basic weaves and their compositions. Sections 1 through 7 of this chapter are devoted to this subject.

ANALYZING THE DESIGN OF A WOVEN FABRIC

Often a weaver wishes to copy a pattern from an attractive piece of material. Sometimes it is possible to find a printed draft of the pattern selected, and so the problem of copying is facilitated. If no draft is available, the weaver must analyze the sample in order to determine the structure of the weave. A few suggestions may help with such an analysis.

First, find the right side or "face" of the fabric; texture and weave are usually more prominent on the face than on the back. Next, determine which yarns are warp and which are weft. If there is a selvage, the warp will be apparent. The yarns of the warp are usually more numerous, tighter in twist, and higher in number of plies than are the weft yarns. Stripes are usually in the warp, and checks are slightly longer in the warp.

The sample should be properly prepared for the analysis. Using a 3″ x 3″

sample, remove the fuzz, brush on a coating of weak starch solution, and press. Make a 1/8-inch fringe in the warp across one end. In one of the weft repeats, make a slit weftwise twice as long as a warp repeat and about 1 1/2 inches above the fringe. Remove a few wefts from around the cut. Remove a few warps from one part of the fringe, leaving an isolated area of weft. Finally, stretch the sample and tack it down.

The weave structure can now be analyzed: Using a stylus or other pointed tool, pull the weft yarns into the fringe, one at a time. With a magnifying glass note the interlacings and jot these down in their proper order on graph paper. Recheck the accuracy of the draft. Note if the selvage is formed at the same time as the pattern weave or separately; in other words, observe whether the same harnesses as the pattern or separate harnesses were used for weaving the selvage.

DRAFTS USED IN WEAVING

Three types of drafts are used in weaving: pattern drafts, heddle-threading drafts, and tie-up drafts. (See Fig. 132.) A treadle plan, listing the order of lifting the heddle harnesses, may also be necessary. (See Fig. 124.) For a discussion of tie-up drafts and treadle plans see pages 216 and 218.

Drafts are plotted on graph paper. The most satisfactory kind for this work is that marked eight squares to the inch.

THE PATTERN DRAFT

An experienced weaver is often able to dispense with pattern drafts, copying patterns directly from woven samples and photographs; the beginner, however, usually has to depend on printed drafts for assistance. The truly creative weaver will eventually wish to create his or her own designs, plotting them on graph paper.

The making of a pattern draft is not difficult, but there are a few limitations which must be considered: The pattern is limited to some extent by the type and the size of the loom, by the number of shafts on the loom, and by the structure of the heddle-threading draft, if the loom is already set up and threaded. Because the average weaver will be using a jack-type or a counterbalanced foot-power loom, pattern-making processes have been described for these looms; the same basic principles, however, can be applied for designing pattern weaves for other looms.

Most designs are planned in units made up of a number of blocks, or small repeat patterns, which take unique, or individual, positions in the warp of the fabric. New blocks formed must not lie directly beneath the last block formed, but must incorporate the use of an additional heddle harness on the loom. Therefore, one limiting factor in designing is that *there cannot be more pattern changes—blocks in unique positions in the pattern—than there are heddle harnesses on the loom.* When the design is put in entirely by hand with pick-up work, there is, of course, no such limitation; this technique is discussed in Chapter IV. Instructions for preparing a pattern draft are as follows:

1. Find the number of block changes in the prospective pattern—that is, count the number of unique blocks in one complete repeat of the pattern—those that do not lie immediately below one another. Study the small heddle-threading draft (see Fig. 132) on which the two block patterns are encircled; each block engages two heddle harnesses.

2. Find one complete repeat of the pattern—this may be made up of several unit patterns or blocks. Count the number of block changes in all the different unit patterns, measuring from and including one center block of one unit pattern to, but not including, the center block of the next similar repeat. In other words, measure from unit center to unit center of one complete pattern repeat to find the number of pattern variations or block changes.

3. If the pattern is found to be within the scope of the loom—that is, if there are no more block variations than the loom has heddle harnesses—the heddle-threading draft can then be made.

THE HEDDLE-THREADING DRAFT

The heddle-threading draft is a plan drawn on graph paper to assist the weaver in threading the heddles. It is also known as the draft, the chain draft, the thread draft, and the threading-in draft. There must be as many horizontal bands on the graph paper as there are heddle harnesses on the loom. They are numbered from bottom to top, counting the front harness on the loom as No. 1. Some weavers black in the squares of the graph paper to lay out the heddle-threading plan; others save time by marking small crosses, circles, numbers (the number of repeats to be used), or checks in the proper squares.

Heddle-threading drafts are classified according to the manner of arranging patterns: *Straight drafts* have a consecutive arrangement of pattern blocks—that is the blocks are arranged in a regular sequence as in the overshot drafts described below. *Point* or *centered drafts* have a pyramid-shaped pattern plan; the treading plan also works to a point and then reverses directions. (See the drafts for the Summer and Winter weave, page 245.) Large patterns can be woven with only a few heddle harnesses when this system is used. *Mixed* or *compound drafts* combine straight and point drafts. *Intermittent drafts* are straight drafts on which certain sections are skipped at regular intervals. In *broken drafts* plotting is based on diagonals running alternately at angles to one another. In *grouped drafts* the heddle pattern shows groups of yarns threaded first in the front and then in the back shafts. The front and back groups are separated by threadings which go across all the shafts. *Corkscrew drafts* have groups of colored yarns threaded in alternate twill lines in a variation of a straight twill. In *scattered* or *satin drafts* the yarns are arranged at random to prevent any semblance of pattern. *Skipped-shaft drafts* are plotted so that each warp threaded on the loom skips past one harness. For example the threading pattern for a plain weave is 1, 3, 2, 4 instead of the regular 1, 2, 3, 4 sequence. A very clear shed is made with this threading when the harnesses are raised—1 and 2 together and 3 and 4 together—for a plain weave.

PLOTTING HEDDLE-THREADING DRAFTS FROM PATTERN DRAFTS

A weaver who is experienced enough to plot her own pattern drafts will also be able to plot her own heddle-threading drafts. The beginner, however, can turn to any good book on weaving and find many heddle-threading drafts ready for use. A heddle-threading draft for overshot weaving is made as follows:

1. Draw a true diagonal through the pattern draft from the upper right corner to the lower left corner. As noted earlier, the pattern draft should be on graph paper.
2. About an inch above the squares of the pattern draft, plot the squares of the heddle-threading draft. Start with any harness on the loom, providing that the squares blacked in on the graph paper follow the regular sequence of the tie-up of the loom—on the four-harness counterbalanced loom this sequence is 1–2, 2–3, 3–4, 1–4, or the reverse. Suppose we start with harness 1, heddle 1, and black in the squares necessary for the first block of the pattern; we will then be blacking in squares 1, 2, 1, 2, etc., as many times as the first block on the pattern requires.
3. Black in the second block of the pattern. The pattern blocks must overlap; that is, the last square of the first block on the threading draft automatically becomes the first square of the second block. This second block would therefore be 3, 2, 3, 2, etc., as many times as are needed.
4. The other blocks move forward above or below the second block in the same manner.

272

THE TEXTILE ARTS

PLOTTING A PATTERN DRAFT FROM A HEDDLE-THREADING DRAFT

When a loom is already set up and the heddles are threaded, a weaver may want to weave a different pattern from the one first planned. She will then have to prepare a pattern draft from a heddle-threading draft —a process just the opposite of the one described above. To plan a new pattern for this loom, or to establish new pattern possibilities for the loom as set up for overshot weaving, the process is as follows:

1. Copy the heddle-threading draft on the upper right-hand corner of a piece of graph paper. Immediately below it draw a diagonal line on the graph paper, starting at the upper right-hand corner. (See the illustration in the upper right-hand corner of Fig. 132.)
2. On this diagonal, starting at the upper right-hand corner, black in as many graph paper squares as are found in the first block of the heddle-threading draft. Remember that a block represents a sequence of blacked-in squares which have the same intervals—note those circled on Fig. 132. The blocks should be completed from right to left, one at a time, down the diagonal. Blocks are always one square wider than they are high, to allow for the necessary transition when weaving. They thus overlap by one square in the pattern, and by one thread in the weaving.
3. Black in the second block, and so on, working down the diagonal, and placing the first square under the last square of the block above.

This pattern will comply with the heddle-threading draft and will, therefore, be plotted as drawn in. Weaving such a pattern is called "weaving as drawn in." In weaving, however, since weight of yarns differs, it may take more or fewer throws of weft to form the squares shown on the pattern draft; this will necessarily alter the treading plan. In actual weaving, the blocks are formed by starting at the lower right-hand corner and working diagonally up toward the left. If woven correctly, a true 45° diagonal will run upward through the centers of the blocks. (See page 243.)

Sometimes the pattern drawn in is not the most interesting one, or we may desire to alter it. This can be done by increasing or decreasing the height of the blocks of the pattern, or we may weave in a rose pattern, described on page 245. The pattern can also be varied in other ways: the loom can be threaded on opposites, small segments of the pattern can be threaded on opposites, or the treading plan may provide for accidents on a loom threaded on opposites. These terms are explained in the next paragraph.

When we have selected a pattern draft but have not yet threaded up the loom, we may be able to make the pattern into a more clear-cut design

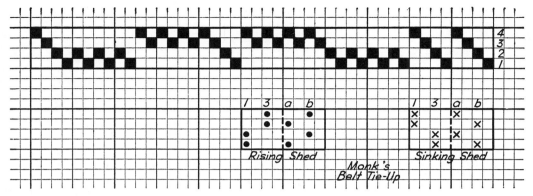

Fig. 141. Monk's Belt Weave. Heddle draft shows pattern blocks with no overlapping warp yarns as was true of draft on Fig. 132.

by threading it up on opposites. To do this, we retain the regular sequences
of the blocks on the heddle-threading draft, but eliminate the overlap.
This is illustrated in the Monk's Belt design, Fig. 141. We thread up the
loom, therefore, with clear-cut blocks: instead of the 1, 2, 1, 2; 3, 2, 3, 2
sequence pattern of the regular overshot heddle-threading draft, we use
the 1, 2, 1, 2; 3, 4, 3, 4 sequence, etc. We can likewise vary the pattern by
threading in opposites only the small connecting intervals, those between
the unit patterns of an overshot weave. The overlapping of two blocks
threaded on opposites caused by treading harnesses 2 and 3 simultaneously will cause an accident or a shadow pattern to appear in the woven
fabric. Sometimes these accidents are deliberate, to give certain effects
to a pattern.

274

PART TWO

NONWEAVING STRUCTURAL PROCESSES

VIII

Nonwoven Fabrics—The Single-Element Processes

Fabrics may be constructed by means other than weaving; the various braiding, knotting, and looping processes are examples of nonwoven structuring. The difference between nonwoven and woven fabrics is that only one set of yarns, either warp *or* weft, is required for most of these nonweaving techniques, whereas two sets—warp and weft—are needed for weaving. Nonweaving methods are called single-element processes. In braiding, meshwork, and in some knot work, the single element is the longitudinal warp. In other knot work, and in knitting, crocheting, and needle looping, the single element is a pseudo-weft; it is carried horizontally back and forth across the fabric, looping into itself as it goes.

Single-element processes have been dear to the hearts of textile craftsmen since ancient times. The origin of these textiles is not known, but since knotted netting has been found in very ancient occupation sites and since it is often the sole textile method used by a primitive group, it is quite possible that knot work was the first single-element process. In more recent historic epochs, the early Egyptians constructed nets and "networks"; the early Norsemen relied a great deal upon their knot work, braiding, and meshwork; and the early Peruvians practiced a variety of braiding, looping, and knotting techniques. During the Middle Ages women in the convents and in the fortress castles occupied themselves with crocheting and loop work. During the Renaissance, both peasant women and ladies of the court busied themselves with knot work, crocheting, and lace making. In our own period, both in Europe and in the United States, knitting is the most popular of these particular processes. In many other areas of the world, such as Mexico, knot work, meshwork, and other of the single-element techniques are still basic to the economy of the people.

1. Braiding and Meshwork

Before discussing braiding and meshwork, let us distinguish between the two processes. While they have elements in common, the basic structures are different. They are similar in that both produce an open lacelike effect; both may be made on stick looms and with the help of shed sticks; in both processes, warp yarns are crossed over and under other warp yarns. However, the two processes differ in several respects. In braiding, the "warp" yarns pass in a diagonal direction until they reach a border, then they reverse directions and pass diagonally to the opposite border; in meshwork, the warp yarns twist back and forth in a limited area and cross adjacent warp yarns. Color patterns on all braids run in diagonal directions; those on meshes run vertically or longitudinally. With the exception of a 1–1 braid, a braided fabric has considerably less stretchability than a mesh fabric. The two techniques may be further distinguished by the openings between the yarns; the interstices in braids are diamond-shaped; those in meshes tend to be hexagonal. In true weaving the interstices are square, because yarns cross one another at right angles.

Both braiding and meshwork are related to several other interlacing processes. For example, braiding closely approaches weaving in technique, except that here the warp yarns serve as both warp and weft as they interlace into one another. The terms braiding and plaiting are almost synonymous, but plaiting has come to mean more specifically the making of straw hats and straw mats, usually from unspun plant fibers, such as palm leaves, canes, and grasses. (See Fig. 142.)

Trimmings and passementeries are often called braids; however, they are usually made of two sets of yarns, one either interwoven or sewed onto the other. (See page 340.)

Meshwork, too, is related to several other processes. Certain forms of meshwork and certain forms of bobbin lace are identical in structure. Likewise, the 1–1 mesh is identical in structure to the simplest form of knotless netting. However, the methods used for constructing the last named fabrics are different: meshwork is made by the intertwisting of lengthwise warp yarns, whereas knotless netting is made by the intertwisting of crosswise *weft* yarns.

BRAIDS AND BRAIDING

Braiding is at times called plaiting, finger weaving, interweaving, webbing, intercrossing, and interlacing. It is one of the textile arts first learned by children, and may have been one of the first textile processes mastered by primitive man. Simple three-strand braids are easily made; five- and six-strand braids are more difficult. It is quite a surprise, therefore, to find that the ancient Egyptians (*111*) and ancient Peruvians (*26*) braided fabrics 18 inches wide!

Before the arrival of the white man in America, braiding and plaiting were carried on in many areas. Braids which have been dug up from ancient Peruvian burial sites show remarkable craftsmanship; many of the pieces were made in the very difficult warp-twined braiding. The Prado Museum, in Lima, has an especially good display of ancient Peruvian braids and meshwork. Many of the pieces are so beautifully patterned that the visitor views with amazement this finery of a time long past. Braided textiles have also been found in ancient burial sites in North America. Amsden dates some braided fabrics found in Bas-

Fig. 142. Plaiting. A palm leaf matting braid made into a bag; from the Tongan Island, South Pacific.

ketmaker sites in the southwestern part of the United States as belonging to the beginning of the Christian era. It is thought that the Hopi Indians of the Southwest learned how to braid from the Basketmaker people; Hopi men still braid white cotton wedding sashes for their brides. On the Eastern Seaboard, the Algonquin and other tribes braided bags and belts, using a hemplike fiber for their work. On the Great Plains Indian tribes made buffalo hair fabrics by the braiding process (*1*). After the arrival of the white man, braid making continued in many parts of the Americas. The peoples of Central and South America still produce great quantities of plaited straw hats and mats which are for sale in all native markets.

279

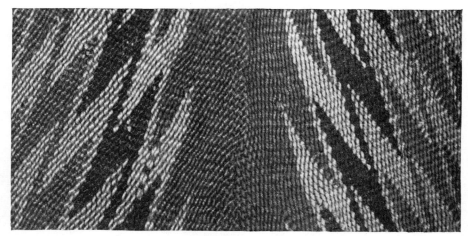

Fig. 143A. Braiding from the Center. Detail of a braid from Coureurs des Bois, Canada. This method was also used by the Osage Indians.

Fig. 143B. Braiding from the Center. Drawing showing the method of procedure of braiding from the center. See Fig. 143A.

At the present time interesting braids are being made in various areas; the Arabs, certain groups in Europe, weavers in eastern Canada, and other peoples throughout the world produce attractive and unique braids.

Some braiding techniques are very intricate. For example, elaborate braids, patterned with allover parallelograms, are made and worn in Coureurs des Bois, Canada. (See Fig. 143A.) Warp-twined braiding is another example of complicated braiding; in this technique, used in ancient Peru, the warp yarns are twisted between each diagonal crossing of the braid. (See page 73.) The 3–3 twill braids made by the Hopi and by the ancient Pueblo and Peruvian Indians appear to be more complicated than they actually are; these braids are described later.

Braids may be made with or without shed sticks. Those made with shed sticks are flat; those made without may be either flat or round. Both methods

THE TEXTILE ARTS

are described in the following pages. Some writers designate the yarns which are either above or below the shed in a braid as the active warp, and those inside the shed, that act as weft, as the passive warp.

BRAIDING WITHOUT SHED STICKS

When braids are made without the aid of shed sticks, the warp may be stretched between two rods, but more often it is allowed to hang from one rod only. The fingers hold the sheds open and cross the yarns to form the braid.

The pattern of the braid is affected by the direction in which the yarns are crossed. Braids can be made by working across the warp from one edge, working across the warp alternately from one edge and then the other, working from both edges as far as the center, and working from the center toward both edges. These four processes are described below.

BRAIDING FROM ONE SIDE OF THE WARP

This striking one-directional diagonal-striped braid was once made in ancient Peru. (See Fig. 144.) The colors selected for it should be dark, in full intensity, and arranged in interesting color groups. When setting up the yarns for braiding, divide one block of one of the colors into two parts and place them on the outside edges of the belt. For example, for the belt described here, the colored yarns are arranged as follows: 3 red, 5 blue, 5 green, 5 purple, 2 red.

Cut 18 of the yarns about 3 1/2 times the length needed for the belt; this takes care of the doubling of the yarns, described below, and of waste. Cut two of the outside red yarns from one side of the belt 12 inches longer than the other yarns; double them, stretch them between two vertical supports, and fasten them there. These four strands, now stretched between the supports, serve as heading cords for the other yarns. These other yarns are now doubled, dropped over, and interwoven into the heading cords, passing over two and under two of them. The four ends of the heading cords which fall down one side of the warp are interwoven back into the belt as the braiding proceeds. The doubling of the yarns makes a total of 40 yarns in the warp. If a medium-weight yarn is used the belt will be about 1 inch wide.

After all the belt yarns have been interwoven into the heading cords, insert a strong string into the loop end of the cords, and tie another string to the four yarns forming the open end of the heading cords. These two strings may be tied together and slipped over a peg to hold the warp yarns during braiding, or they may be attached to a rod which in turn is attached to a supporting cord. The strings are removed when the belt is finished.

281

When all is ready, the warp yarns are braided according to the following directions.

1. Form a shed below the heading yarns, picking up every other yarn. *Always pick up the yarns from right to left.*

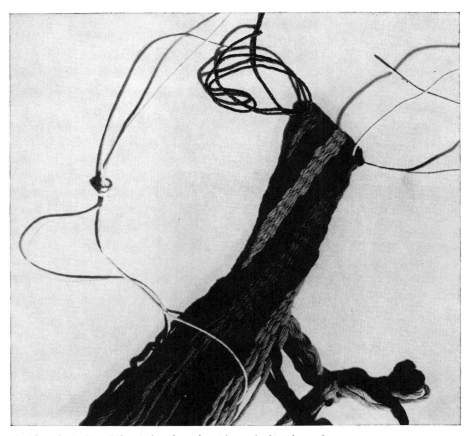

Fig. 144. Braiding from One Side. A braid made without shed sticks and braided from one side.

2. Through this shed, draw two of the warp yarns from the outside left edge. *Always pull the yarn through the shed from left to right.* These two yarns could be called the wefts, since they now take the position of weft. Again, working from right to left, form another shed and pull two more "wefts" through. Loop these four "wefts" together temporarily with a slip knot. Draw two more wefts through the next shed.

3. Now untie the top four yarns—the first two pairs pulled through the sheds. Starting with the top one, interweave them singly down the side of

the belt into one another and over and under the other wefts. Tie the last two wefts into a slip knot.

4. Repeat steps 1 through 3 until the braiding is finished. Always push the "weft" firmly up against the finished braid. The belt should be firm and compact. Be careful not to let the vertical warps cross out of order during the interweaving process.

5. Finish off the ends of the belt with fringe or stitch across with a sewing machine and sew on a buckle.

BRAIDING FROM THE CENTER TOWARD BOTH EDGES

A braid made by working from the center of the warp outward toward the edges is often called an Osage braid, though the method is used by peoples other than the Osage Indians. (See Fig. 143B.)

Bright rich colors make the most attractive belts. The colors for the warp are arranged in groups. The grouping used in the belt described here is as follows: 11 red, 11 purple, 22 blue, 11 purple, 11 red—a total of 66 yarns. When medium-weight worsted yarn is used, a belt 2 1/2 inches wide is made.

The warp for this belt should first be wound around the pegs of a warping board. No cross need be formed during warping, unless the weaver feels it necessary to keep the yarns straight. One complete circuit around the pegs should equal the length wanted for the belt, allowing for take-up and waste. Before the warp is removed from the pegs, several rows of compact twining are made in the end of the warp opposite the starting point, using the same color of yarn as the dominant color of the belt. The other end of the warp, opposite the twining, is then cut across and the warp removed from the pegs.

The center of the belt, the twined area, is now stretched across a horizontal rod. This may be done in a number of ways: the warp yarns to the back of the twining may be looped around the rod (see the illustration) and then tied close to the rod in one big loose slip knot; or a cord can be wound through the warp binding it to the rod; or the strands of twining cords—the ends of the yarns used for twining—could be used to fasten the warp to the rod. In the last two methods the yarns to the back of the twining must be looped into a chain to prevent tangling; those in front are allowed to hang downward from the rod. The rod is now tied to a vertical support, and the braiding is begun in the front yarns.

The warp is now about ready for braiding, but before it can be braided two sheds must be stabilized in it. This is done as follows: the warp yarns are divided in half; in the right half every other yarn is picked up, working from right to left, and a shed is made under them. A cord is slipped into this new shed and the ends are tied into a bow knot. Now pick up the yarns on the left half of the warp, again working from right to left, slip in another cord, and tie as before. To prevent the loss of the shed pattern it is recommended that these shed cords be placed in the warp and kept a little below the area being braided. When braiding, pick up every other shed by hand and use the shed cord to form the alternate sheds. At intervals, as the braiding progresses, the warp in these shed cords must be adjusted.

The sheds are always made *from right to left*. The center yarns are always crossed and one is carried into the shed *from left to right*. The warp yarns which are pulled through the sheds act temporarily as weft and are so-called in the description which follows. Always work on the right half of the warp, turning the belt to make this possible.

1. Make a shed through the right half of the warp, *working from right to left* as far as the center. Cross the left one of the center pair over the right one and carry it through the shed just made in a *left to right* direction. Make a new shed. Turn the belt over and slip the left hand into this last shed, which will now be on the left side of the loom. Note: After each weft yarn is thrown into a shed from the center, a new shed is always made; when it is opened, the weft above it is pushed upward firmly. The belt is then turned and the left hand slipped into this shed. Later, when the belt is reversed again, the shed is ready for a new throw of yarn. This new shed always prevents the weft from falling out; it also acts as a battening agent.

2. Leaving the warp in the turned position just described, make a shed in the right half of the warp as far as the center, again working from right to left. Pick up the left yarn of the center pair, cross it over the other yarn of the pair—the one which was interwoven into the preceding shed—and run it through the shed from left to right. Make a new shed. Turn the warp over, back to its first position, and slip the left hand in this second shed.

3. Repeat steps 1 and 2 once more, and with a slip knot tie the weft yarns that hang at the selvage into pairs. After four weft yarns have been braided into both sides of the warp, untie the top pair; beginning with the top yarn, interweave the two down the edge of the belt into each other and into the other two wefts at the selvage.

4. Beginning at this point, in order to save time, interweave two rows of weft into each half of the warp before turning the belt.

5. The width of the belt must be kept uniform. Measure frequently.

6. Repeat the above steps until half of the warp—that on the front side of the twining—has been braided. Then turn the belt around and braid the

warp to the back of the twining in exactly the same manner. When finished, the belt has a diamond design in the center with chevron patterns which face this diamond on either end of the belt.

BRAIDING FROM BOTH SIDES TOWARD THE CENTER

In a method of braiding used in Sweden, the warp yarns are carried into the sheds from the outside edges of the warp toward the center. The warp yarns which act as wefts are twisted around one another when they meet at the center.

BRAIDING FROM ALTERNATE SIDES INWARD AND ACROSS THE ENTIRE WARP

Hair is braided into a 3-strand plait by bringing the outside strand inward, working first on one side and then on the other. Five-strand and double-strand braids may be made by the same method. This is the process which is popularly associated with the term *braiding*.

OTHER BRAIDS AND CORDS

Warp-twined braiding is described in the discussion of warp twining, page 73. Other braids and cords[1] are described in the last section of this chapter.

USE OF SHED STICKS FOR BRAIDING AND MESHWORK

GENERAL DIRECTIONS

When planning a design for either a braided or a mesh belt, remember that both braids and meshes are more attractive if they are made with at least three contrasting colors. The stripes formed by the braid or the mesh are more evident when contrasting colors are used. A suggested color grouping is turquoise, white, and black.

Both braiding and meshwork are facilitated if the warp is stretched on two-stick looms and shed sticks are used—small polished rods slipped into the warp to maintain a series of sheds. (See Fig. 66.) Any of the braids described below may be made with the help of shed sticks.

After the color plan has been selected, the warp yarns are cut according to the arrangement desired, and tied between the sticks of a two-stick loom. They may be attached by means of slip knots or strung on heading cords which in turn are attached to the sticks. Sometimes the sticks are slipped into the end loops of a continuous warp. Whatever the method, when the warp is

---

[1] For a careful study of round braids and cording, see also Raoul Graumont and John Hensel, *Encyclopedia of Knots*, Cornell Maritime Press, 1946.

on the two sticks of the loom, the loom is stretched either vertically or horizontally between two supports. Whichever position is used, the tension must be made adjustable, which is done by tying one of the loom bars to its support with a knot which can easily be untied. Any adjustment needed can then easily be made.

Before the braiding or meshwork is started, a few rows of plain weaving are generally made at either end of the warp. If each shed formed is opened the full length of the warp, a weft yarn can be inserted at each end.

The use of shed sticks for making braids and meshes has a distinct advantage. When one row of braiding or meshwork is made at the front of the loom, another row can automatically be made at the back of the loom. It happens this way: Certain warp yarns are picked up and a shed is formed. A shed stick is slipped into it in the front of the warp. Using the left hand, the shed is then opened and cleared through the warp to the very back of the loom, where a second shed stick is slipped in and pushed as far back as it will go. In this way shed sticks are placed in the front and back of each shed formed, until about five sticks are anchored in each end of the warp.

On the sixth row of braiding and thereafter, the shed sticks nearest the loom bars on each end of the loom are removed, and the other sticks are pushed toward the loom bars, one at a time. The two shed sticks which were removed from the warp are now set to the front and back of the newly formed shed.

Always check to see that the yarns are crossing properly; in the case of braids, always check to see that they are progressing diagonally.

When the center of the length of warp is reached, the sheds will be too small to insert the fingers. When this point is reached, take out of the warp all of the shed sticks except the last two put in. Then, with a tapestry needle threaded with some of the warp yarn, make a few rows of plain weaving through the last few sheds. Carry the yarn ends back into the warp to insure a smooth selvage.

BRAIDING WITH SHED STICKS

DIRECTIONS FOR STANDARD SWEDISH 1–1 BRAIDS

The same color arrangement may be used for this braid as that described for 1–1 meshwork, or any other color plan may be used. Any number of warp yarns can be used. (See Fig. 145, left bottom.) Shed sticks can be used as described in the preceding section.

Fabric made by this process has great stretchability—it may be stretched twice its original width.

1. Weave a few rows of plain weaving. The outside warp on the right should be in the down position on the last weave shed formed. Now slip the fingers of the left hand from left to right into this last weave shed; push the top right warp *toward the right*, pick up the first right bottom warp in the space made, and lift it above the fingers of the right hand. At the same time, drop the top right warp, the one you pushed toward the right, and place this warp beneath the fingers of the right hand. As the warps are crossed, they are transferred from the left to the right hand. The right hand is held in the new shed as it is formed.

2. Continue working across the warp from right to left, pushing one top warp down under the fingers of the right hand, and lifting one bottom warp up above them. When one row has been completed, put the two shed sticks into the shed as described in the preceding section. Note that the fingers of the left hand hold the old shed and those of the right hand form the new shed.

3. On the second row, push the first top right warp *toward the left*, pick up the *second* warp on the bottom from the right side and place it above the fin-

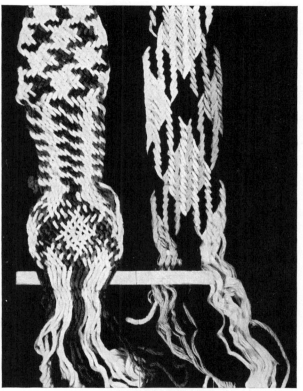

Fig. 145. Braiding and Meshwork Techniques. Left strip: top, Mexican 2–2 braid; center, Mexican 2–2 mesh; bottom, Swedish 1–1 braid. Right strip: Hopi 3–3 braid.

gers of the right hand. The warp just pushed toward the left is now dropped below the fingers of the right hand. Continue across the row, alternately raising one bottom warp and lowering the top one. When the shed on the row is completed, slip the shed sticks into the front and back of the warp.

4. On the third row, push the top right warp *toward the right* and continue as in steps 1 and 2 above. On the fourth row, proceed as in step 3. Continue in this manner until the center of the length of warp is reached, then weave a few rows of tabby as described in the general directions.

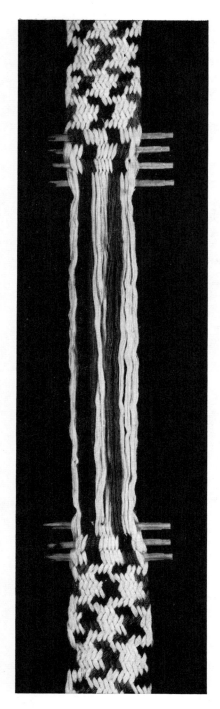

DIRECTIONS FOR MAKING MEXICAN 2–2 BRAIDS

An even number of yarns are used in this braid. The colors may be arranged about as follows: 3 blue; 10, 12, or 16, etc., white; 6 red; 10, 12, or 16, etc., white; and 3 blue. (See Fig. 146.) If the first figures in the series are used, the belt will be about 2 inches wide.

At first glance this braid appears to be a little difficult, but it is really easy if the instructions given below are followed carefully. On both ends of every row of braiding, three strands of warp are left unbraided; these yarns will later have to be "corrected" or incorporated. If they are corrected *after* picking up the yarns entirely across one row and while the yarns are still above the fingers, there will be no difficulty. A general rule to follow for making this correction is as follows: When the three outside warps are *down*, the one on the outside crosses *under* and comes up between the other two; when the three outside warps are *up*, the one on the outside crosses *over* and goes down between the other two.

The general directions for braiding with shed sticks apply to this braid.

1. Before starting the braid, be sure that the outside warp on the right is in the *up* position. Now slip the fingers of the left hand in a left to right direction in the last weave shed. Push the three top right warps toward the right and pick up the first bottom right warp in the space made. Drop the *three* warps below the fingers of the right hand and raise the *one* warp above the fingers of that hand. Continue across the row, dropping one warp from the top and picking up one from the bottom, and transferring the shed from the fingers of the left hand to those of the right as the work progresses.

Fig. 146. Mexican 2–2 Braid, made with shed sticks and braided from both ends of the warp toward the center.

2. When the row is finished there will be three warps down on the right side of the row and three warps up on the left side. The correction must now be made. While the warp is still on the right hand, correct the left side of the warp, using the left hand. To do this, take the outside warp across and over toward the right; push it down between the next two warps, putting it *under* the fingers of the right hand. Now transfer the entire shed from the right hand to the left hand, and correct the three warps which are *down* on the right side. With the right hand, grasp the bottom right warp, passing it under toward the left, and bring it up between the next two warp yarns. Put this warp above the fingers of the left hand.

3. With the right hand, slip in the shed sticks. Open the warp as far back as possible and put one shed stick in each end of the shed.

4. On the second row, the first warp to the right is in a down position. Now pull out the three bottom right warps and push down the top right warp in the space made, bringing up the three bottom warps above the fingers of the right hand and dropping the top warp beneath the fingers of that hand. Continue across the row, picking up a bottom warp and dropping a top one. This time the left three warps will be in the down position. To correct the row, take the left bottom warp, pass it to the right *under* one warp, bring it up between the other two warp yarns, and put it over the fingers of the right hand. Now transfer all the shed to the left hand and correct the three warp yarns on the right by bringing the outside top warp *over* toward the left, pushing it down between warps two and three, and putting it under the fingers of the left hand. From this point on, remember to braid a row and then make the needed corrections.

Note: Before beginning to braid a new row always check the position of the outside warp yarn. If the outside *right* one is in the *up* position, start the braiding by pushing the three top right warps toward the right and putting them down below the fingers of the right hand; then bring up the first bottom right warp in the space made to the left of the three. After the three outside warps have been put beneath the fingers, the one on the outside edge is always passed toward the left under the next one and brought up between the other two.

If the first right outside warp is *down*, always pull out the three bottom right warps, lifting them over the fingers of the right hand; push down the outside top right warp in the space to the left of the three.

After the three outside warps have been lifted from the bottom to the top, the yarn on the outside edge is always passed toward the left *over the top of the next one* and pushed down between the other two. *The yarn on the outside edge is always the one corrected; it always moves in a direction toward the center of the loom and is brought back into the weave.*

5. Repeat steps 1 through 4 until the center of the length of warp is reached. Finish off the center of the braiding with a few rows of plain weaving.

DIRECTIONS FOR MAKING THE GUIANA 2–2 BRAID

Another interesting 2–2 braid, much easier to manipulate than the Mexican one, is one made in the northern part of South America by the Indian women of the Guianas. They carry their babies in slings braided this way. The appearance of the braid is practically identical to the Hopi 3–3 braid; see Fig. 145, right belt.

There should be an uneven number of warp yarns for this braid. They are usually arranged in pairs of alternating colors with one extra warp included. A suggested arrangement is: 1 white; 2 red; 2 white; 2 red; 2 white; etc. The yarns are put on the loom in this order from right to left. For the belt described below, 17 pairs of each color are used; with the extra yarn, a total of 69 warp yarns is needed. The general directions given for the use of shed sticks apply to this braid.

Before beginning the braid, make three rows of basket weaving at each end of the loom as follows: Starting from the right, drop one warp, pick up two warps, drop two, and continue thus across the warp. Open the shed the length of the warp and put in a weft yarn at each end of the loom. For the second row, pick up one warp, drop two, pick up two, etc., across the loom; again put in a weft yarn at each end of the loom. Make one more row of this weaving, dropping one, picking up two, etc., and then begin the braiding.

1. Slip the fingers of the left hand into the last basket weave shed. The outside warp on the right should be in the down position. Push the *two outside top right* warps *toward the right* and in the space thus made pick up the two outside bottom right warp yarns. Drop the two top warps below the fingers of the right hand and lift the two bottom warps above the fingers of that hand.

2. Push the next two top warps, the third and fourth from the right, toward the right and pick up the corresponding pair of bottom warps. Drop the top pair.

Note: The top pairs always cross over a bottom warp and *go down as pairs,* but the bottom pairs are always split; the right one of the bottom pair is picked up to become the left one of the pair at the top; the left one is crossed under a top pair to become the right one of the pair at the top.

3. When the shed is finished, transfer it from the right to the left hand; disregarding the outside bottom warp on the second row of braiding, pick up the second warp from the right on the bottom. Pass the *two top warps toward the left* over the third bottom warp from right. The third bottom warp is also picked up and the two top warps are pushed to the left and dropped beneath the fingers of the right hand. The warp now stands one down, two up, two down. Continue across the row so that two are up, two are down, etc.

   Note: The pattern for this row is as follows: the first two top pairs of warp yarns on the right of the shed are always pushed to the left and go down in pairs; the bottom warp pairs are again split as in 2 above, but in the opposite direction. The left warp of a pair on the bottom is picked up to become the right warp of a pair on the top; the right bottom warp passes under and to the right of the upper pair to become the left warp of a top pair. When the warps are all crossed on the row, transfer the shed from the right to the left hand.

4. On the third row repeat 1 and 2 and on the fourth row repeat 3. When the center of the length of warp is reached, put in a few rows of basket weaving, using a tapestry needle for it.

DIRECTIONS FOR MAKING A HOPI 3–3 BRAID (A DIAGONAL TWILL)

The 3–3 braiding technique is a favorite of the Hopi Indians. It is used by the men to weave the white wedding sashes for their brides. Braids of this type have been found in ancient graves at Paracas Cavernas in Peru.

The 3–3 braids are made by lifting three warps up and pushing three down. The braids have a particularly interesting feature: in addition to the diagonal direction of the warp, which forms diamond patterns as the colors cross, there is also a vertical pattern composed of chevronlike stripes. (See Fig. 145, right belt.) These are more apparent in a braid of one color than in a multicolored braid.

The color sequences for the 3–3 braids should be arranged in multiples of three with one extra yarn added. A suggested color arrangement for a belt is 1 white, 12 white, 12 black, 12 turquoise. Put these yarns on the loom in a right to left direction. Yarns of one color may be put on the loom as a continuous warp.

The general directions for braiding with shed sticks apply here also.

291

Before beginning to braid, make three rows of three up and three down plain weaving, as follows: on the first row, drop the first warp, pick up three, drop three, etc. across the warp. Open the shed the entire length of the warp and put a weft yarn in each end of the shed thus made. On the second row, pick up one, drop three, pick up three, etc., across the warp, again putting in a weft yarn in each end of the shed. On the third row, repeat the first row.

1. To start the braid, slip the fingers of the left hand into the last weave shed made. The outside warp on the right should be in the down position.

2. Now push the *three top right warps to the right* and pick up the three right bottom warps in the space thus made, lifting them above the fingers of the right hand. Drop the three top warps beneath the fingers of that hand. Push the second group of three top warps over to the right and pick up three bottom warps—the fourth, fifth, and sixth on the bottom of the original shed. Drop the top three. The pattern to this point will be three down, three up, three down, three up, counting from right to left. Continue across the row and when finished put the shed sticks in the front and back of the shed. Transfer the shed from the right to the left hand.

3. On the second row, the process is the reverse of the first row. The top warps are now shifted *to the left*, and the bottom warps are split and passed to the right as follows: Push the first three top right warps *to the left* and, disregarding the first right outside bottom warp, pick up the next three bottom warps and put them over the fingers of the right hand. The top three are then dropped under the fingers of the right hand. Continue across the row, picking up three and dropping three, and transferring the yarns from the left to the right hand.

   Note: The three warps in each top group always go down together as a group. On the first row, they go down to the right, and on the second row to the left, of the bottom warps picked up. The three warps in the bottom groups are always split. On the first row, the two right warps are lifted to become the two left warps of a top group; the left warp of the original bottom group is lifted to become the right warp of another set, the next group of three on the top row. On the second row, the three bottom warps are split in the reverse direction: that is, the two left warps of the bottom being picked up to become the two right warps of a top group of three, and the right bottom warp passes to the right under a top group of three and is lifted to become the left warp of another top group of three.

When the three bottom right warps are in the extreme right position on the loom, the outside warp farthest to the right is always disregarded—that is, it is never picked up when undertaking the next row of braiding.

4. Repeat steps 1, 2, and 3, continuing until the center of the length of warp has been reached. Then weave a few rows of three up and three down plain weaving to match that made at the beginning. This will probably have to be undertaken with the help of a tapestry needle.

MESHWORK

One of the most interesting of the ancient textile techniques is that generally called meshwork, though it is also known as sprang-work, knotless netting, net, interlocking, and bobbin lace. Examples of it are to be found in many museums. On display in the Cinquantenaire Museum in Brussels is the photograph of a linen mesh bag of an Early Dynastic period; one writer (104) has suggested that it was made with bobbins.[2] A net bobbin dated *ca.* 2000 B.C. is in the Egyptian collection of New York's Metropolitan Museum; it is similar to a lace bobbin in appearance. M. Bixio, excavating at Claterna, near the old Roman city of Bologna, came upon a set of bone bobbins lying in pairs (104) which could have been used for mesh making.

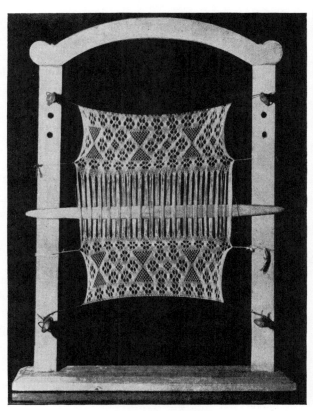

Fig. 147. Meshwork Frame. The meshwork on this frame resembles bobbin lace. (From Gertrude Whiting, *Tools and Toys of Stitchery*, Columbia University Press, 1928.)

Some fine meshwork has come from ancient Peru. How it was made is not always clear. In the Columbia University collection of Paracas Cavernas artifacts the author found some 200 little sticks about 3 inches long, each of which had a strand of yarn

[2] This is not necessarily true, since some elaborate meshwork made in the finger technique is illustrated in *Egyptish Vlechtwerk* (111).

NONWOVEN FABRICS—THE SINGLE-ELEMENT PROCESSES

wedged in the end. These sticks may have served as bobbins for meshwork. A center chain in some pieces indicates a method similar to that of Fig. 147.

Paintings on early Greek vases show women making open mesh by a similar process. Instead of using bobbins, they are working on small frames which appear to be about 12 by 18 inches in size (*101*). (See Fig. 147.) A frame of this type was found in an ancient Viking burial site, the Osberg ship burial, dated at about A.D. 800–840 (*101*).

It should thus be evident that a mesh fabric can be constructed by various methods and with different types of tools and equipment. When it is made either with or without the help of shed sticks, on either two-stick looms or small frames, the process is somewhat related to braiding; but when it is made on a lace pillow with the help of bobbins, the process resembles bobbin lace. Meshwork made on a large rectangular frame with the help of a small weft shuttle is known as knotless netting. The techniques referred to above are described elsewhere in this book, under the various related processes.

MESHWORK MADE WITH SHED STICKS

The meshes described below are made on two-stick looms with the help of shed sticks.

DIRECTIONS FOR MAKING A 1–1 MESH

The 1–1 mesh can be made by two entirely different processes, with the help of shed sticks as described below, and by the knotless netting technique, described later in this chapter.

A 1–1 mesh has tremendous stretchability. The Indians of Mexico use it for market bags and hammocks. One of their mesh bags made of sisal fiber is illustrated in Fig. 148.

The colored yarns for this type of meshwork should be selected and arranged in groups of two or four. The following color arrangement makes an effective belt: 2 blue; 2 white; 4 blue; 6 white; 4 red; 6 white; 4 blue; 2 white; 2 blue. The general directions for using a shed stick in braiding and meshwork (p. 285) apply here, and should be reviewed before starting the meshwork.

1. Pick up the warp to form the sheds and make a few rows of plain weaving, ending with the outside right bottom warp in the down position. Slip the fingers of the left hand from left to right into the last weave shed made. Start the mesh by picking up the yarns at the right

and putting them over the fingers of the right hand as follows: Push the right outside top warp to the right over and across the bottom outside warp, pick up that bottom right warp in the space thus made, and drop that first top right warp. Continue across the warp yarns, dropping a top warp *beneath* the fingers of the right hand and lifting a bottom warp *above* them. When the row is finished, slip shed sticks into the front and back of the shed.

2. Repeat the above procedure for the second row.

3. On the third row, the top right warp is pushed to the *left* and the *second* bottom warp is picked up, the first one being left down. Continue across the loom picking up a warp and dropping one until the row is finished. Again slip shed sticks into the front and back of the shed.

4. Repeat this procedure on the fourth row. *Note that the first outside bottom warp is still left floating.*

5. Repeat steps 1, 2, 3, and 4. Note that the top warp goes twice to the right and twice

Fig. 148. 1–1 Meshwork. A market bag from Oaxaca, Mexico. The top of the bag is done in needle looping (knotless needle netting). The bag is shown upside down in order to show pattern to advantage.

to the left. When it goes to the left, it crosses over the *second* bottom warp, which is picked up; the outside bottom warp is left floating. When the center of the length of the warp is reached, finish with a few rows of tabby weaving, using a tapestry needle if necessary.

DIRECTIONS FOR MAKING A MEXICAN (AND SWEDISH) 2–2 MESH

Pairs of colored yarns or groups of yarns in even numbers should be selected for this mesh. (See Fig. 145, center of left belt.) A belt may of course be made in any color harmony selected. Again, the general directions for braiding with shed sticks apply and should be reread before starting the mesh.

1. Weave several rows of tabby weaving, ending with the outside warp on the right in the *up* position. Slip the fingers of the left hand from left to right into the last weave shed. Push the three top right warps to the right, bring up the right outside bottom warp in the space left, and drop the first three below the fingers of the right hand; the bottom one is now above the fingers. Continue across the row, dropping a top warp and picking up a bottom warp. When the left margin is reached, there will be three warps on the bottom; these are raised together.

2. There will now be three warps below the fingers on the right margin of the warp and three above them on the left margin. This grouping must be corrected. Since the warp is all on the right hand at this point, the correction will first be made on the left side of the warp. To do this, take the outside left margin warp, bring it to the right over the next warp, push it down between the second and third warps from the left, and place it beneath the fingers of the right hand. This correction is made only on this row; after this time, no corrections are necessary.

3. Now transfer the entire warp shed to the left hand and correct the three bottom warps on the right side. Take the outside bottom warp, cross it *under* the next (the second) bottom warp, bring it up between the second and third bottom warps, and place it over the fingers of the left hand. The corrections are now complete; starting at the right, the warp has one down, one up all across the shed. Slip shed sticks into the front and back of the shed.

4. To make the second row of mesh, slip the fingers of the left hand into the last shed made. Push the two top right warps to the right, picking up the outside bottom right warp in the space made. Drop the two top warps below the fingers of the right hand and lift the bottom warp above the fingers of the right hand. Continue across the row, dropping one top warp and lifting one bottom warp. Again set in the two shed sticks.

5. To make the third row, slip the fingers of the left hand into the last shed and push the top right warp to the right, over the two bottom right warps, and pick up the outside bottom right warp in the space made. Continue across the warp, dropping a top warp and lifting a bottom warp. Set in the two shed sticks.

6. Repeat steps 4 and 5 until the mesh is finished. Note that when a row starts two down it ends with the two up. The process is two over one to begin one row, one over two to begin the next row, then two over one, etc. When the center of the length of warp is reached, finish

296

it off with a few rows of tabby weaving, using a tapestry needle to help put in the weft.

MESH MADE WITH BOBBINS

DIRECTIONS FOR MAKING A SIMPLE BOBBIN "WARP" MESH

Lace bobbins are used to make this simple mesh or knotless net. (See Fig. 169.) Each warp is attached at the back of the "loom" to a bar, passed over a drum, and weighted down in front of the weaver with a bobbin. These yarns can be stabilized by having them pass over a revolving drum with projecting pegs spaced in the same diamond pattern as the mesh; the mesh is formed over the pegs, and the action of the drum is controlled with a rachet wheel and dog. An easier method for making a narrow mesh is to work on a hard lace pillow, using strips of cardboard or lightweight wood as gages over which the rows of twists are made; pins can be used to stabilize the meshes as formed. After several rows of mesh are made the gages are withdrawn. A simple net is made as follows.

1. Twist each pair of warp yarns together twice all the way across the warp. This is done by throwing the two bobbins over one another twice in the same direction.
2. On the next row, separate the two warps just twisted together and combine each with one warp of an adjacent pair—the right one with the left warp of the adjacent pair to the right, and the left one with the right warp of the pair to the left. Twist each of these pairs together twice by throwing the bobbins over each other.
3. Recombine the original pairs and twist them together twice.
4. Repeat until the fabric is finished. End by knotting the pairs together.

A 1–1 "weft" mesh is described under Knotless Netting, page 315. Fabric made by this process can be identical to the 1–1 warp mesh described above.

2. Looping Techniques

Sometimes we become so involved with one textile technique that we fail to notice its close relationship to others. For example, such entirely different tools are used for knitting, crocheting, and needle looping that we often overlook the relationship between these single-element processes. Fabrics made by these processes have only a weft, or are made of horizontally aligned yarns which pass from side to side across the fabric; they do not have the warp and weft of woven fabrics. Knitting, crocheting, and needle

297

looping, then, have three things in common: they are all looping processes, they are all single-element processes, and they are all structured solely of horizontally aligned or "weft" yarns.

The tools used for these processes differ according to the technique employed, each being specific to a particular method. Blunt sewing needles, known as tapestry needles, are used for most half-hitch looping; knitting needles and crochet hooks are used for knitting and crocheting respectively; and lace bobbins and shed sticks are used for making several varieties of knotless netting. The first three of these tools are used for weft-structured loop work and the last two for warp-structured loop work. Each technique is described briefly here, but no detailed instructions are given for specific articles, since many pamphlets on knitting and crocheting are available in the art needlework sections of department stores.[3]

KNITTING

There seems to be no general agreement as to the origin of knitting. One of the earliest known examples, a small piece of tan wool fabric, dated at *ca.* 200 A.D., was found at Dura-Europos near the Euphrates River. Knitted red sandal socks dated about 350 A.D., reputedly from Arabia, are on exhibit in the Victoria and Albert Museum, London. Some fine Arabian silk knitting made during the seventh to ninth centuries was found at Fustat. Ancient knitting needles are said to have had hooks on one end, resembling crochet hooks.[4]

The people of Europe became aware of the art of knitting at a rather early date. At least, two German authors (*94*) who studied this problem claim that knitting was introduced into Italy and Europe by the Arabs sometime around the fifth century A.D.[5] Since the first knitting guild in Paris was named after St. Fiacre, a Scotchman who died in Paris in 670 A.D., another theory is that he invented knitting (*113*). During the Middle Ages, knitting guilds controlled the manufacture of knitted goods; each guild member had to pass a rigid test which included an elaborate piece of pat-

---

[3] Crochet and knitting stitches of many kinds are described and specific instructions for many articles given in such manuals as: *Star Beginner's Manual*, The American Thread Company, New York; and *The Vogue Knitting (and Crocheting) Book*, Condé Nast Publications, New York.

[4] Mary Thomas, "Knitting," in *Chambers's Encyclopaedia*, Oxford University Press, New York, 1950. Her information was taken from: *The Excavations at Dura-Europos conducted by Yale University, and the French Academy of Inscriptions and Letters. Final Report IV, Part II: The Textiles,* by R. Pfister and Louisa Bellinger, Yale University Press, New Haven, 1945.

[5] By communication with Regina A. van Bültzingelowen who, with Dr. Edgar Lehmann, is publishing *Nichtgewebte Textilien vor 1400*, Verlag dr. ell, Tübingen, Germany.

tern knitting. Hand knitting has been a favorite art of the peasant folk of Europe ever since that period.

At the present time many Indian peoples of the Western Hemisphere work in the knitting technique. The Pueblo Indians of the Southwest knit leggings (41), the Guatemalan Indians of Solola and other villages knit underarm bags (see Fig. 149), and the Indians of the high Andes knit stocking caps and sweaters (see Fig. 150). The art of knitting may well have been taught to these Indians by the Spanish; however, since most of their designs are definitely non-Spanish, the origin of knitting on the Western Hemisphere may well be questioned. Pseudo-knitting, which closely resembles regular knitting in appearance, if not in technique, was made by the ancient peoples of Peru.[6] (See p. 303.)

The word "cnyttan" was mentioned in England in 1492. Nearly a century later, in 1589, the knitting of stockings by machine methods commenced in Nottingham. Reverend William Lee is reported to have invented the machine. Other English developments include a ribbing device invented in 1758, a warp-knitting machine invented in 1775 by a Mr. Crane, and a circular knitting machine invented in the nineteenth century.

Knitting, both by hand and machine, has been a very important textile process in the United States. In the early part of the eighteenth century Mennonites established a stocking knitting industry in Germantown, Pennsylvania, using stocking frames brought from Germany. Another small knitting factory, known as the Wakefield Mill, was established in Germantown by one Thomas Fisher. Many English knitters came from Nottingham and Leicester to work in the Fisher Factory and in other knitting mills. Machine knitting processes have come a long way since these early beginnings. In the present century, the invention of tricot knitting and advances made in the process have greatly improved the quality of machine knitted fabrics.

KNITTING METHODS

Knitting may be divided structurally into two classes, warp or tricot knitting and weft knitting. The former type must be done by machinery; loops formed in the warp are similar to those of a crocheted chain, but they are connected from side to side and diagonally by accessory yarns.

In weft knitting—the regular hand knitting process—knitting needles are used to hold and to loop the yarn, which is carried back and forth across the fabric in a horizontal direction. Various types of weft knitting are listed and described below.

---

[6] Gayton (23) quoted Crawford as saying, "knitting was common in ancient Peru." The reference may have been to needle knitting or pseudo-knitting.

Knitting with Knitting Needles

Weft knitting is customarily done with knitting needles. These needles come in various lengths and sizes, are made of various materials, and are finished with one or two pointed ends. On standard needles one end is pointed; two of them are needed for flat knitting. Three double-pointed needles are usually used in knitting socks, and circular double-pointed steel needles are used for knitting tubular skirts.

In hand knitting a weft yarn is carried across the fabric and looped, by means of a knitting needle, into previously looped stitches held on a second knitting needle. Each new stitch or loop made on one needle releases a loop from the other, and the released loop is automatically locked into a chain stitch. (See Fig. 149.) The process is further described at the end of this section.

Fig. 149. Knitting from Guatemala. This interesting pattern comes from Solola, Guatemala.

Knitting Spools and Circular Knitting Frames

Knitted tubing, done without needles, can be made on spools, on circular frames, or on oval frames. The yarns are held on a row of pegs which project from and surround the center opening of the spool or frame. Wooden pegs are easiest to work with, but since it is impossible to drive wooden pegs in a spool, finishing nails must be hammered around the spool's center opening.

Knitting spools and frames are used as follows: A yarn is wound around the circular enclosure, passing around each of the pegs from right to left in a counterclockwise movement; it goes across the inside, around the outside, and again across the inside of each peg. *These crosses must face the inside opening on the frame.* After the first circuit, the yarn is carried once again around the enclosure in the same manner as before, making two loops

300

Fig. 150. Knitting from Peru. Upper left, detail of a cap from the high Andes; pattern yarns float on the back. Upper right, detail of a sweater in natural llama wools; from Huancayo. Lower right, detail of a natural colored vicuna wool sweater from the southern Andes of Peru. The pattern of the knitting is reversible; like double cloth, the colors on the opposite side are in reverse combinations.

around each peg. Using a stylus or a crochet hook, lift each bottom loop over the top of the peg and let it drop to the inside of the spool, onto the "necks" or crosses of the top loops. A new row of loops is then formed, and the lower loops again lifted over the new loops, over the pegs, and dropped inside the spool. As the work progresses, a column of tubular knitting drops down the center of the spool or circular frame.

Knitting on Straight Frames

A heavy, double-faced fabric may be knitted between two boards set about 1/3 of an inch apart parallel to one another in a frame. A row of upright projecting pegs is driven in along each edge of the inside opening. Starting at the left side of the frame, the yarn is carried diagonally from side to side across the center opening, passing around every other peg on both sides of the frame: that is, one peg is wound with yarn and the next peg is left free, on both sides and across the entire frame. The yarn passes around the pegs on one board in a clockwise direction and on the other in a counterclockwise direction. The crosses in the yarn must be on the inside of the pegs—that is, facing the inside of the frame. When the end of the row is reached, the yarn is returned across the frame in the same manner, except that this time it is carried around the pegs that were omitted on the previous passage. When this is finished, another complete circuit is made over and back across the frame. There should now be two loops on every peg on the frame. At this point, use a stylus or crochet hook to pull each loop on the bottom row over the one above it on the top row and then over the top of the pegs, where it is released or dropped onto the "necks" or crosses of the top loops. The process of winding the pegs and releasing the loops is continued until the fabric is finished. Note that different procedures can be used to wind the yarn onto the pegs, resulting in different knitted effects. A knitting machine can now be purchased for this type of work. (See Fig. 151.)

Mechanical Knitting Frames

A hand knitting machine known as the Texilia,[7] invented in Italy, resembles two parallel bars, each equipped with a border of small close-set hooks along one side. One bar is stationary and the other is fastened to the loom with pivot arms which can lift or lower it. At its left end is a crank or lever. (See Fig. 151.) The hooks on the two bars dovetail; those on the

---

[7] The Texilia is distributed by Jacob Goldfarb and Company, New York. Necchi-Elna and Pfaff, sewing machine companies, are distributors for knitting machines made in Switzerland.

movable bar can slip between those on the stationary bar and ensnare a strand of yarn. These bars are about 24 inches long and 4 inches wide.

This knitting device is used as follows: A length of yarn is thrown entirely across the stationary bar in front of the hooks. The lever is then lifted and the yarn is pulled into loops by the hooks on the movable bar. Another yarn is thrown along the first bar in front of the hooks, the lever is again raised, and the hooks of the movable bar pull the first loops over those just formed. A row of knitting is made very rapidly by this process.

Fig. 151. Knitting Machine. Woman using knitting frame, the "Texilia." (Manufactured by Negri Freres, Milano, Italy.)

Pseudo-Knitting or Needle Knitting

This is a looping process which is actually a knotless-netting technique, though it is sometimes mistaken for regular knitting. However, neither the structure of a pseudo-knit fabric nor the process used is the same as that of regular knitting. In pseudo-knitting the yarns cross beneath each loop formed as a result of the half-hitch stitch used. Then, too, pseudo-knitting is made with a tapestry needle threaded with yarn; it can be duplicated on knitting needles by reversing the regular direction of yarning over. If the stitch forms a three-dimensional fabric, it is a looping technique; if made upon and attached to a fabric, it is an embroidery technique. The terms *free pseudo-knitting* and *embroidered pseudo-knitting* should distinguish the two types. Because of its use in ancient Peru, it is called the Paracas pseudo-knitting stitch. (See page 355.)

Pseudo-knitting is done as follows: a row of small backstitches with long loops between them is sewed across the edge of a fabric, or a set of half-hitch loops is made over a cord. Upon either of these foundations, and around the back of the necks of the loops thus made, a second row of loops is coiled, again using the backstitch or the half-hitch stitch. When the yarn is carried across the fabric from left to right, the looping is counterclockwise; when the yarn is carried from right to left, the looping behind the previous row of loops must be clockwise. (See Fig. 157, No. 4.)

In very ornate pseudo-knitting, several tapestry needles are used, each threaded with a different colored yarn; the colored yarns are manipulated to form small pattern areas in the work. The loops of the various colors interlock, so that a solid fabric results, and the joints between the colors are not visible. Between the pattern areas, the yarns are floated on the back of the fabric when not being used. The ancient Peruvians have become famous for their achievements in this technique; they used it to depict figures of men, animals, and plants. The work looks very much like that in Fig. 149.

KNITTING STITCHES

A number of different knitting stitches can be used singly or combined to give various effects to knitted fabrics. There are, however, three stitches which are considered basic to the work: (1) plain, in which the wales appear on right side of the fabric and the courses on the wrong side; (2) purl, in which the courses appear on both sides; and (3) rib, in which the wales appear on both sides of the fabric. Other stitches are more or less variations of these three. Directions for these and other knitting stitches are given below:

Casting On Stitches

The number of stitches needed per inch for a piece of work will vary according to the size of the needle, the size of the yarn, and the firmness of the work desired. A small swatch should therefore be made to determine the number of cast-on stitches which will be needed for a given task.

Select a larger knitting needle for casting on than will be used for the rest of the knitting. Two methods of casting on are described below.

Method I. A slip-knot loop is made in the end of the yarn and slipped onto a knitting needle. The needle is then transferred to the left hand. The point of a second needle, held in the right hand, forms the second stitch in this way: The point of the right needle passes through the slip-knot on the left needle, moving from left to right and from front to back. A yarn is then thrown over the point of the right needle and drawn back with it; this loop now rests on the shaft of the right needle and it is transferred to the left needle by inserting the point of the left needle from right to left in the loop. Other cast-on stitches are formed in the same way, each new loop passing through the loop made last, and each in turn being transferred to the left needle.

Method II. Make a slip knot for the first stitch and half-hitch knots for the remainder of the stitches, slipping each one as made over the point of a knitting needle held in the left hand. To make half-hitch knots, form a counterclockwise loop in the yarn by wrapping the yarn toward you on top of the coil and transfer this loop to the knitting needle.

Knit Stitch

This stitch is also called plain stitch, garter stitch, and plain knitting. It is the standard knitting stitch. In regular flat knitting, when the stitching moves back and forth across the fabric, the knit stitch is horizontally ribbed on both sides of the fabric. (See Fig. 152A.) In circular knitting, it is vertically ribbed on one side and horizontally ribbed on the other.

In making this stitch the yarn is kept at the back of the work. The knitting needle, holding the right number of cast-on stitches, is held in the left hand. Hold the last

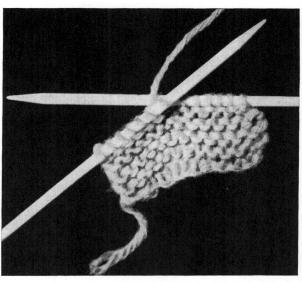

Fig. 152A. Plain Knitting.

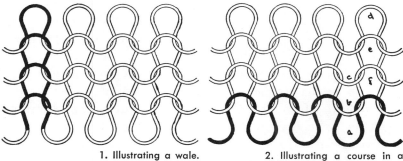

1. Illustrating a wale.

2. Illustrating a course in a plain circular knit fabric.

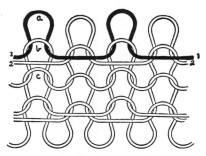

3. Illustrating a "run-resist" circular knit fabric.

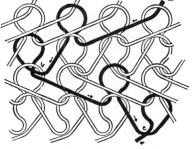

4. Illustrating a simple warp (one bar) tricot fabric.

Fig. 152B. Detail Studies of Knitting Stitches. 1, 2, and 3 are made by weft-knitting; 4 is a detail of a machine-made, warp-knitted, tricot fabric. (Courtesy, American Bemberg.)

NONWOVEN FABRICS—THE SINGLE-ELEMENT PROCESSES

cast-on stitch near the point of the needle by the index finger of the left hand. Hold the free needle like a pencil between the thumb and index finger of the right hand. Place the yarn over the index finger, under the third finger, and over the fourth finger. Bring the two needles together. Insert the point of the needle held in the right hand from left to right into the front of the end cast-on stitch, the last one made, and bring the point out of the back of the stitch. Pass the yarn first under the point of the right needle, wrap it over the point, and draw it through the stitch that is on the left needle. Slip the old stitch off the left needle onto the neck of the newly made stitch. Carrying the yarn over the needle is called "yarning over."

This new stitch is retained on the right needle. Continue across the knitting, forming new stitches, until all of the cast-on stitches have been removed from the first needle. Turn the needles around and form new stitches on the next row, removing the stitches from the left needle one at a time as just described. Repeat the process until the knitting is finished.

Purl Stitch

When the purl stitch is carried back and forth across a piece of flat knitting, the resulting fabric is horizontally ribbed on both sides. In circular knitting, the purl stitch makes a fabric which is vertically ribbed on the front and horizontally ribbed on the back.

In making the purl stitch the yarn is kept in front of the work. Holding the work, or the cast-on stitches, in the left hand, insert the right needle from right to left into the front of the first stitch, wrap the yarn over and under the point, draw the loop formed through the stitch on the left needle from front to back, and slip the stitch on the left needle off onto the neck of the new stitch which is now on the right needle. Continue across the row of stitches on the left needle until all the work is on the right needle. Turn the work around and repeat for the next row.

VARIATIONS IN KNITTING

Stockinette Stitch

This stitch produces a flat vertically ribbed knitted fabric with a horizontal ridge on the back. It is made by knitting one row and purling the next. On circular work, the knitting progresses continuously around.

Rib Stitch

Double ridges separated by deep grooves, called double reversed ribs, are accomplished by knitting two, purling two on both sides of the fabric. The order must be reversed in the return direction to maintain the ribs. The yarn is brought to the front for purling and placed to the back for knitting.

Tuck Stitch

Two or more stitches on the left needle are combined and dropped into one stitch on the right needle.

Open Stitch

Yarn is wound twice around the right needle, so two loops in place of one are formed on it. On the next row, the double wound loop is picked up as only one stitch.

Pattern Knitting

Bobbins of different colors are used for pattern work, and the yarn from each bobbin is incorporated into the knitting as that color is needed for the design. The design appears on the front and the yarns float on the back of the fabric from pattern to pattern.

Northern Europeans are very skillful knitters of pattern work. Sweaters from Austria, Norway, and Sweden are especially popular with skiers. The Indians in the highland of Peru and Guatemala also make attractive knitted bags and sweaters, using ancient Inca and Mayan designs in their work.

Argyle Knitting

Argyle bobbins each carry a different color, but since the colors are kept in separate vertical columns, no floats appear on the back of the fabric.

Cable Stitch

This stitch requires a third needle, a double-pointed one, which makes a separate piece of knitting on top of another similar piece of knitting, forming a twisted cord on the surface of the fabric. Use an even number of stitches in multiples of ten, plus four extra stitches. Working on the wrong side for the first row, knit four, purl six; repeat as many times as needed; end with knit four. On the second row, purl four, knit six; repeat as many times as needed; end with purl four. Continue alternating in this way for seven rows. On the eighth row, purl four, then slip the next three stitches to a double pointed needle and hold them in back of the work. Knit three on the regular needle; knit three on double-pointed needle; repeat this series across the row; end with purl four. Continue to repeat rows one through eight.

Moss or Seed Stitch

Using an even number of stitches knit one, purl one, alternately across row. On the next row, purl one, knit one, alternately across. Alternate these two rows for the rest of work.

Lock Stitch or Tricot Knitting

In this complex structure two or more warps running in different directions are knitted together; one is the regular warp and appears as regular knitting; the others run diagonally and/or vertically across the fabric and interlock into the first. Unraveling or runs are prevented by this means. This type of knitting is usually machine-made.

Milanese Stitch

This work also has two sets of warp, knitted simultaneously but in opposite directions. Like the tricot, it is also usually machine-made.

CROCHETING

Crocheting, like knitting, is a looping process; it is sometimes defined as "knitting with a hook." In crocheting, the loops are made with a hook, one at a time. Since a hook is used to form the loops, the stitch is more versatile than knitting—a crocheted chain can meander at will over or around the pattern. (See Fig. 156.)

Little can be said concerning the history of crochet work, for little is recorded on the subject. Ancient braids and cords have been found which were made by finger crocheting. One method of twining is based upon the use of a chained weft; this is a very ancient method of fabrication. During the Middle Ages crocheting was known as nun's work, because it was popularly used by nuns in convents. In 1820, the people of Ireland began making a lovely crocheted lace which is now known as Irish crochet (see p. 340).

NAMES OF CROCHET STITCHES

The most important crochet stitches are listed below, but only the basic stitches are described here. For information concerning other stitches, refer to a manual on crocheting; see the footnote on page 298.

1. Chain
2. Single crochet
3. Half-double crochet
4. Double crochet
5. Treble crochet
6. Quadruple crochet
7. Filet mesh
8. Ribbed afghan stitch

9. Pineapple stitch	15. Bean or popcorn stitch
10. Moss stitch	16. Rib stitch
11. Moss afghan stitch	17. Picot stitch
12. Double-moss afghan stitch	18. Slipper stitch
13. Cross-stitch afghan stitch	19. Star stitch
14. Shell stitch	20. Cluster stitch

GENERAL DIRECTIONS FOR CROCHETING

A crocheted chain may be hand-chained or it may be made with the help of a crochet hook. To make it with the fingers, first make a slip knot and draw a loop of yarn through it. Continue to draw another loop through each loop made until the chain is completed.

In order to produce the beautiful lacelike work we usually associate with crocheting, a crochet hook is needed. This is held in the right hand just as a pencil is held. The yarn is wrapped around the fingers of the left hand in a characteristic fashion. It passes under and around the little finger, over the ring finger, under the middle finger, and over the forefinger; it is then grasped between the thumb and the middle finger. The hook engages the part which stretches between the thumb and the index finger.

All crochet stitches are based upon variations of the single chain. When fine yarns are used and an intricate pattern is selected, the work may appear quite complicated. Directions for the basic stitches used in crocheting follow:

Chain Stitch

Make a slip knot in the yarn. Run the crochet hook through the loop of this slip knot, catch hold of the strand of yarn, pull it back through the loop, and leave it on the neck of the hook; as in knitting, this process is called yarning over. When this procedure is continued through every newly made loop, a chain results. The stitch is, therefore, called the chain stitch. The expression "chain one" is often used to mean "make a chain stitch."

Single Crochet

Make a single crocheted chain of the desired length. Starting back through the *second* loop of that chain, insert the hook, yarn over, and draw the yarn through the loop. There will now be two loops on the neck of the hook, one which was there originally and the one just made. Using the hook, pull a loop of yarn *through these two loops*. There will now be but one loop on the hook. Repeat this process through each loop along one edge of the original chain. At the end of each row chain one before returning across the next row.

309

Half-Double Crochet

This process is also called short double crochet. Make a single chain the length desired. Wrap the yarn once around the hook; there are now two loops on the hook. Turn back and insert the hook through the *third* loop on one side of the original chain; yarn over and pull the new loop onto the neck of the hook. There will now be three loops on the neck of the hook. Yarn over and draw the yarn through all three loops. There will now be but one loop on the hook. Repeat this process through each loop along one side of the entire chain. Chain two before returning for the next and succeeding rows.

Double Crochet

Make a single chain of the desired length. Wrap the yarn once around the hook and insert the hook in the *fourth* loop at one edge of the single chain. Yarn over and pull this loop through; there should now be three loops on the neck of the hook. (See Fig. 153.) Yarn over and draw the yarn through two of these loops; yarn over and draw the yarn through the remaining two loops. There is now but one loop on the hook. To start the second double-crochet stitch, again throw the yarn once around the hook; insert the hook in the next loop of the single chain, on the same side and beside the last stitch made. Repeat for all the stitches. When the end of the row is reached, chain three before returning back across the next row. Start each new row in the top of the second double crochet of the previous row.

Fig. 153. Double Crochet. (Courtesy, Mrs. Zelpha Moench.)

Treble Crochet

Make a single chain of the desired length. Wrap the hook twice with yarn and insert it in the fifth loop of the chain. Yarn over and pull the loop through. There should now be four loops over the neck of the hook. Yarn over and pull the yarn through two of them; yarn over and pull the yarn through two again; yarn over once more and pull the yarn through two loops. There is now but one loop over the hook. Continue in this manner through each loop along one side of the original chain. Before returning over the next row, chain four, beginning the work in the second and subsequent rows in the top of the second treble crochet of the previous row.

Filet Crochet

This interesting technique is achieved by making solid areas of double crochet on a square-mesh ground, also formed by bars of double crochet. (See Fig. 154.)

VARIATIONS OF CROCHET

The crochet technique encompasses several novel processes. Two of these are described below.

Hairpin or Maltesse Lace

Hairpin lace is a crocheted loop braid which is made over a metal hairpin-shaped frame (see Fig. 155). Whiting (113) calls this frame a fringing fork; sometimes it is called a staple, since it is staple-shaped. A wider rectangular crochet frame may also be used for this type of work. The width of the work depends on the width of the frame. A simple frame can be made by bending a 12-inch piece of heavy wire into a U-shaped staple. A clip across the open end will keep the yarn from slipping off. Hairpin lace is made as follows.

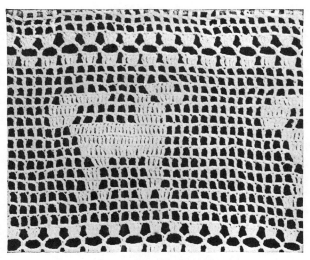

Fig. 154. Filet Crochet. This interesting work is from Cuenca, Ecuador.

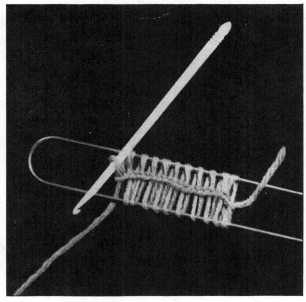

Fig. 155. Hairpin Frame.

1. Make a slip knot, place it over the left prong of the frame, and pull the knot to the center of the opening. Carry the yarn over and then under the right prong bringing it on the under side to the center of the opening. Place the hook under the top yarn of the loop on the left prong and draw a loop of the free yarn through it; yarn over and chain one. Slip

the hook out of this last loop, turn the frame over a half-turn toward the left, and pick up this same loop again on the other side.

2. Carry the hook under the top yarn of the loop on the left prong and pull a loop of the free yarn into a loop on the hook. There are now two loops on the hook. Yarn over and draw the yarn through both loops, forming a single crochet. Slip the hook out of the loop and again turn the frame over one half-turn toward the left. Pick up the loop again after the frame is turned. Repeat this process until the piece is finished.

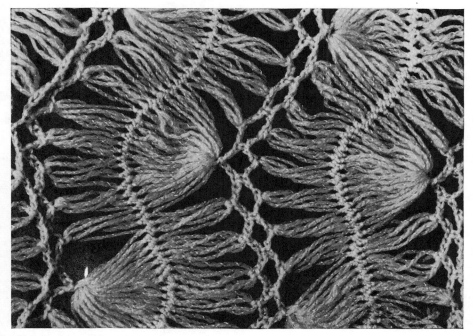

Fig. 156. Hairpin Lace. This pattern was made by Mrs. W. H. Leonard, Salt Lake City.

The crocheting is done first on one side of the frame and then on the other, as the frame is turned continuously toward the left; it is always done in the center of the top side of the frame. The free yarn always comes under the left edge and is always on the under side of the frame. The free yarn is wrapped around the little finger and carried over the index finger of the left hand as for regular crochet; with the left hand it is pulled taut against the left edge of the frame. The right hand holds the hook. Two stitches are made on each side of the frame after each turn; the first one holds the bottom free yarn in place and the second forms a single crochet by passing into the two loops on the hook. On large frames, the crochet

THE TEXTILE ARTS

hook is pulled through as the frame turns; on small frames, it is removed from a loop on one side of the work and replaced in the same loop after the frame is turned to the other side. The crocheting progresses toward the closed, or curved, end of the hairpin. As the work piles up on the frame, the clip at the bottom is removed and part of the work is pushed off the open end; the clip is then put in place again.

Several different stitches can be used in the formation of hairpin lace. (See Fig. 156.) Ornamental effects are produced by making supplementary rows of chain stitching around the center chain of the braid or lace while it is still on the frame. Strips of the hairpin lace may be crocheted together by a crocheted chain to form laces, shawls, stoles, bags, etc.

Daisy Medallions

A looped yarn "flower" can be constructed on a Daisy frame—a small round frame, bordered with projecting spokes which radiate from a center axis or lever. The yarn is carried around the entire frame, crisscrossing from side to side and going around the back of each spoke. Several rows of chain stitching are then made around and into the center of the flower to hold the yarn petals in place. When all is ready, the axis is pressed down, pulling the spokes in; this action releases the yarn flower.

Circular medallions made in this way, are often crocheted together to form various objects. Bags, belts, stoles, and place mats can be made by laying the flowers side by side and joining them with chain stitches.

NEEDLE LOOPING AND KNOTLESS NETTING

In studying fabrics made by early primitive peoples, we discover that looping techniques were among the first textile processes employed by man,[8] though we cannot be certain whether the word "net" in ancient writings refers to knotted net, knotless net, or some other textile technique. Isaiah spoke of "they that work in fine flax and *weave* networks" (19–9); and Homer wrote of veils of net *woven* of gold and worn by the early Aegeans (96). Since the only openwork *woven* fabric which could be called a net is gauze, could these men have been speaking of gauze, or the related leno weaving? Or were they speaking of meshwork, twining, loop work, bobbin net, or knotted net? We will actually have to find some of their "net" textiles before we know.

---

[8] See Amsden's (1) discussion of the basket-maker culture and O'Neale's (48) discussion of the early Nasca culture. This technique was also employed by the early Hopewell culture.

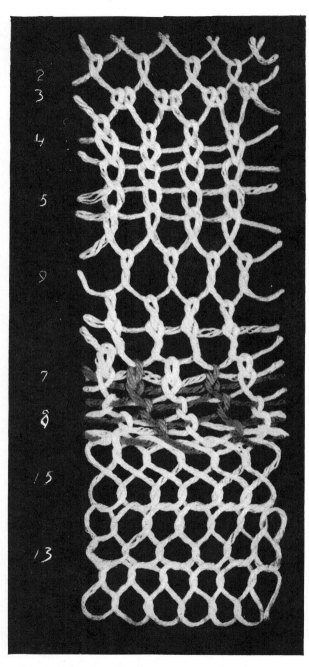

Fig. 157. Knotless Needle Netting. A description of these various needle-looping techniques is given in the text.

In archaeology needle looping processes are variously called half-hitch looping, coiling without foundation, knotless needle netting, or needle knitting—the latter is but one variety of the process. Fabrics formed by needle looping belong to the class containing a single-element structure, which was discussed at the beginning of this section. In needle looping, the weft—or yarn carried horizontally—is the "single element" that forms the structure of the fabric. It is usually necessary to use a tapestry needle to carry the yarn.

The loop used for most needle looping is the half-hitch. A half-hitch loop is one which crosses upon itself, resembling the upper three-fourths of the figure 8. (See Fig. 157, No. 2.) This stitch, which is used for most needle-made knotless netting, is much like the buttonhole stitch, except that the yarn is carried through previously formed loops of yarn instead of through the edge of a fabric; the top of the buttonhole stitch is the bottom of the needle-netting stitch.

Accessory weft yarns are sometimes used in the structure of this looping process, in which case the half-hitches pass around the accessory weft as well as back into a previous row of half-hitch loopings. Various knotless needle nets are listed in order of complexity and described. (See Fig. 157.)

SIMPLE NEEDLE-MADE MESH OR KNOTLESS NET

Type 1

Some meshes are made without the use of the half-hitch loop. In this simple meshing process, the cord or yarn is run through the loops of the stitches of the preceding row in a forward direction only, never twisted or crossed. This method simulates a 1–1 mesh as described on page 297. The yarn for this mesh is sometimes carried on a small shuttle instead of a tapestry needle.

SIMPLE HALF-HITCH LOOPING TECHNIQUES

Type 2: Simple Half-Hitch Looping

Half-hitches are made back into the free loops which hang from and between the half-hitches of the preceding row.

Type 3: Multiple Half-Hitch Looping

Two or more half-hitches are made into each free loop that hangs from and between the half-hitches on the preceding row.

Type 3-B

These half-hitches may be arranged in increasing numbers on progressive rows and in this way form patterns.

Type 3-C

Two half-hitches may be made to face one another, forming a lark's head knot.

Type 4: Pseudo-Knit Looping, also Called the Ceylon Stitch, and Needle Knitting

Half-hitches are made to encircle the back of the neck of half-hitches on the preceding row. (This method was also described under knitting.) As a variation of this stitch, the new stitch may encircle half-hitches which are back two or more rows. (See page 303.)

Type 5: Intra-Half-Hitch Looping

Half-hitches are carried through the half-hitches on the preceding row, intersecting them. As a variation, the new stitches may intersect half-hitches two or more rows back.

Type 6: Fagoting

Fagoting is a simple loop embroidery technique—a figure 8 stitch—related to the half-hitch looping. It is used for joining two edges of cloth to-   **315** gether. The stitch is made up of two loops, reversed in direction, one attached to one edge of the cloth and the other to the other edge. (See Fig. 179, No. 4.)

ALTERNATE TWO-STRAND HALF-HITCH LOOPING TECHNIQUES
Type 7

Any simple half-hitch looping techniques previously described can also be made with two alternating strands of cord or yarn. These may be of the same or different textures and colors. They may be carried entirely across the row, one at a time, or carried at varying lengths across one or more rows of the work.

Type 8

This is like Type 7, except that the two yarns are carried across the row simultaneously, crossing one another at every half-hitch. In a variation of this stitch, the two yarns alternately form half-hitches into the loops between the half-hitches of the preceding row, at the same time encircling the *two* loops which hang from the two half-hitches on the preceding row. (See Fig. 157.)

TWISTED HALF-HITCH LOOPING TECHNIQUES
Type 9

The yarn may be twisted once, twice, or three times around itself between half-hitches. Any of the half-hitch methods described may be treated this way. The various combinations possible are classified according to number of twists and type of loops: one such technique could be listed as "single twisting between single half-hitch looping."

INTERLOCKED HALF-HITCH LOOPING TECHNIQUES (CIRCULAR LOOPING)
Type 10: Single Half-Hitch Interlocking

In this stitch each half-hitch, after passing through the loops between half-hitches on the preceding row, loops or interlocks back into the adjacent half-hitch, the one just formed on this new row.

Type 11

The yarn, entering from the back, bisects the joint between the half-hitches on the preceding row; it then passes downward and interlocks into the adjacent half-hitch on the new row.

Type 12

Before the half-hitches on the same row interlock as in Type 10, they pass into the loops at the bases of the two half-hitches immediately above on the preceding row. The yarn goes into the bottom loop of the right half-hitch and out of the bottom loop of the left half-hitch.

REVERSED AND INTERLOCKED LOOPING TECHNIQUES

The following processes are concerned not so much with making half-hitches as with making reversed loops which interlace into one another and automatically form two half-hitches, each being a part of the other, but in reversed positions to each other. The process is similar to fagoting, only the loops are interlocked top and bottom.

Type 13: Hour-Glass Looping

The yarn is carried forward in a left to right direction, through the bottom loop of an hour-glass-shaped loop on the preceding row. It is then carried downward and interlocked into the bottom loop of the preceding hour-glass loop on the same row. It is then turned upward and interlocked into itself, before again passing into the bottom loop of the next hour glass on the preceding row.

Type 14

Like Type 13, except that the upper loop of each hour glass being formed passes through the bottom loops of two adjacent hour-glass structures on the preceding row.

Type 15: Complex Interlocked Hour-Glass Looping

In this very complex technique, the new hour-glass loops are made by first interlocking the bottom loop back into the bottom loop of an hour glass formed two or three stitches back on the same row. The rest of the hour glass is made as in Type 13.

Type 16: Figure 8 Looping

This is similar to hour-glass looping, except that the yarn is first taken in a downward direction from back to front into the bottom loop of the preceding figure 8 loop on the same row; it is then carried in an upward direction from front to back through the top loop of the same figure 8 loop, before continuing on through a bottom loop of the figure 8 on the previous row.

Type 17

Like Type 15, except that the loop passes through two adjacent bottom figure 8 loops on the preceding row.

Type 18: Complex Interlocked Hour-Glass and Figure 8 Looping

The top loops of either the hour-glass or the figure 8 structures are carried up and through the bottom loops of structures on two or more rows back instead of the preceding row.

COMPLEX COMBINED LOOPING PROCESSES
Type 19: Twisted Interlocked Looping

Many of the looping processes just described are varied by multiple twisting or by combining several types of loops, such as the single half-hitch, the hour-glass loop, and the twisted loop. (See Fig. 158.) In another combination, the yarn coming from a single half-hitch is reversed to form an hour-glass loop, and then twisted twice around the bottom loop of the previously made hour glass. Many other combinations are possible. (See Fig. 159.)

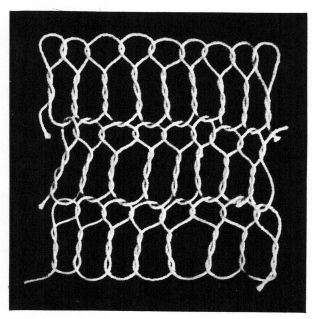

Fig. 158. Ancient Peruvian Netting. Twisted hour-glass needle netting found in Huaca Prieta excavation. (Courtesy, The American Museum of Natural History and Junius Bird.)

LOOP-KNOTTED TECHNIQUES
Type 20

One of the knotting processes made by the ancient Peruvians is closely related to the half-hitch looping technique. The work, done with a needle and heavy yarn, proceeds from left to right across a netting frame. The needle is carried from the back into a loop of yarn which hangs between the knots on the preceding row. It is then brought forward, carried to the left, taken around and across the back of the loop, and finally brought forward and inserted into the loop from front to back. When the yarn is pulled tight, a square or reef knot is made.

A square knot is also made by carrying the yarn into the loop on the preceding row from the front; it is then taken back toward the left, brought around forward, crosses the front of the loop, and is then inserted in the loop from back to front. The ancient Peruvians used both these knots; by insert-

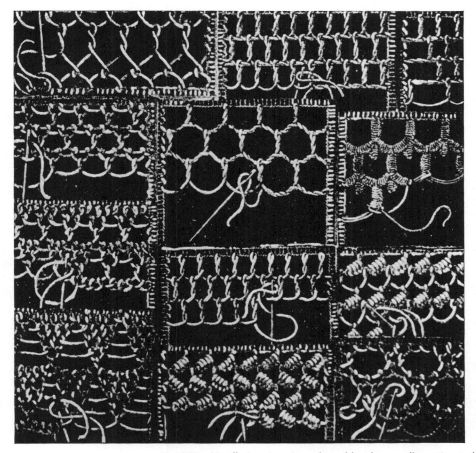

Fig. 159. Needle Looping. A number of knotless needle netting techniques are shown here. (From C. R. Clifford, *The Lace Dictionary*, Clifford & Lawton, 1913.)

ing pieces of yarn into such knot work they were able to make knotted pile fabric (*26*).

Type 21: Knotted Half-Hitch Stitch

After each half-hitch on the previous row has been made into a loop, the yarn is passed around the back of the half-hitch, encloses the two yarns of the half-hitch, and forms a loose knot. When this stitch is made in the edge of a fabric it is called the knotted blanket stitch.

Type 22: Knotted Diamond-Mesh

Fine knot work can be made with a needle and thread, in about the same manner that coarse knot work is made with a mesh pin and a netting needle.

319

The knots are formed in the loops between the knots in the preceding row, working from loop to loop as in half-hitch looping. This knotting technique was another achievement of the ancient Peruvians (*46*).

MACHINE-MADE KNOTLESS NET

Machine-made net and tulle are popularly used as dress fabrics. These machine-made knotless nets have both a warp and a weft, and closely resemble nets made by hand by warp-twisted twining. In machine-made net the weft

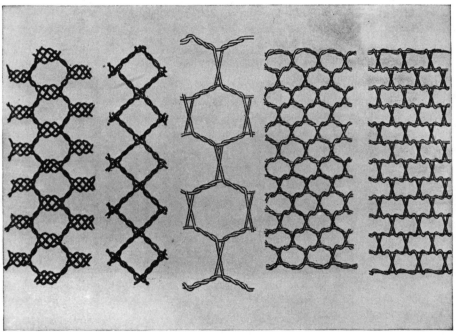

Fig. 160.   Machine-Made Knotless Netting. This is a combined warp-weft mesh.
(From C. R. Clifford, *The Lace Dictionary*, Clifford & Lawton, 1913.)

is arranged on bobbins set in two rows of carriages. These carriages are so manipulated that the weft yarns drop and twist around the warp yarns; then, going in opposite directions, the two carriages twist the weft yarns around each other. (See Fig. 160.)

The first steps toward making machine-made net (7) came in England. The first machinery for knitting hosiery had been invented by William Lee, in 1589. Nearly two centuries later, in 1758, Jedediah Strutt fashioned a net on this stocking machine and made ornamental clocks in stockings. Two years later net was being made without reference to stockings. In 1775, Crane in-

320

vented a warp knitting and webbing machine which was later adapted to the weaving of net patterns. John Heathcoat conceived several ideas which in 1808 culminated in the net machine. A year later he invented a wide bobbinette machine for net making which was entirely separate from the older stocking machine. Later he invented another bobbinette machine which operated in much the same way that bobbins are used to make pillow lace. At first only narrow edgings of bobbin net could be made on net machines, but after the machines were enlarged, it was possible to manufacture wider nets. The inventors next turned to lace making and in 1813, John Leavers and his brothers developed a lace-making machine; in 1837, they adapted the Jacquard loom to their machine.

3. Knot Work

Knot making was not only one of the first accomplishments of prehistoric people, but through the ages has never ceased to intrigue man's curiosity. The ancient Egyptians knew the art of knot making—King Tutankhamen's tomb door was tied closed with a sailor's knot. In ancient Greece the reef knot was called the knot of Hercules, in the belief that Hercules originated it. This knot is used on Mercury's staff. In the writings of Oribasius, Greek names were given for 18 kinds of knots used in surgery.

Many superstitions and myths have surrounded the art of knot making. The Koran states that the Prophet Mohammed was bewitched by a Jew who tied magic knots; when the Angel Gabriel found these knots in a well, Mohammed's illness was cured. During the Middle Ages persons were condemned to death in France and Scotland for practicing knot sorcery.

There are many, many types of knots.[9] Some of the better known are sailors' knots, builders' knots, fishermen's knots, and weavers' knots. Some of the knots used in weaving are illustrated in Fig. 23; others are shown in Fig. 122A and 122B.

KNOTTED NETTING

Primitive peoples were often dependent upon knotted fabrics for many of their needs. Excavations have uncovered ancient knot work made into fish nets, net bags, and other articles. The ancient Swiss lake-dwellers and others practiced knot making (100). The ancient Peruvians made intricate knotted fabrics (see Fig. 161A). "Nets of checker work" were spoken of as

[9] See *Webster's Unabridged Dictionary* for illustrations of various knots. Also see Graumont and Hensel (100).

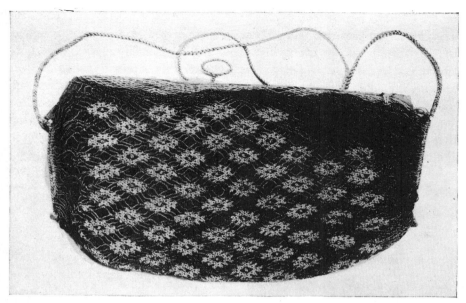

Fig. 161A. Knot Work from Ancient Peru. A bag or hairnet. Embroidery on a knotted net ground. (Courtesy, The American Museum of Natural History.)

decorating Solomon's temple (I Kings, 7–17). In 1913, Clifford found knotted network at an ancient site in Thebes, which he dated *ca.* 1000 B.C. The women of ancient Egypt wore knotted network called shebetz, sometimes ornamented with beads and charms, over their hair and breasts.

WARP-KNOTTED NETTING

The natives of South Sea Islands use simple knot work for making bags and grass skirts. (See Fig. 161B.) This work is based upon the knotting of warp fibers which hang from a cord, similar

Fig. 161B. Knot Work from the Tongan Island. Knotted fiber bag ornamented with shells.

to those on a warp-weighted loom. The yarns are knotted together in diamond-shaped meshes; sometimes shells and beads are incorporated. When correctly made, the knot used has a smooth band across the front surface of the strand. The knot is formed as follows: two warp strands are held together at the point where the knot is to be located; they are drawn up and over and toward the left of the double strand held in the fingers. A loop is formed and the two strands are pulled through the loop. The loop is then pulled tight into a knot. This is known as an overhand knot.

A warp-knotted fabric is made as follows:

1. Two adjacent warps are knotted together as described, then the next two are similarly knotted together, and the process is continued around or across the warp.
2. On the second row around, one warp is selected from each of two adjacent knots, and they, in turn, are knotted together. This is again repeated across the warp. (See Fig. 162.)
3. On the third row the original pairs are reunited and knotted together.
4. The process is repeated until the knotting is finished. A cardboard strip can serve as a gauge over which the warps are knotted.

WEFT-KNOTTED NETTING
Knotted Netting Made with Mesh Pin and Netting Needle

More often than not, native peoples make their fish nets by a weft-knotting process which requires the use of two netting tools, a mesh pin, and a net-

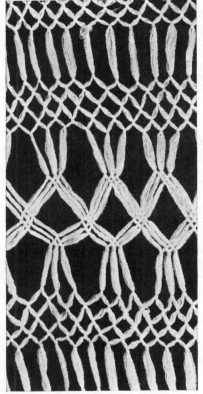

Fig. 162. Knotted Fringe. Detail of knotted fringe from Mexico.

ting needle. The mesh pin is a flat piece of polished wood about 6 inches long. The netting needle is a flat stick shuttle pointed at one end and with an opening in the center, from one end of which a spine projects. (See Fig. 163.) The netting needle should be slightly narrower than the mesh pin: for example, a 3/4-inch netting needle is used with a 1-inch mesh pin.

The netting needle is wound with weft as follows: The weft cord is carried lengthwise over the front of the needle, around the back of the spine, and back to the starting point. The needle is turned over and the same winding is made on the back. First one side and then the other side is wound until sufficient cord is on the needle.

323

Knot work is done on a simple netting frame, which consists of a removable rod held between two vertical supports; notches cut at the top of these supports hold the rod. The diameter and length of the rod and the size of the frame depend upon the type of work to be done. Large frames are needed for making fish nets, small ones for making bags.

A knotted net is made from left to right across the frame, working first on one side of the frame and then on the other. The process is as follows:

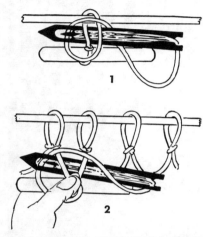

Fig. 163. Knot-Work Technique. (1) Netting needle and mesh pin in place for first row of knotted netting. (2) Position of these two tools on the second and subsequent rows.

1. Tie the end of the weft cord around the mesh pin. Holding the pin below the rod of the frame, a little lower than the width of the needle, carry the cord from the back of the pin to the back of the rod. Bring it forward over the rod and let it drop down in front of the rod and the pin. Hold the end of the cord against the pin with the thumb and throw the cord in a clockwise circular loop over the thumb. Pass the netting needle *under* the two strands of cord hanging from the rod and *over* the left end of the circular loop. (See Fig. 163.) Pull the loop up to a knot, holding the thumb in place as long as possible. The first knot is now on the mesh pin.

2. Preparatory to making the second knot, carry the cord down the face of and under the bottom of the mesh pin; take the cord up the back of the pin and over the top of the rod, from back to front as before. Drop the yarn down the front of the rod and the front of the mesh pin, and make a knot, using the same procedure as for the first knot.

3. Continue knotting across the frame until a sufficient number of knots has been made, slipping the finished knots off the end of the mesh pin as the work progresses.

4. To start the second row of knots, turn the rod around if the frame is small, or walk around it and work on the other side if it is large. Always work from left to right. The knots on the second row are made in a slightly different manner than those of the first row. The cord is passed down in front of the mesh pin and up the back as before, but this time it does not go over the rod. Instead, carry the needle with its attached cord through the first loop, which hangs between the first two knots on the previous row. Now pull the cord tight, at the same time pulling the bottom of the loop flush with the top edge of the mesh pin. Holding the

thumb on the cord that went through the loop, make a clockwise circle in the cord and throw the needle through it as described in step 1. Pass the needle behind the two cords which hang from the upper loop, and over the end of the clockwise circle of yarn, just as on the first row. Pull the knot tight and remove the thumb. Continue to form the knots in this way until the second row is completed. Turn the work around or walk around it and start the third row—this and all subsequent rows are made like the second row.

Knotted Netting Made by Needle Looping

The ancient Peruvians made a knotted netting by a looping process similar to half-hitch looping. This was described on page 318.

WARP AND WEFT INTER-KNOTTED NET

A knotted net with square meshes is formed by using a netting needle to carry the weft across the warp, which may be a free warp, a weighted warp, or a warp strung on a loom. A square mesh can also be made by knotting the warp on a free-warp loom around the weft; in this case the weft is pulled straight across the warp and enclosed in the knots of the warp.

MACRAMÉ

Macramé[10] is an Arabic word meaning "fringe trimming." Macramé is a "true" knot technique in which two yarn ends are locked around one another. This was probably one of the oldest types of fringe lace and may have an Arabian or some other Near Eastern origin (96). This work was introduced into Spain by the Moors as the Spanish name, Fleco Morisco, indicates. In Genoa, macramé knot work reached a peak of excellence in the commercial establishment of Albergo de Poveri. Macramé fringed towels became important commercially along the French Riviera. Much of the work now comes from Algiers, Morocco, and Italy (see Fig. 164), but islands in the South Pacific, especially Tahiti, also excel in macramé.

Many different types of articles are made in macramé today, including mats, purses, bags, caps, and box covers. As this suggests, macramé is not only the basis for a knotted fringe, but it can also be utilized to make an allover knotted fabric. The latter is usually done on a hard lace pillow with the help of pins.

[10] Graumont and Hensel (100) devote 100 pages, 45 of them are full-page plates, to the subject of macramé.

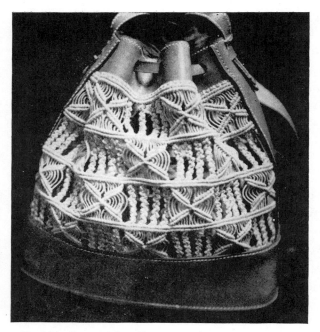

Fig. 164. Macramé Bag. Macramé work from Italy.

A macramé belt is made as follows: Pieces of firm linen dreadnaught cord about 20 inches long are stretched between the two upright supports or over the top of a hard lace pillow. The number of lengths needed is determined by the width of the belt to be made; 15 is an average number. The cords, which should be seven times the length of the belt to be made, are doubled and attached to the stretched cord by means of lark's head or slip knots. One method of procedure, that for a simple knotted belt, will be described presently. As experience is gained, more intricate patterns and other knots can be tried. (See Fig. 165.)

Carry one of the outside cords clear across the warp; as it crosses each warp, knot that warp in a half-hitch around it. Make four rows of such half-hitch knots across the warp. Now make a series of square knots by combining and separating pairs of cords on alternate rows across the warp for eight rows. Make four more rows of half-hitches. Continue alternating the two areas until the belt is finished. End with four rows of half-hitch knots.

Some of the knots commonly used in macramé work are the square knot, half-hitch knot, spiral or waved knot, small shell knot, lark's head knot, beaded knot, and the collecting knot (*100*). Most of the knots are made by hand, but sometimes a crochet hook is used to assist in pulling the cord through the knots. The macramé patterns are usually in geometric shapes such as squares, diamonds, chevrons, and crosses.

Macramé belts can be very interesting, especially when two or more colors are used to form the chevrons, diamonds, or zigzag lines on the belt.

Fig. 165. Macramé Knotting. Detail of the customary method of beginning a piece of macramé work. (After Graumont and Hensel, *Encyclopedia of Knots and Fancy Rope Work,* Cornell Maritime Press, 1946.)

326

TATTING

Tatting may have been another of those textile arts which sprang from the creative fountain of the Near East; its actual origin is unknown. Tatting work is generally classified as lace, and really deserves this classification, especially when it is made of very fine tightly twisted yarn such as fine crochet cotton. Tatting is also classified as one of the knotting processes. The knot used is made in two parts, an *over* knot and an *under* knot. Each is a half-hitch; together they make up one hitch knot. The knotting in tatting work is done with the help of a small specially designed shuttle. The position of the hands and fingers is important in tatting.

THE POSITION OF THE LEFT HAND

The yarn is wound on a tatting shuttle and the free end is thrown in a loop around the fingers of the left hand. This loop is held firmly in place with the thumb and forefinger, and the yarn is stretched in the space between the second and third fingers.

THE POSITION OF THE RIGHT HAND

The shuttle is held in the right hand between the thumb and forefinger. The yarn from it is held above the little or fifth finger; it is an easy matter to slip the little finger under the yarn and lift it up.

DIRECTIONS FOR TATTING

Simple tatting is made as follows:

1. Loop the yarn over the left hand and have both the hands in the positions described above. The yarn above the fifth finger on the right hand must be held above or higher than the yarn on the left hand. To make the first half-knot, slip the shuttle *under* the yarn held between the second and third fingers of the left hand and pull it back *over* that yarn but under the yarn held above the fifth finger of the right hand. Now pull up on the yarn with a slight jerk, thus forming a knot on the loop held on the left hand. This knot—a half-hitch—must slip easily along the yarn.

2. To make the second half of this knot, repeat step No. 1, but this time hold the yarn on the right hand *below* that on the left hand. Slip the shuttle *over* the yarn held by the left hand and pull it back *under* that yarn, but *over* the yarn held by the fifth finger of the right hand. (When more experience is gained, it will not be necessary to put the yarn over the fifth finger of the right hand for the "under" knot.) Again pull the yarn up with a jerk to form the second half of the tatting knot. The two half-

hitch knots form a hitch knot. Both of them must slip easily on the yarn on the left hand.

3. Repeat the knotting process until the desired number of knots have been formed along the looped yarn; then pull up on the loop and push all the knots together into a small tight circle. (See Fig. 166.) Continue to make knot-covered circles, spacing them evenly along the yarn.

The process described gives the method of making a very simple tatted edging. Tatting is usually ornamented with picots. A picot is made by allowing a length of yarn to "float" between one hitch knot and the next. When all the knots are pulled together into a circle, these floats loop up and form picots. Very intricate tatted lace can be formed by combining the tatted circles into various combinations.

Fig. 166. Tatting. Tatting shuttle and simple tatting.

4. Lace

Lace is defined as an ornamental open network fabric containing a design. The Italians called it *Punto in Aria*, meaning "work out of the air." The word "lace" is an English derivative of several closely related fifteenth-century words: *laces*—darned netting; *lacez*—a braid trimming; *lacer* or *lacier*—to lace together; and *lace*—braids or ties for binding.

Lace consists of a pattern, called the flower, a background, called the ground, and brides, or webs, which join the patterned areas together. The pattern can be an integral part of the background, appliquéd or embroidered onto the background, or set into a background which is then made around it.

Lace is generally classified as being embroidered on net, needle-made, bobbin-made, or composite.

The origin of lace making is unknown. Most writers of the nineteenth century claimed that it evolved from the embroidery skills of the fifteenth and sixteenth centuries. The Italians claimed to have originated the point laces, and the Germans the bobbin laces; the subject is discussed further when these laces are described.

Lace is not in itself an entirely unique art, and may have been developed from one or more of a number of the textile techniques, such as twining, drawnwork, cutwork, hemstitching, knot work, filet work, needle looping, crocheting, braiding, meshwork, leno and gauze weaves, wrapped weaves, and other open-structure weaves. Renaissance artisans surely found sufficient inspiration from existing textile arts to develop the art of lace making.

DEVELOPMENT OF LACE

From the late Middle Ages through the Renaissance there was evidence of a gradual shifting in the style of lace from large heavy patterns toward light fine work. From 1480 to 1590, the laces now known as Gothic laces contained geometric patterns without connecting webs or brides. In the next half-century Renaissance laces contained floral patterns made with connecting webs or brides. From 1720 to 1780 most laces consisted of little bouquets and sprigs of flowers scattered over net grounds. The sixteenth and seventeenth centuries are known as the lace centuries, when lace was widely used to ornament altar cloths, collars, cuffs, fans, diadems, petticoats, garters, skirts, and even shoe buckles.

The Italians were the first to produce lace on a commercial basis; they developed the beautiful Point Venetian laces, first mentioned in 1654, which became the finest of all laces (*109*). (See Fig. 167.) The important lace-making centers were Venice, Genoa, Milan, and Naples.

Spain became so extravagant in the use of lace that in 1623, Philip III had to pass an ordinance curtailing the wearing of lace. It is said that some of the women of Spain at that time were wearing as many as a dozen underskirts of handmade lace. The outstanding lace-making centers of Spain were Barcelona, Talavera de la Reyna, Valencia, and Seville.

Flanders learned the art of needle lace from Spain and in turn the Flemish taught the Spanish how to make pillow lace. Flemish laces were some of the most beautiful of Europe. Brussels lace was particularly famous; its thread was so fine that it had to be spun in dark, damp, underground rooms, because any contact with the dry air would have caused it to break during spinning. Naturally such lace was extremely expensive. The principal lace centers of Flanders were Ypres, Antwerp, and Brussels.

The marriage of Catherine de Medici to Henry II of France in 1533 accelerated the flow of Italian laces into France to such an extent that, to prevent bankruptcy, many French edicts were directed against the use of foreign laces. Ten such edicts were made between 1549 and 1583. Later, in 1613, an edict prohibited the use of all lace; another in 1660 prohibited the importation of all foreign laces. After the edicts were passed much foreign lace was smug-

329

gled into the country. In 1665, under Colbert and during the reign of Louis XIV, France began to make her own laces; Italian and Flemish artisans were brought to France to teach the art of lace making to French weavers.

Fig. 167. Venetian Gros-Point. (From the collection of the Musée de Cluny in Paris. Courtesy, Ministère de l'Éducation nationale.)

Lace continued to be smuggled into France, however. One story tells of French dogs being taken to Flanders, starved, sewed into loose skins filled with lace, and sent back to France. Even as late as 1820, 40,278 of these dogs were reportedly caught crossing the border (*109*). After the French lace-making industry was solidly established, a very disastrous ordinance was passed which threatened not only the entire lace industry of France, but many of her other textile enterprises: The revocation of the Edict of Nantes, in

THE TEXTILE ARTS

1685, forced 300,000 persons of all walks of life out of France; some 4000 lace makers left Alençon alone.

England profited by the errors of her neighbors and welcomed French weavers and lace makers, many of whom settled in Honiton and Devonshire, which became lace-making centers. Nevertheless, Brussels lace continued to be smuggled into England, where it was sold under the name of Point d'Angleterre; England finally passed a number of edicts in an attempt to protect her own lace industry. Although much lace was produced, England did not excel in the production of the really fine laces.

Though most of the other countries of Europe continued to produce the lacelike embroideries so prevalent in the Middle Ages, some similar coarse laces, such as Battenberg, Cluny, and Torchon, were made in Germany in such cities as Dresden, Hamburg, Potsdam, and Brandenburg. Peasant types of laces were also made in Holland, Switzerland, Scotland, Ireland, the Scandinavian countries, and Russia.

On the Western Hemisphere, during the Colonial period, Brazil became an important center for handmade cotton laces. Lace was also made in Paraguay, Chile, and Mexico. All of these districts still produce a coarse but pleasing handmade lace. In the United States during Colonial times the making of handmade lace was very limited, though a few housewives attempted making tape laces.

A word should be said about the lace industry of China. Some time around the beginning of the nineteenth century, the Chinese started copying the beautiful European laces, especially Venetian Point. The expensive handmade laces of the Continent could be reproduced by hand in China at a very low cost; for example, a Venetian cloth that cost $1000 could be duplicated for less than $300. Only rarely, however, were the Chinese laces as fine in quality as those of their European counterparts.

Handmade lace is still being made on a limited scale in some of the old European lace centers, and can still be purchased by those willing to pay the price. In dark workshops in Venice and elsewhere in Italy, the glorious point laces are still being made by girls, whose eyes soon weaken under the strain. Belgium, France, and Spain also still produce some fine handmade laces. The intricasies of lace have long intrigued the fancy of mankind and handmade lace will continue to be one of the most cherished of the textile fabrics.

MACHINE-MADE LACES

England led the continent in the development of lace-making machinery: the stocking knitting machine invented by Lee in 1589 led to the invention by

331

Robert Frost in 1740 of a machine for making knitted lace. Heathcoat's invention of a machine for making net, in 1808, was of utmost importance. In 1813, John Leavers, sometimes called Levers, invented a machine that made 18-inch lace. In 1834, Draper adapted the Leavers' machine[11] to the Jacquard loom (95), thus making it possible to weave lace almost 230 inches wide, the full width of the machine. This is still the largest of all textile machines, covering an area of about 500 square feet. It has been described as having the bulk of an elephant and making lace with the daintiness of a spider. It can make many strips of lace at the same time; when the work is done, the strips are cut apart, either through a series of binding stitches or through the net separating the strips. England still produces the bulk of the world's lace-making machinery.

As soon as the Napoleonic Wars were over, lace machines were smuggled from England into France, part by part. Heathcoat established a factory in Paris in 1818 and another in St. Quentin in 1826.[12] France was soon excelling England in the production of fine lace and is still one of the world's largest producers.

Lace machinery was imported into the United States as soon as possible. In 1818, Dean Walker established at Medway, Massachusetts, the first lace machinery on American soil. In 1884, Loeb and Schoenfeld began manufacturing tambour lace curtains in Camden, New Jersey; in 1885, John Willoughby opened a factory in Fordham, New York, to make Nottingham lace. There are now more than 75 lace factories in the United States, operating some 837 Leavers machines. The Schiffli factory on the Hudson River is perhaps the largest. These factories employ more than 10,000 people and do an annual business of more than $35,000,000.00.

TYPES OF LACE

It is difficult to list the different types of lace; actually any filmy fabric which has a definite pattern worked upon an open ground could be called lace. Laces are made by various methods. Some very beautiful fine knotted laces are made in Switzerland and Austria; some of the work is so fine that it could compete with a spider's web. On the other hand, the same technique can be employed to make heavy coarse fish nets out of strong cordage. Tatting is another knot process which produces beautiful laces; macramé, too, is a knot work process that produces lace, but in this case the lace is

[11] *American Fabrics*, Reporter Publications, Inc., Fall, 1952. A picture of the Leavers' machine is in this issue.
[12] *Ibid*. See also Frances Morris, *Notes on Lace of American Colonists*, William Helburn, Inc., New York, 1926.

THE TEXTILE ARTS

usually very coarse. Macramé is also used for headings on fringe. When crochet work is fine and open it is called crocheted lace; Hungary is noted for fine crochet. Hairpin lace is another version of crocheted lace. Some knitting is open and lacelike; Spain makes machine-knit lace for gloves and shawls. Fine meshwork made on frames was a very ancient art and is still made in northern Europe today; some of it has the appearance of bobbin lace. (See Fig. 147.) Appliqué upon net can be so fine as to be classed as lace. Some weaves are so open as to simulate lace; for example, the Guatemalan Indians of Coban combine swivel weaving, done upon a fine transparent background, with gauze weaving; the resulting fabric is very lacelike. There are also the regular bobbin- and needle-made laces, often called true laces, which are made upon perforated paper patterns.

This section of the present volume is chiefly concerned with the structure of these so-called "real" laces, bobbin-made and needle-made laces, which can be classified as embroidered on net, bobbin-made, needle-made, or composite.

EMBROIDERED AND APPLIQUÉD LACES

A lacelike fabric can be formed by embroidering or appliquéing motifs upon a net or mesh background. Outstanding laces of this type are the following:

Type 1: Regular Filet

Conventional or geometric designs are formed upon a knotted-net ground by filling in certain meshes with solid darning stitches which simulate weaving. This is sometimes called darned lace. (See Fig. 170, No. 2.)

Type 2: Needle-Looping Filet

The mesh may be bobbin-made, but the filet is made in needle looping.

Type 3: Buratto Filet

On a basic ground of woven gauze, filet is put in with a needle, interweaving over and under the weft and keeping the filling yarn parallel to the twisted warp.

Embroidered Net or Tambour Work

This is a lacelike fabric composed of meandering lines of chain stitches which form floral and curvilinear designs on a knotless-net ground.

Appliquéd Net

A very fine lawn is appliquéd onto a knotless-net ground, usually in a design in the form of little sprigs of flowers. Brussel's appliqué and English

Honiton appliqué are two examples of this work. This is one of the last types of lace to be developed.

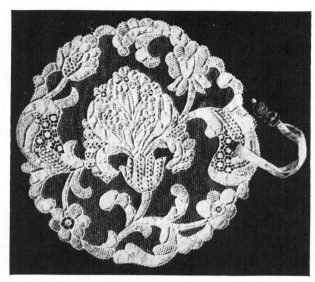

Fig. 168A. Point Lace. A sample of Queen Marguerit coronation veil, Barono school, Italy.

Fig. 168B. Viennese Lace. Needle-point lace.

NEEDLE OR POINT LACE

Needle lace, also called point lace and needle-point lace, is made with a needle and thread.[13] Patterns perforated in parchment are used for much of the work; sometimes the patterns are printed on a shiny white fabric which is cut away when the lace is finished. Burned-out work is lace made on a stamped wool or silk fabric, which is burned away with lye when the lace is finished. The ties which connect the pattern units are twisted, knotted, overcast, looped into thorns, or made into picots. The flower or other design of the lace is usually heavier than the background.

As we have noted earlier, the Italians claimed the invention of the needle or point laces; it is now quite evident, however, that they developed this art from cut-work embroidery, called reticella, which was practiced earlier among the peoples of the eastern Mediterranean. The Italians may have learned the work from Syrian artisans who moved from Syria to Byzantium, then to Sicily, and finally to Italy, carrying with them the knowledge of the

[13] Powys (*110*) has a chapter devoted to the detailed method of making needle-point lace (Chapter XI).

textile arts of the Near East. The various types of needle laces appeared historically in approximately the following order: reticella, punto de aria, raised Venetian point, tape lace, d'Angleterre lace, Alençon, Brussels, Argentan, and Argentella. (See Figs. 167 and 168 A, B.)

BOBBIN LACE

Bobbin lace is often called pillow lace because it is made over a fabric-covered barrel-shaped frame or a heavily stuffed hard round pillow. (See Fig. 169.) Bobbin lace is said to have been invented in Germany in the six-

Fig. 169. Lace Pillow with Bobbins. Showing position of bobbins. (From Gertrude Whiting, *Tools and Toys of Stitchery*, Columbia University Press, 1928. Courtesy, B. Altman and Co., N.Y., and Gertrude Whiting.)

teenth century by Barbara Uttman, who adapted meshwork techniques to lace making. Others say that she learned the craft in either France or Italy, and still others claim (*109*) that she learned the basic process from a Flemish refugee from the Inquisition and later perfected the method. We know that the first pattern book for bobbin lace was printed in Italy in 1557—a fact which has led many to believe that bobbin lace was invented there. Actually, the historic background of bobbin lace in both the Old and New Worlds may reach as far back as pre-Christian times; see the discussion of meshwork, page 293.

Bobbin lace is made as follows: Over a hard pillow is laid a piece of parchment in which the pattern is traced in small holes. Pins are stuck into the holes as they are "worked." The thread is wound on small lace bobbins and is then twisted around the pins to form the ground; as many as 300 to 400

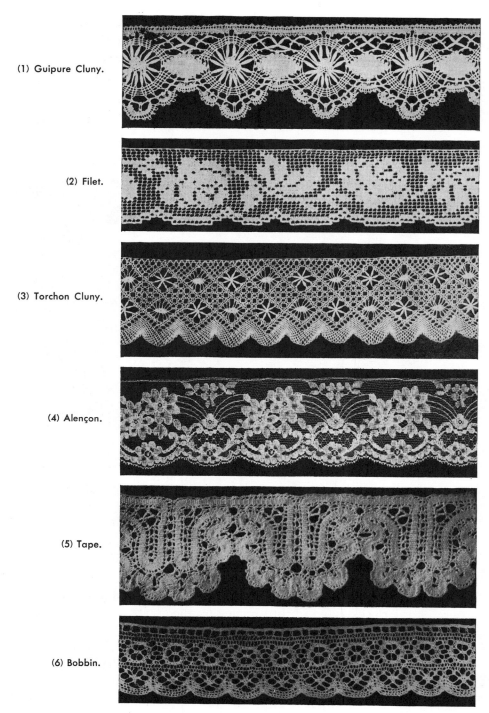

(1) Guipure Cluny.

(2) Filet.

(3) Torchon Cluny.

(4) Alençon.

(5) Tape.

(6) Bobbin.

Fig. 170.   Narrow Lace Edgings.

bobbins are used in a complicated pattern. Most often the pattern—or flower as it is usually called—is made of a heavier thread; it is formed at the same time as the background. The background brides or webs are columns of twisted warp. When background and pattern are made simultaneously, the product is called straight bobbin lace. Sometimes a "free" medallion is set in and filled around with the background; such a structure combines needle and bobbin lace techniques.[14]

The types of bobbin lace appeared historically approximately in the following order (96): Aloe, Binche, black silk, blonde silk, Brussels, Cluny, duchesse, Lille, Maltese, Mechlin, plaited, simple bobbin, tape lace, Trolle Kant, Valenciennes, and Honiton. (See Fig. 170, Nos. 1 and 3.)

COMPOSITE LACES

A number of laces are made by combining two or more of the lace-making techniques. A few of these laces are listed below.

Tape Lace

Tape can be made by either the needle or bobbin techniques; usually, however, bobbins are used. The joining webs connecting the tape patterns can be made by either needle or bobbin methods; usually they are made with the needle. (See Fig. 170, No. 5.)

Appliquéd and Embroidered Laces

The needlework of these laces is usually done upon a bobbin-net ground.

Filet Lace

The needle-filled or darned-in meshes of this lace are usually made upon a knotted-net or bobbin-net ground.

GLOSSARY OF LACE STRUCTURE

Laces are usually named for the locality of their manufacture—a confusing system, since the same lace made in different regions is often called by different names. Laces are also named according to their method of construction. Sometimes the name of the lace stands for both a locality and a structure.

APPLIQUÉ. Fine muslin motifs are appliquéd on a net or muslin ground, such as carrickmacross, or used as the flower for a needle lace.
A'JOURS. Ornamented openwork.

[14] The book by Mincoff (107) is devoted to patterns and methods of making pillow lace. **337**

BOBBIN LACE. A pillow lace; a lace made with bobbins.

BURNED-OUT WORK. The lace is made on a fabric, such as wool or silk, which is then dissolved away by lye.

BURRATO. A filet design on a background of crossed or gauze-treated warps.

BRIDES. The ties, pearl ties, legs, webs, meshes, or nets which hold the lace flower or pattern in place.

CORDONNET. A heavy cordlike thread which outlines the pattern or flower on the right side of some laces.

DENTELLE. The French word for lace.

EMBROIDERED NET. A lacelike pattern embroidered on net; see *Tambour lace.*

FILET (OR LACIS). A pattern filled into a net or netlike ground.

FLOWER. The pattern of a lace; also called a gimp.

GIMP. See *Flower.*

GROS POINT. Venetian point, a strong needle-point lace. Flower is partially made in buttonhole stitch.

GROUND. The background of a lace pattern.

GUIPURE. A flat, tapelike flower or pattern connected by open web work of coarse yarn. Originally a bobbin lace, webs are now often needle-made.

MALINE. The name of a Belgian town called Mechlin by the English; a net of warp yarns which has a diamond-shaped mesh.

NEEDLE LACE. A lace made with a needle and thread; also called point lace. The stitches used are called fillings, modes, or *a'jours.*

PEARL. Picot or loop on edge of lace.

PILLOW LACE. See *Bobbin lace.*

POINT LACE. See *Needle lace.*

RESEAU. A twisted or braided net or mesh ground used as a background for the lace pattern.

RETICELLA. A lacelike web and ornamental pattern, worked over large cut-out areas of fabric.

SHADOW LACE. A wide bobbin Alençon lace without the cordonnet on the flowers.

TAMBOUR LACE. Chain-stitched embroidery on net.

TAPE LACE (MESSO PUNTO). A lacelike tape, usually bobbin-made, is basted to a parchment pattern and a background worked around it; this can be of mesh-work, fagoting, or bride work, and is made with bobbins combined with needlework or solely of needlework.

TIES. See *Brides.*

TORCHON. Coarse flat bobbin lace, also known as peasant lace.

TULLE. Bobbin-made net with hexagonal openings, composed of a set of longitudinal warp yarns and a set of diagonal warp yarns; usually machine-made.

VAL. Narrow bobbin lace; a short term for Valenciennes.

TYPES OF LACE ACCORDING TO AREA

Only a few of the many laces are listed below. They are grouped by countries.

ITALIAN

ALOE LACE. Bobbin lace made from aloe fibers.

BURATTO. Crude embroidered lace with the warp done on a gauze-woven ground.

LACIS. Darned netting or filet; a long-pointed edging.

PUNTO IN ARIA. A needle lace made on yarns previously couched down.

PUNTO CONTATO. A lace made upon a warp and weft, in which the design is put in by counting the yarns.

PUNTO FOGLIAMI. Most famous Venetian point.

PUNTO A GROPPO. Macramé lace.

PUNTO TAGLIATO. Cutwork.

PUNTO TIRATO. Drawnwork and cutwork.

PUNTO RESEAU. Bobbin net.

PUNTO RETICELLA. Free cutwork, also called Gotico and Greek lace.

PUNTO VENECIA. Venetian needle point; Rose point is heavy and more compact. Both have highly raised flowers done in buttonhole stitch.

FLEMISH

ANTWERP LACE. Similar to Mechlin; a bobbin lace.

BINCHE. Resembles Valenciennes.

BRUGES. Bobbin lace, a coarse Duchesse lace.

BRUSSELS APPLIQUÉ. Similar to British Honiton appliqué.

BRUSSELS BOBBIN LACE. Resembles French Cluny lace.

BRUSSELS POINTS. Rare and beautiful laces.

DUCHESSE LACE OR OLD BRUGES LACE. Looks like tape lace; a bobbin lace.

GUIPURE DE FLANDRE. Fine tape lace; the tape was usually bobbin-made, the brides either needle- or bobbin-made, usually a combination of both processes.

MECHLIN LACE. Pretty, fine bobbin lace with flat flower design.

OLD FLANDER'S POINT. Original Belgium lace.

SPANISH

POINT DE'ESPAGNE. Gold and silver lace.

BLONDE. Silk bobbin lace; a bobbin Chantilly lace.

SPANISH MILANESE. A pillow lace.

SOL LACE. A knotted net made in the shape of wheels or suns; part of the pattern is filet-filled.

FRENCH

ARRAS. Fine net bobbin ground; see *Lille*.

CAMPAGNE. Narrow bobbin lace sometimes used as tape for other laces.

CHANTILLY. White and black silk bobbin lace made at Caen. Has cordonnet.

CLUNY LACE. Has Guipure wheels raised on a torchon lace; formerly was a square-knotted net ground with raised wheels.

GUESE. Coarse bobbin lace, sometimes called beggars lace.

LILLE. Fine net ground bobbin lace; the pattern is outlined in heavy thread and stands out in relief. Similar to Arras's lace of southern France.

MIGNONETTE, OR BLONDE DE FIL. Bobbin lace 1 or 2 inches wide.

POINT D'ALENÇON. The flower is made over horsehair which tightens when the lace is washed: has a needle-looped mesh ground.

POINT D'ARGENTAN. Large six-sided mesh ground on lace.

POINT DE FRANCE. Imitation Venetian point.

POINT DE PARIS. Ornamental bride ground on bobbin lace.

POINT DE SEDAN. Resembles Venetian Gros point.

VALENCIENNES. Bobbin lace: the pattern and net are made with same thread.

BRITISH

APPLIQUÉ. A fine cambric laid over net; cut-out areas allow the net to show through.

BEDFORDSHIRE. Flemish type of bobbin lace, like Devonshire.

BUCKINGHAMSHIRE. Pattern and ground are made at the same time; a bobbin lace.

HONITON. The most beautiful of English bobbin laces. Flower sprigs are connected with a bobbin-net ground.

HONITON APPLIQUÉ. Similar to Brussels appliqué; fine bobbin-made sprigs appliquéd on fine bobbin-made net.

HONITON GUIPURE. Bobbin-made sprigs connected with needle-made brides or fine bobbin-made tape.

TROLLY. Copied after Flemish *Trolle Kant;* bobbin-made lace in which groups of yarns form heavier twists.

SCOTTISH

BUNT LACE. A bobbin lace.

IRISH

CARRICKMACROSS. There are two types: guipure and net appliqué.

IRISH CROCHET. A famous crocheted lace with raised rose flowers joined by many brides which have large picots along their stems.

IRISH POINT. A needle lace, an imitation of Brussels and Venetian point.

LIMERICK. Embroidery on net; also Tambour embroidery.

GERMAN

BATTENBERG. A coarse lace made of Battenberg tape—a bobbin tape—made in curvilinear patterns connected with needle-made brides and wheels.

5. Trimmings (Passementerie)

Fringes, tassels, cords, and braid trimmings are usually considered ornamental rather than functional. However, ornamentation may be an important functional part of an article—for example, cords used as handles on bags

340

and braids used to connect two pieces of fabric may be both ornamental and functional.

FRINGE WORK

A fringed edging is often added to such hand-woven pieces as belts, mats, bags, and rugs. Fringes can be made by braiding, knotting, and looping techniques.

Fringe may be a component part of the warp of a fabric, or it may be added to the finished fabric. When it is part of the fabric allowance is made for it by inserting a strip of cardboard in the warp before weaving commences.

A fringe may be added to the edge of the finished cloth in various ways:
1. By knotting in the yarn. A crochet hook is used to pull a double strand of yarn into and through the fabric. This strand is then made into a slip knot and secured over the edge of the fabric.
2. By darning in the yarn. Yarns can be darned into the fabric with a needle, either parallel or diagonal to the warp.
3. By looping in the yarn. Yarns can be sewed into the edge of a fabric by using the back stitch of the needle-looping process. The ornamental part of the fringe can be further enhanced by additional rows of half-hitch loops, into which the fringe yarns are then slip-knotted.

Fringe is named after its basic structure as follows:
1. Macramé fringe.
2. Knotted fringe, made as for warp-knotted netting. (See Fig. 162.)
3. Looped fringe, made by any of the knotless netting processes.
4. Gauze or leno fringe. A leno weave is made in the regular warp at the end of a piece of woven fabric, above a knotted fringe. The yarns of an added fringe can also be twisted into a leno weave, using an accessory weft to hold the twists in place; the ends of the fringe are then knotted.
5. Braided fringe. Various braiding techniques are used as a foundation for a fringe. For example, here is one: Make a series of four-strand braids for a given number of turns across the end of the free-hanging warp. Separate the yarns and rebraid two warp yarns of one braided strand with two yarns of an adjacent braided strand. Recombine the original four strands and braid together. End with a few rows of knotted fringe.

The 1–1 and 2–2 braiding is often used by the Guatemalan Indians to finish the ends of woven scarfs.

TASSEL MAKING

Tassels are often used to trim the bottom of a fringe, or to terminate bag and belt cords. They are made as follows:

1. Wind the yarn around a cardboard strip of the desired length. Fasten the yarns together securely by tying a yarn through the loops at one end. Cut the yarns at the other end.
2. Bunch the yarns at the tied end and wind several strands of yarn around them about 1/3 to 1/4 of an inch from the end.
3. Cover the top of the tassel with blanket stitching, needle knitting, braiding, or with a Turk's knot. This knot is made with three needles threaded with yarn which are interlaced into a three-strand braid as they circle round and round the tassel head.

CORD MAKING

Cords are used for handles on bags, for ties, and for many other purposes. They are made by processes described here.

Braided Cord (Sennit Braiding)

This cord can be square-braided (four strands); round-braided (four or more strands); flat-braided (three, five, or more strands); or interlock-braided (four or eight strands). To make the interlocked braid, tie the ends of four strands of yarn together; two are crossed and the other two, one from the back and one from the front, are then crossed through the opening below the first cross. The first two are then recrossed, again one from the back and one from the front, through the lower part of the opening made by the cross of the second pair. Repeat this alternate crossing until the cord is finished. Tie the ends.

Knitted Cord

Spool knitting or needle knitting can be used to made a round cord. (See page 300.)

Twisted Cord

To make this cord, double two long yarns, put a pencil or stick in the end loops; tie the open ends and put them over a knob; by twisting the pencil, twist the yarn. Carefully remove the twisted yarn from the knob, holding the two ends together. The two twisted strands will now automatically retwist around each other to make a four-ply cord. Tie the cord at both ends.

342

Crocheted Looped Cord

A two-strand cord can be made by crocheting together two strong stiff yarns, either by finger crocheting or with the help of a hook. To make this cord, tie the ends of the yarns together and make a loop in one of them; then reach through this loop and pull the other yarn through. Continue to loop each yarn into the other until the chain is finished. Tie the ends.

Double-Wrapped Cord (Coxcomb Braid)

A bag handle can be made by tying two strong cords together and wrapping them with a third yarn or cord, passing it over and under the cords in a figure 8 movement. (See page 195.)

Blanket-stitched Cord

A number of yarns are held together and wrapped with the buttonhole stitch—a half-hitch stitch.

Peruvian Braided Cord

Six strands of different colored weft yarns are interwoven into two or more heavy cotton longitudinal warp cords tightly stretched. The weft yarns are interwoven into the warp cords, one at a time, and in the same direction, going over and under alternate warps entirely across the cords. They are turned and interwoven back across the warp in reverse order: that is, the last weft yarn woven may be taken back as the first weft of the new group. They may be returned, however, in the same order as originally carried through. Whichever system is used, at each return back into the warp they form a fan; this effect gives a scalloped finish to the edges of the cord. (O'Neale, *46.*)

Embroidery and Needlework

Embroidery is an art of Oriental origin, but whether the first impetus toward it took place in the Far or the Near East may never be known. In the Far East embroidery is still very close to the life of the people. The Chinese believe that embroidery was practiced in their land as early as 3000 B.C. Until recent times this was one of the first arts taught to young Chinese girls; a girl's marriageability often depended upon the embroidered trousseau she made. Some of the best embroidery work in the world today still comes from China and Japan. (See Fig. 171.) India also claims the origin of the embroidery arts; elaborate embroideries, ornamented with precious stones and interlaced with gold and silver thread, have long been used in the temples and in the homes of the rulers of that land.

In the Near East, on the other hand, murals on the walls of Egyptian tombs demonstrate that the ancient Egyptians also excelled in the embroidery techniques. Perhaps the Hebrews learned this art during their captivity in Egypt; in any event, they were very appreciative of it. Ezekiel (xxvii) spoke of the "fine linen with broidered work from Egypt." The veil with which Moses covered the Holy of Holies was "of fine linen embroidered with cherubim of blue, purple, and scarlet." Solomon ordered an embroidered curtain for the temple.

Ancient Persia, Babylon, Sidon, Israel, and Damascus were producers of fine embroideries. We must also remember that the Greeks accredited Athena with the invention of embroidery. When Alexander conquered Persia, he was amazed at the splendor of the embroideries he found there. To show his countrymen what elaborate needlework came from the Near East, he sent home the embroidered tent of Darius that all might see and

344

Fig. 171. Chinese Embroidery. Emperor's Dragon Medallion, of silk and gold, Ming Dynasty. (Courtesy of the Metropolitan Museum of Art.)

wonder! The Phrygian embroideries were so famous in ancient times that the work became known to the Romans as Phrygian. The Romans imported many embroideries from Babylon and elsewhere in the Near East.

Embroidery was one of the most important textile arts of the Byzantine Empire. Byzantine embroideries copied the ornate designs of Persia in rich colors, often enhanced with gold and silver threads and pearls; for many centuries they were considered of superior quality. Much of the energy of embroiderers was spent decorating ecclesiastical garments; the influence

345

EMBROIDERY AND NEEDLEWORK

Fig. 172. Ancient Peruvian Embroidery. A detail from a Paracas embroidery. (Courtesy, Museo Nacional de Antropología y Arqueología, Lima, Peru, and A. Taullard, *Tejidos y Ponchos*, Guillermo, Buenos Aires.)

of Byzantine design may still be seen on vestments of the Catholic Church.

After the Byzantine period, embroidery continued to be of great importance in both the Near East and southern Europe. The Mohammedans, who usurped the Byzantine power, were great lovers of embroidery. During the Middle Ages in Europe embroidery was ranked as a fine art and given the same recognition now accorded to painting and sculpture—in fact, portraits were often worked out in embroidery. Many monasteries and convents had rooms set apart for embroiderers. Throughout the Renaissance period the convents continued to specialize in the teaching of embroidery.

Embroidery was exceedingly important in the fourteenth and sixteenth centuries. Every nobleman had his own personal embroiderer. The royal embroiderer of Henry IV of France was given a special service: flowers were planted in the royal gardens that he might have a direct source for designs for the royal robes. Men's costumes of this period were as highly embroidered as women's.

In England embroidery was extensively used for textile decoration. The Pope called gifts sent to him "a fountain of embroidery from England." Mary, Queen of Scots, was a skilled embroiderer; she is said to have learned this craft during the happier days of her youth in France. Queen Anne was also noted for her embroidery work, especially for her excellent petit point. Three types of embroidery should be mentioned in connection with England: Crewel embroidery was much in evidence during the Elizabethan

346

and Jacobean periods; a special inlay appliqué was an important textile art of the latter part of the seventeenth century; and "turkey" work, an Oriental knot technique, became popular during the nineteenth century.

Although embroidery was used extensively in Europe during the Renaissance, the rich woven fabrics of Italy—the velvets, brocades, and damasks —soon began to supplant embroidery in popular favor. In the early part of the eighteenth century Chinese embroideries began to find a market in Europe. European artists often sent their designs to China to be embroi-

Fig. 173. Guatemalan Embroidery. Satin stitch embroidery from Mexico-Guatemala border district, actually from Guatemala.

dered. The peasant peoples of Europe are still fond of embroidery, and ornament their clothing and household effects with gay, pleasant patterns.

On the Western Hemisphere the art of embroidery has a very old heritage. In South America the ancient Peruvians were skilled artisans, contributing some of the world's rarest embroideries. (See Fig. 172.) The Indians of Peru still do beautiful work. Those in northeastern North America worked porcupine quills in leather in geometric patterns. Before the coming of the white man the Indians of North America embroidered on doeskin, incorporating beads of shell, bone, and stone in their work. After the white man came, the Indians used glass beads. In the far north, the Eskimos made patterns from dyed strips of leather and appliquéd them on fish skins and

347

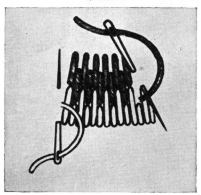

Fig. 174. Machine-Made Embroidery. Top, work of the Mayan Indians of Yucatan; made on a sewing machine, using flame stitch. Bottom, detail of handmade flame stitch. Note the manner in which the colored yarns dovetail.

leather of various types. In tropical areas the Indians sewed brilliant feathers onto fabric in unusual patterns.

When the Spanish came to Central and South America, they taught the Indians European methods of needlework and put them to work embroidering materials for Spanish use. Today the Mexican and Guatemalan Indians excel in the embroidery arts, still using many of the designs taught them by the Spanish. (See Figs. 173 and 174.)

Many of the early colonists of New England were skillful embroiderers, and their samplers are seen in many museums today.

At the present time most of the embroidery used in the United States is machine-made. (See Figs. 174 and 184.) In a cluster of little towns along the Hudson River in northern Hudson County, New Jersey, known as the "embroidery center," many emigrants from Switzerland and Germany carry on their traditional embroidery crafts in a very untraditional way: the machine does the work in place of the original hand processes. Sewing machines and other special machines are today able to imitate many embroidery stitches. The marvelous Schiffli machine, for example, with its versatile 682 to 1020 needles and its little boatlike shuttle (Schiffli means "little boat") is responsible for 90 percent of all of the machine-made embroidery in the United States. Machine-made embroidery, however, can only imitate; it can never equal the exquisite work of a skilled hand embroiderer. Consequently, lovely handwork will always find a market among discriminating people.

1. General Directions for Doing Embroidery

Many pleasant hours may be spent "painting with a needle"—the title the Romans gave embroidery. Individuality of design is as important to the embroiderer as it is to anyone working in the other fields of art. Learn to be original and create your own designs. The "theme" used for a design may come from a variety of sources—floral arrangements, portraiture, scenery, historic tableaus, samplers, abstract compositions, etc.

After deciding upon the design for your embroidery, select the proper treatment and equipment:

1. To transfer the design to the fabric, you will need tracing paper, pencil-blackened paper, or perforated paper; or you can draw the design onto the material free-hand.
2. Choose an appropriate color harmony for the design. If the piece is to be washed, use colorfast yarns. Select the proper yarns or floss according to the type of the material and the type of the design. Yarns of wool, silk, mercerized cotton, linen, raffia, and sisal can be used, either alone or in combination.
3. A combination of embroidery stitches can sometimes be put together to add interest to a piece of work. Select those most feasible. Variation may also be accomplished by padding certain areas, by the use of different types or weights of yarn, and by adding beads, ribbons, and braid to the work.
4. Needles come in different sizes; heavy yarns require needles with large eyes set in deep grooves. Select needles according to the character of the fabric, the weight of the yarn, and the type of stitches to be done.
5. To maintain an even surface in your work, use a hoop or tambour, or attach the fabric to an embroidery frame. (See Fig. 101.)
6. Small embroidery scissors are helpful.

Keep the work clean. Remember to keep the hands clean while working.

2. Embroidery Stitches

Embroidery stitches can often enhance an otherwise plain fabric with color and pattern. Although there are a great many of these stitches, a creative worker is always seeking new variations and combinations. Most of the important embroidery stitches are listed and described below, but it would hardly be feasible to include the great range of possible variations. Some of these stitches are illustrated in Figs. 175 and 179.

ARROW. The arrow stitch imitates the feather at the end of an arrow shaft. It is made up of a series of overlapping cross-stitches, each laid down just a yarn's width beneath the preceding one. The stitch is made as follows: bring the yarn out of the fabric in the upper left-hand corner of the pattern, carry it diagonally down to right margin and insert the needle about 1/4 inch from the top; cross

349

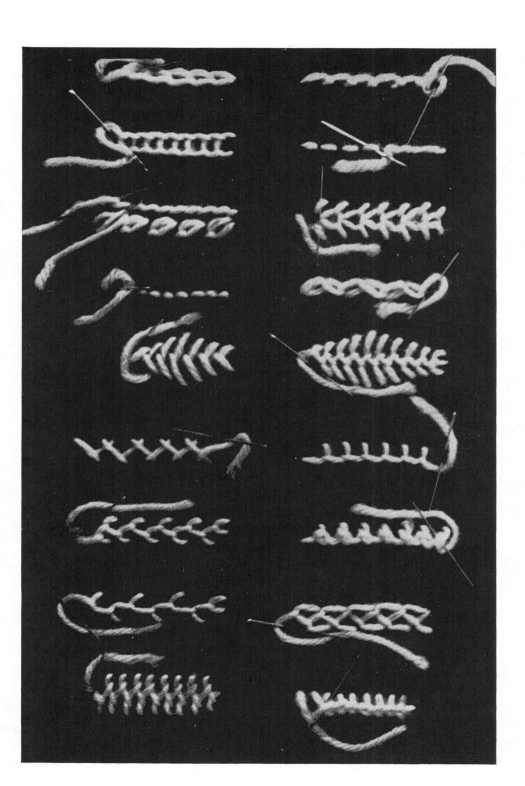

it beneath the fabric and bring it out again on the left-hand margin about 1/4 inch down from the top; cross the yarn diagonally upward on the face of the fabric and insert the needle in the top right-hand corner; this completes the first cross-stitch. Now bring the needle out at the upper left-hand corner immediately below the yarn where the work first began and repeat the stitch, always inserting the needle immediately below the points of the previous stitch. The stitching is continued in this way to form a rectangular column.

ARROWHEAD. Arrowheads are used to reinforce the corners of pockets, the arrow stitch being made to fit into a small triangle, accenting the top or apex of the triangle. A *crow's foot track* is another triangular reinforcement, but here each corner is given the same treatment as the apex of the arrowhead.

BACKSTITCH. A series of line stitches. The needle passes a two-stitch length under the fabric and then a one-stitch length backward above the fabric. This forms a line of even stitches which touch end to end on the right side of the fabric.

BACKSTITCH CHAIN. A widely spaced row of short backstitches is laid down over a row of chain stitches, covering just the loop where two chain stitches join. The result resembles a cable chain stitch.

BASKET WORK. Wide-spaced satin stitches, alternating in vertical and horizontal blocks.

BERRY. The berry stitch is composed of two separate chain stitches, one surrounding the other, but both having the same starting point.

BLANKET STITCH. A wide-spaced buttonhole stitch. The yarn is looped under the point of the needle to form half-hitches and carried along the edge of the fabric from left to right.

BRAID. Imitation plaiting made by close-set Van Dyke stitches.

BRICK. A series of long and short stitches on alternate rows, spaced to dovetail like bricks.

BRICK AND CROSS. Blocks of horizontal, wide-spaced, satin stitches alternate with crosses to form a background filling.

BULLION KNOT. A short stitch is made, leaving the needle in fabric; yarn is wrapped five or six times around the end of the needle, which is then pulled through the fabric.

BUNDLE. Three wide-spaced vertical satin stitches are pulled together by a yarn wrapped once or twice around them in the center.

BUTTONHOLE. Same as blanket stitch, except that stitches are placed very close together.

CABLE. Sometimes called a cable chain stitch. A chain separated by a short backstitch, made as follows: Make a chain stitch and bring the yarn up in the loop as usual. Make a short backstitch to the front of the chain stitch, letting the yarn extend from the right; make another chain stitch, inserting the needle in the same hole but to the left of the backstitch; repeat.

Fig. 175. Embroidery Stitches. Left column, top to bottom: Chain or crewel; open chain; stem, outline, or Paracas; lazy daisy, also called detached chain, railway, or petal stitch; backstitch; open fishbone; herringbone; feather; open feather; and backbone, a version of feather. Right column, top to bottom: Cretan; scroll; wheat ear; open zigzag chain; feather (long and short combination); buttonhole; Antwerp edge (knotted buttonhole); closed feather; and Van Dyke.

EMBROIDERY AND NEEDLEWORK

CATCHSTITCH.   See Herringbone.

CEYLON.   A half-hitch, pseudo-knitting stitch. See page 303.

CHAIN.   A stitch that resembles a crocheted chain, made as follows: A loop of yarn is thrown in front of the needle as it emerges from the fabric; the needle then pierces the fabric close to the point of emergence, and the point is brought up in the left center of the loop. On the next stitch, and on all subsequent ones, the needle pierces the fabric on the right center of the preceding loop on a line with the adjacent stitch, and emerges on the left center of the new loop. The stitch can be opened wide or closed, and can be made any length desired. It can also be made backwards. A "heavy chain" stitch is a chain made backwards. See also *Backstitch chain*, and *Cable Double chain, Feathered chain*, and *Scattered chain*, and *Crewel*. There are many variations of the chain stitch, some of them very complex.

CHEVRON.   A zigzag stitch with a bar at each end. To make it, bring the needle to the surface of the fabric; insert it a short distance to the right and bring it to the surface between these two points. This short outline stitch brings the yarn up in the center of and just below the stitch. Carry it diagonally downward toward the right; make two stitches from right to left as on the first row, and bring yarn up on top center of stitch. The work proceeds toward the right; the yarns pass diagonally upward and downward alternately between the two rows of stitches. There are two stitches on each row, the second one emerging where the first was inserted; actually one outline stitch is formed.

CLOSED FEATHER.   Feather stitch with the ends partially closed.

CLOUD FILLING.   Background stitches. Small running stitches are made in vertical columns, and in alternating positions in adjacent columns. A yarn is then threaded back and forth crosswise through the columns and then vertically up one column and down the next, threading through the stitches. Eventually two yarns run through each stitch.

CONE.   Same as open fishbone stitch, but conforming to a cone shape.

CORAL.   A simple knot stitch. The yarn is held flat and looped back; the needle pierces the fabric outside the loop and emerges inside it. When pulled tight, the yarn of the loop forms a knot.

COUCHING.   Any of a number of methods used to hold a yarn or yarns on top of the fabric. Whipping stitches, cross-stitches, invisible stitches, etc. are used to hold the yarns down. Also called the Oriental stitch.

CRESTED CHAIN.   See *Wheat ear*.

CRETAN.   A stitch made by reversing alternate blanket stitches: one is made from left toward center, the next from right toward the center, and each is set slightly in front of the other. This stitch is also called a flattened-out feather stitch; it varies with length of side area and slant of the needle.

CREWEL.   See Crewel embroidery, page 361.

CROSS-STITCH.   Described on page 364.

CROSSED BACKSTITCH.   See *Double backstitch*.

CROSSED BLANKET.   Blanket stitches placed along edge of fabric so that alternating angles are formed as ends of stitches cross.

DANISH KNOT.   A variation of the blanket stitch in which the needle enters the *back* of the loop of the blanket stitch.

DARNING. A pseudo-weft woven into a pseudo-warp raised above the fabric.

DETACHED CABLE. See *Cable*.

DETACHED CHAIN. Each chain stitch is completely separated from the next. Also called scattered chain.

DOT. Small backstitches spaced far apart. See *Seed*.

DOUBLE BACKSTITCH. A backstitch is made first on one side of an area and then on the other, passing back and forth across the center and thereby forming cross-stitches. This stitch is also called the double herringbone, the plaited Algerian, and the crossed backstitch.

DOUBLE CHAIN. The chain loops are formed first toward the right and then toward the left, the needle emerging twice in the same place in the same loop. In one version the stitches are placed at right angles and the upper end of one stitch becomes the starting point or lower end of the next stitch.

DOUBLE FEATHER. See *Feather*.

DOUBLE HERRINGBONE. See *Double backstitch*.

DOUBLE RUNNING. A second set of running stitches fills in the gaps made by the first.

FAGOTING. See page 369.

FALSE SATIN STITCH. A stitch which floats on the face of the fabric, drops below the fabric at the end of the float, and rises near by to form the next stitch, which goes in the reverse direction. The stitches shuttle back and forth, connecting at their corresponding ends under the fabric and forming vertical columns of stitches on top.

FEATHER. A chain stitch is made with the ends left open; another is made above and to the right, the next above and to the left, etc. In the double feather two such stitches are made on the right and left. Closed feather is same as feather except that the loops are longer and nearly closed at the ends.

FEATHERED CHAIN. A series of open chain stitches placed alternately at right angles to one another with their closed ends inward. Each stitch is connected to the next by a short plain stitch which gives the appearance of winding between the stitches. The whole chain looks like a vine with leaves.

FERN. Two separate line stitches of the same length fan out at the same angle from the center, and are connected to the next pair below by another line stitch. There are, therefore, three stitches in each unit.

FISHBONE. The same as the arrow stitch, except that the lower stitches are smaller and cross in the center of the area, while the upper ones are wide and follow the outline of the pattern. The yarn passes horizontally across the back of the fabric between the wide and narrow ends. The stitching can be made from top to bottom or bottom to top. If worked from bottom to top, the smaller cross-stitches can be put in in the form of a chainlike band which runs up the center of the wider side arm stitches. This stitch is often used to fill in leaf areas in an embroidery pattern.

FLAME. Long and short stitch, usually made in graded colors. (See Fig. 174.)

FLAT. A running stitch or any flat stitch taken back and forth over an area. A slanted flat stitch can be used to fill leaf patterns; the bars do not cross at the center as in the leaf stitch.

FLY. See Y stitch.

FOUR-LEGGED KNOT. One stitch is crossed at right angles by another which knots around the center of the first stitch.

FRENCH KNOT. Bring thread to surface, twist the yarn around the needle several times near point of emergence, pierce fabric again close to point of emergence.

GOBELIN. A stitch which passes diagonally over two intersections of a buckram fabric. A long tent stitch.

GUILLOCHE. An interlocked figure 8 border stitch.

HEAVY CHAIN. A chain stitch made in reverse order, the loop passing beneath the legs of the preceding loop.

HEMSTITCHING. See page 370.

HERRINGBONE. Sometimes called catch stitch. A variation of the outline stitch. There are two rows of stitches, and the yarn zigzags back and forth between them in a series of cross-stitches, proceeding from left to right. The needle is inserted into the fabric horizontally from right to left. Alternate stitches are placed on alternate rows.

HOLBEIN. A two-direction line stitch; horizontal courses of stitches are crossed by vertical courses, forming open blocks.

HUNGARIAN. Sets of three vertical canvas stitches—short, long, short—arranged in dovetailing blocks.

INSERTION. Any type of stitching, such as fagoting, twisted fagoting, etc., used to join the edges of two pieces of fabric.

KENSINGTON. See *Long and short.*

KNOTTED BLANKET. Same as blanket stitch, except that the yarn is passed through the top loop again, encircling the two yarns.

LADDER. There are several versions of this stitch: (1) A columnar arrangement made up of stitches which pass from side to side, each one making a half-hitch loop around the back of the previous half-hitch loop on each side of the column. (2) Double hemstitching, in which both sides of an opened strip are hem-stitched. (3) A widespread chain stitch. (4) A column of parallel flat stitches, both ends being covered with close-set Van Dyke stitches.

LAID-IN WORK. Any stitches above the fabric and not attached to it.

LATTICE. Yarns that cross at right angles, sometimes interwoven, sometimes couched down at the intersections.

LAZY DAISY. Detached chain stitches rotated around a center to form petals for a flower. The loop ends form the circumference.

LEAF. The leaf stitch is worked from bottom to top. The yarn is brought out left of center near the bottom of the pattern and carried diagonally up to the right edge. It passes under the fabric and emerges right of center slightly above the origin of the previous stitch, but on the lower side. It is then carried diagonally up and over the previous stitch and enters the fabric at the left margin. The yarn emerges to the left of center slightly above the center origin of the previous stitch, but again on the under side of that stitch. This process is continuously repeated.

LINE. A straight stitch.

LONG AND SHORT. Parallel rows of alternating long and short satin stitches, dovetailed so that the stitches form a column.

LONG-ARMED FEATHER. A feather stitch in which the center stitches are small and rather straight while the side arms are long.

LONG FRENCH KNOT. See *Bullion*.

LOOP. The stitch starts in the center, passes to the side next to the previous stitch, passes under the fabric to the opposite side, emerges and makes a half-hitch loop around the back of the previous half-hitch loop at center.

MILLE FLEUR. A series of single stitches radiating from a center.

NEEDLE KNITTING. See *Pseudo-Knitting*.

NEEDLE WEAVING. A figure 8, wrapped-warp technique used in drawnwork.

OPEN CHAIN. A chain stitch in which the needle always slants from right to left, spreading the loop end.

OPEN FISHBONE. An open-stitched version of the fishbone stitch. The small cross-stitches in the center dovetail into the crouches of the wider side arms.

ORIENTAL. See *Couching*.

OUTLINE. The reverse of the backstitch. The long floats are on the outside of the fabric instead of underneath as in the regular back stitch.

OVERCAST. Small stem stitches placed diagonally side by side over a running stitch.

PADDING. Filling under a pattern. Some embroidery work, such as scalloping, is firmer or more attractive if done over padding. Outline stitches are generally used as padding stitches.

PARACAS. An attached needle-knitting stitch. Named by Lila O'Neale.

PARACAS PSEUDO-KNITTING STITCH. Named by author. See page 303.

PEARL (or PICOT). A whipped stitch made through a small stem stitch.

PEKINESE. A half-hitch looping made into adjacent backstitches.

PETAL. A stem stitch made with a detached chain stitch on one side. In another version, a buttonhole stitch is made adjacent to a detached chain stitch.

PLAITED ALGERIAN. See *Double backstitch*.

PLAITED STITCH. See *Braid*. Columns of braid stitches are made next to one another in half-drop positions which give the appearance of solid plaiting.

PSEUDO-KNITTING. A process of half-hitch looping which may be entirely free of the fabric or partially or entirely attached to it. See page 303.

RAISED FISHBONE STITCH. Same as arrowhead stitch, except that it conforms to a leaf shape instead of an arrowhead triangle. Upper and lower stitches both conform to the outline of the leaf, passing horizontally underneath the fabric. Work proceeds from top to bottom or from left to right.

RAMBLER ROSE. A solid area built up with the stem stitch, which starts at the center and rotates around and around in a clockwise direction.

ROPE. Buttonhole stitches worked downward instead of in the usual manner. The stitches are placed diagonally side by side and close together. The second stitch laps back partially over the first, making a raised or padded effect.

ROUMANIAN FERN. A continuous column of fly stitches connected by line stitches.

ROUMANIAN. Long stitches placed side by side, each one crossed at the center by a short stitch.

RUNNING. A sewing stitch or simple line stitch. These stitches have uniform narrow spaces between them; they are worked from right to left.

355

SATIN. Over-and-over stitches placed side by side.

SCALLOPING. Buttonhole stitches used to finish off the edge of a fabric. The edges so treated are usually drawn in a series of curves and rather heavily padded before being embroidered.

SCATTERED CHAIN. Single chain stitches scattered over fabric at even intervals; also called detached chain.

SCROLL. The needle is inserted into the fabric at a diagonal angle toward the left, and emerges into a complete loop formed by the yarn. The work proceeds from left to right.

SEED. Small, even, single or paired stitches made in all directions; also tiny wide-spaced backstitches or tiny detached chain stitches.

SHADOW. A cross-stitched filling made on the back of a transparent fabric. Only the tiny back stitches which outline the pattern show on the right side.

SHEATH. See *Bundle*.

SINGHALESE CHAIN. Two colored yarns are couched down along the outside edges of an open chain by the stitches of the chain.

SOUMAK. See page 169.

SPLIT. A backstitch in which the needle forming each new stitch pierces the yarn of the last stitch, bisecting it.

STEM. Stitches which run forward at a diagonal slant parallel to one another. Each time the needle is inserted half a stitch above the previous stitch and brought out even with its center. The yarn must always be kept on the same side of the needle. The ancient Peruvians used this stitch; they went forward over four and back under two of the warp or weft yarns in the fabric, forming a slanted pseudo-Soumak stitch. See Fig. 172.

SWORD EDGING. One vertical stitch twists back into another vertical stitch to form a twisted cross-stitch or mesh stitch above the fabric.

TENT. Half of a cross-stitch.

TÊTE DE BOEUF. A single line stitch, caught and drawn down at the center by a single detached chain stitch, thus giving the appearance of the horns on a bull's head.

THORN. Widely separated fishbone stitches, used to couch down a yarn.

THREADED. A yarn run along and through any set of embroidery stitches.

TRELLIS. Similar to the lattice.

TWISTED CHAIN. To make this stitch, form a clockwise loop in front of the needle. Working from right to left, insert the needle slightly below and behind the front of the preeceding stitch and make a diagonal stitch upward toward the left. Bring the needle out of the loop. Repeat.

TWISTED RUNNING STITCH. A second yarn is carried through the stitches of the running stitch, entering two adjacent stitches from the same side.

WAVE FILLING. A row of open-ended detached, chain stitches set side by side, loops up. Subsequent rows form pseudo-chains, each loop running under the legs of the loop above.

WHEAT EAR. This stitch resembles a loop with two antennas. It has two parts: (1) Two short diagonal stitches are made to fan out a short distance apart on the same level; (2) a reversed chain is looped under the base of the stitches.

356 VAN DYKE. Related to the open fishbone. The short stitch at the center is always even with and under the fabric at the point where the previous stitch crosses. Work proceeds from bottom to top.

VAN DYKE ROUMANIAN. A series of dovetailed Y-stitches.

Y-STITCH. A very open-ended chain stitch with a short running stitch to hold the loop end down. The stitch looks like a Y.

ZIGZAG CHAIN. A chain stitch in which alternate stitches pass first to the right and then to the left, or up and down, depending upon the direction of the work. A zigzag cable chain is a cable chain made in this same zigzag manner.

ZIGZAG CORAL. Coral stitch knots are placed at the outside points of a zigzag line.

3. Types of Embroidery

Special handling of certain embroidery stitches by national groups has resulted in what have come to be known as national "types" of embroidery. Some of these are the specialized work of one particular area and are used only in that area; others have been borrowed widely, or have been independently invented in many areas, and are in general use. The better-known types of embroidery are described below.

APPLIQUÉ

Appliqué is generally classed as a form of embroidery. The term refers to the superimposition of one piece of material upon another; usually the two are sewed together with ornate stitches.

Appliqué is a very old form of ornamentation, though little is known of its history. Various references to it occur in historical writings; for example, reference is made in the Bible to "Joseph's coat of many colors" —the work was probably either appliqué or patchwork. The funeral tent of the Egyptian Queen Isi-em-keb, dated 980 B.C., was made in inlaid appliqué. It is in the Boulak Museum in Cairo. The Egyptians still enjoy doing appliqué. (See Fig. 176.)

Many mummy bundles of the pre-Columbian Indians of Peru have appliquéd copper masks and eyes. A popular method of ornamentation in both ancient Peru and Egypt was the sewing of metal spangles onto scarves and clothing. Even today in the Near East, as well as in Europe and America, many garments are ornamented with spangles.

A patchwork type of embroidery was used by the Persians for saddle cloths and horse trappings. It was composed of small pieces of broadcloth cleverly combined, the seams being covered with variously colored needle work.[1] These Gul-Duzi-i-Resht cloths, as they are sometimes called, are

---

[1] Sir R. Murdock Smith, *South Kensington Handbook on Persian Art*, Committee Council of Education, Chapman and Hall, London, 1876.

still being made at Rescht and in a few other cities. Many patchwork quilts of the American colonists were made in this same technique.

Appliqué was used by the Crusaders for ornamenting horse trappings, knights' surcoats, etc. The Spanish and Italians used it with great skill in the sixteenth century. The British Museum has examples of work done by Mary, Queen of Scots, while she was a prisoner in England; it consists of small velvet inserts set into a similar fabric of a contrasting color. The pieces are combined so cleverly that the piece seems to be one multicolored fabric. In Belgium the appliqué principle was applied to lace making in 1661. The early colonists in America used the process to decorate clothing and linens; examples of their work can be seen in many American museums.

Fig. 176. Egyptian Appliqué.

Appliqué is widely used today to decorate textiles. Much of this work has a peasantlike quality, but some of it is very intricate and formal.

TYPES OF APPLIQUÉ
Superimposed Appliqué

In superimposed appliqué, one piece of fabric is placed above and attached to a second piece of fabric. There are a number of ways of doing this work:

Type 1. The Darien Indians of Panama make bright allover appliquéd fabrics. Irregular curvilinear patterns are dovetailed on a bright-colored fabric in such a way that a margin of the fabric shows around each pattern. Sometimes several patterns are superimposed one above the other, the edges of each showing beneath the one above it. The Seminole Indians of Florida do a similar type of appliqué.

Type 2. Hawaiian natives make quilt tops in appliqué; a large foliate design, the size of the quilt, is cut out and appliquéd to the quilt.

Type 3. A shadow type of appliqué is made in the Madeira Islands. Semitransparent material is used for both basic fabric and pattern pieces.

358

Foliate borders, appliquéd on the wrong side of the material, show through the material sufficiently to give a charming effect to the work.

Type 4. Another similar type of appliqué also comes from the Madeira Islands. In this case, a contrasting color is used for the pattern pieces and they are attached to the right side of the fabric. Switzerland also produces this type of appliqué.

Type 5. On the European continent, small patterns of very fine white cotton are occasionally appliquéd on net. The work resembles Irish carrickmacross lace.

Type 6. The appliqué work of the peasant folk of Europe usually consists of small naïve designs, often made of several superimposed pieces, sewed to a solid piece of fabric. This work is popular in both Europe and America.

Inlaid Appliqué

Here the background and pattern fabrics are both cut out. The pattern fits flush into the background and is finished with couching or other embroidery stitches. In cutting, allowance must be made for hems on both fabrics.

Patchwork

In Colonial days patchwork quilts were made by sewing together material of various shapes, colors, and sizes. Frequently the pieces of fabric were sewed onto a background foundation. In patchwork all of the background must be covered. A visit to any county or state fair today will show that this type of work is still popular.

Complex Appliqué

Any of the foregoing appliqué techniques can be combined, and they can also be combined with other types of embroidery.

ATTACHING APPLIQUÉD PIECES

Much of the charm of an appliquéd pattern depends upon the contour of its separate pieces; this fact should be kept in mind when planning the pattern. If the article to be made is to be washed, the fabrics must be washed and ironed before the appliqué patterns are cut out; this prevents puckering and insures even shrinkage. In cutting the pieces allowance must be made for suitable hems. The location of the pattern pieces should be outlined on the base fabric.

The cut-out pieces are sewed to the base fabric with any of the following methods:

Sewing-Machine Stitching

The appliquéd pieces are stitched down on the machine, the edges being first turned under and basted.

Blind Stitch

Small hidden stitches can be used where no further elaboration is needed. For this stitching, the needle is brought up through the fabric and pushed down at almost the same spot, making the stitch practically invisible.

Blanket or Buttonhole Stitch

Small even buttonhole stitches can be used, with the heading threads running parallel to the outside edges of the appliquéd pieces.

Miscellaneous Stitches

Other embroidery stitches can be used around the outside edges of the patterns and/or to accent details within the patterns.

Adhering Solutions

In some cases pattern pieces are glued to the base fabric.

COUCHING

In both the Near and Far East intricate allover curvilinear designs often form a background for a highly padded embroidered motif; these designs are frequently formed by metal yarns which are couched onto rich fabrics.

Yarns which are too heavy or too stiff to be otherwise used in embroidery may be couched to the surface of a fabric. The stitching which holds these floating yarns in place may be invisible or it may play an important part in the design. In the Orient two or more yarns are often laid close together and held in place with couching stitches. The stitching methods most frequently used in couching are as follows:

The Invisible Stitch

The couching stitch may catch only the very bottom edge of the laid-on pattern yarn; it is therefore practically invisible.

The Loop Stitch

The couching stitch may loop over the top of the laid-on floating yarn; it may be carried in diamond, diagonal, or other patterns over the laid-on yarn; it may be of contrasting color and thus add interest to the embroidery; it may even wrap around and entirely cover the laid-on yarns.

Interlaced Yarns

In this method long running stitches are laid down first; and the pattern yarn is then threaded in and out through them. If this pattern yarn is carried through the same side of all the stitches, a twisted cord is formed above the fabric. If it is drawn alternately through consecutive stitches, first from one side and then from the other, it forms loops on alternate sides of the running stitches.

CREWEL EMBROIDERY

A very attractive type of embroidery, known as crewel work, has enhanced Asiatic fabrics for centuries. China may have been its initiator, since it has been done there for hundreds of years. Some of the work is so fine that it takes a magnifying glass to discern the stitches. (See Fig. 177.) The fineness of the work caused many to go blind, and it is now prohibited by law in most of China.

Other countries have also produced excellent crewel embroidery. India is especially noted for her felted Numdah rugs embroidered in bright crewel-work patterns. (See page 196.) In Persia and other eastern Mediterranean lands, crewel embroidery enhances many soft-colored leather bags and slippers. The work has

Fig. 177. Crewel Embroidery. Detail of a piece of fine Chinese crewel work.

Fig. 178. Detail of Crewel Embroidery. The chain stitch is one of the important stitches of this work.

been made in England since the Jacobean period, when it was used to decorate bed and chair coverings. It was occasionally used in the American colonies to ornament quilt tops. According to d'Harcourt (*26*), the ancient Peruvians also used the stitch in some of their embroideries.

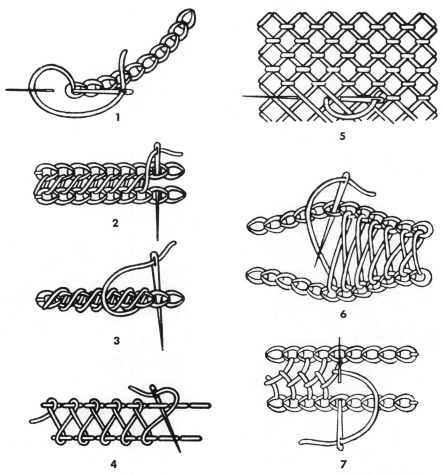

Fig. 179. Stitches Used in Crewel Embroidery. (1) Chain stitch. (2) and
(3) Chain stitch and overcast stitch. (4) Backstitch combined with fagoting.
(5) Lattice work. (6) Chain and fagoting stitches. (7) Chain and feather stitches.
Note: The chain stitch is often called the "crewel" stitch.

The chain stitch is the basic foundation stitch of crewel embroidery (see
Fig. 178); other stitches used to supplement it are the herringbone, satin,
cross, outline, filling, and couching stitches (see Fig. 179). In crewel embroidery the pattern areas are often filled in solidly with rows of chain
stitches, usually rotating from the center, around and around, toward the
edge of the area. Or parallel lines of chain stitches are set close together.
A crewel needle, a large-eyed embroidery needle, is used for this work.
Beads and other ornaments are often stitched into the embroidery.

363

CROSS-STITCH WORK

For at least 300 years cross-stitch embroidery has been a popular type of folk art. European embroiderers have long been famous for the fine *petit-point* with which they decorate evening bags and other articles. The peasant peoples of Europe use a coarser type of cross-stitch work to decorate blouses and linens.

In America needle point has been popular since Colonial days. In this type of embroidery small cross-stitches of woolen yarns are stitched into a buckram base; the heavy fabric thus made is used for upholstery.

Fig. 180.   Cross-Stitch Embroidery. Cross-stitch work on fine huck toweling, from San Miguel Allende, Mexico.

The Indians of Central and South America probably learned cross-stitching from the Spanish; at least, there seems to be no record of this type of work being done before the arrival of the Spaniards. The Indians of Mexico are especially fond of cross-stitch work, using it to decorate blouses, shoes, bags, and skirts with bright patterns. Some of the best work comes from San Miguel Allende and from Merida, Yucatan. (See Fig. 180.)

Cross-stitching is sometimes called canvas work, because it is often done on a specially prepared canvas, buckram, burlap, or huck. The fabric selected for cross-stitch work should have an open warp and weft structure, so that a needle can pass with ease through the fabric, at the crossing points of the warp and weft.

Designs for cross-stitch work should be plotted on graph paper. There are two types of cross-stitch designs, positive and negative. In positive cross-stitch, the pattern proper is done in the cross-stitch technique; in negative cross-stitch, only the background around the pattern is done. Positive cross-stitch is used for petit-point, a very fine type of work; needle point, a medium-fine work; regular cross-stitch, a medium type; and gros-point, a large type, made on burlap and used for rugs and upholstery material. Negative cross-stitch is used for Assisi work, which is always done in two tones, such as brown yarn on beige linen. (The Holbein stitch is also often used as a background for negative pattern work.)

There are several ways of doing cross-stitch. The easiest method is to make one-half of the stitch entirely across one row of the pattern —half of a cross-stitch is a tent stitch—then reverse the direction, returning across the row with the other half of the stitch.

Fig. 181. Drawnwork and Cutwork. A linen fabric from Italy.

CUTWORK

Cutwork is a very old form of embroidery, thought to have originated in the Near East. It became very popular on the Continent and in England in the late Middle Ages. In his chronicle of King Richard's reign, Harding said: "Cut werke was greate both in court and townes."

Cutwork is a type of free embroidery; it is a lacelike web made above the surface of the fabric; at its outer edge it is stitched firmly to the fabric with a buttonhole stitch. When the pattern web is finished, the fabric under the web is cut out, leaving the lacelike web inserted in the solid fabric. (See Fig. 181.) Many historians think that cutwork was the immediate predecessor of needle-point lace. The principal types of cutwork are the following:

Simple Cutwork

Fabrics stamped for the cutwork that is described above can be purchased.

Renaissance

The same as simple cutwork, except that brides or bars are used to connect the elements of the design.

Richelieu

The same as Renaissance, except that the bars have picots on them.

Italian Cutwork

The brides are heavy and form a lacelike web cross the open areas. This form of cutwork later became reticella lace.

Hardanger

Made in Norway, this type of cutwork is combined with solid areas of satin-stitch embroidery. This work is also known as Kloster blocks, because the alternating cut-out and solid areas are in small squares.

Cluny

A web of heavy thread is made above the cut-out area, with the yarns radiating from the center in a spider web type of pattern.

Hedebo

A Danish type of embroidery in which cutwork, drawnwork, and other types of embroidery stitches are combined.

DRAWNWORK

Pieces of ancient fabrics containing areas of drawnwork have been found on both Eastern and Western Hemispheres. It is apparent from studying these fabrics that several methods of work were used. In some cases open nonwoven areas had been left through the warp during weaving—this process is described under hemstitching; in other cases yarns had been drawn out of the woven materials. Occasionally, both warp and weft yarns had been pulled out, and in these openings various types of needlework had been done. Work of this last type has been found in both ancient Peruvian burial sites and in Egyptian tombs of the Graeco-Roman period.

Drawnwork gets its name from the fact that yarns, warp and/or weft, are pulled out of a fabric, and in the open areas thus created weblike embroidery is done. Many stitches can be combined to enhance drawnwork; some frequently used are the following:

Simple Hemstitching

This is described later in this section.

Gauze Stitches

Leno and gauze twists are made in the warp, using an accessory weft. This technique is described in the discussion of gauze weaving.

Knot Work

The warps are grouped together and held in place with fancy knots.

Russian Work

A solid pattern is silhouetted against a background of meshlike drawnwork.

Bavarian Work

The fabric appears to have alternate squares of plain weave and open areas, the latter adorned with needle-made wheels like those on Cluny lace. Both warp and weft yarns are drawn from the fabric at even intervals: for example, 1/4 inch will be drawn out and 1/4 inch left intact, both warpwise and weftwise. Large floral patterns, highly padded and worked in the satin stitch, are often placed upon the same cloth that has areas of this particular drawnwork. This type of work is also made in Majorca. (See Figs. 182 and 183.)

Fig. 182. Drawnwork. Drawnwork, known as Bavarian work, from Bavaria, Germany

Needle Weaving

Patterns are woven into opened warp areas. Tapestry needles are used.

EYELET EMBROIDERY

Eyelet embroidery, often called Madeira work, is used to adorn cottons and linens. The openwork effect is obtained by punching small holes **367** or eyelets in the fabric and finishing their edges with satin stitches. This type of embroidery can be machine-made and is produced commercially in large quantities. It is used most on flounces and edgings but is also produced in wide yard goods.

Before punching or cutting out any of the holes, small running stitches are sewed around the areas to be opened. A small stiletto is used to punch

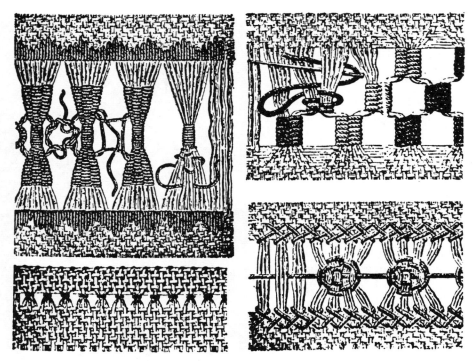

Fig. 183. Drawnwork Techniques. Upper right, the fagoting stitch being used. Lower left, an example of hemstitching. (C. R. Clifford, *The Lace Dictionary*, Clifford & Lawton, 1913.)

the smaller holes, and scissors or double-bladed knives to cut open the larger areas. These large holes are cut in a special fashion: the fabric is slit across the center of the area to be opened; for square holes other slits are made to the corners; for round, oblong, or other shapes, slits are radiated from the center to the sides. The surplus fabric is then folded back and the edges finished with the satin stitch.

Designs for eyelet embroidery usually include daisylike flowers with open pointed petals. Some of the cut areas are highly padded before edging with the satin stitch. The stem stitch and the buttonhole stitch are also used to cover and to strengthen the edges of the cut out areas. The buttonhole stitch is usually used to cover the scalloped edge which finishes the outside edge of the piece. (See Fig. 184.)

FAGOTING

Fagoting is both a type of embroidery and an embroidery stitch; it is used to join together two pieces of fabric. The fagoting stitch is related to several other stitches. For example, it is a combination of a backstitch and a loop; it is also two reversed half-hitch stitches; it is made the same as the herringbone, except that smaller catch stitches are

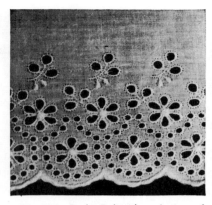

Fig. 184. Eyelet Embroidery. A piece of machine-made work.

taken. The work progresses from *left to right*, but the stitch is made from *right to left*, moving back and forth across an opening, first in the hem of one fabric and then in the hem of the other. Each backstitch is laid down slightly forward of the position of the last stitch on the opposite side of the opening. As the stitches pass over the opening, they automatically cross. (See Fig. 179, No. 4.) For variation the fagoting stitches may be twisted around one another or knotted as they cross. Fagoting is used in various ways, some of which are described in the following paragraphs.

Type 1: Open Lacelike Braid

For this work, a pattern delineating the strips to be fagoted is first made on heavy paper and a second pattern traced from it. The second paper is cut into its respective parts, laid on the fabric, and the fabric cut out to conform to the shapes of the pattern. The edges to be joined are then turned under and a narrow hem basted in them. Next the fabric pieces are tacked or basted onto the heavy stiff paper pattern so that the spaces between them are uniform and of the right width; usually, the edges to be fagoted are basted about 1/3 of an inch apart. Regular backstitch fagoting stitches, made about 1/8 of an inch apart, are used to join the edges.

Type 2: Solid Binding Braid

In this technique figure 8 stitches placed close together interlace back and forth between the edges of two adjacent pieces of fabric. Unlike regular fagoting, the backstitch is not used; the needle penetrates through one edge and then through the other, always entering the fabric from the back. The

369

Indians of Guatemala use this technique to bind together the two strips of material used in their skirts.

Type 3: Wrapped-Cord Braid

Although this work is listed here because it is done with a needle and thread, it resembles tapestry weaving more than it does embroidery. The Indians of ancient Peru and Mexico (26) used this special type of fagoting in constructing certain braids and trimmings. In this work, the yarns are carried back and forth in a series of figure 8 loops, wrapping over and under two adjacent cords. To facilitate handling, the cords are sometimes couched lightly to a basic fabric. This is the same method used in wrapped-warp tapestry weaving to cover groups of warp. (See Fig. 183.)

HEMSTITCHING

Hemstitching is an embroidery technique closely related to drawnwork. Here uniform groups of yarns in an open area in the fabric are pulled together by means of a needle and thread. Between each group of constricted yarns, the thread pulling them together is carried through the adjoining edge of the fabric. Hemstitching is sometimes made in the warp during weaving, or in openings reserved for it during the weaving process. To provide space in this way while weaving, a cardboard strip, wider than the width of the fabric, is slipped into the warp during weaving. Hemstitching is also made in open areas formed by drawing out from a woven fabric some of the warp or weft yarns, or even some of both. (See Fig. 183.)

MOCK WEAVING

A number of embroidery types closely resemble weaving in appearance. In mock weaving, a tapestry needle carries the yarn in a running stitch, either through the meshes of a loosely woven fabric or under the floating yarns of a specially structured fabric, such as huck toweling.

MOCK WEAVING ON PLAIN-WEAVE FABRICS

Tourists in Mexico have been delighted with the beautiful embroidered dresses in the shops there. Much of this embroidery is in the form of "mock weaving" and is done in wool on coarse hand-woven cotton fabrics. (See Fig. 185.) Various stitches are used for this work, some of the more important being the running stitch, the false satin stitch, and the darning stitch.

Fig. 185. Mock Weaving. Running-stitch embroidery—the stitching runs around the fabric row by row. The work looks like brocade. Made in Mexico.

The Running Stitch

This is carried along the back of the fabric in long skips, showing also in long skips in the design areas on the face of the fabric. The work is done one row at a time, entirely across or around the fabric. (See Fig. 185.)

False Satin Stitch

The false satin stitch is used to make ornamental patterns arranged in wide bands; it is used to ornament skirts, blouses, jackets, and other garments. The regular satin stitch can be used too, but the stitches should be widely spaced for this type of work. The false satin stitch is described on page 353.

The Darning Stitch

This is a running stitch which is used on huck toweling and similar fabrics; it is carried under the floating yarns of such fabrics.

371

MOCK WEAVING ON HUCK TOWELING AND WAFFLE-WEAVE FABRICS

One mock weaving process is used effectively on huck towels; yarns are run through their floating warp loops. When fine huck toweling is embroidered with fine embroidery floss, a dainty open design results; but if the huck is coarse and the design is worked in heavy wool, a woven effect is produced. If woolen yarn is to be used, a coarse huck fabric should be chosen; otherwise, it will be extremely difficult to pull the yarn through the huck loops. Abstract designs are generally used for this work. (See Fig. 186.) Mock weaving on huck toweling is done in the following manner:

Fig. 186. Mock Weaving. Waffle-weave embroidery from Germany. (Courtesy, Rozina Skidmore.)

1. Count the number of huck loops on one row across the surface of the towel; mark the center loop. Count the number of loops needed for one complete repeat of the pattern. Dividing this number into the total number of available loops will determine the number of possible pattern repeats. Arrange the pattern so that one unit will be centered on the toweling. The design may be a spot pattern, a border pattern, or an allover pattern.

2. Use a tapestry needle to carry the yarn, taking it across the fabric one row at a time. If the pattern requires it, the yarn may skip across certain of the loops, or may even be carried several rows upward.

3. The background of the design is filled in either as the work progresses or after the design areas have all been finished.

BUCKRAM EMBROIDERY

Colored woolen yarns form effective geometric patterns when laced through buckram, burlap, or tapestry canvas. (See Fig. 187.) The fineness or coarseness of this work depends upon the texture of the fabric and the weight of yarn selected. Any of the stitches used for mock weaving on plain-weave fabrics can be used, and cross-stitch work is often done on buckram. The designs are usually geometric—squares, diamonds, frets, and step patterns. Buckram embroidery is simple to do.

1. Cut out the article to be made, allowing for suitable seams.
2. Count the number of holes across the fabric and find the center hole. Plot the design so that it will be centered on the fabric.
3. Choose the type of stitch to be used, and embroider the center first; this insures a symmetrical design.

QUILTING

The tufted work known as quilting is made by stitching designs into padded areas on a fabric. It is used to ornament quilts, clothing, upholstery, etc. The designs may be geometric, curvilinear, abstract, or realistic. The running stitch is generally used for the work.

The effects obtained in quilting depend upon the type of material and kind of padding used. Padding may be made out of a variety of materials. First in importance is cotton batting, which is laid be-

Fig. 187. Mock Weaving. Running-stitch embroidery on rayon burlap.

tween the surface fabric and the backing cloth. Cotton batting sometimes comes enclosed in cheesecloth; in this case no backing cloth is necessary. Next in importance as padding material are cords; these are arranged between the surface fabric and the backing cloth and are generally outlined in the running stitch. Tufts of hair, wool, and cotton are also sometimes used for padding; they are pushed between two rows of stitching as the work is being done.

PUNCH WORK

Punch work is an allover, lacelike, openwork embroidery—really a kind of allover background treatment. The area to be treated is perforated with small holes, made by a large needle. The holes are kept open by sets of yarns which are pulled between the holes and connect them. Unlike eyelet embroidery, the edges around the holes are left unfinished. Directions for punch work are outlined below:

1. Mark the pattern areas of the material with dots placed equally distant apart.
2. Using a large three-edged sail needle threaded with embroidery floss, perforate the first dot from the back of the fabric and bring the needle through the fabric. Perforate the next dot on the same horizontal row, pushing the threaded needle below the fabric.
3. The third dot to be perforated is the one immediately below the first dot. Bring the needle up through it and carry it across to the fourth dot, the one immediately below the second dot; push the needle below the fabric. Come up again in the fifth dot, below the third dot. Continue in this manner down the column of dots. Pull the yarn taut, so that the holes are opened, but not tight enough to pucker the cloth. When one column is finished, start the next.
4. After all the stitches connecting the horizontal dots are made, turn the fabric. Perforate the dots again and open them still wider by making stitches at right angles to those first made.

SMOCKING

In smocking fancy stitches are used to hold down folds of a soft material. The process is as follows:

1. Mark the material in the areas to be smocked, using dots about 1/4 of an inch apart to mark off the folds. Transfer patterns may be purchased for this work. It is usually recommended that the fabric be stamped on the wrong side.
2. Run gathering threads through the dots across each row of these dots. Pull up the gathers in each row to the width desired, taking care to arrange the folds in vertical columns. Usually the fabric is pulled up about two and one-half times or to a width somewhat less than half the original width of the fabric.
3. Turn the fabric to the right side and arrange the top edges of the folds in place. The folds are then fastened permanently in place by means of special embroidery stitches. When the work is finished the basting stitches are removed.

Many different embroidery stitches are used in smocking; those most frequently used are the outline, cable, chain, herringbone, feather, stem, and Van Dyke stitches, and French knots. The stitches are usually arranged in

374

patterns; they can form straight lines, diamonds, chevrons, zigzags, honey-combs, and latticework. Directions for a few popular types of smocking are given here.

Basket or Cable Pattern

The stitching runs straight across the plaits.

Chevron Pattern

The stitches zigzag up and down from one fold to the next and the joining thread shows on the outside of the work. (See Fig. 188.)

Honeycombing

Alternate folds on alternate rows are caught with a small couch stitch. In this case the joining threads run on the back of the fabric. The folds are not basted in for this work.

Herringbone

This is a variation of the outline stitch. Since this is one of the most popular stitches used for smocking, detailed instructions for it are given. For the first stitch, throw the thread to the left, above the needle, and combine two folds. For the next stitch, throw the thread to the right below the needle, drop down 1/8 of an inch, and combine the right half of the last fold with the next fold to its immediate right. Repeat, passing up and down between two rows.

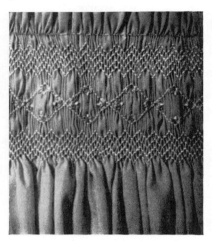

Fig. 188. Smocking.

MISCELLANEOUS TYPES OF EMBROIDERY

APPENZELL EMBROIDERY. (Switzerland) Satin stitches laid end to end.

ARASENE WORK. Embroidery made with a mixed thread, as silk and wool.

BERLIN WORK. Wool embroidery on canvas. The designs were formerly printed in Berlin.

CANDLEWICKING. A loop work made by bringing the yarn over a little rod and then securing the loop with a few running stitches. See the discussion of tufting, page 189.

DARNING. Four general types of darning are used in embroidery: plain darning, in which a warp and weft are interwoven above the surface of a fabric; filet darning, in which a warp and weft are darned into the holes of an open net; interweaving darning, in which a weft is darned over and under into an open warp on the loom; and mock weaving, in which a weft is darned into the warp of a woven fabric.

FLORENTINE WORK (FLAME STITCH). An irregular satin stitch is done in stair-step combinations that dovetail. Various colors, usually grading from dark to light, are combined. See *Flame stitch*, page 353.

ITALIAN RELIEF WORK. The pattern area is embroidered with an alternating purl buttonhole stitch—one stitch passes left to right and the next from right to left. Each row loops back over the loops of the last row.

MORAVIAN WORK. Immigrants from Moravia, a part of Czechoslovakia, made pictures of Biblical scenes in embroidery.

SHADOW WORK. Fagoting stitches fill in each pattern, worked across the pattern from border to border on the back of transparent material.

STUMP WORK. A heavily padded embroidery in which wads of hair or wool are used as padding.

TAMBOUR WORK. Tambour work was introduced into France by Madame de Pompadour. It was popular in America for many years after the Revolution. A notched or tambour needle—a special kind of crochet needle—is used for this work; it is manipulated so that a chain or crochet stitch is formed on the fabric. The yarn is held under the fabric with the left hand; it is caught by the hook and pulled up to the top of the fabric, and is then drawn over the last loop made; this forms a crocheted chain stitch.

TURKEY WORK. This is a cut knot-pile work made on an open scrim burlap. The English were very fond of Turkey work in the past century. The Ghiordes knot was used for the work. Rows of knot work stood in contrast to rows of cross-stitch (*113*).

PART THREE

NONSTRUCTURAL ORNAMENTATION

CHAPTER X

Dyes and Dyeing Processes

Man learned early that color improved the appearance of his possessions. In very old archaeological sites, simple fabrics have been found which still possess traces of applied color. O'Neale (*46*), in discussing the range of colors found in ancient Peru, mentions 190 different hues! Apparently dyeing had reached a peak of excellence on the Western Hemisphere at a period roughly corresponding with the beginning of our Christian era. (See Figs. 189 and 190.)

Many dyes of the early historic period came from the ancient Near East, purple, red, and blue being the colors most favored. At an early date the Phoenicians gained a monopoly of Tyrian purple, trading it widely in the Mediterranean area. In early historical writings the dyeing of fabrics is mentioned frequently. A number of verses in the Bible are concerned with the use of dyes: from Exodus comes, "rams skins dyed red"; from Isaiah, "dyed garments from Bozrah"; and from Ezekiel, "images of Chaldeans portrayed with vermillion—with dyed turbans." Herodotus, the Greek historian, told of the red dyes of Libya; and Pliny, the Roman historian, described the ancient Egyptian methods of dyeing and mordanting.

During the Middle Ages and into the early years of the Renaissance, the dye industry spread from the eastern Mediterranean centers toward the west and then gradually northward into Europe. It is reported that there were some 200 dye enterprises in Jerusalem in the twelfth century (*136*). In 1160 A.D., Jewish dyers, extending their influence westward, gained control of most of the Italian dye industry. In the fourteenth century Florence was especially famous for her many dye works. As the Renaissance progressed and Europe began importing indigo and other dyes, many controversies arose concerning the handling and control of foreign dyestuffs.

379

Fig. 189. Ikat Dyeing from Ancient Peru. Peruvian shawl from Viru, Peru. (Courtesy, The American Museum of Natural History.)

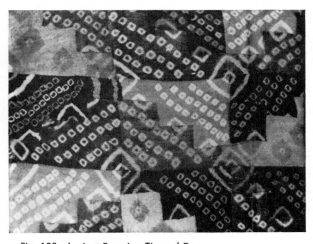

Fig. 190. Ancient Peruvian Tie and Dye. Ancient patchwork tie and dye from Chanca, Peru. (Courtesy, Museo Nacional de Antropología y Arqueología, Lima.)

Up to the middle of the nineteenth century natural dyes were the only ones available. Since 1856, when W. H. Perkins made his discoveries concerning aniline dye, synthetic dyes have gradually replaced natural dyes.

The history of the dye industry in the United States is interesting. Two world wars were largely responsible for making this country independent producers in the dye market. At the beginning of World War I the United States found herself in the embarrassing position of being without dyes, since she had been entirely dependent upon the European dye market, and principally the German market. At that time Germany held most of the dye patents and produced most of the synthetic dyes for the world market. Fabrics dyed in the United States during the first part of the war often lost their color in the first laundering. Experimental work was quickly undertaken to correct this condition. In 1917, certain companies in the United States were issued licenses to use dye patents formerly held by enemy aliens; by 1919, the Chemical Foundation Incorporated had licensed the use of some 4500 basic German patents on drugs and dyes. These licenses made possible the manufacture of vat dyes and dyes of faster colors. After the war, the dyes being produced within the country supplied over 60 percent of those needed for home consumption. In 1921, the importation was forbidden of any dye that was produced in this country. High protective tariffs levied on all other dyes allowed the young American dye industry to forge ahead.

By 1940, the United States was well established in the dye industry, but still not completely independent. The revived German chemical drug and dye industries were again a potent force in the world dye market. At the beginning of World War II the patents held by German dye companies in eastern cities in the United States were again confiscated and distributed among the leading American dye manufacturers. The result is that the United States has now become an independent producer of dyes.

Although the discovery of dyes has been of tremendous importance in the history of a culture, of no less importance is the manner in which these dyes have been put to use. Over the ages special textile design processes, dependent upon the particular use of dyes, have been developed by various peoples in different lands. In south-

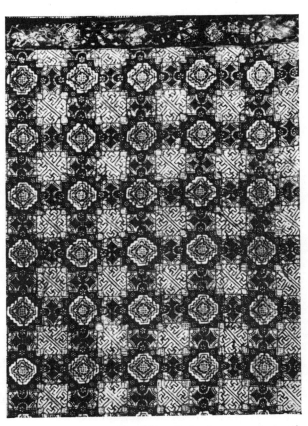

Fig. 191. Batik. Javanese nineteenth century printed and painted cotton. (Courtesy of the Metropolitan Museum of Art.)

eastern Asia, for example, dyeing techniques were eventually perfected to the degree that they became fine arts. Very beautiful textiles have been produced by such processes as tie and dye, batik, mordant pattern dyeing, and discharge dyeing. (See Fig. 191.)

1. Color—What It Is

Nature is the source of all of our colors and dyes; she has literally sheathed herself in the colors of the rainbow. What a dreary world this would be without this array of color! Of even more interest is the fact that these colors can be extracted from nature—from plants, flowers, and other organic substances—and transferred to materials of our own choosing. Any discussion of the transfer of color automatically enters the realm of dyes. But we cannot discuss the subject of dyes, without discussing color; nor can we understand color unless we know something about the structure and reaction of dyes.

Color is the result of complex physical and chemical phenomena. Three different kinds of activity are involved: the eye or receptor, the light or transmitter, and the object or reflector.

There is an interaction between light waves and the retina of the eye. The eye is so constructed that it can distinguish color. Color therefore has a personal interpretation. Both eye and light are required to make color possible; without either there is no color. But there is also more to color than meets the eye.

White light is composed of all the colors—when white light passes into and is dispersed by a prism, it is separated into its many parts, and each color has a different wave length and a different frequency. Color also results when light is subjected to interference, refraction, diffraction, and reflection.

When light strikes an object, it is absorbed or reflected, and transmitted. If all of the light is absorbed, the result is no color or black; if all of the light is reflected, the result is total color or white. Gray is a slight reflection of all the colors. When the light strikes an object, the usual reaction between the two is chromatic: that is, part of the light is filtered out or absorbed by the object and part is reflected, the part reflected constituting the light waves rejected by the object. In general, the reflected light becomes the color of the object. There is an interrelation, then, between the light and the object: the light furnishes the original source of color and the object by selectivity reflects the secondary source. The secondary source then is transmitted to the eye by means of light.

There are several theories to explain these reactions, most of them based upon the electrical energy of the molecule. It has been suggested that the electrons vibrating at a certain frequency within a molecule absorb color waves of the same frequency. Since each molecule is composed of a special structure of positive and negative particles, and since light rays range from short ultraviolet to long infrared, this theory is plausible.

From this standpoint, bleaching is explained as a shifting of electrons from one compound to another, with a resulting change in the physical structure and chemical composition of the molecule. Bleaching is also described as resulting from the breakdown or splitting-up of the double bonds in the chromophore, or color-giving group, within the molecule.

382

To the textile design student, there is still another phase of color which is of tremendous importance. This concerns the chemistry and other properties of dyes; for example, each dye has a different chemical composition, and each reacts differently when it comes in contact with the various fibers. More information on this subject is given later.

COLOR IDENTIFICATION

Color identification and color matching have become important to both industry and science. Since a verbal description of a color seldom conveys the same message to two individuals, the standardization of color has been of tremendous importance. Although there are a number of color identification systems on the market, they all depend upon a graded arrangement of colors which are numbered in sequence. Sets of color cards are available to many special interest groups; for example:

Archaeologists. The colors of ancient artifacts can be accurately described.[1]

Geologists. Soil colors can be accurately recorded.[2]

Designers. Costume designers, interior decorators, stage-set designers, and all artists who sell their work for commercial duplication are greatly helped by being able to tabulate definite color arrangements.[3]

Manufacturers. Manufacturers of carpets, drapery, and upholstery materials, and other furnishings are able to produce fabrics of the same or related colors.

Retailers and consumers. Through the retailer, consumers are now able to order from the manufacturer colored fabrics which will match identically those already in use in the home.[4]

Stylists. The world of fashion has for a number of years been able to use a color tabulation system which is published annually; this consists of a large folder containing color tabs which keynote the style preferences for the coming seasons.[5]

2. Sources of Dyes

The dyes we use come from many different materials scattered about the world at large. The sources of dyes are generally classified as being either

---

[1] A. Maerz and M. R. Paul, *A Short Dictionary of Color*, McGraw-Hill Book Company, New York, 1950. This book contains actual color cards.

[2] Munsell Soil Color Charts, distributed by Munsell Color Company, Inc., Baltimore, Md.

[3] Munsell Color-Card System, distributed by Munsell Color Company, Inc., Baltimore, Md.

[4] Color Index (dye formulas), Society of Dyers and Colourists and American Association of Textile Chemists and Colorists, Lowell Technological Institute, Lowell, Mass., 1956.

[5] Standard Color Card of America, 9th ed., The Color Association of the United States, Inc., New York, 1941; published in 15 year intervals. A series of special color cards is also published; these come out biannually.

natural or man-made. Natural dyes are divided into animal, vegetable, mineral, and metal dyes; the man-made or synthetic dyes, which can be broken down into many complex chemical divisions, are generally considered as being derivatives of the double-bond, six-carbon, benzene-ring molecule.

NATURAL DYES

Prior to the discovery of synthetic dyes in the last half of the nineteenth century, only natural dyes—animal, vegetable, metal, or mineral—were used. Many of these natural dyes were difficult to secure and were therefore very costly. The story of some of the more important of them reads like a novel.

One of the most important dyes of the Near East was a red dye secured from the Kermes, a scale insect (coccus ilicis) which lived on oak trees in the Mediterranean region. The dye was made from the dried bodies of the female Kermes.

The most cherished dye of the ancient Near East was Tyrian purple—a dye extracted from the murex brandaris and murex trunculus, shellfish similar to snails. According to legend, about 1000 B.C. a young couple on the coast near Tyre noticed that their dog's throat was spattered with a purplish-red dye after killing a shellfish—an event that is supposed to have led to the discovery of the dye. A colorless liquid, found in a little vein in this particular shellfish, oxidizes in air to become a red-purple.

Sometimes Tyrian purple was extracted by hand, but usually it was prepared in large vats. The shellfish were crushed, soaked in salt water three days, and strained. More salt was added to the liquid, which was heated and allowed to ripen. It was reheated to a moderate temperature over a period of six days, and finally evaporated to a dry powder. It is said that 12,000 of the little shellfish were needed to produce 1 1/2 grams of coloring matter—and there are 31.2 grams in an ounce. The shell middens or heaps of discarded mollusk shells left by the ancient dyers can still be seen near the former sites of Tyre and Sidon.

In his *Life of Alexander*, Plutarch told of Greek soldiers finding purple fabrics stained with this dye in the tomb of Darius; the fabrics had still retained their beautiful color after 190 years. Purple dye became so costly that in 301 A.D. an edict in Rome set the price of wool colored with it at $350.00 a pound and decreed that only members of the nobility could wear purple *(141)*. All this perhaps explains the old phrase "royal robes of purple."

There is evidence that the ancient Peruvians and Mayans used a purple dye secured from a similar variety of shellfish, the purpura lapillus, which lived along the west coasts of the Americas *(5)*. The Quiché Indians of

384

Guatemala still demand a higher price for any textile that contains even a few threads dyed with this purple.

A half-century ago, Dr. Paul Friedlaender, of Biebrich-on-the-Rhine, discovered that this purple dye is a brom-indigo color, bromine and indigo base. Many synthetic purple dyes on the market at the present time are superior to this famous ancient dye.

India is usually spoken of as having first developed the full resources of the dyeing trade. Her early dyers were familiar with the madders, nutgalls, blue and green vitriol, and indigo. The Romans gave the name of indicium to the blue indigo dye, reflecting its Indian source. Later it came to be known as indican and finally indigo. The indigo plant, indigoferae, a member of the pea family, has a yellow juice that oxidizes to blue upon exposure to air. For commercial use the blue indigo paste must be reduced to a yellow fluid before yarn or cloth is dipped into it for dyeing. In the old world the reducing agent for this was fermented urine. The Spanish taught its use to the Indians on the Western Hemisphere, though long before the arrival of the Spaniards, the Incas were dyeing fabrics with indigo as were the Indians of Central America and the West Indies. What they used as a reducing agent is not known. The plant from which indigo is obtained in the West Indies is anil.

The Chinese were also skillful dyers and users of indigo. Marco Polo, in his description of Kanbalu, now Peking, said: "Indigo also of an excellent quality, and in large quantities, is made here. They procure it from an herbaceous plant, which is taken up by the roots and put into tubs of water, where it is suffered to remain until it rots, when they press out the juice; this on being exposed to the sun and evaporated, leaves a kind of paste which is cut into small pieces of the form which we see it brought to us."

Indigo was rarely used in Europe prior to the latter half of the sixteenth century, at which time the Dutch and Portuguese imported it from India. Its introduction was strongly opposed by the growers of woad, which had hitherto been the chief material for blue dye in Europe, though it had only a tenth the dyeing strength of indigo.[6] In the reign of Elizabeth I, a law was passed forbidding the use of indigo in order to protect the home woad industry.

Another dye which has been of extreme importance since ancient times is madder, a red dye extracted from the root of the madder plant. This dye is also known as dyer's root; the Arabs call it alizari; it is also known as the famous Turkey red. The process of dyeing a fabric with Turkey red

[6] When the Romans arrived in England, they found that the ancient warriers of Briton dyed their bodies blue with woad (5).

was once a lengthy one, requiring about three months to go through all the steps. The fabric passed through several color-setting or mordanting processes. It was first soaked in rancid fatty oil, then in a bath of alum, and then in limewater. These steps were repeated. The material was then boiled in fine ground madder root, after which it was boiled and washed in a soap solution. The entire cycle was repeated until the color was sufficiently dark. When alizarin dye was eventually made synthetically, the formula duplicated the chemical and physical composition of the madder dye. Where the ancient dyeing process had taken months to complete, the modern method using the new Turkey red, a synthetic alizarin, is now only a matter of hours. Consequently, synthetic alizarin has practically replaced madder dye.

From the Western Hemisphere came cochineal, a beautiful red dye which became the first product to be exported from the New World to Europe. This dye comes from cochineal insects (coccus cacti) that grow on several species of cactus in Central America. The cochineal grains, the dried bodies of these insects, run 70,000 to the pound. For a long time, the Navahos unraveled European woolen fabric dyed with cochineal and rewove it into their Bayeta blankets. They apparently found it more convenient to do this than to secure the cochineal dye. The dye still has a considerable amount of prestige—for example, the coats of Britain's Royal Guard are still dyed with cochineal.

A very important scarlet dye comes from the lac, a scale insect (tachardia lacca) which lives on trees, especially on certain species of the genus ficus. These insects are extensively cultivated in northern India. The color resembles cochineal and was formerly used with cochineal. Another variety of this insect is the garnet lac, named because of its deep red color (169).

IMPORTANT NATURAL DYES

Name	Color	Source	Location
Vegetable Dyes			
Alder	Red	Bark	U.S.
Avocado	Brown	Seed	Tropical districts
Archil	Purple	Lichens	Scotland
Barwood	Blue, black	Wood	Africa
Birch	Yellow, brown	Bark	U.S.
Blackberry	Black	Young shoots	U.S.
Black Oak	Black (with alum)	Bark	U.S.
Brazilwood	Red-purple	Wood	Brazil
Broom	Yellow	Flowers	Scotland, U.S.
Curcumin	Yellow	Root	Asia
Cutch (Acacia)	Brown	Wood	India
Dandelion	Yellow	Flowers	U.S.

Name	Color	Source	Location
Elderberry	Blue	Berry	U.S.
Elder	Black (with copperas)	Bark	U.S.
Fungus	Orange	Mold	U.S.
Fustic	Yellow	Wood	Cuba, West Indies, Europe
Hops	Yellow	Fruit	U.S.
Huizachi	Black	Pod	Mexico
Indigo	Blue	Plant juice	West Indies, Central America, China, etc.
Logwood (+mordants)	Purple, black, or red	Wood	Campeche, Mexico
Onion skins	Yellow	Skins	Universal
Madder	Red	Root	India and Near East
Maple bark	Purple (with copperas)	Bark	Eastern U.S.
Quercitron	Brown	Bark	America
Rabbit bush	Yellow	Flowers	Western U.S.
Saffron (yellow crocus)	Yellow	Flowers	China, Egypt
Mango	Golden brown	Bark	India, etc.
Sandal wood	Red	Wood	Tropical districts
Sorrell (wild rhubarb)	Yellow	Flowers	Western U.S.
Sumac (aromatic)	Black	Twigs	Western U.S.
Tumeric	Yellow	Root	India, China
Walnut	Brown	Nut husks	Italy, U.S.
Water Lily	Brown	Root	U.S.
Weld	Yellow	Plant	France, Italy
Whortle (blueberry)	Blue, purple	Berry	U.S., etc.
Woad	Blue	Leaf	England, Europe
Wolf moss	Yellow	Lichen	N.W., North America
Yellow Iris	Blue	Root	U.S.

Animal Dyes

Name	Color	Source	Location
Cochineal	Red	Insect	Central America
Kermes	Red	Insect	Near East
Lac	Red	Insect	India, East Asia
Murex	Purple, red	Shellfish	Mediterranean Coasts
Purpura	Purple	Shellfish	West Coasts of America
Cuttle fish (squid)	Black	Cephalopod	Widespread

Metal and Mineral Dyes

Name	Color	Source	Location
Iron (oxide)	Red	Metal	
Copper (sulfate)	Blue-green	Metal	
Chrome (sulfate)	Yellow	Metal	
Sulfur	Black, etc.	Mineral	

ARTIFICIAL AND SYNTHETIC DYES

Research in the possibilities of new dyes started as early as the beginning of the eighteenth century. In 1704, Diesbach produced the pigment Prussian blue; in 1771, Woulfe discovered picric acid in indigo; in 1817, Stromeyer produced cadmium yellow; in 1824, Guimet achieved artificial ultramarine blue; in 1834, Runge discovered the use of nitric and rosolic acids in dye preparations; and in 1838, Guimet produced artificial viridian. However, important as such experiments may have been, they were but forerunners of the great aniline dye discoveries made in the last half of the nineteenth century. The principle highlights of the aniline dye story are as follows:

1826: Aniline first discovered by Unverdorben in Holland as a product of indigo. It seems likely that the name, aniline, was derived from the American indigo plant, anil. (Now the process is reversed and indigo is synthesized from an aniline compound!)

1856: W. H. Perkin, an English chemist, accidentally discovered the first synthetic aniline color, a mauve (27).

1858: A magenta was discovered by R. W. Hoffman, whose name is largely associated with the napthalene colors, of which there is a wide range.

1859: Fuchsine, a magenta dye, was discovered by Vergiun.

1862: Nicholson discovered a blue acid dye for wool.

1862: Lightfoot discovered aniline black.

1864: Griess discovered azo dyes.

1865: The Kekule benzene theory was established.

1867: Poirrier and Chappat discovered methyl violet.

1868: Graebe and Liebermann discovered the alizarine colors. These have the same chemical composition as the natural madder dyes.

1880: Baeyer synthesized indigo.

1873: Croissant and Bretonnière developed sulfur dyes, the thionation of aromatic hydrocarbons.

1879: Nietzki developed Biebrich scarlet.

1884: Bottinger discovered the direct dye, congo red.

The above list is not complete, nor does it suggest the extensive experimentation which has taken place since 1884. Many large corporations now maintain specialist staffs who seek to perfect various aspects of the dye industry. One of the world's largest laboratories for industrial chemical research is the Jackson Laboratory of the Du Pont Company. A problem with which most technicians are currently concerned is the dyeing of synthetic fibers.

The synthetic dye industry is indeed a highly technical one. The so-called artificial dyes are synthetized coal tar products made from benzene, anthacene, naphthalene, toluene, xylene, and other related compounds.[7]

Synthetic dyes can be produced more easily and cheaply than natural dyes and can also be standardized to a dependable color range. Since the

[7] The chemical formula for aniline is $C_6H_5NH_2$. The aniline compound is a derivative of benzene, C_6H_5; the carbons in benzene are arranged in what is known as the benzene ring, a hexagonal structure which has a carbon located on each point.

middle of the nineteenth century, when synthetic colors were first discovered, they have gradually been replacing natural dyes, though some natural dyes are still used, especially in the Near and Far East.

3. Properties of Dyes

Dyes are rather complex chemical compounds which react in a number of ways. Dyes can be defined as a class of substances known as colloidal electrolytes, their conductivity depending upon the mobility of the ions present. The general public thinks of dyes as a class of coloring compounds, and that may be sufficient for us, since we are not going into the chemical background and reactions of dyes.

In order to have even a rudimentary understanding of dyes, it is necessary to know something of their properties and reactions. Dyes can be classified according to source, physical structure, chemical composition and structure, color quality, color fastness, toxic effect, affinity for certain fibers, methods of application, dependence upon auxiliary agents, and reactions with mordants. All of these topics are discussed in this section.

PHYSICAL STRUCTURE

Technically, fibers are colored by either pigments or dyes. Pigments are made up of larger molecules than dyes. The pigment carries or imparts its own color; the dye transfers its color to a solid. Pigments generally have to be adhered to fibers by means of special resins or adhesive agents. Both dyes and pigments have natural and synthetic sources. Pigments are suspended in solutions, dyes are dissolved in solutions.

CHEMICAL COMPOSITION

Dyes are classified according to chemical composition into acid dyes, basic dyes, developed or diazo dyes, direct cotton or substantive dyes, naphthol or azoic dyes, sulphur dyes, chrome dyes, vat dyes, indigosol dyes, union dyes, direct acetate dyes, mordant or adjective dyes, and other dyes for special synthetic fibers. Such a classification is obviously a superficial one. In scientific circles, dyes are classified chemically into many complex divisions according to the arrangement of benzene-ring molecules, linkages, double bonds, and substituted chromophore and auxochrome groups.

COLOR QUALITY

The range of hue, value, and chroma of dyes has considerably increased since the advent of synthetic dyes, but in many instances there has been less improvement in color quality. A comparison of a fabric dyed with

389

natural dyes and one dyed with synthetic dyes quickly shows the difference. Textiles from Guatemala, woven from yarns dyed with natural dyes, seem to have a soft full-color quality. When synthetic dyes are used the colors are often harsh and garish.

COLOR FASTNESS

The color fastness of a dyed fabric depends upon the permanency of the dye. Few dyes are absolutely color fast under all circumstances. To be entirely permanent, they must be fast to light, to washing, to perspiration, to acid fumes, to steam, to ironing, and to crocking. Few dyes can qualify to this standard, though most are permanent to one or another of these items *when used on certain fibers*. Wool combines with the greatest number of dyes for a permanent effect, cotton with the least. When in doubt, tests must be made with the dye and the fabric. Many otherwise fugitive dyes become permanent with the use of mordants. These are discussed later in the present chapter.

TOXIC EFFECTS

Some dyes are toxic and should not be used for dyeing clothing. Some of the toxic dyes, such as chrome, crock, which makes their use very limited.

AFFINITY FOR CERTAIN FIBERS

Successful dyeing depends upon the selection of the correct dye for the particular fiber used. The specific use of certain dyes for particular fibers is indicated in the discussion which follows.

Wool and Silk Fibers

These animal or protein fibers combine chemically with acid and basic dyes. Wool can also be dyed with chrome and direct dyes, and with leuco-vat dyes—also known as thioindigo—when it is processed with a minimum of alkali damage.

Cotton, Rayon, and Linen Fibers

Direct, developed, sulfur, and vat dyes are used for dyeing cotton, rayon, and linen. Naphthol dyes can be used on cotton and rayon, but not on linen. If a mordant is used, basic dyes can also be used satisfactorily for dyeing these vegetable fibers.

Acetate Fibers

The dyes used commercially on acetate fibers are direct acetate dyes, developed acetate dyes, naphthols, acid dyes, vat dyes, and pigments. The direct acetate dyes include azo dyes (40). For more permanent results, the coloring matter can be added to the solution before it passes through the spinnerettes and is formed into fibers.

Synthetic Fibers

Many synthetic fibers can be dyed with naphthol or azoic dyes and acid dyes, with direct dyes if acid is added to the dye bath, and with vat dyes if a mordant is used (53). This is the area receiving most research emphasis at the present time.

When material woven of different fibers is dyed with special dyes, certain fibers dye and others do not. Such *cross-dyeing* sometimes helps to give design to a fabric. Some dyes, such as specially prepared union dyes, are capable of dyeing animal and vegetable fibers at the same time.

METHODS OF APPLICATION

Textile fibers and fabrics are colored by various processes: direct physical action, direct chemical action, and the intermediary chemical and physical actions of mordants, developers, and binders.

Direct physical action refers to the fact that particles of color may be trapped by hairs or other structural elements of fibers or may be absorbed into the body of a fiber.

Direct chemical action refers to the chemical affinities of some dyes for certain fibers. For example, as mentioned previously, when wool and silk are dyed by acid or basic dyes they unite chemically with the dyes.

Intermediary action refers to the fact that many particles of color are adhered to textile fibers by intermediary chemical or physical assistants. For example, mordants unite chemically with dyes to form insoluble salts; the coloring matter is then physically bound to the fiber. A similar situation occurs when developers are used; particles of color may be adhered to textile fibers by means of such binders as albumin, glue, or resin. Albumin coagulates with direct or substantive dyes and leaves a coating on the fiber; both actions are physical. Resins in emulsions with color particles bind the color to the fiber, which is then heat-treated for more permanent results. There are three types of emulsions: water in oil, oil in water, and binder with thickening agent. Many emulsions are permeable; that is, the emulsion is able to penetrate membranes of textile fibers and so is trapped when the liquid is removed. Some emulsions are nonpermeable, and the pigment is then coated only onto the outside of the fiber. Binders may be dissolved in volatile organic solvents; when the solvent evaporates, binder and pigment are left on the fiber. There is today a marked increase in the use

391

of pigment coloring, because of the brilliancy of the colors themselves and the uniformity of coverage.

AUXILIARY DYE AGENTS

Successful dyeing does not depend wholly upon the dye, or even upon the interaction between the dye and the fiber. A number of other factors must be taken into consideration. Before they will properly react with fibers, dyes may require a particular acid or alkali pH concentration, some type of mordanting treatment, a particularly high or low temperature, or the assistance of a special developer. Some dyes must be reduced before they will react. Some dyeing takes place rapidly, some is a very slow process. The composition, concentration, and temperature of the dye bath are very important. Each dye has its own idiosyncrasies—the novice soon discovers that dyeing can be a very complex undertaking. For the most part, the layman is spared many of these technical considerations, because the ordinary household dyes available at most drugstores are especially prepared to facilitate general dyeing.

A number of chemical agents, generally called auxiliary agents, are used in dyeing to increase the efficiency of particular dyes. A textile auxiliary agent is any substance which generally assists in dyeing, bleaching, and printing. Agents are also used to improve the hand and appearance of a fabric. Since 1920 more research has been concerned with auxiliary dye agents than has been undertaken on dyestuffs (*131*). Among the commonly used agents are the following, to list only a few:

Sulphuric acid, an acidifier and exhausting agent.
Hydrochloric acid, a stripping agent which also forms tin salts.
Organic acids, activators in dye penetration and mordanting.
Glauber's salt (sodium sulfate), a retarding and leveling agent.
Common salt (sodium chloride), an exhausting agent.
Sodium carbonate, a neutralizer and fixative agent.
Sodium hydrosulphite, a reducing agent for vat dyes.
Soap, a wetting agent. Many nonfatty wetting agents now replace soap.

MORDANTS

These chemical compounds are used to set color and at times to change the color of a dye. Mordants are discussed at some length on pages 399–402.

4. Methods of Handling Yarns and Fabrics During Dyeing

Certain terms are used in the dye trades to describe the form, condition, or arrangement of the material being dyed. This phase of dyeing is generally considered the *handling* process. The various methods used to handle the dyeing of fibers, yarns, and fabrics are now considered here.

Dyed in the solution. Coloring matter is placed in the viscous liquid of the synthetic fibers before this liquid is exuded through the spinnerettes. This method is also called dope-dyeing.

Dyed in the stock. Natural textile fibers are dyed before being spun.

Top-slub dyeing. Fibers are dyed after carding and before being pulled into roving. Thick strands of these fibers are coiled around perforated spindles.

Dyed in the yarn. Yarns are dyed in hanks or skeins, wound onto special spindles—this is called package dyeing—or dyed on beams or drums.

Dyed in the warp. Prepared warps are dyed before being woven. They are hung over beams or drums.

Dyed in the piece. In piece dyeing fabrics are handled in many ways. Several of these methods are described here:

In *kettle dyeing* small pieces of material are dropped into a kettle of dye and stirred with a rod during dyeing. They are also sometimes put in revolving drums or in washing machines, which give the needed motion.

In *vat dyeing* large or small pieces are treated in vats as in kettle dyeing. Vats are often made of wood.

In *rack dyeing* large articles are fastened to a chain rack and pulled back and forth through a long trough of dye.

In *chain dyeing* separate pieces are fastened together into a long chain and dyed as any other long length of fabric.

In *cylinder dyeing* one length of cloth is sewed end to end to form a loop; this loop is then rotated continuously around the outside of rollers which carry it into and out of the dye bath. In another version the fabric passes under and over a series of rollers, with most of the fabric remaining in a slackened state in the dye bath; this process is called winch, reel, or beck dyeing.

In *jig dyeing* a large piece of fabric is rolled through a dye bath back and forth from one warp beam to another.

In *pad dyeing* the cloth is stretched open, run through a trough of dye, and rolled between cylinders which force the dye into the fabric.

In *multilap continuous-process dyeing* the cloth is put through a series of rollers which heat-treat the dye or the pigment-resin application.

In *pressure dyeing* cloth is dyed under pressure in a machine called the Baroter (*133*).

Other special processes are used, especially for synthetic fibers. For example, the fabric is dyed in cabinets containing steam or hot air, or in vats containing hot oil or molten metal. Air brushes, paint brushes, and paste printing are also used to put dye onto fabrics.

5. Dyeing Procedures—for Home and School Use

GENERAL DIRECTIONS

1. Use rubber gloves.
2. Since certain metals precipitate certain dyes, a porcelain vessel is best to use for dyeing. Copper boilers are often used if porcelain is not available.
3. A wooden rod and a large spoon are needed.
4. A few large saucepans should be on hand.
5. Use soft water or water artificially softened. A few drops of acetic acid or vinegar will sometimes soften hard water.
6. Since soap softens fibers and makes them more permeable, a little is often added to help the dye job along, especially for light colors.
7. Always dissolve the dye thoroughly and strain it before diluting. The dye is usually dissolved in hot water and cheesecloth is usually used for straining it. However, since the cheesecloth is bound to extract some dye, a strainer of a plastic material, such as vinyl plastic, is preferable. Metal strainers should not be used, as they are likely to precipitate the dye.
8. If batik or tie and dye work is to be done, choose a dye that does not need to be boiled. Special dyes can be purchased for batik.
9. Thoroughly wash and wet out the material to be dyed before immersing in the dye bath. (To wet out material, soak 10 minutes in warm water.)
10. Have a sufficient amount of liquid in the dye bath to cover completely the article being dyed.
11. Follow instructions carefully for particular dyes. Maintain temperatures prescribed, etc.
12. Keep the material in the dye bath continually agitated.
13. It is usually better to dye a fabric several times to get a dark color, rather than to try for it at one dyeing; this is true of vat dye.
14. Rinse thoroughly in cold water unless a mordant rinse is called for. Rinse well after being mordanted. The hydro-rinse is recommended for most cold dip-dyed pieces. (See page 401.)
15. Open the fabric, carefully shake out the wrinkles, and stretch upon a drying rack. The dye must be squeezed gently from a dyed fabric; if the fabric is wrung tightly, the dye has a tendency to settle in the deep wrinkles formed. Drying racks should be made of glass, baked

394

porcelain, or plastic, or any material which will not change the color of the dye or will not absorb it. Use plastic clothespins.

16. Dyes may be removed from the hands with Lava soap, lemon juice, or weak solutions of bleaching agents.

6. Formulas for Dyes, Dye-Pastes, and Paste-Paints

Even though it is now possible to purchase satisfactory textile dyes and paints, it is worth while to know a few of the basic formulas used in coloring textiles. This knowledge serves to promote a better understanding and appreciation of the coloring processes.

PREPARATION AND USE OF NATURAL DYES

VEGETABLE DYES

The preparation of the dye bath for dyeing with natural dyes can be very involved. Besides collecting materials and preparing the dyes, most plant dyes have to be mordanted (see pages 384–387).

It is quite exciting, by way of experiment, to test the dyeing qualities of various plants, berries, and blossoms. Many common household foods and spices, such as coffee, tea, and cinnamon bark have dyeing properties. Many Central American teas and spices, such as manzanilla tea, are also dyes. It is also challenging to test the color changes brought about in dyes by certain mordants (see pages 399–402).

When natural dyes in the form of flowers, bark, twigs, roots, and berries are used, they are generally crushed, steeped in a small amount of water for about two hours, and strained. A porcelain or granite vessel should always be used both for extracting the dye and for dyeing.

Formulas for making natural dyes are given in several of the books listed in the bibliography—for example, Pope (*142*), Young (*143*), and Owen (*140*). The following are typical formulas:

Dyeing black with alder bark: Use 1 lb. of bark and twigs of the alder tree to 1 lb. of wool. Break and shred the twigs and bark, steep in sufficient water, strain, add the wet-out wool, boil slowly two hours, add 1 oz. of iron sulfate, and boil lightly for 15 minutes.

Dyeing yellow-green with Oregon grape: Crush and shred about 4 lbs. of the roots, leaves, and stems. Steep in sufficient water for two hours, and strain. Add 1/4 lb. of alum and boil 10 minutes. Add the wet-out yarn and stir well. Leave in the dye bath over night.

The last formula is one of the Navaho dyes. A variety of colors used by the Navahos are obtained by substituting other plant products for the Oregon grape. For example, for yellow rabbitbrush blossoms and twigs are used; for orange-tan juniper bark and twigs; and for a rich brown wild walnut hulls.

Certain qualifications apply to the use of vegetable dyes with fabrics. Many of the plant products mentioned give their best results in either a neutral or a slightly sour bath. A slightly sour bath is especially preferred for wool; a little vinegar added to the dye insures this condition. Silk dyes best in soapy water. Cotton often needs an alkali medium such as lime. Some products such as indigo, logwood, and mountain mahogany root must be reduced by fermentation or reduction before dyeing will take place. Primitive peoples obtained their lime for mordanting from wood ashes, such as the ash from green juniper needles.

As noted earlier, cotton and wool are often soaked or mordanted in alum before dyeing. Some natural dyes such as tumeric, catechu, fustic, and logwood will dye cotton without a mordant. Linen must be boiled in a solution of 1/2 cup bicarbonate of soda for each pound of fabric.

ANIMAL DYES

The principal animal dye still used is cochineal. This dye produces a range of colors according to the mordant used with it: red is obtained with alum, scarlet with tin, and purplish grey with iron. Two formulas are given for using it. Animal dyes are also discussed on pages 384–387.

Dyeing cotton red with cochineal. For 1 pound of cotton use 150 grams of sumac, 100 grams alum, and 20 grams cochineal, using sufficient water to cover the garment. Soak the cloth 1 day in the sumac, soak and stir 2 to 3 hours in a hot alum solution, then boil slowly in the cochineal solution for about an hour.

Dyeing wool red with cochineal. For 1 pound of wool use 1 ounce stannous chloride, 1/2 ounce cream of tartar, and 40 grams (about 2/3 ounce) cochineal, with enough water to cover the garment. Mordant the wool for 1 hour in the stannous chloride and cream of tartar and rinse thoroughly; boil the fabric in the dye bath for 1 hour. In both cases put the wool into the solutions when the water is warm; gradually raise the temperature to boiling and keep at a slow boil or just below boiling. Stir occasionally. Remove and rinse in warm water. Always handle wool gently.

PREPARATION AND USE OF ARTIFICIAL DYES

Although natural dyes are used in some parts of the world and in some rural areas in this country most of the dyes used now, in both industry and the home, are the artificial dyes. Grocery stores and drugstores carry various prepared household dyes which are easy to use. The majority of these dyes are direct union dyes which color most types of fibers. No mordants are needed. The only product used in addition to the dye is common salt, which is added to certain dye baths to exhaust the dye from the bath. Directions for using the dyes usually come with the dye.

No such general statement can be made concerning the synthetic dyes used in the textile industry. Vat dyes, developed dyes, and naphthol dyes, as well as other synthetic dyes, often require many accessory agents and rather elaborate equipment in order to carry a dyeing process to completion.

PREPARATION AND USE OF TEXTILE DYE-PASTES AND PASTE-PAINTS

For many textile design processes, mordants, discharge chemicals, and coloring matter must be applied to the fabric in a thickened or paste form. A thin dye or paint solution would run beyond the pattern boundaries and ruin the appearance of the fabric. It is interesting to note that the hand-painted textile designs of the ancient Peruvians had clear-cut outlines, indicating that the coloring matter was applied in a paste or gum form; what they used is not known, but it was probably an algarroba gum.

Textile paints are as a rule either dye-pastes or paste-paints. Formulas are given for both types. The coloring matter in the two differs. In the dye-pastes it is a dye dissolved in a thickened solution. In the paste-paints it is a pigment held in suspension in an emulsion. The paste-paints ordinarily contain a binder which holds the pigment on the fabric.

Although there are several satisfactory textile paints on the market,[8] some designers prefer to prepare their own. A few formulas are given here which can be used for painting, printing, stenciling, and silk-screen printing.

The following materials are used as thickening agents for dye-pastes and paste-paints: corn starch, wheat starch, gum tragacanth, dextrin, locust-bean gums, gum arabic, some soluble vegetable gums, and synthetic resins. Gum tragacanth can be purchased from any drugstore. It is prepared as follows: 70 grams (2 1/4 oz.) of tragacanth are put to soak in 1 liter (4 1/4 cups) of distilled cold water. The gum is soaked for one day with occasional stirring. It is then beaten with an egg beater and heated in a double boiler at a slow even heat until it is clear and transparent. The heating sometimes takes as long as six hours; water is added to the top and bottom of the double boiler as needed. After the thickened solution is cooled and strained, it is put in a jar and tightly sealed. Before it is

[8] The better-known textile colors are Prange and Alpha colors. There are also some emulsified resin colors on the market.

used, the skin which forms on the top must be removed and the solution strained again.

DYE-PASTE FORMULAS

A dye-paste consists of a combination of a dye, a thickening agent, and a preservative. Sometimes a mordant is added. The dye selected for the paste must be one that has an affinity for the fibers in the fabric to be painted or printed. For this reason, union or all-purpose dyes, such as regular household dyes, are generally used for these simple formulas. Household dyes can be purchased at grocery stores and drugstores.

Formula I

Use 1/2 to 1 oz. powdered tragacanth gum (sold at drugstores), 1 quart cold water, and one of the following: 1 teaspoon formaldehyde for vegetable fibers; 10 drops carbolic acid, 10 drops acetic acid, or 4 tablespoons white vinegar for wool or silk. Add the formaldehyde or acid, whichever is needed, to the prepared tragacanth already described. To this thickened solution add the dye, which has previously been dissolved in about 1/2 cup of boiling water and strained through several layers of cheesecloth; a fine plastic sieve is better than cheesecloth, but it is not always available. Use soft water for dyeing; water containing metallic elements will precipitate the dye. Add enough water to the ingredients to make a paste the consistency of a thick cream. Cool and strain.

Formula II

Use 1 to 2 parts of direct or household dye, 10 parts glycerine, 30 parts distilled water, 1 part sodium phosphate, and tragacanth gum to thicken. Prepare the tragacanth as described above. Dissolve and strain the dye as for Formula I. Mix together the dye, glycerine, and sodium phosphate, and bring to a boil; remove from heat and add enough tragacanth to thicken to the consistency of a thick cream; cool. This formula can be used only on cotton and rayon; if wool or silk is to be printed substitute 10 parts vinegar for the sodium phosphate and use 20 parts of water instead of 30 parts.

CHEMICAL PASTES USED IN DYEING PROCESSES

In printing fabrics chemical pastes are used to change the color or to entirely remove the color of a dyed fabric. This treatment is one type of textile design. Mordant pattern dyeing is discussed on pages 399–402; here a paste containing a mordant is painted or printed onto a fabric before it

398

is dyed. The many pastes used in discharge printing are other examples of the use of chemical pastes. A discharge paste is used to remove the color from a dyed fabric.

PASTE-PAINTS

A paste-paint is composed of a pigment color, a thickening agent, a binder, an indelible agent, and a solvent. Most paste-paints are emulsions. The pigments of paste-paints are coated onto the fiber or fabric to be dyed with a binder. All types of fibers can be colored when pigments and binders are used.

Formula I

Use 1 part glycerine, 3 parts tragacanth paste, 2 parts satin-finish varnish or other binder, 1/10 part of H. P. Indelible Dryer or oil of wintergreen, and Alpha textile color or other dry pigment powder as needed.

Prepare the tragacanth as already described. Mix together the glycerine, tragacanth, and Indelible Dryer or oil of wintergreen. Mix the dry color in a little of this paste until smooth and add to the rest of the paste, mixing well together. Blend in the varnish or resin binder, beating well with a spoon. Thin to the consistency of very thick cream with mineral spirits.

Formula II

Regular oil paints in tubes can be used for textile painting. In this case a few drops of H. P. Indelible Dryer should be added to each tablespoon of paint. The dryer makes the paint colorfast. Another indelible solution which can be added to oil paints is made by mixing 3 tablespoons of mineral spirits, 1 teaspoon of oil of wintergreen, and 4 to 6 drops of either lemon juice, vinegar, or acetic acid. This, however, is not as effective as the H. P. Dryer.

7. Mordants and Mordant Pattern Dyeing and Printing

Many centuries before the advent of Christianity, mordants were being used to control the color of dyes and to make them permanent. The fact that certain mordants change the color of dyes was known by the ancient Egyptians, according to a description given by Pliny: "Garments are painted in Egypt in a wonderful manner, the white clothes being first smeared, not with colors, but with drugs which absorb colors. . . . Although the dyeing liquor is of one color, the garment is dyed several colors, according to the different properties of the drugs which have been applied to the different parts: nor can this dye be washed out."

The dyers of the Near East knew that mordants could change the color of dyes, and that one dye could therefore serve in many capacities. They found, as we know, that when alizarin is treated with different mordants, different colors result: with zinc or nickel acetate the color is blue; with stannous chloride the color is yellow; with stannous salts (citrate, lactate, etc.) it is red; with potassium bichromate it is mauve; and with tannic acid it is brown.

The Japanese invented a novel method of mordant-print dyeing. They discovered that when they placed leaves between two layers of cloth and pounded the cloth with padded mallets, the imprint of the leaves took a different color when the fabric was dyed. After the fabric was steamed, dried, and dipped into dye, the areas where the leaves had been placed were a darker color than the other areas. The tannin in the leaves had mordanted the dye. This process is still used to some extent.

COMPOSITION OF MORDANTS

The word mordant is a derivative of a French word meaning *to bite;* that is, the dye bites into the fiber. A chemical reaction takes place between the mordant and the dye, the mordant combining with the dye to form an insoluble salt. This salt coats the fibers being dyed. Ancient peoples of the Middle East often used lime and alum as mordants.

Some common natural dyes and the mordants generally used with them are:

Fustic, a yellow used with aluminum or tin mordants.
Logwood, a dye of various colors depending on the mordant; mordanted before dyeing with salts of iron, chromium, or tin.
Madder, a red when the cloth is soaked in oil, alum, lime, and chalk before dyeing.
Black oak bark, a green used with alum.
Maple bar, a purple used with copperas.

The following chemicals are used as mordants or to assist in the mordanting action by promoting dye penetration or exhaustion:

Inorganic acids, such as sulfuric acid.
Organic acids, such as acetic, tannic, and tartaric acid.
Bases, such as lime and the caustic soda in soap.
Soap, which helps to set the colors.
Slightly basic salts, such as ammonium acetate, aluminum acetate, sodium or potassium dichromate, and tartar emetic (potassium antimony tartrate).
Acid salts, such as copper sulfate and alum (aluminum-potassium sulfate).
Neutral salts, such as Glauber's salt and sodium chloride.
Metals, such as iron, chrome, tin, copper, and zinc.

DIRECTIONS FOR USING MORDANTS

A fabric may be treated with a mordant before, during, or after the dyeing process. Since chrome is often used in mordant dyeing, the methods of applying mordants are sometimes called bottom chrome, metachrome (or synchromate or monochromate), and top chrome. Other terms for these three methods are (1) premordanting and bottom mordanting; (2) process mordanting, single-bath mordanting, and parallel mordanting; and (3) top mordanting and post-mordanting.

A Bottom Mordant, for Batik, Tie and Dye, Etc.

Fabrics may be mordanted before dyeing as follows: wool is wet out and mordanted in a solution made up of 4 ounces alum and 1 ounce cream of tartar to 4 gallons of soft warm water. The wool is put in the warm mordant, which is brought slowly to a boil and boiled slowly for an hour with occasional stirring. Silk is wet out, is allowed to stand overnight in this same mordant, and is then dyed. Cotton, linen, and rayon can be boiled in a mordanting solution for an hour and allowed to stand overnight in the solution, which is made up of 4 ounces alum and 1/4 ounce sodium carbonate to 4 gallons of soft water. The above formulas are for one pound of fabric (*142*).

It is also possible to print or paint a mordant paste onto a fabric before dyeing; any of the printing or painting processes can be used to apply it. When the fabric is run through the dye the mordanted areas take a different color than the rest of the fabric. The hand painting and printing processes of the ancient Egyptians and Japanese, mentioned earlier, were both bottom-mordanting processes.

A Parallel-Mordanting Process, for Oil Paints

As already noted, a fixative agent such as H. P. Indelible Dryer or oil of wintergreen should be added to oil paints when they are used for textile printing and painting.

The Hydro-Rinse, a Top-Mordanting Process

This is a process for setting the color for both batik and tied and dyed work. After the material is removed from the dye bath, it is first put in a 5% solution of tannic acid for 30 minutes, then in a 5% solution of tartar emetic for 15 minutes, and finally rinsed thoroughly.

A Top-Mordanting Process—Vinegar Press—for Home Use

A mordant can be pressed into a fabric. For example, painted and stenciled fabrics are covered with a damp cloth wrung out of a dilute solution of

401

white vinegar and pressed with a warm iron. The solution is composed of about 4 tablespoons of vinegar to 1 cup water.

A Top-Mordanting Process, a Steam Bath Process

A steam bath process is often used commercially for setting the colors of printed and painted fabrics. Sometimes the cloth is stretched on steam tables for this procedure, sometimes it passes over rollers and thence through a steam chamber, and sometimes it is folded between clean sheets of cloth and placed in open-mesh metal baskets which are then hung in a steam bath. Vinegar or acetic acid is often used in these steam baths.

Thermal Finishing Process, Steam Press

Prepared textile paints are often set by pressing the design on the fabric with a damp cloth for 3 minutes with the heat set at 350° F. for cotton and at 250° F. for rayon.

Thermal Finishing Process, Hot Dry Press

Some manufacturers recommend that printed and painted designs be pressed with a moderately hot iron for a few minutes to set the colors.

8. Discharge Dyeing and Printing

Discharge dyeing and printing, sometimes called extract printing, is used to remove dye from certain areas of a dyed fabric. A paste is used for this work which contains either an oxidizing or a reducing agent. Reducing agents are generally preferred for discharge printing, because oxidizing agents more readily affect the strength of the cloth. Discharge pastes are painted, stenciled, stamped, or printed onto a fabric. One formula for a discharge paste, a citric acid discharge, is as follows:

300 gm.	citric acid crystals
130 gm.	water
70 gm.	caustic soda 33% solution
500 gm.	starch thickening
1000 gm.	

Two methods are generally used for discharge print-dyeing:

Method I

A discharge paste is stamped onto the cloth before dyeing. The chemical substance in the paste counteracts any dye action which might take place;

the areas treated remain colorless or white. The pattern then appears as a white silhouette upon a colored ground.

Method Ii

A chemical discharge paste is stamped onto the cloth after it has been dyed. In the presence of moisture or steam, this discharge removes the dye from the areas treated. One of the first attempts to design textiles in the United States was by discharge printing. A justified complaint of discharge printing is that it often tenders the fabric; a humorous story from the Colonial period illustrates this well. A certain Mrs. Robinson, author of the book *Loom and Spindle* and a worker in one of the first textile mills in Lowell, Massachusetts, said that clothes made from fabrics first printed in the mill were "garments of humiliation," because the white spots washed out, cloth and all, leaving the wearer covered with eyelet holes (*64*).

Some of the important methods used to apply the discharge paste to a woven cotton or rayon fabric are as follows:

Discharge Tie and Dye

This technique is described later in the chapter as one of the variations of tie and dye work.

Discharge Stencil Work

A paste is made of wheat flour boiled in a saturated solution of zinc sulfate and chalk. Using a stencil and palette knife, a pattern is stenciled onto cloth with this paste; the cloth is then dyed in a vat or sulfur dye. The insoluble sodium sulfite which is formed resists the dye. The material should be kept flat during dyeing.

Discharge Painting and/or Stencil Work

A thin paste made of wheat flour boiled in a concentrated solution of citric acid is painted or stenciled in a pattern on a fabric. The cloth is then dipped into a bleach composed of 2 tablespoons sodium hypochlorite or clorox to a gallon of water, plus enough baking soda to nullify the smell of chlorine. As soon as the pattern is bleached the cloth is removed and washed immediately. This is usually considered a reduction process.

Discharge Painting Work

A thin paste made of sodium hydrosulfite and flour is painted or stenciled onto a cloth previously dyed with either acid or direct dye. The material is placed in a steam bath until the dye is reduced in the pattern areas. In another method a wet cloth is placed over the pattern, which is then steamed by ironing.

Discharge Printing

Certain chemicals, mixed with a paste, are printed onto a dyed fabric by the roller printing process. The chemicals remove the dye in the printed areas. In some cases the discharge paste is printed onto the fabric before it is dyed; it then counteracts the dye in the areas so treated.

9. Tie and Dye Work

Tie and dye work is one of the resist-dyeing textile processes, the resistance being accomplished by binding or knotting the cloth tightly to prevent the penetration of the dye. A Malay term, "plangi," is increasingly being used in place of "tie and dye" to designate this process. Tied and dyed cloth is known in India as "bhandana work," from the Hindu verb *bhanda*, meaning to tie; and as *chundari* or *chunari*. In Japan it is known as *shibori*. Some of the work has as many as 30 knots to the inch.

It is difficult to trace the origin of tie and dye work. Since the peoples of southeastern Asia employ the greatest variety of techniques to do this work and produce the greatest number of pieces, this area is often assumed to be its place of origin. Diffusion undoubtedly played a part in the spread of this technique, but, on the other hand, the fact that such widely separated lands as Asia, Africa, and the Western Hemisphere did tie and dye work indicates that independent invention also may have occurred long ago in these areas.

Ancient Chinese silks found in Sinkiang testify to early tie and dye work in China. It also appears to have been done anciently in Japan. Persia, Syria, and Cyprus are reported to have used this technique. On the Western Hemisphere in pre-Columbian times, tied and dyed fabrics were made in the areas now comprised in Arizona and New Mexico, and more especially in Peru (*130*). (See Figs. 189 and 190.)

Varieties of tie and dye work are being produced today in India, Siam, Cambodia, Indonesia, Mindanao in the Philippine Islands, and in parts of China, Japan, and Africa. On the Western Hemisphere various types of the work are found in the United States, Mexico, Guatemala, Peru, southern Ecuador, and Argentina.

GENERAL DIRECTIONS FOR TIE AND DYE WORK

The best material to use for tied and dyed work is a lightweight pure silk cloth or a silklike fabric such as rayon. The fabric should be washed and ironed before beginning the work. The design is planned and marked on the fabric by means of dots or running stitches, or the points to be tied are marked by small steel safety pins pinned into the material. Perforated-paper designs can be transferred to cloth by dusting colored chalk over the perforations.

After the design is plotted on the cloth, the marked points of the material are picked up and wound tightly with waxed thread or string—points can be formed over toothpicks, which are then left in the cloth until after dyeing. To make a uniform sunburst pattern, the cloth should be evenly distributed in each fold. When all the ties have been made the cloth is ready for dyeing.

1. The general directions for dyeing given on page 394 should be followed.
2. After wrapping and tying the marked places, soak the fabric in water a few minutes before putting it in the dye bath. Squeeze out excess water and put the cloth in the dye. The dye will take better if it is warm, but not to exceed 40° C. (104° F.), or the wax on the strings will melt. Leave the fabric in the dye as short a time as possible; in intricate work, remove immediately. Squeeze out excess dye and rinse. Additional touching-up may be done with a brush.
3. It is recommended that the cloth be treated with a mordant either before or after being dyed. Bottom mordanting is preferred. (Mordants are discussed on page 399.)
4. Rinse thoroughly and hang to dry. Remove strings and press with a warm iron while the material is slightly damp; if it is entirely dry use a steam iron or press with a damp cloth.

VARIATIONS OF THE TIE AND DYE PROCESS

THE TIE AND DYE PROCESS APPLIED TO FABRICS

Twist Dyeing

The cloth is folded into small pleats and then twisted, giving an irregular repeat design to the fabric.

Dip Dyeing

The wet cloth is dipped into a series of dye baths containing increasingly darker values of the same or related color. The entire piece of cloth is first dipped into water and then into the lightest value of the dye; part of it is then dipped in the next darker value, still less of it in the next darker dye, etc., the bottom part alone being dipped into the darkest value dye. This shade dyeing gives a graduated effect to the material.

405

Knot Dyeing

Tying the cloth in knots before dyeing it often produces strong, bold patterns.

Tuft-Tie Dyeing

The material is stretched over a rectangular metal plate and tied down securely crosswise and lengthwise with evenly spaced waxed-cord bindings. Starting at the center the material is then pulled into tufts and dyed on the plate. This method produces a very interesting irregular allover pattern.

Line-Tie Dyeing

The material is folded lengthwise or pulled to a center point and folded, and bound tightly at intervals with a waxed cord. This makes horizontal stripes across or around the material.

Object-Resist Dyeing

Seeds or other objects, such as spools and buttons, are tied in the cloth to provide a variation of pattern.

Point-Resist (Diamond) Dyeing

"Points" of material are drawn up and twisted about with thread. They resist the dye and appear as diamonds on the finished fabric. (See Fig. 190.) For fine designs the material is dampened and pressed down over a pattern arrangement of nail points projecting from a board (136). The cloth is allowed to dry, and then these little points are lifted from the rack, one at a time, and wrapped with a fine waxed cord which floats from point to point instead of being cut. When the points have all been tied, the material is wet out and dyed. In some places the natives use grasses and various fibers as ties.

Spider Web and Tied and Dyed Work

The Japanese make unusual tied and dyed patterns with a variation of the point method just described. Instead of one solid wrapping, they carry the waxed string down the point, twisting it around in a spiral arrangement. The cloth must be carefully folded for this method, so that the spiral resist pattern will be continuous. (See Fig. 192.)

Tritik Dyeing

Intriguing bisymmetric designs can be made on a fabric by combining the techniques of stitching and dyeing, a process known as stitch-resist tie and dye or tritik dyeing. Tritik is a Javanese word which designates this particular stitch-resist process. Beautiful pieces of tritik, as well as combinations of tritik and plangi dyeing, are made in Java, Cambodia, Sumatra, and India.

For tritik work the fabric is folded in half and the design is drawn on

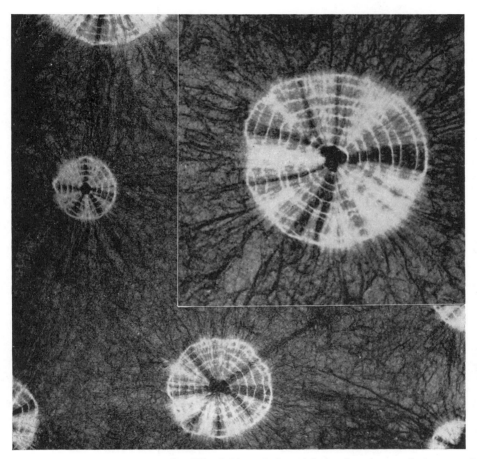

Fig. 192. Spider web tie and dye work on heavy soft rice paper from Japan.

the top surface. The design which is composed of many small parts, is then outlined with small running stitches, using waxed thread and sewing through the two thicknesses of cloth. When an area is outlined, a few inches of thread are left hanging free. When all of the stitching is finished, these hanging threads are pulled up to make tight gathers around all patterns. The threads are then secured, either by sewing them into the fabric or by tying them to other threads. The fabric is covered with little points or

407

puffs. (See Fig. 193.) To vary the pattern some areas may be wrapped solidly with waxed cord. The fabric is then wet out and dyed. When it is dry and the ties are removed and the fabric opened, the same design appears on both halves. Tritik can be used to form circles in a fabric.

GRILLE (AND BRUSH) DYEING

The dye is brushed along the folds of an intricately folded fabric.

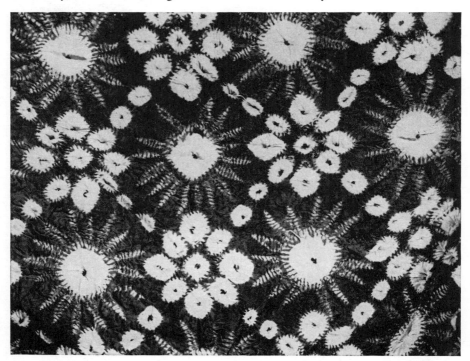

Fig. 193.   Trikit Dyeing from Indo-China. The work is done in a stitch-resist technique.

Discharge Tied and Dyed Work

A dyed cloth is tied and dipped into a solution of sodium hydrosulfite, 2 tablespoons to the gallon of water. The chemical bleaches all the exposed color.

Screen-Print Tied and Dyed Work

Silk fabric to be used for silk screen printing (discussed later) can be treated so as to print a pseudo-tie and dye design. Before the silk is stretched on the frame, it is tied in the pattern and dipped into benzene-

408

soluble tusche;[9] the ties are then taken off and the silk stretched on the frame. A layer of some water-soluble medium, such as glue, is coated over one side of the screen. The tusche is then removed with benzene. Fabric printed from such a screen resembles tie and dye work.

THE TIED AND DYED PROCESS APPLIED TO YARNS
Ikat and Double Ikat Dyeing

The type of tie and dye work called ikat—also known as Khanjari, Kasuri, Chiné, Jaspé, and color-space dyeing—may have originated in south-eastern Asia; at any rate, skillful dyeing of yarns in this technique is done today in Java, Bali, Sumatra, southern Borneo, in the Philippine Islands, and other adjacent lands. The Dyaks of southern Borneo do especially beautiful ikat work.

It is interesting to learn that ikat dyeing was known to the ancient inhabitants of Peru, since pieces of this work have been found in pre-Columbian cemeteries. Although ikat work is no longer done in Peru, it is possible that the knowledge of it diffused from there to other centers. For example, the Indians of Guatemala and Ecuador do outstanding ikat dyeing today. (See Figs. 189, 194, and 195.)

Fig. 194.   Ikat Dyeing from Guatemala. Detail from a skirt with tied and dyed weft yarns. Some skirts are in double ikat.

In ikat dyeing, sections of the warp and/or the weft are tied and dyed before these yarns are put on the loom or woven. When both the warp and weft are so treated, the work is called double ikat. There are two types of double ikat: the patterns may be independent or they may coincide.

In preparation for ikat dyeing, the warp yarns are wound into hanks of the length needed for the loom. If the weft is to be treated instead of the warp, the hanks are made the width of the fabric to be woven. These hanks are then stretched over a frame and the yarns are wrapped and tied

[9] For an explanation of tusche see page 442.

with waxed cord at intervals determined by the pattern. The hanks are then removed from the frame and dyed. When the ties are removed and the yarns put on the loom and woven, the patterns can clearly be discerned. In Guatemala the Indians stretch their yarns between telephone poles on the streets and then walk along these lines to put on the ties.

Fig. 195. Ikat Dyeing from Ecuador. Section of a shawl which has an ikat-dyed warp.

Meissen Dyeing (Double-Ikat Dyeing)

In Japan, a very difficult tied and dyed work is done, using the same method as in ikat dyeing with one important exception: both warp and weft yarns are tied and dyed, in such a manner that later, when they are crossed during weaving, the tied pattern areas of warp and weft coincide. Clean-cut light pattern areas are thus formed in the fabric. The Japanese stretch their yarns between poles to do the preliminary tying and carry small trays of dyes along the yarns to do the dyeing.

Dyed-in-the-Warp or Printed-Warp Fabrics

A warp-printing process that is usually machine operated is also related to ikat dyeing. After the warp yarns are wound onto the warp beams preparatory to being put on the loom, they are run through a roller printing press and a pattern is print-dyed onto them. Patterns can also be applied by free-hand painting or block printing. When the warp is finally installed on the loom and woven into cloth, an indistinct pattern, often called a shadow print, results. (Fig. 196.)

Drum Dyeing

For velvet and tapestry carpet weaving, the pattern is dyed onto the warp-pile yarns on drums before they are woven into the carpet. These

410

drums are usually about 39 feet in circumference and wide enough to carry 330 turns of the yarn side by side. As the yarns pass over the drum, the pattern is printed on them (86). Each 39-foot turn of the yarn about

Fig. 196. Dyed-in-the-Warp Print. A shadow print which is made by weaving into a machine roller printed warp.

the drum will appear in the same warp row in each of 330 rugs of the same design. For a run of 9′ x 12′ velvet rugs over 400 drums must be printed.

10. Batik

Hot wax is used as a "resist" element on fabrics and on pottery in two closely associated color processes. When hot wax is applied to a fabric with a brush or a tjanting, and the fabric is dyed, the resulting design is

411

silhouetted against a colored background. This process is known as batik. (See Fig. 199.) The same process applied to pottery is known as negative painting.[10]

There are evidences of the use of both batik and negative painting in widely separated areas of the world. Perhaps Asia was the original home of this art, since "batik" is an ancient Malayan word signifying to trace, to paint, or to design. The name applies to the fabric as well as the process. Batiks are widely worn in the Near East, the Orient, India, and the islands adjacent to India.

Batiks are still made by hand in parts of Java and Indo-China. Javanese batiks are famous for their design and color quality. Many of the patterns used today are the same as those found on robes of prehistoric idols. The traditional batik designs of India and Java are composed of intricate curvilinear patterns; typical patterns are floral designs interspersed with fruits, birds, animals, and Buddhistic symbols. Special designs, often outlined in gold, are worn by those of high or priestly rank. Batiks are very specialized in Java; each community makes and wears its own particular patterns and colors; for example, Pekalongan batiks are cream and blue, while those of Solo are golden tan and deep blue. Batik designs are used on the sarong —a strip of cloth twisted about the body; the slendang—a scarf similar to the Mexican reboso; the kemban—a narrow girdle; the sarong kapala —a head kerchief, formerly used by men to designate their village; and on other articles of clothing.

Dutch traders brought back the knowledge of batik in the middle of the seventeenth century, and many people in Holland started working in this medium. European batik work, however, never found a favorable market; the charm and richness of the native Javanese batiks were missing in their European counterparts. Early in the present century Dutch traders introduced batik into the United States. Several American artists became interested in the technique, but their work also proved to be clumsy in comparison with that of India and Java, and their designs were definitely sentimental and trite.

The making of batiks by hand is much too slow and too expensive for profitable large-scale production in the United States, but in the last few years many imitation batiks, some fairly attractive, have been turned out by roller printing presses and also by the silk-screen process.

[10] In ceramic work the design is painted on pottery with oil, hot wax, fat, paste, or other resist material; the pottery is covered with a colored slip or glaze, and then is fired or smoked. In the firing, the resist material is loosened or burned off, and a pattern is left silhouetted on the colored background.

DIRECTIONS FOR DOING BATIK—JAVANESE METHOD

The ancient oriental methods of doing batik remain unchanged; attempts to shorten the process have only resulted in inferior and cheaper fabrics.

The Javanese method today is as follows: Cotton cloth is cut to size, washed thoroughly in cold water and dried in the sun. It is then soaked for several days in cocoanut oil, boiled to remove the oil, and again dried in the sun. This oil process may be repeated

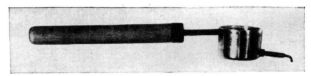

Fig. 197. Tjanting. A small kettle used for applying the wax for doing batik in the Javanese method.

several times. The cloth is then pounded with wooden beaters. The oil and beating processes soften and mellow the cloth. Sometimes a weak solution of rice water is used to give the fabric enough sizing to prevent the wax from spreading too quickly. Usually the design is drawn on with a pencil or charcoal.

A tjanting is used to apply the hot wax. (See Fig. 197.) This little vessel, which looks like a tiny tea kettle, which measures 1 or 1 1/2 inches in diameter, has a 4-inch handle. The fine stream of wax[11] which issues from the spout outlines the design and makes the little dots characteristic of this work. (See Figs. 191 and 198.)

The Javanese put in the dark colors first. The cloth is hung over a frame and both sides are waxed. When the wax is all on, the cloth is dyed. It is then dried and the wax boiled out. It is dried again, restarched, and rewaxed. This second application of wax covers both the new pattern and the first pattern. The fabric is then dyed the second color and the process is repeated. The work is long and time-consuming. Waxing is usually done by women and dyeing is done by men.

Fig. 198. Batik. A small sample of a piece of batik cloth from India. Use of the tjanting and also tjap blocks.

An inferior imitation batik product made by using tjaps is sold to the poor. A tjap is a block provided with ridges made out of thin brass strips arranged to conform to the outline of the design.

[11] A Javanese formula for wax is 6 parts of resin (melam geplak from Borneo mixed with animal fat), 1 part of beeswax, and a little reused wax from previous batik work.

When the tjap block is pressed upon a hot waxed pad—usually made of jute covered with muslin—and then pressed upon the cloth, a wax print is made. It often takes 13 to 15 tjap blocks to make a complete design. The fabric is dyed and the wax removed as in the batik process.

Vegetable dyes are used in Javanese batik. The principal colors used are indigo blue, golden tan, and black. The tan is made from the bark of the mango tree, and the black is made from the blue and the tan. Most batiks are dyed in these three colors. The soapy boiling bath used to remove the last wax also sets the color. The indigo dye is usually a monopoly of one dyer, who does all the blue dyeing for the town.

EQUIPMENT NEEDED FOR BATIK—AMERICAN METHOD

Wax

Pure beeswax, with a little resin added, is used for fine batik work. For ordinary work the proportion can be approximately 5 parts beeswax to 1 part paraffin, or even 2/3 beeswax and 1/3 paraffin. Crackle work can be done with about 2/3 paraffin and 1/3 beeswax. The new hydrogenated waxes, though called paraffin, are not as brittle as paraffin and cannot be used for crackle work.

Brushes

Fine but durable brushes are needed; Japanese brushes are especially good. In most of the batik work done in the United States brushes are used instead of the tjanting.

Frame

A frame is necessary upon which the material can be stretched; a shoe box or a small adjustable frame like a quilting frame can be used.

Wax Container

A small deep pan is needed for heating wax; a No. 2 1/2 tin can makes a good container.

Dye Container

Large enamel vessels are needed for dyeing.

Heating Unit

A portable electric plate is satisfactory for heating wax.

Dyes

The dyes used must be cold—at least they must be kept at a lower temperature than will melt wax. Batik dyes may be purchased.

Fabric

Fine silk or silklike material is recommended for batik work.

Miscellaneous Supplies

Pins are needed for stretching the fabric, an apron or smock to protect the clothing, and rubber gloves to protect the hands.

Designs

The best batik designs are small, ornate, allover patterns in which minute dots play an important part. However, every conceivable type of design —scenic, floral, or abstract—can be executed in batik.

DIRECTIONS FOR DOING BATIK—AMERICAN METHOD

1. The general directions given for dyeing, page 394, apply also to batik dyeing. They should be reviewed before beginning batik work.
2. Always wash and iron material before waxing and dyeing.
3. Designs can be drawn or traced on the cloth lightly with pencil or painted with wax in a free-hand style.
4. Stretch the material tightly over a frame of the proper size—a small quilting frame is good; a shoe box can be used for small pieces.
5. The temperature of the wax must be maintained at the degree best suited for application. This is soon learned by the worker. If the wax is too hot, it will run out of control; if too cool, it will pile up on the fabric. Do not let the wax smoke. Application on very thin fabrics is easier to control if the fabric is lightly starched and ironed first.
6. Apply wax only to that part of the design which is to remain the original color of the cloth. Waxed areas resist the dye. (See Fig. 199.)
7. Thoroughly wet out the fabric before dipping it into the dye.
8. The dye pan must be large enough to receive the cloth satisfactorily. Be sure the dye is thoroughly dissolved, strained, and evenly distributed in the dye bath. The dye bath must be agitated before adding the cloth. The cloth is added to the bath and removed as soon as the proper tint is acquired. The dye takes best when the temperature is as warm as the wax will stand without melting. However, if a crackle effect is desired, the dye has to be very cold. Uneven dye jobs are the result of

415

too strong a dye, too small a vessel, not enough stirring while dyeing is in process, or insufficient rinsing.

9. After dyeing, rinse the fabric in fresh water and dry.
10. Wax in the areas which are to be second lightest in value and dye the cloth again. Repeat the process as many times as necessary.
11. Remove the wax as described in the following paragraph.

Fig. 199. Batik. American silhouette method of doing batik.

In the American batik method, the wax is not removed from the material between each application of dye. Instead, the colors and values of the pattern are built up from light to dark in the waxing-dyeing procedure. Since colors add during dyeing—for example, blue dyed over yellow forms green—care must be taken to build up good colors. Avoid dyeing colors over their complements—for example, blue over orange turns an ugly brown.

After the final dyeing the fabric can be treated with a mordant such as a hydro-rinse before the wax is removed.

When the material is dried the wax is removed. Place the fabric between clean sheets of plain absorbent paper laid upon a *thick pad of newspaper* and press with a moderately hot iron. Repeat the process until most of the wax has been removed from the fabric, changing the papers as necessary. Remove the remaining wax with a cleaning fluid. Remember to use precautions when handling a cleaning fluid; always work out of doors or in a well-ventilated room. In Java the wax is removed by boiling and hence can be used again. However, this technique can be used only when the dye used is fast to boiling. A little soap or alum in the water will help stabilize the dye. Dyes can be removed from the hands with Lava soap, lemon juice, or a weak solution of a bleaching agent.

VARIATIONS OF THE BATIK PROCESS

A number of wax-resist techniques, in addition to the regular methods described above, closely related to batik are listed and described here.

Outlined and Tinted Batik

The design on the cloth is outlined with a brush and hot wax in a line 1/8 to 3/16 of an inch in width. The cloth is then wet and excess moisture

416

removed by patting it between two towels, without bending it. Each little enclosed area is colored, using a brush. The fabric is dried and the wax removed as in the methods already described.

Crackle Batik

Crackle work requires a wax that contains a large percentage of paraffin. Both surfaces of the cloth are painted with a layer of melted wax, or else the fabric is dipped into it. If the second method is used, remove the wax from the heat before dipping the fabric, and use a pair of plyers to remove it from the wax. When the wax is cold, crush the stiff cloth in the hands to crackle it well. *Be sure the wax is cold*; dip the fabric in cold water to cool it if necessary. Dip the fabric in the dye, remove, and rinse. Some of the veins in the crackle can be painted with an additional color for a variegated effect. (See Fig. 200.) Dry the fabric and remove the wax as before.

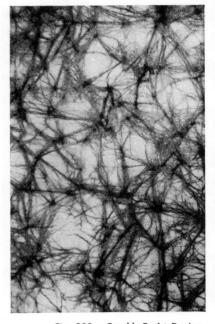

Fig. 200. Crackle-Resist Dyeing.

Crayon Batik

The design is drawn or traced on the material and then filled in with colored wax crayons. The wax is removed as before. The design may be mordanted: place a dampened cloth, one wrung out of a dilute white vinegar solution, over the fabric and press with a warm iron.

Dyed Crayon Batik

To dye a fabric on which a crayon pattern has been drawn, the pattern must be applied to both sides of the fabric. This is done by holding the cloth against a window pane and applying the crayons to the back as the design shows through, or by painting the back of the design with hot wax and a brush, as in batik. The material is then wet thoroughly, dyed, and the wax removed as for regular batik.

White Line Silhouette Batik

White crayons or wax pencils are sometimes used to draw single curvilinear patterns on a light-colored cloth. It is usually necessary first to outline the design with a pencil. The cloth should then be held up to the window and the same design applied to the back with crayons, wax pencils, or hot wax. The cloth is then wet thoroughly and dipped into the dye. The process of drawing and dyeing may be repeated several times to obtain variations of color. The wax is removed as for regular batik.

Pinpoint Printing

A print may be made by waxed pinpoints. A design is first drawn on a square of heavy cardboard approximately 4″ x 4″. The cardboard is laid on a pillow or a sandbag and the design outlined with large pins poked *entirely through* the cardboard at even intervals. A second square of cardboard or a piece of plywood is glued on the cardboard design over the pinheads; this holds the pins firmly in place. For printing, the pinpoints are dipped into hot wax and pressed against the cloth. When the fabric is dyed, a shadowlike effect results. The wax is removed as for batik.

Commercial Silk-Resist Printing

Silk is sometimes printed by using a resist process. The silk is bleached or whitened, dried, and then printed by machinery with a wax or resin all-over design. It is then dyed and dried, and the wax is removed.

Tjap-Resist Printing

The tjap method of printing, another variation of the batik, has been described under the Javanese batik method.

CHAPTER XI

Textile Painting Processes

No doubt some form of hand painting was the first color work done by man. Prehistoric cave paintings found in Spain and France show that man early discovered how to express himself graphically. Painting with colored clay on damp pieces of pottery was another early art expression.

Actual examples of early textile painting are found in both the Old and the New Worlds. Patterned fabrics painted on the ancient Egyptian murals show examples of what is possibly fabric painting; a mural dated *ca.* 2500 to 2300 B.C. illustrates fabric which appears to be the oldest known example of painted cloth. A fabric wall-hanging found near Thebes, dated *ca.* 1594 B.C., is an example of an early attempt to paint a pattern on fabric. Painting on silk was anciently practiced in China; the beautiful landscapes of the Ming Dynasty, many of them painted on silk, are considered among the world's finest art. On the Western Hemisphere large bold patterns painted on cloth have been found in many ancient Peruvian burial sites. (See Fig. 201.)

Recently there has been a strong revival of interest in the art of textile painting. Many factors share in bringing about this new accent on hand-painted fabrics: modern art influences, emphasizing "free" expression; improved methods of reproducing hand-painted textiles through the medium of the silk screen; and new demands for textiles which are suited to modern casual and outdoor living.

Some credit, too, should be given to the influence Mexico has had on textile design. About 1940, many little workshops in the town of Cuernavaca began to produce fabrics with colorful hand-painted designs. The demand for them increased to the point that manufacturers in the United States be-

Fig. 201. Hand-Painted Fabrics from Ancient Peru. Different types of hand-painted designs. Top and bottom left, from Huara, Peru, (Courtesy, Museo Nacional de Antropología y Arqueología, Lima.) Bottom right is from Surco. (Courtesy, The American Museum of Natural History.)

gan producing cloth with similar designs. Most hand-painted patterns are now reproduced by the silk-screen process.

1. Direct Hand Painting

Hand painting of cloth is not difficult; it takes only a little practice and patience. (See Fig. 202.)

Much thought should be given to the structure of the design. Often the

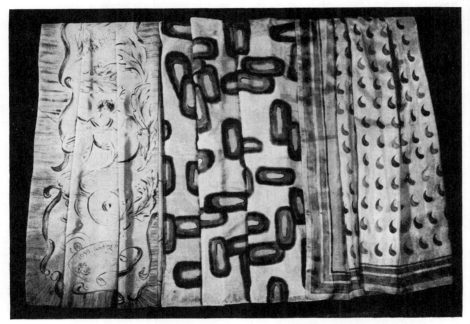

Fig. 202. Hand-Painted and Stenciled Fabrics. Left and center pieces are hand painted; the right piece is stenciled.

charm of a hand-painted design comes from the character of the lines used; free-flowing lines, tapering lines, broken lines, and other special line treatments add interest to patterns. Solid unbroken outlines should never be used. The design must be carefully plotted for space relationships. Contrast of value is another essential consideration; dark accents give strength to a design. Subtle balances of color and value and careful treatment of line are important factors in hand painting of textiles.

Designs used on textiles may be geometric, abstract, nonobjective, peasantlike, historic, or scenic—in fact, there is practically no limit to the scope or treatment of subject matter which may be used for textile designs. (See p. 6.)

421

Modern hand-painted textiles should reflect the free expression now found in so many phases of modern art. Textile designs with a modern flair should appear to have been painted with a light, free, and playful brush; they should also be dynamic in structure, spacious in feeling, and appealing in subject matter. They should be in the spirit of casual living. There is no place in the modern setting for the little prosaic designs so popular in the first quarter of this century.

When hand painting is done on a commercial scale, the silk-screen process must be used. The design is painted directly on a silk screen with tusche; the silk screen is further prepared and the tusche is removed; when the screen is printed, the hand-painted design is authentically duplicated.

EQUIPMENT RECOMMENDED FOR HAND PAINTING

Good Sable Brushes

Since line control is essential to good hand painting, brushes which will give good performance are needed, especially brushes which form good points. An assortment of sizes is helpful.

Stiff Brushes

These are important when working for texture treatments.

Blotters or Absorbent Paper

These are necessary for backing very fine material during painting.

Cardboard

The fabric is often stretched over cardboard during painting.

Palette Knife

This tool is helpful in mixing textile paint.

Textile Paint

There are a number of good textile paints on the market. Formulas for homemade textile paints are given on page 399.

Miscellaneous items such as pins, thumbtacks, Kleenex, a smock, and mineral oil or other cleaning solvents are useful.

GENERAL DIRECTIONS FOR HAND PAINTING ON FABRICS

1. Make a suitable design. Practice painting it with water color paint on large sheets of newsprint until you acquire some skill and self-assurance in handling the paint.

2. Wash and iron material before starting to paint.

3. Stretch the material tightly over a frame or pin it tightly over cardboard. When thin cloth is stretched over cardboard, blotting paper or absorbant paper should be placed beneath it.

4. Light pencil guide lines or dots can be marked on the fabric to chart the course of the design.

5. Use white plates to hold and mix the colors, or small sauce dishes or coffee cans if large amounts of color are needed. A palette knife is useful in mixing the paint.

6. Test paint for right consistency; if it is too thick, it is hard to apply; if it is too thin, it runs beyond control.

7. The painted design should appear spontaneous and free-flowing. Avoid painting areas solidly with paint. Use a stencil if necessary. Stencil painting and free-hand painting can often complement one another; the stencil may offer a touch of control to an otherwise free pattern. Keep all work open and free in appearance.

8. Let the paint dry and then set the color by pressing with a warm iron. It is a good idea to cover the design with a cloth dampened in a medium solution of white vinegar (4 tablespoons to 1 cup of water) and press it again.

9. Hand-painted fabrics should be dry-cleaned or washed in cool water with a mild soap. If possible, paint a sample swatch and test the washability of the paint before attempting to launder a piece.

VARIATIONS OF DIRECT HAND PAINTING

Dry-Brush Painting

An unusual texture is obtained by using a wide, stiff-bristle paint brush on fabric; the regular 2-inch brush used by house painters works very well. Mix the paint thoroughly to the right consistency and spread it out in a thin layer on a sheet of glass, using a palette knife to spread it. Touch the tips of the bristles into the paint, rub the brush on a sheet of paper until the individual bristles show in each brush stroke, and brush the color lightly over the fabric with straight, wavy, or zigzag strokes. Use large, bold strokes to fill in the background around other design units. See the border of the left fabric in Fig. 202.

Finger-Painting Techniques

Finger painting can be used in textile design. Make a finger-painted design on a large sheet of glass, using a dye-paste paint such as that described on page 399. Thoroughly wet the cloth to be painted and squeeze out excess

423

water. Open it out, lay it face down on the finger-painted design, and pat it gently. Remove cloth and use the hydro-rinse described on page 401. Dry and press.

Hot Wax Painting

The method used in the United States to do batik work constitutes a form of hand painting, hot wax being used in the brush in place of paint. The cloth is then dyed. This process has been described in some detail (page 415).

Warp-Painted Designs

Designs can be painted, stenciled, or printed onto the warp yarns which have been placed on the loom but not yet woven.

Air-Brush Painting

An air brush with a fine nozzle can be used to apply a "free-hand" pattern to cloth. Stencils are often used to limit the range of the spray.

2. Stencil Painting

Stencil painting is one of the resist processes of textile design (see Fig. 203), the resist in this case being the stencil itself, which prevents the paint from spreading beyond the margin of the cutout pattern. The name "stencil" seems to have been derived from the old French word, *estencillas,* which probably came from the Latin word, *scentillo,* both meaning to sparkle.

Very little is known about the historic background of stenciling. It is said that the Egyptians used stencils as early as 2500 B.C. (*121*). The Romans are reported to have been versed in stencil craft, but little is known of their work. Some writers claim that the Chinese were the originators of the process. The Japanese, however, have long been noted for their fine stencil work. They had a unique method of constructing stencils, known as the Yuzan process. In this process, the stencils are cut in duplicate out of thin rice paper. A number of hairs are laid crisscross between the two stencils and across the openings. When the stencils are then lacquered together, the hairs hold them in place but do not prevent the paint from passing through the openings. The Japanese use a soft rabbit-hair brush to paint their stencils. They sometimes touch up weaving patterns with small colored stencil designs.

During the Renaissance the Germans used stencils on furniture to imitate hand painting. Stencils were regularly used by early New England house-wives.

Commercial stencils were first used in the United States about the time of the Civil War to mark packages for shipping. Stencils have been used for this purpose ever since. A stencil cutting machine was perfected in 1894. Thick cardboard stencils are usu-ally cut out with a jig saw. Some 40 curved and straight sten-cil "chisels" are now available to professional stencil cutters. Metal stencils have been in use about 50 years. In the hands of an experienced artist-cutter stencil-ing can be a "fine art."

Since about 1925, many com-mercial stencil prints have been made with the aid of an air brush; the process has also been success-fully used in commercial illustra-tion work for grading tonal val-

Fig. 203. Stencil Painting. Two stencils were dovetailed to make this formal de-sign.

ues and colors. The silk screen stencil process is now extensively used for most commercial duplication work. It is discussed at some length later.

THE STRUCTURE OF THE STENCIL

Stencils can be made out of heavy waxed paper, cardboard, or metal. Metal stencils are the most durable and are used for commercial work. Sten-cil paper may be purchased or made at home. To make it, heavy wrapping paper is waxed for heavy-duty stencils, and lightweight paper for fine stencil work. To do the waxing, place the paper to be waxed on a thick pad of newspaper on an ironing board, sprinkle small pieces of paraffin on the sur-face, cover it with another similar sheet of paper, and run a moderately hot iron over all. Separate the two top sheets; this provides two sheets of stencil paper. Repeat the process if more wax is needed.

The charm of a stencil-painted pattern lies in the contour of its outline and the variation of the sizes and shapes of its openings. If there is but one stencil pattern, all open areas must be held together by ties or stays. (See Fig. 204, right.) If there are many of these intricate parts, the sten-cil becomes very complicated and difficult to handle. Because of this, mod-ern stencil designers no longer use these difficult stencils; they recommend instead the use of multiple stencils, giving each part of the design its own

425

stencil. In use, the parts fit into one another or are superimposed upon one another. A control pattern must be maintained to keep the stencil parts in order. The rooster on the left of Fig. 204 was made with multiple stencils.

Positive and Negative Stencils

When the paint is applied around the outside of a pattern, the stencil is said to be a negative stencil; when it is applied to the inside of the cut-out openings, the stencil is a postive stencil. (See Fig. 204.)

Fig. 204. Equipment for Stencil Work. The illustrations shows a stencil knife, a round type of stencil brush, two simple stencils, a piece of work from one of the stencils made with an air brush, and a cock painted in the dry-brush technique.

CUTTING THE STENCIL—STEP-BY-STEP PROCEDURE

1. Select a suitable weight of paper for the stencil, according to the usage it will have.
2. Trace the design selected for the work onto the stencil paper. If the stencil paper is transparent, place the design beneath a piece of glass. Using masking tape, secure the glass to the table and the stencil paper to the glass. Then trace the design on the stencil paper.
3. Select an Exacto knife, a Sloyd knife, or a Speed Ball pen knife. Keep the blade sharp while working. (See Fig. 204.)
4. Cut out the areas designated in the design. It is a great help to shade the areas that are to be cut out. Cut out small areas first.

426

DIRECTIONS FOR STENCIL PAINTING

Method I

The first and newer method of stencil painting, and the one generally used at present, is a combination of dry-brush work and stencil painting. The stencil is held firmly on the area to be painted, and the color applied with a flat, stiff oil-painting brush. The brush contains very little paint; it is pulled across the stencil paper and carried lightly over the cloth, using the dry-brush technique. The strokes are pulled from the edges of an opening toward the center. Various directions of brush strokes can be used. (See the rooster, Fig. 204.) The dry-brush technique is described on page 423.

Method II

The second method of stencil painting is less frequently used now. A regular round stencil brush is employed for the work. (See Fig. 204.) It is "inked" by dotting it up and down on a sheet of glass on which paint has been spread, taking care not to get paint on the sides of the brush. The stencil is held firmly in place on the material; in most cases it is safe to fasten it down with thumbtacks. The color is applied to the open areas in the stencil by briskly dotting the brush up and down. The brush is held firmly in a vertical position; it is not rubbed across the fabric, since this would push the paint under the edges of the stencil.

Using Method I or Method II, proceed as follows:
1. Always wash and iron cloth to be stenciled, unless the article is to be dry-cleaned instead of washed.
2. Stretch the material tightly over a base table or a sheet of cardboard and pin it down.
3. Mix the paint thoroughly. It must be just the right consistency. If too thin, it will run under the stencil; if too thick, it will look "boardy" and stiff on the fabric. Test the color and consistency of the paint by spreading a thing coating on a piece of glass, using a palette knife. Use either standard textile paints or mix your own paint according to the formulas on page 399.
4. Always make a sample print on a small piece before doing the actual printing on the large fabric. Carefully stencil the design on the fabric. Take care not to rub the color under the edges of the stencil.
5. Clean the stencil carefully, before each application of paint, especially the side next to the cloth. Keep Kleenex on hand for this work.
6. Let the paint dry on the fabric 4 to 6 days before setting the color. The color may be set by simply pressing with a moderately warm iron, but

it is better to cover the stenciled fabric with a damp cloth wrung out of a white vinegar solution (4 tablespoons to a cup of water) and then press.

OTHER METHODS OF APPLYING PAINT TO STENCILS

1. An air brush can be used to paint or fill in the stencil design. (See Fig. 204, center.) This is especially useful with a stencil made of shellacked lace.
2. An inked pad can be used to pat color over the stencil and thus to do the printing.
3. A small sponge, inked with the paint, can be used to stipple in the stencil design.
4. Textile crayons can be dragged into the pattern area in a sort of dry-brush technique.
5. The stencil can be filled in by using a palette knife to apply a dye-paste containing acetic acid. The whole thing then may be steamed thoroughly and washed. This is a Japanese stencil method.
6. A discharge paste can be stenciled onto the material. This is a stencil-resist paste-dyeing method. The fabric is then dyed. (See page 402.)
7. A design can be stenciled onto a prepared warp before it is woven into cloth.

CHAPTER XII

Textile Stamping and Printing Processes

Man has long been intrigued by the process of printing. Footprints and handprints may well have been his first introduction to the printing arts. Prehistoric peoples in both the Old and New Worlds stamped red clay handprints on cave walls. It is possible that the first actual use of stamps for printing was attempted in Mesopotamia some 5000 years ago. Cylinder-shaped, rocker-shaped, and flat stamps, some of the latter containing a clutch or handle in the back, have been found in ancient sites in that area. Brass signature seals have also been found in the Near East, but these date only from *ca.* 300 B.C.

How far the influence of Mesopotamia spread throughout the ancient world has never been ascertained. A mural in Egypt dated *ca.* 2500 B.C., shows a fabric with a repeat-design which undoubtedly was printed with stamps. The first recorded occurrence of block printing in Egypt appears in historical accounts of the fifth century B.C. (*149*). In the opposite direction, India also has an ancient heritage of printed fabrics. Some wooden blocks found in India obviously had had either hand knobs or clutches on the back, similar to those found in early Mesopotamia (*147*). Long before the beginning of the European Renaissance printing on fabrics had become a fine art in India. In fact, block printing on textiles in Europe was the direct result of the importation of patterned fabrics from India. In the New World ancient baked-clay stamps have been found in both Central and South America. There is evidence that these stamps were sometimes used for body decoration as well as for ornamenting pottery and textiles.

429

The commercial production of printed textiles no longer depends upon the block printing process. Other more efficient methods, such as roller printing and silk screen printing, have practically replaced the use of blocks. But the engraved rollers of the great roller printing presses of today are but modern developments of their ancient prototypes, the clay roller stamps of Mesopotamia.

1. Stick-Stamp Printing

Stick-stamp printing is a form of block printing. The earliest record of printing which has the appearance of having been done with stick stamps is a mural painted in Egypt *ca.* 2500 B.C.; the painters apparently used small stamps to place ornamental patterns on the clothing of the figures in the mural. Since the Egyptians used this stamping process on wall paintings, a similar manner of painting could easily have been utilized in textile design. It is known, however, that they were printing with stick stamps during the Roman period. The method they used was rather cumbersome. Most of their designs required an assortment of stamps; for example, instead of making a diamond design of one solid block, they would make a stick stamp equal to one side of the diamond and use it four times to print a diamond pattern.

It is likely that other areas around the Mediterranean also made use of small stick stamps. Figures on Greek vases dated *ca.* 500 B.C. appear to be wearing clothing decorated with stick stamps.

EQUIPMENT

Very little equipment is needed for stick-stamp printing.

Stamps

The stamps are made from dowel sticks, meat sticks, or small cubes of wood, or from such varied materials as rubber Artgum erasers (see Fig. 205), rubber corks, and even vegetables. Metal stamps can also be used if they are first covered with shellac and flock to give them a suitable surface.

A Knife or Chisel

A small knife or chisel is needed for carving the stamps. A vice for holding them during carving also comes in handy.

A Felt Pad

A well-inked pad is needed for the printing. It can be prepared by cutting several thicknesses of felt, flannel, or fine wool, stacking them on top

430

of one another, and stapling them together. The pad is laid on a piece of glass or tacked to a board and saturated with the printing paste or paint.

Textile Paint

Any of the standard textile paints, together with their binders and reducers, can be used for inking the pad.

Cardboard

The fabric is stretched over cardboard to keep it stabilized during the printing.

Miscellaneous equipment such as pins, Kleenex, a smock, and mineral spirits are also needed.

DESIGN

In planning a design for stick-stamp printing, a definite center of interest should be arranged; one stamp should be designed for this purpose. Other stamps should reinforce this center of interest and give color contrast and variety of shape to the pattern. The stamps can be planned for border designs or for allover patterns. Although there is a certain rela-

Fig. 205. Stick-Stamp Printing. The sample was printed with two stamps made on Artgum erasers.

tionship between stick-stamp printing and block printing, the character of the two processes is entirely different; block prints are often heavy and formal, while stick-stamp prints are gay and childlike in appearance.

DIRECTIONS FOR MAKING STICK-STAMP PRINTS

1. Always wash and iron the material before starting the stamping process.
2. Plan the design, carve the stamps, prepare the paint, and apply it to the inking pad.
3. Make a few test prints on sample swatches. (See Fig. 205.)
4. Stretch the material over a piece of cardboard and mark in lightly, with pencil or chalk, the areas to be stamped.
5. Stamp the material by pressing the stamps first against the pad and then on the fabric. Keep the stamps in line and evenly spaced.

431

6. Let the stamped fabric stand for a few days and then set the color as for block prints.

7. Clean the stamps thoroughly and store them away.

2. Block Printing

China is thought to have been the initiator of block printing. It is said that China employed earth pigments to paint block prints on textiles in 400 B.C. However true this may be, the National Museum in the Forbidden City does have some wooden blocks dating from 200 B.C., much later than the records of the use of clay stamps in Mesopotamia. Block printing on paper has a history somewhat parallel to that of block printing on cloth. Paper making was invented in China in 75 A.D. and block printing on paper began there soon afterward; by the sixth century, it was firmly established. The oldest known printed book, made from blocks, was printed in China between 850 and 1050 A.D. The earliest known piece of block-printed cloth was one, belonging to the ninth century A.D., found in a Coptic tomb in Egypt. Many of the Coptic print designs were ornamented with gold and silver; the process was called tinsel work and was done on brilliantly colored cottons and silks.

The knowledge of block printing spread northward from the Mediterranean area into Europe. Fabric that appears to have been block printed was found in the tomb of Bishop Caesarius, who was buried in Arles, France, in 543 A.D. Another piece of this type of work was found in the tomb of St. Cuthbert, who was buried in Durham, England, in 1104. A thirteenth century record mentions that block printing was being done in Italy at the time (*117*). In Germany, early in the Renaissance, craftsmen began using block prints to imitate Florentine velvets; in other European centers the weaves themselves were being copied.

Ever since the period of the crusades, Europe had been somewhat aware of the printed cottons of India and Java. It has even been said that America was discovered because Columbus was searching for the block-printed fineries of the Far East. A considerable quantity of block prints from India appeared in Europe in 1592, when the British captured a Portuguese vessel loaded with India prints.

As early as 1619, England was using blocks for printing cloth. About a decade later permission was given to the East India Company, a British industry, to import cottons from India. These cottons were called India prints and Chints, and became very popular in England. In 1676, William Sherwin was granted permission to print on cloth in the manner being used in India;

432

before long the copying of India prints and calicoes became an important English enterprise. The first calicoes were cotton prints from Calcutta, made principally by the block print, batik, and tjap processes. In 1720, a law was passed in England prohibiting the wearing of printed calicoes. Defoe, writing about the law at the time, commented that Queen Mary had so influenced the importation of fine calicoes from East India that Parliament, in order to protect the home industries, had been obliged to prevent further importation. The law remained in force 56 years.

The blocks the English workers used to print their fine fabrics had clutches or handles placed on the backs to assist in handling. The faces of the blocks were carved, coated with a varnish made of oil and gold size, and dusted with a fine wool flock. Several coatings of varnish and flock were applied. The blocks were printed by first pressing them against a well-inked pad. Silk-screen printing has now practically replaced block printing in England.

During the seventeenth century, France, too, began importing printed cottons from India, and attempts were made to duplicate them. Around 1675 there was such a great vogue in printed fabrics that the weavers began to complain loudly that the imported and homemade prints were ruining their business. The result was laws to protect the established textile enterprises. In 1686, Claude Lepeletier, Colbert's successor, issued an edict prohibiting the importation of fabrics from India; he also ordered the destruction of all blocks used in printing, and prohibited the sale of all printed cottons, whether imported or of home manufacture. In addition, he decreed that any such merchandise and print blocks found would be burned and the affected establishments fined 3000 livres. Naturally, many workmen left France and established themselves in other countries, especially in England, Switzerland, and Germany. This little industrial war lasted nearly a century; the restrictions were removed in 1759.

THE BLOCK PRESS

The history of the block press somewhat parallels that of fabric printing. As far back as during the Roman Empire the screw press was being used by cloth pressers. The first letterpress was established in Germany about 1450. The Gutenberg Bible, the first book printed in the Western world, was printed on it. Some writers claim that Rhenish monks had used block prints at least 100 years before this; they are even credited with introducing block printing into Europe. At any rate, there is no denying that block printing reached the status of a fine art in the work of the German artist, Albert Dürer (1471–1528).

433

The first letterpress was installed in England in 1475. In 1539, the first one in American was installed in Mexico; the first letterpress in the United States was installed in Massachusetts in 1639.

Ireland is reported to have been printing from copper plates in 1751; but the initial use of the block printing press for textile printing is usually credited to Switzerland, and the date is set at sometime between 1760 and 1770.

Fig. 206. Block Print. This fabric from Mexico was actually done by the silk-screen process. The blocks were printed onto the screen which in turn printed the fabric. The stamps were copied from ancient Mexican stamps. (A series of these stamps are pictured in *Sellos del Antiguo Mexico*, by Jorge Enciso, pub. by author, Mexico, 1947.)

In 1770 Oberkampf installed presses in his establishment at Jouy, France. (See Fig. 215.) Soon after this, the first block printing press was constructed in England; copper plates were used. In 1811, the first steam power press was installed. In 1834, Perrot of Rouen, France invented a mechanical press, the Perrotine block printing machine, which was later extensively used in France, Germany, and Italy.

Very little block printing on a commerical basis was done in the United States until 1772, when Benjamin Franklin invited one John Hewson to come from England to America and establish a printworks; most of the tools for

434

it had to be smuggled out of England. Martha Washington wore dresses made from fabric printed in Hewson's Philadelphia shop. In 1790, as a result of a survey of American manufacturing made by Alexander Hamilton, a factory was erected in Paterson, New Jersey, which spun, wove, bleached, and printed fabrics. In that same year H. Vendausen, a German, established a block-printing plant in East Greenwich, Rhode Island. By 1811 eight printing establishments were operating in Philadelphia.

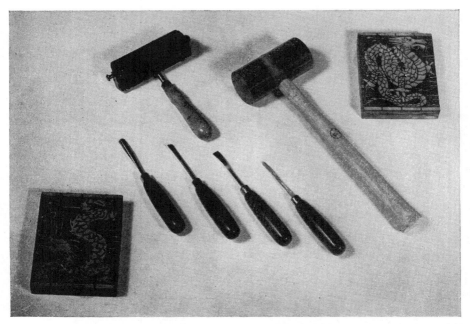

Fig. 207. Block-Printing Tools. Top, a brayer and a mallet. Bottom, a series of tools—gouge, chisel, curved-neck chisel, and veiner.

Block-printed fabrics were still produced and still in demand as late as the beginning of World War II. The silk-screen process has now almost completely replaced the use of blocks for printing, and few hand-block-printed materials are now made commercially. The charm of block-printed fabrics has been preserved, however, through the medium of the silk-screen process. Blocks are now printed directly onto a silk screen which prints them. The final product appears to be a true block print. (See Fig. 206.) Blocks, plates, and cuts are still being used, however, on letterpress machines for printing commercial stationery.

EQUIPMENT NEEDED

The equipment needed for block printing (see Fig. 207) includes a linoleum block, a set of linoleum carving tools, a set of textile paints and fluids, **435** a 12-inch square sheet of glass, a brayer, a mallet, a sheet of heavy cardboard, pins or thumbtacks, Kleenex, clean cloths, and a pad of newspapers. (A brayer is a rubber roller about 6 inches long, attached to a short handle. It serves as the tool for rolling ink or paint onto the block.) The best fabric to use for block printing is a cotton with a close fine weave, though other types of fabrics can be used.

DESIGN

A design for block printing should generally conform to the size and shape of the linoleum block; it is poor planning to make a design which uses only a small part of the block.

Designs for linoleum blocks should be bold and direct (see Fig. 208), with special attention given to the various parts of the pattern. It is important that there be a variation in the size and that the shape of these parts should have interesting contours. Textured areas should be balanced against plain areas. There should also be an attempt to balance light and dark values in the pattern. Stick stamps are often used with linoleum blocks to give added sparkle and variety to the pattern.

Fig. 208. Block-Printed Fabric. Two blocks were used to print the linen for this jacket.

PREPARATION OF LINOLEUM BLOCK
Structure

Although the block for printing can be made from wood or various other materials, it is ordinarily carved from linoleum. A linoleum block can be purchased or made at home. If the block is to be made, select a piece of heavy battleship linoleum which is free from blemishes and cut it to size. It must be glued onto a piece of plywood, but this can be done either before or after carving the design in it. When carved linoleum is tacked onto the wood, the tacks must be placed in the cut-out areas. If very large sheets of linoleum are used, it is not feasible to mount them on wood. One corner of the linoleum block should always form a right angle so that the position of the block can be stabilized during printing. Remove the surface wax on the linoleum with alcohol or lightweight sandpaper, and coat the surface with a white paint; casein paint makes a good coating.

Transferring the Pattern

There are three methods of drawing or tracing the pattern on the block: (1) Hold the paper on which the design is drawn up to the window and

436

with a soft pencil trace the design on the back of the paper; when the paper is laid on the block and the design retraced, the pencil lines on the back surface transfer the pattern to the block. (2) The entire back of the paper on which the design is drawn can be blackened with pencil; this will serve as a makeshift carbon. (3) The design can be traced onto the block with regular carbon paper.

Cutting the Block

Assorted knives, gouges, and veiners are needed. (See Fig. 207.) They should always be kept sharp.

Warm the linoleum to soften it; this will make it easier to cut. Do not let the fingers get in front of the tools; use a bench hook. Outline the pattern with the tip of a fine sharp knife, working slightly outside of the edge of the actual outline; cutting directly on the edge narrows the pattern. In cutting, take care to slant the knife slightly *away* from the design; if the pattern is undercut, the edges will chip and break off. Cut out the larger areas with a gouge; use a veiner for small areas. Cut off troublesome corners and high background projections. Make a trial print and correct any errors or uneven edges.

Flocking the Block

English block printers put flock on their blocks to insure a better print. This is described on page 433.

DIRECTIONS FOR BLOCK PRINTING

1. Always wash and iron the material before printing.
2. Stretch the fabric to be printed over a sheet of cardboard. This acts as a pad and insures more even printing.
3. Mark lightly, but accurately, the areas to be stamped; pencil dots are satisfactory. Use a yardstick or a stick marked off in the unit measurements of the block to help calculate the placement of the blocks on the cloth.
4. Prepare the paint. Place some on a sheet of glass, mix the desired color, and spread it out on the glass, using a palette knife for the work. Be sure the consistency is right. If it is too thin, the brayer will slip over the glass; if too thick, the paint will pile up on the brayer. The brayer should make a humming sound as it rolls back and forth over the paint. Standard commercial textile paints can be used or the paint can be made from formulas given on page 399.
5. Ink the linoleum stamp with the brayer by rolling it back and forth over the face of the block. Wipe off any paint that may have touched the

437

background. Make several trial prints to test the consistency of the paint and to practice the methods of application.

6. Hold the block firmly on the material and tap it with a mallet, first in the center and then on each corner. Blocks that do not register when printed may be reprinted. When very large sheets of linoleum are used for block printing, the sheets are inked with large brayers and laid face down on cloth stretched over a blanket for padding. The linoleum is then trod upon; that is, the worker, either barefooted or wearing soft buckskin moccasins, walks over the back of the linoleum until he feels sufficient pressure has been exerted to print the pattern.

7. Let the stamped material stand for a few days and then set the color by pressing the piece with a cloth wrung out of a solution of white vinegar (4 tablespoons to 1 cup of water).

8. The block should be cleaned thoroughly and stored.

3. Silk-Screen Printing

Silk-screen printing, which started so modestly in the early part of the twentieth century, has become one of the most important methods of printing textiles; it is also extensively used for printing wallpaper and for commercial printing.

The first patent for silk-screen process printing was issued in England in 1907, to Samuel Simon of Manchester. The following year a patent was issued in the United States to the New York Reproduction Company, which used the process for printing on pennants. About 1912, in San Francisco, F. O. Brant and J. A. Garner organized the Velvetone Poster Company, which claims to be the first to use the silk-screen process on paper and cardboard for advertising. At first the stencils were cut and processed by hand, but later the Selectasine Printing Press was devised to obviate this. (See Fig. 209.)

Patents were issued in 1915 and in 1921 for a process of silk-screen printing which employed a photographic compound, potassium bichromate and gelatine, for coating the screen. In 1920 the carbon-tissue stencil-screen method was patented in England. In 1921, the first successful stencil silk-screen printing press was invented; it could make as many as 1500 impressions per hour. Finally, in 1930, the stencil-film process was patented.

As this account shows, it took a quarter of a century to adapt the silk-screen process to commercial needs. At first it was used to make posters, signs, pennants, and banners. In the late 1930's experimentation began to extend its use to other fields. It was discovered that the silk-screen medium was fine for making art prints, and these prints, or serigraphs as they are called, are now competing successfully on the market with other types of prints. Serigraph prints are especially adapted to modern interiors and are being used in place of modern painting. Silk-screen printing is also now being used for printing wallpaper and textiles.

But we are primarily concerned here with the adaptation of the silk-screen printing process to textile design. In 1925, a silk-screen stenciling apparatus was invented for printing on bolt lengths of cloth, probably for use for banners and advertising. It is not known when the process was first employed as a medium of textile design.[1] The first process-printing on cloth is thought to have been done in France (*161*). Screen-printed fabrics were not much in evidence in clothing before 1940.

An enterprise undertaken at about this time helped to promote the popularity of the silk-screen process for use on textiles. In the early 1940's, James and Leslie Tillett, two brothers who were fabric printers in England, visited Mexico

Fig. 209. Silk-Screen Process Printing. Printing advertising material by the Selectasine process. (Courtesy, Velvetone Co., San Francisco, Calif.)

and decided to remain in Cuernavaca. Here they started a small factory using Mexican labor. Using the silk screen and other processes, they printed gay skirts and blouses for the tourist trade, simulating both free-hand painting and block printing. The project was such a success that Leslie Tillett opened another factory in New York. In the meantime other individuals in the United States and abroad began to realize the value of silk-screen process printing in duplicating hand-painted textiles and established their own textile printing factories.

The development of commercial methods of printing has been rapid. At first, only small screens were used, no wider than the reach of the individual who did the printing. These screens were hinged to a base table and the fabric was pulled under them as the printing progressed. One of the first improvements made in commercial printing was the use of tracks or rails to move the screen above fabric stretched over a long base table. At first this

[1] The author of this book, using the silk-screen process in 1931 for the printing of textiles, was perhaps the first person in Salt Lake City to do this work.

arrangement required two people to operate the squeegee: one pushed it toward the center of the screen and the other then pulled it toward the opposite side. Later, a wide squeegee was developed which could be held by two persons, one on either side of the screen, and pulled lengthwise down the screen frame. (See Fig. 210.)

In modern well-equipped factories the printing is now controlled by electrical devices. The squeegee, operated mechanically, slides back and forth

Fig. 210.   Silk-Screen Printing. Printing drapery material by the silk-screen method; an eighteenth-century design fabric is being printed. This method was used in 1951. (Courtesy, Scalamandré Silks, Inc., N.Y.)

in grooves along the screen frame. (See Fig. 211.) One recent type of silk-screen process machinery has electronic devices which control the entire process. It was developed in Switzerland by the Fritz Buser Engineering Company and is now being installed by many textile plants. In this process the cloth itself is drawn along a table; as it travels it is printed from screens with mechanically operated squeegees. Eight colors can be printed simultaneously. The fabric moves on from the printing table to the drying box. This process operates with great precision and turns out such perfect prints that the fabrics retain the character and appearance of hand painting or printing.

Silk-screen process printing has been heralded as a revolutionary development in the textile industry, especially since its conversion to electronic op-

440

eration. Its advantages over roller printing are discussed later in this chapter. Silk-screen process printing has grown into a multimillion dollar network of enterprises.

SILK-SCREEN METHODS

A number of different methods are used in silk-screen printing to transfer the design to the screen: the stencil-film method, the tusche method, and the photographic method. These methods differ so markedly that each is generally considered a type of silk-screen process printing. Each type has its own specific equipment. Some are best adapted to one type of work and some to another. All are within the capacities of home craftsmen, but some are considerably easier than are others. All of the silk-screen methods described here are also adapted to machine printing, but the emphasis in this book is upon processes which can be used at home or at school. The author strongly recommends the stencil-film method to those who wish to work for the first time with the silk-screen medium of printing.

Fig. 211. Mechanical Silk-Screen Printing. Two views of the all-electric Buser machine for silk-screen printing of fabrics. (Courtesy, Northern Dyeing Corp., Washington, N.J.)

THE STENCIL-FILM METHOD

The stencil-film method is closely related to stencil painting. As the name implies, a stencil is made for the screen. Stencil-film papers are constructed in such a way that a layer of film coats a layer of transparent backing paper. A number of satisfactory lacquer-soluble stencil-films are available.[2]

Cutting the Stencil-Film

Designs selected for silk-screen work should have clean-cut well-delineated contours. Turn the design face up on a smooth-surfaced table or a piece of glass and secure with masking tape. Blacken or otherwise mark the areas to be cut out. Cut a piece of stencil-film paper large enough to cover the screen, or at least to form a 4-inch margin around the design; place it

[2] Lacquer-soluble films are sold under various trade names. Some of the better known are: Nu-film, Blu-film, Pro-film, and Ulano Speed-cut film. Craftint Cut Film is a water-soluble film which must be adhered to a damp screen; it is satisfactory for small patterns, such as Christmas cards, but is unsatisfactory for large screens such as those used in most textile design work.

on the design with the film surface on top and secure it with masking tape. Since the stencil paper is transparent, the design will show through.

Using a sharp fine-pointed knife, cut out the marked areas of the design, being careful not to cut through the backing paper. Remove the cut-out sections of the stencil-film and make small slits through the backing paper in these areas; these slits allow air to escape during the adhering process.

Adhering Stencil-Film to Screen

Place the film layer of the stencil-film paper containing the cut-out design next to the screen on the front outside surface. Take care to place it in the correct position, with the design parallel to or at right angles with the sides of the frame. Tape the film paper in place.

Now turn the frame over so that the design and the screen are flat on the table and, working from the inside of the frame, start adhering the film to the screen. This is done with an adhering fluid. This liquid is different for different films. For lacquer-soluble films it contains lacquer thinner. Actually, lacquer thinner may be used alone, but it is usually recommended that its strength be reduced with a small amount of alcohol to prevent a burning-out or loss of part of the design.

Tear a clean cotton cloth into pieces about 2 inches square. Dampen one of the pieces with the adhering fluid, squeeze out excess fluid, and, starting at one corner, press the dampened cloth against the screen, holding it there a moment. Take one of the pieces of dry cloth and press it against the ad-hered area. Repeat the process on an adjoining area. *Never rub the screen*, or the film will dissolve. Always work diagonally across the cloth and always adhere adjacent areas in order to prevent wrinkles and air bubbles. Adhere only a small section, about 2″ x 2″, at a time. Continue the process until the entire stencil has been adhered to the screen.[3]

Check to see that the film is entirely adhered to the screen, applying more fluid to any area that may need treatment. Carefully remove the backing paper. Should any loss occur to a part of the design through the use of too much fluid or too much rubbing, make the needed corrections, using a fine paint brush and lacquer paint. If the background contains air holes, cover them with lacquer or masking tape. When the outside edges of the screen are sufficiently masked, the screen is ready for printing.

TUSCHE METHOD

Tusche is a thick opaque paintlike liquid available in either water-soluble or benzene-soluble form. Benzene-soluble tusche is usually a black oily

[3] It is possible that brayers with soft padded rollers, similar to those used for applying paint to walls, could be used for applying adhering fluid to large screens.

substance. (The same tusche is used in preparing a stone for lithography.) Water-soluble tusche is usually a dark brick red, somewhat like poster paint. It is well to have both types on hand for use in patching up screens, even, if they are not needed as media for applying the design to the screen.

Method I: Benzene-Soluble Tusche

When benzene-soluble tusche is used, the design is painted directly onto the inside of the screen with it. When the tusche is dry, spread a thin coating of glue entirely over the screen, on the side with the tusche painting LaPage's glue is used for this, in a proportion of about 2 parts full-strength glue to 1 part cold water. Tilt the screen and pour the glue along one end. With a piece of cardboard quickly pull the glue lengthwise in several strokes and then crosswise in several strokes—actually it is best if the glue can be put on with one complete stroke. Nothing must be allowed to touch the screen until the glue is dry.

When the glue is dry, remove the tusche with benzene. Any corrections needed can be made with a water-soluble tusche. After the edges of the screen are masked, the screen is ready for printing. Oil paints or lacquer must be used for printing, since water-soluble paints would dissolve the glue.

Method II: Water-Soluble Tusche

Coat the outside face of the screen with a thin solution of either dextrin or cornstarch boiled in water a few minutes. Then carefully paint the design on the inside of the screen with water-soluble tusche. When the tusche is dry, quickly drag a thin coat of transparent lacquer over the screen with a squeegee, or paint it on with a brush, on the same side of the screen as the tusche. If a caustic dye-paste is used for printing, a caustic-resisting bakelite varnish should be used in place of the lacquer.

When the lacquer is dry remove the tusche with water. When corrections are made, using lacquer as the medium, and the screen is properly masked, it is ready for printing. In this case water-soluble paint or dye-paste can be used for printing, or any oil paint which does not soften the lacquer coating on the screen.

Method III: Tusche or Lithographic Crayons

A very easy and quick way to make a silk-screen pattern is to draw the design with tusche or lithographic crayons, which are available at supply stores. A glue solution can be pulled over a tusche crayon drawing on a silk screen as it was over the benzene-soluble tusche in Method I. The tusche is then removed with benzene.

443

The photographic process was one of the first methods used for preparing the screen. Any of the following photosensitive processes can be used to sensitize the screen.

Method I: Potassium Bichromate Method (Direct Method)

The screen is coated directly with a sensitizer. The following formula is sufficient for a screen 24 inches square: photographic gelatin, 113.6 grams; potassium bichromate powder, 14 grams; distilled water 400 cc. Place the gelatin in the top of an enamel double boiler, add water, stir, and soak for 20 minutes. Place over boiling water and heat until 65° C. (150° F.) is reached; add the potassium bichromate dissolved in a little warm water; 10 drops of ammonia and 20 drops of glycerin may also be added. Coat the screen while the solution is still warm.

Coating the screen. To coat the screen, either place it upright in a vertical position or tilt it slightly backward; put the warm gelatin solution on the back with a 2-inch painter's brush. Barely overlap brush strokes, taking care to keep the brush warm, and not working back over an area already coated. Let the screen dry slowly and then coat the other side. Some workers use horizontal strokes on one side and vertical on the other. Two coats are often given to each side. The coating should be applied in a rather dark place or in a darkened room lit only by a 60-watt lamp covered by a yellow filter. Set the screen in a completely darkened ventilated room to dry; use as soon as possible after it is dry.

The design and its application. Make the design on either heavy transparent tracing paper or acetate film, using a special negative opaque black ink or India ink mixed with a little paste. (The design can also be a high-contrast positive.) Adhere the design to the side of the screen with white vaseline. Spread the vaseline on the screen and lay the design on top of it. Press gently from the center out so that no air pockets will let the light under the pattern area. When acetate film is used, transparent scotch tape is sometimes sufficient to keep the design flat. All of this work must be done in semidarkness or in a dark room. Use black cardboard or felt to cover the side of the screen not to be exposed, the side opposite the design.

The exposure. Expose the side of the screen upon which the design rests to the light according to the following table:

> bright sunlight, 10–13 minutes
> bright daylight, 10–30 minutes
>
> 300-watt lamp at a 24-inch distance, 20–22 minutes
> carbon lamp at a 20-inch distance, 24 minutes

The potassium bichromate in the coating changes color on exposure. A small area which has been covered by tape may be used as a control for the color change. When the potassium bichromate has turned a bronze color, clean off the vaseline and wash the screen, first in cold and then in hot water, letting the water run first on one side of the screen and then the other. The gelatin area which was below the design will give away because it was not exposed to the light and is still soft. When the gelatin is all dissolved from the design areas, let the screen dry. When it is properly masked it is ready for printing.

Method II: Direct Lacquer Method

The screen is thoroughly coated on both sides with one or two coats of a gelatin solution of 1 part gelatin to 6 parts water. The design is painted directly on the inside of the screen, rail side up, with one or two coats of black lacquer, or it is painted on acetate film and attached to the inside of the screen as described under Method I. A 10 percent solution of potassium bichromate is painted on the outside surface of the screen, opposite the side with the design. The screen is exposed to light as in Method I. The unexposed areas are washed out with warm water, and any remaining lacquer is removed with lacquer thinner. When properly masked, the screen is ready for printing.

Method III: Carbon Tissue Stencils

This process of photography was invented in England in the middle of the last century; after the first World War it was developed in the United States for silk-screen work. This is the easiest and most accurate of the photographic methods so far described. (The new sensitized films, Method IV, are even better.)

Paper coated with a gelatinous emulsion can be purchased under various trade names. Working in a dark room, coat the paper with a liquid sensitizer just before using. This sensitizer is also available in a prepared form. When the film paper is sensitized, press it flat on a second backing sheet to give it additional support. Place the design, the positive, on top of the film paper, place both in a photographic contact frame, and expose them. Immerse the film paper in hot water (110° to 120° F.) for about 5 minutes, film surface downward, and then turn it over. The unexposed areas of the paper should dissolve away. Agitate the water a little to help remove the film from these areas. Rub lightly with the fingers if some areas of the design appear to resist. As soon as the negative is ready, adhere it immediately to the screen—it is sticky when wet. When it is dry, carefully remove the

445

double backing sheet. When the edges of the screen are masked it is ready for printing.

Method IV: Sensitized Silk-Screen Film

This photographic silk screen-process is the most satisfactory yet developed. It consists of a prepared sensitized film: the screen is ready for exposure when purchased. The film, which may be purchased in sheets or rolls, is acetate coated with a sensitized film. There are several varieties of this film on the market, each sold under a special trade name, and each developed according to the specific formula of the manufacturer. Instructions for each film should accompany the purchase. In general, the film is exposed, developed, and adhered to the screen in essentially the same way as the carbon tissue method.

ADDITIONAL SILK-SCREEN METHODS

A number of other silk-screen methods might in some cases be better suited for a particular purpose than those described.

Shellac Film

This film corresponds to that used in the stencil-film method, but the adhering is done with alcohol.

Paper Stencils

Paper stencils can be made from a heavy fine-grained paper. The paper is cut to the size of the screen, the design is drawn on, and the paper is coated with lacquer or shellac. The design is cut out and the paper adhered to the screen with lacquer thinner (for lacquer) or alcohol (for shellac).

Glue-Paper Stencils

Stencils made out of paper which has a coating of glue can be adhered to the screen by covering the screen with a damp cloth on the side opposite the stencil and then pressing with a warm iron.

Typewriter Stencils

Mimeograph stencils cut on a typewriter can be treated exactly like paper stencils.

Lithography

Lithographic processes are discussed at the end of the chapter.

446

GENERAL DIRECTIONS FOR SILK-SCREEN PRINTING

PREPARATION OF THE FRAME

Size of the Frame

The frame should be large enough to provide a clearance, beyond the design to be printed, of at least 1 1/2 inches on two sides and 4 inches on the other two sides of the frame. The wider margins hold the paint; these then should be arranged on opposite sides, at right angles to the hinged end of the frame. For most purposes, a frame of approximately 20″ x 30″ is a good size; for printing yardage, the frame should be at least 30″ x 42″.

Structure of the Frame

A wooden frame for silk-screen printing can be purchased at an art supply store, constructed at a lumber mill, or made at home. For a long-wearing non-warping frame beech or sycamore should be selected, though frames which are to be used only a few times can be made of pine. The corners of the frame must be

Fig. 212. Screen and Base Table. The simple silk-screen equipment used for home and school. Note squeegee at top of the base table.

accurate right angles; they must be reinforced with metal cleats. Homemade zinc triangles or regular corner braces will also help to reinforce the corners. The frame should be hinged to a base table; this table is described later. (See Fig. 212.)

PREPARATION OF THE SCREEN

Selecting the Fabric for the Screen

The frame should be covered with silk-screen mesh, such as No. 12 silk bolting cloth or a fine open-mesh nylon. Any fabric other than the specially prepared silk-screen mesh should be washed and ironed before being stretched on the frame.

Stretching the Silk-Screen Fabric on the Frame

Tack the material to the frame by starting from the centers of the four sides of the frame and working first on one side and then on the opposite side, tacking two to four tacks on one side at a time. Work gradually toward the corners, keeping the material stretched so that it is taut, smooth, and free of wrinkles. The fabric can, if desired, be pulled over the edges and tacked to the sides of the frame, but usually it is simply tacked to the top.

There are other methods of stretching the material onto the frame: Slots can be cut in the frame into which the fabric is pushed and held by

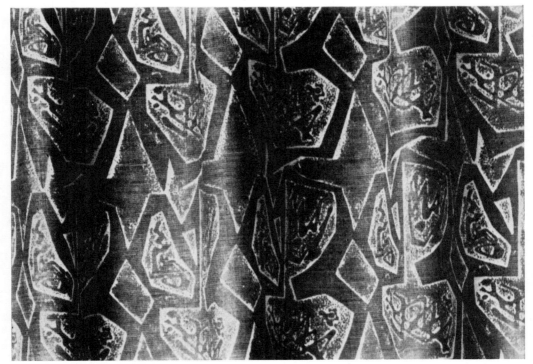

Fig. 213. Silk-Screen Printed Fabric. "Crocus," by Ruth Reeves. (Courtesy, Rowen, Inc., N.Y.)

wedges; this frame is similar in principle to an embroidery hoop. Another frame is similar to a quilting frame; it is bordered with strips of heavy material; the fabric is stretched across the face of this frame, folded back into a double edge, and pinned to the heavy material on the borders. With either of these two systems, the screen with its design can easily be removed from the frame and stored for future use.

PREPARATION OF THE DESIGN

Versatility of Silk-Screen Designs

Top ranking artists and designers have been attracted to the field of silk-screen printing because of the very adaptable nature of the technique. (See

448

Fig. 213.) Hand-painted designs, with distinct brush strokes, can be accurately duplicated. In fact, practically all known textile design processes, can be duplicated by the silk-screen process. (See Figs. 206 and 214.) The following are some of the techniques that are readily imitated by the silk-screen process:

Block Printing. Block prints are stamped onto a silk screen using the tusche method. When the screen is printed, the similarity of the fabric to that printed directly by block printing is amazing.

Fig. 214. Imitation Prints. A series of silk-screen process prints made to imitate other textile processes. Left, imitation of hand painting. Center, imitation of block printing. Right, imitation of tie and dye work.

Tied and Dyed Work. The silk for the screen is tied and dipped into tusche before it is stretched on the frame. When the screen is prepared according to the tusche method and printed, the resulting fabric has the appearance of an actual piece of tie and dye work.

Batik Work. A batiklike design is prepared and printed with the screen. The tusche method is usually used.

Hand Painting. Hand-painted designs are accurately duplicated with the silk-screen process. The design is painted onto the screen, using the tusche method.

Stencil Painting. A stencil is made by one of the stencil-film processes described earlier.

Roller Painting. Roller-printed designs are duplicated by the photographic method of silk-screen printing.

Photography. Any of the above processes can be duplicated on the silk screen by the photographic process. Likewise, actual photographs of scenery, animals, people, or of any design, can be duplicated by the photographic process of silk-screen printing and printed upon fabric.

Suitability of the Design

The subject and treatment of the design should be in harmony with the fabric to be printed and its intended use.

Structure of the Design

Since so many types of design can be adapted to silk-screen printing, the structural requirements of the design differ accordingly. Interesting lines, as well as variation in sizes and contours are essential. A general discussion of design is given in the Introduction of this book.

Constructing a Repeat-Pattern

The silk-screen process is often used to print allover designs. Here the handling of repeats is very important. The sides of the design should be checked accurately to make certain that the repeats will match during the printing. (See Fig. 216.) A repeat design is prepared as follows:

1. Cut a piece of heavy wrapping paper the size of the silk-screen frame, plus suitable margins. Divide it into exact vertical and horizontal sections and break these sections into bricks, or divisions of even size which alternate in position on alternate rows. This arrangement makes it possible to form half-drop or stair-step sequences in the repeats of the design.
2. Lay a piece of heavy tracing paper over one section of the marked wrapping paper and make one repeat of the pattern. Try this in other sections to make sure that the pattern dovetails accurately. Again check the spacing carefully to be sure that the design units will match along the margins during printing.
3. Trace the repeat into the section on the wrapping paper.

Two-Tone or Multicolor Designs

A design of two or more colors can be printed, if a frame and screen are prepared for each color. The designs must be carefully made to dovetail on the different screens. To insure accurate placement, the frame should be hinged to the base table before the design is adhered to the screen. The original design is then taped to the base table, and the sections are checked against it.

In common practice, however, one screen may serve a dual purpose: a two-color print may be made by blocking out one part of the screen during the first color printing and the other part of the screen during the printing of the second color.

450

TRANSFERRING THE DESIGN TO THE SCREEN

The manner in which the design is put upon the screen differs according to which silk-screen method is used. These methods were described earlier, page 441. The design should be arranged on the screen so that there are 2-inch margins on both ends and 4-inch margins on both sides. The wider margins hold the paint. One of the ends will be hinged to the base table, as described a little further on.

MASKING THE SCREEN

After the design is put on the screen, the screen is masked; that is, all open areas not to be printed must be blocked out. Some silk-screen methods, such as the photographic and the tusche methods, require very little masking, because the solution used covers the entire screen. More masking is required for the stencil-film method. The amount of masking needed will depend upon how the size of the stencil compares with the size of the screen.

Materials Used for Masking

Wide paper tape can be used for masking, but brightly colored synthetic Scotch tapes are better. Paper tape often buckles and comes off; synthetic tape remains permanently fixed. Synthetic tape is more expensive, but the cost is warranted.

Masking Procedure

The masking is done on the outside face of the screen, though some printers mask both inside and outside. The tape should lap over the stencil backing film about 2 inches; it should be carried across the screen between the design and the frame and then up the outside of the frame about an inch or more. If a large area is to be blocked out, wide strips of newspaper, four or five sheets in thickness, or strips of acetate can be taped down overlapping the film and the sides of the frame.

PREPARATION OF THE BASE TABLE

One end of the silk-screen frame should be attached to a base table with open pin-type hinges. The base table may be merely a sheet of plywood 6 inches larger than the screen on three sides; on the fourth side is fastened a strip of lumber as long and as thick as the frame of the screen. (See Fig. 212.) The hinges are fastened to this strip and to the silk-screen frame. They stabilize the position of the frame during printing, and are especially necessary in making a two-color print pattern or in using two or more screens for printing.

451

Preparing the Base Table for Printing

Cover the base table with wrapping paper and tape it down. The area beneath and around the screen on the base table must be charted and marked carefully, so that the fabric will be placed in the correct position beneath the design during the printing.

SELECTING THE FABRIC TO BE PRINTED

Select the fabric with care; it should of course be appropriate for its intended use. A smooth-surfaced fabric will produce more clear-cut prints. Transparent material is hard to work with because the paint goes through the fabric; this makes it necessary to put a backing cloth or a clean sheet of paper under the fabric for each print made. A medium or a light-colored fabric provides the best background for a printed design.

The paint selected for the pattern should be darker than the fabric, in order to insure a good transition between pattern and background fabric. If a very dark fabric is used, a light-colored paint must be selected; this combination is not advisable, however, because light paint often looks chalky and heavy on a dark background. It is always better to work toward a dark value in the design than to attempt to put a light value over a dark one.

Preparing the Fabric for Printing

The fabric must always be washed and ironed before printing. It should be cut in appropriate sizes if individual pieces are to be printed. If several yards of material are to be printed as a single piece, the fabric should be folded into large accordionlike pleats and placed across chairs or on a low stand at one side of the base table.

PAINTS USED IN SILK-SCREEN PRINTING

When choosing the paint for silk-screen printing, it is most important to select a type of paint that will not dissolve the particular coating used on the screen. The fabric used for the screen must also be considered, since some printers use nylon in place of silk for covering their frames. Water-soluble paints or pastes, many of which are on the market, cause nylon to stretch and, therefore, cause the screen to buckle during printing.

Commercial Textile Paints

There are a number of good textile paints on the market. In using Alpha colors for silk-screen work, select the large economy cans of the dry colors. Mineral spirits used with the regular textile liquid will keep the Alpha textile paint the right consistency during painting. Other types of paints can be used for printing on textiles: lacquer, auto body paint, regular oil paint, and resin-based paint can all be used if a small amount of H. P. Indelible Dryer is added to the paint mixture. Of course, lacquer paint cannot be used if the design has been put on the screen with any of the lacquer-soluble stencil-film materials.

Homemade Dye-Pastes and Paste-Paints

If a homemade paste-paint is to be used, a sample of the mixture should be tested on the screen and on the cloth before too much paint is mixed. Dye-pastes and paste-paints contain water, which may buckle the screen. Formulas for these pastes and paints are given on page 399.

OTHER EQUIPMENT NEEDED

Squeegee

The most important single tool for silk-screen printing is the squeegee. A squeegee is a strip of board-inch lumber with a strip of rubber 1/4 inch thick inserted lengthwise along one edge. (See Fig. 212.) (Squeegees are commonly used for washing windows.) The squeegee should be about 1 inch shorter than the width of the silk screen frame if it is to be pulled lengthwise of the screen. When this tool is pulled over the screen, the paint is pressed through the openings in the pattern and onto the cloth. When material is printed by the yard, it is often more convenient to use a squeegee which passes *across* the screen; in this case, the squeegee should be 1 inch less than the length of the frame. Squeegees can be purchased at any length desired, cut to customer's specifications.

The following miscellaneous supplies are also needed: Kleenex, clean cloths, a stack of newspaper, solvent for cleaning hands and screen, masking tape, a few empty coffee cans, and a clothes rack. If a mordant, such as white vinegar, is to be used, this should also be included in the equipment.

PRINTING BY THE SILK-SCREEN PROCESS

Before starting to print all details should be carefully planned and all equipment systematically arranged. The design is upon the screen, the screen is masked, the frame is hinged to the base table, the base table is marked for printing, the fabric to be printed has been washed and ironed, the paint is mixed, and all supplies needed are arranged for convenience. Whichever type of paint is used, enough should be on hand to print the

453

entire project. A convenient way to handle it is to put it in a coffee can and bend the can to form a spout for pouring. The paint should be the consistency of thick cream. The screen is inked by pouring the paint across one of the wide-margin sides; it should not be allowed to run down into the design area.

Before starting to print, make one or more test prints to check the location of the design, to try the consistency of the paint, to test the efficiency of the masking, and to determine the amount of pressure needed on the squeegee. Also check the base-table markings carefully to be sure that the fabric is correctly placed under the design. In two-color printing, the position of the two frames on the base table should be carefully checked and a test print made to test the accuracy of the register.

Printing is considerably facilitated if two or three people share the work —three are a minimum if yardage is being printed. The division of labor and the plan of operation should be systematized before the printing is undertaken. It is especially important to arrange the location and handling of the paint in advance, or you may have paint spread on tables and chairs as well as on the fabric. Have Kleenex readily available to keep the equipment clean and especially to keep the hands clean.

To print the design, pull the paint firmly over the screen with a squeegee, pulling in one direction for one print. For the second print pull the squeegee back to its original position. If small sections of material are to be printed, each section should fit into the area marked on the base table. If yardage is being printed, pull the cloth forward to the marker on the base table after each printing. In printing yardage, it is usually considered wise to print every other design unit first then to print the alternate units on a second printing. This prevents smearing the pattern. If this is not possible, lay strips of newspaper under the edges of the frame to prevent smearing. In printing thin or transparent material it is often necessary to place a fresh piece of paper under the cloth before each print. If two or more colors are being printed, each color should be allowed to dry before others are printed. It is a good idea to hold the cloth in place during printing with a few strips of masking tape.

As the fabric is printed put it on a drying rack or spread it out on tables. If yardage is being printed, pull the fabric forward and allow it to rest on a long table previously arranged to hold it. (Papers should be spread on drying racks and tables to prevent damage from paint.)

After the fabric has been allowed to dry for 48 hours it can be dry-pressed, steam-pressed, or given a vinegar press to assist in setting the color.

CLEANING THE SCREEN DURING AND AFTER PRINTING

If the paint should run down into the open pattern when the frame is lifted between prints, it may be necessary to wipe off both sides of the screen in the areas affected. Rub with care on the face of the screen, lest the film be loosened. If the paint dries on the screen or clogs it during printing, the screen must be cleaned before another print is made. The solvent used for cleaning must be one that will not dissolve the film coating the screen; the most satisfactory solvent for general use is mineral spirits. Use cloth for cleaning the screen; never use Kleenex for this purpose, as it clogs the mesh.

When the printing is finished, the screen must be cleaned thoroughly. First, scrape as much paint as possible off the screen with a squeegee. Turn the screen face down on several thicknesses of newspaper and pour some mineral spirits onto the back. Using old cloths, wipe off as much paint as possible, continuing until the mesh is clear when the screen is held to the window. Store screens either face-to-face or back-to-back on a shelf or screen rack.

If the stencil-film design is not to be used again, it may be removed from the screen with the special solvent which dissolves the coating on the screen: water-soluble coatings can be removed with water and lacquer-soluble coatings with lacquer thinner or commercial film removers.

4. Textile Rotary Press Printing Processes

The commercial printing of textiles has undergone many changes since its introduction into Europe in the seventeenth century. Carved wooden blocks were first used for printing, then engraved copper plates, and then, late in the eighteenth century, engraved copper rollers were installed on rotary printing presses. In the second quarter of the nineteenth century the silk-screen process was adapted to textile printing.

Most fabrics printed in the United States today are printed by either the silk-screen process just described or by the roller printing process. The silk-screen process has a distinct advantage over the older roller printing method. For one thing, the preparation of the screen for silk-screen printing is considerably less expensive than the engraving of the roller for roller printing. The silk-screen process is therefore preferred for short runs and test runs. But because of the durability of metal rollers, the roller printing process is employed for exceedingly long runs of yardage. In other words, roller printing is still basic to the textile industry. (See Fig. 217.)

It should be kept in mind, however, that conditions in the textile industry are constantly changing; research is continually in progress. As a case in point, the photosensitive process, now widely used for printing textiles by the silk-screen method, may before long be adapted to roller printing. This would lessen the cost of transferring the design to the rollers, and would possibly give roller printing the advantage. It is already the opinion of many European printers that current methods of engraving rollers for roller printing will soon be replaced by some type of photographic process.[4] Photosensitized plates are already established as the basis of lithography, and a very limited number of textiles are being printed by that process.

ROLLER PRINTING—THE ROTARY PRESS

As noted earlier, baked-clay roller stamps were made by the ancient Babylonian peoples. Although many of them were undoubtedly signature stamps used to sign clay tablets, many had such ornate patterns as to suggest their use for printing on cloth. It seems strange that nearly 4000 years would pass before man visualized the application of this principle to large-scale production.

It has been reported that Ireland was printing from copper plates in 1752, but it is a matter of record that in 1770, Thomas Bell, a Scotchman living in Lancashire first started using an engraved metal plate for printing; a few years later he adapted this principle to a cylinder and installed his first roller on a calendering frame (*117*). By about 1780, printing plants using rotary presses were established in England and at Amiens, in France. Oberkampf experimented with roller printing on textiles at Jouy, France, in 1793, and three years later his machine was in operation. It could produce in one day what had formerly taken 42 block printers to turn out (*117*). (See Fig. 215.) Roller-printed fabrics soon began to appear on the market in large quantities. Adam Parkinson, of Manchester, England, then developed a method of keeping the rollers in register so that one color could be printed over another. In 1805, James Burton, of Blackburn, England, combined the use of wooden and copper rollers. In the nineteenth century England led the world in the production of woven and printed cotton goods. (See Fig. 216.)

One of the handicaps of rotary printing was the engraving of the cylinder—some designs required 6 months to engrave by hand. In 1801, Samuel Widmer, working for Oberkampf at Jouy, developed a method by which steel points, operated by machinery, could be used to cut designs onto the

[4] *American Fabrics' Magazine,* Reporter Publications, Inc., Spring, 1954.

Fig. 215. Toile de Jouy Print. One of the famous prints of Huet, made at Jouy, France, for Oberkampf. This is a late eighteenth-century roller print. (Courtesy, Cooper Union Museum.)

copper cylinders. Sometime later the invention of the pantograph, a tracing and enlarging machine, further shortened the time needed for engraving the cylinder.

In the United States the first cylinder built for the rotary printing press—and eventually used for printing cotton—was made by the Baldwin Locomotive Works under the direction of David Mason. In 1810 Thorp, Siddal, and Company in Philadelphia printed the first calicoes in the United States from engraved rollers; 5 years later some 2325 people were engaged in the industry (*117*). Today the huge roller printing enterprises and others concerned with the finishing of fabrics, employ more than 100,000 people.

Fig. 216. Design Repeat. An artist's drawing of one repeat of an early eighteenth century design for drapery material to be printed on the roller printing press.

PREPARING THE ROLLERS

Three processes are commonly used for applying designs to metal rollers before they are installed on the rotary press: the die and mill process, the engraving process, and the photographic process.

The Die and Mill Process

A steel mill containing a raised design, cast from a pattern die, sinks its design into a copper roller as the two turn together under pressure.

The Pantograph Engraving Process

The pantograph has replaced the former tedious process of hand engraving the roller for the roller printing press. With the pantograph a roller is engraved as follows: The design, enlarged with the use of a projector, is corrected if necessary, and is engraved onto a zinc plate. This plate is placed in the pantograph machine; an operator then traces around its design with a needle. As the tracing is being made at the front of the panto-

458

graph, diamond points at the back of the machine cut through the acid-resisting varnish coating the roller and engrave the design into the copper; at the same time the design is reduced to the necessary size. The roller is then etched in acid, the acid affecting only the engraved areas. The varnish is removed and the roller is installed on the press. The dye-paste used in printing adheres to the etched areas.

The Photographic Process

The photographic process is being increasingly used to transfer the design to the cylinder for roller printing. The design positive is fastened with transparent tape around the photosensitized surface of the roller. The roller is then turned slowly, first in the exposure cabinet, next in developing fluid, and finally in etching acid. The hardened film is then scrubbed off and the roller installed on the press. There are a number of ways of transferring the design to the roller by the photographic process; several of them are described in the discussion of lithography which follows. The photographic process has been for a number of years now the established method of preparing metal plates for the rotary presses used in lithography. Its use for transferring patterns to rollers for textile printing may prove to be as revolutionary a development as was the initiation of metal rollers more than 150 years ago.

PRINTING OPERATIONS

As the roller revolves on the press during printing, it comes in contact with a furnishing roller which is partially submerged in a tray of dye-paste. As it turns it transfers the color from the tray to the engraved rollers. (See Fig. 217.) A knife at the back, called a doctor, scrapes off excess color.

Rotary press rollers transfer designs to textiles by several methods: (1) The warp is printed before it is woven, forming what is known as shadow prints (see Fig. 196). (2) Two or more colors are printed in rapid succession by use of a series of self-inking rollers (see Fig. 217). (3) Both sides of the cloth are printed simultaneously by a process called duplex printing. (4) Transparent lacquer or resin printed onto a fabric serves as an adhesive base for the application of ground-wool flock; flock is also sometimes adhered to the resin pattern by an electromagnetic process. (5) Patterns can be removed from a dyed fabric by printing a discharge paste onto the fabric.

After being printed, the fabric is usually run through other rollers and

459

given other finishing treatments; it may be steamed, dried, ironed, plastic-coated, or embossed by being passed over a series of rollers.

OFFSET ROTARY PRESS PRINTING—LITHOGRAPHY

A few words should be said about the process of lithography, which is now very important commercially. Devised in Germany by Senefelder in 1796, it was originally a fine art print-making process in which prints were taken from limestone slabs. Because the right quality of limestone is difficult to secure, the work today is often done on aluminum or zinc plates. The picture is painted or drawn onto the stone with a black oily opaque tusche, a black tusche crayon, or a special tusche pencil. The stone is then etched with dilute nitric acid which hardens the tusche and makes the untreated stone more permeable to water. Ink im-

Fig. 217. Roller Printing Press. A view of roller printing presses in operation. The cloth drum, self-inking rollers, ink trays and other mechanisms are visible. The fabric design is not visible in the picture. (Courtesy, Riegel Textile Corp., N.Y.)

pressions can then be taken from the stone as in ordinary printing; both water and ink are used in the printing. The oil or tusche areas attract the ink and repel the water; the background areas attract the water and repel the ink.

Although the basic principle is still a matter of printing with ink and water, the commercial process today depends upon the use of a photosensitive metal plate. When the plate has been properly treated and is ready for printing, it is attached to a rotary press. Commercially the process is known as offset printing.

Although the metal-plate process of lithography has not as yet been applied to textile design to any extent some efforts have been made in this

460

direction: book bindings are printed by the lithographic method; small articles, such as stiffly starched American flags, are printed on the lithograph press; and some fabrics stretched over a backing canvas have been run through a web-fed lithograph press. Photographs of animals, scenery, and people can be directly transferred to cloth in this way. The use of rotary presses in commercial lithography and in textile painting suggests a distinct relationship between the processes. Lithography is described here in some detail, partly because of this close relationship, and partly because any or all of its processes are prospects for future use in textile design.

THE ZINC-PLATE PROCESS

The use of a grained zinc or aluminum plate, once so basic to lithography, is now of secondary importance. Very briefly, the process is as follows:

1. Make a design and photograph it, using a high-contrast film. Develop the film with a high-contrast developer.
2. In a semidark room, coat a thin sheet of zinc, especially grained and cut to size, with a bichromate colloidal solution made up of potassium bichromate mixed with either gelatin, egg albumin, or some other colloidal compound. For multicolor printing a plate must be made for each color. Dry the plate or plates in a dark place and use immediately— they cannot be stored because the surface coating soon hardens.
3. Lay the high-contrast negative on this sensitized metal plate and expose to light until the light-sensitized material has hardened under the exposed areas of the film. (See page 444 for exposure chart.)
4. Remove the negative and coat the plate with heavy black greasy ink. This coating adheres to the hardened colloid, enables the image to be delineated, and enables the ink in printing to stick to the image patterns.
5. Wash the metal plate in warm water to remove the unsensitized coating which lies below the unexposed areas of the negative. Remove excess water with a squeegee.
6. Place the plate in a dilute solution of weak acid such as tannic or phosphoric, or brush this weak acid over the plate. The acid solution should contain a solution of gum arabic. This process desensitizes the exposed surfaces and changes their chemical composition, making the metal in these areas more sensitive to water and less sensitive to ink.
7. Wipe off the excess solution with a piece of cheesecloth and allow the plate to dry thoroughly.
8. Place the plate around the cylinder on the printing press; sponge it off when ready to print.

461

TEXTILE STAMPING AND PRINTING PROCESSES

9. As the cylinder rotates in printing the plate is exposed first to rollers which give it a coating of water and then to rollers which give it a coating of ink. The water is absorbed by the areas which were not exposed, and the ink is adhered to the areas that were exposed.
10. When not in use the zinc plate is always protected with a thin coat of gum arabic solution, which is washed off when the plate is again put on the press.
11. Zinc plates can be reused if they are ground down and given a new surface grain.

THE PRESENSITIZED ALUMINUM-PLATE PROCESS

The use of presensitized ungrained aluminum plates has now practically replaced the use of the zinc plates in lithography. This is understandable, for the aluminum plates are prepared with a photosensitive coating at the factory and are ready to use when purchased. Plates can be purchased for either positive or negative exposure—most of those sold are for negative exposure.

The sensitized aluminum plates are prepared for the press as follows: The negative is placed over the plate; the plate is exposed to the light, developed, and then completely covered with a dilute gum solution, the formula for which can be secured from the manufacturer. A water-soluble lacquer is next poured over the plate and thoroughly rubbed into the image with a sponge. (This lacquer, which comes in different colors, is another special product of the manufacturer.) The lacquer adheres to the image and not to the background. When the image is plainly delineated, the plate is wiped dry with a piece of cheesecloth.

Aluminum plates need not be coated with gum arabic every time there is a pause in the printing, as is necessary for some plates; this is another of their advantages. However, it must be coated with gum arabic before it is stored. When the design on the plate is no longer needed, the plate is discarded; it cannot be reconditioned and reused.

THE BIMETAL PROCESS

There are several bimetal plates on the market. Printers prefer them for longer printing runs. One type is a copper-plated aluminum; this is not coated with a photosensitive film when purchased. After it has been coated with the proper film, the negative is placed on it and the plate is exposed, developed, and etched. The etching removes the copper in the unexposed areas and the light-hardened coating is then removed with an abrasive

462

cleaner and a bristle brush. In printing, the ink adheres to the copper and is repelled by the aluminum.

THE TRIMETAL PROCESS

Trimetal plates, the most expensive of those used in lithography, are used by printers for very long printing runs; their cost is warranted by the service they give. Printers must coat their own plates with a photosensitive material. Several types of these plates are on the market; one, for example, has an aluminum base which is plated first with copper and then with chrome. In using it, a positive is placed upon the sensitized plate, the plate is developed, and the image is removed. The unexposed metal is then etched with chrome-etch. The hardened gelatin coating is then scrubbed off with an abrasive cleaner. In printing, the ink adheres to the copper and is repelled by the chrome.

THE SELENIUM PROCESS—XEROGRAPHY

This process is known both as the electric-image reproduction process and as xerography. A photoconductive plate is coated with selenium, in place of the customary photographic film (127). Selenium is a nonmetallic element resembling sulfur in chemical properties; it has an electrical resistance which varies under the influence of light. The design on the plate is developed with a special carbon electromagnetic powder.

The process is as follows: The selenium on the plate is given a positive electrical charge. A positive photograph or an opaque design on acetate film is placed on the plate. The plate is then exposed, the light nullifying the charge in the exposed areas. The film is removed and the plate treated with a negative-charged carbon powder, which adheres by electrical attraction to the unexposed or positive design. The ink is attracted to and held' by the carbon-treated areas. The plate is now ready for the press. It is also possible to use the selenium process on specially prepared metal rollers; a very expensive rotary press equipped with such a roller is now on the market.

The selenium plate described above can be used as the master for the preparation of other master plates employed in other methods of printing. The image on the selenium plate can be transferred to a special paper and fixed or fused to it with heat; this paper master is in turn used as a plate for printing. This transfer of image is possible only because the paper has a different magnetic field from the powder on the selenium plate. The image on the selenium plate can also be transferred to a lithograph master and copies of the design can be run off on a lithograph machine. Head-

463

scarfs, large handkerchiefs, and other small pieces of fabric, which have been previously stiffened, can now be printed on a lithograph press by means of the selenium process.

5. Fabric Finishes

One of the most important contributions of the twentieth century to the field of textiles is the development of new coatings for finishing fabrics. A high percentage of fabrics that come from the mills today have been given a series of special treatments or finishes. The majority of these finishes are applied to the fabric by the roller printing process, or at any rate, the roller presses are used at one stage or another during the various steps in finishing. Pressing is considered a finishing process, as are dyeing and printing. Actually, any nonstructural treatment applied to a woven or otherwise constructed fabric is considered a finishing process; the last three chapters have therefore been dealing with finishing processes.

Finishing processes are generally classed as either physical or chemical. Most physical processes are applied by roller presses; some chemical processes can be applied with rollers—discharge printing, for example—but usually the rollers are used to give a final pressing to the fabric after it has had a chemical treatment. (Dyeing of textile fibers is also dependent upon either a physical or a chemical reaction, as mentioned earlier.) Other finishes given to textile fabrics include the following:

PHYSICAL FINISHING TREATMENTS

Singeing and shearing.
Stretching or tentering.
Shrinking or thickening.
Pressing or calendering.
Napping or teaseling.
Beetling or pounding.

Frictioning: Fast-moving rollers give a polish.
Swissing: Special rollers give a nonporous finish.
Chasing: Special rollers give a dull finish.
Schreinering: Engraved rollers give high luster.
Moiré: Engraved rollers give a water-wave finish.
Embossed: Patterned rollers emboss a fabric.

CHEMICAL FINISHING TREATMENTS

Bleaching: Removes color or applies whitening processes.
Caustic soda treatments: Mercerizes cotton, gives a luster to wool.
Crêping: Treats silk with sulphuric acid, etc.

Fulling: Cleans, shrinks, and thickens wool with soap, etc.
Lustering: Treats wool with chlorine.
Parchmentizing and animalizing: Treats cotton with sulfuric or nitric acid.

Various substances are used to give special surfaces to fabrics; some enhance the beauty of the fabric, others add to its serviceability. Some give beauty at the expense of serviceability; for example, cotton fabrics which have been given a synthetic polished surface are weaker than unpolished cottons of the same weight and weave. Most of the substances used for coating textiles are new synthetic compounds, but many have ancient antecedents. For example, fabrics have been treated for centuries with starch of various types and with glue sizing. The important coatings used on fabrics are glues, gelatins, starches, vegetable and mineral oils, rubber, synthetic rubber, resins, and plasticizers.

Some of the latest and most revolutionary developments in the textile industry have been in the field of fabric finishes. A great deal of research has been undertaken in recent years utilizing existing information on resins and plasticizers for developing new fabric finishes. The impetus for much of this research activity was the direct result of wartime—and later peacetime—demands for fabrics which could give specific performances. The list below, in which related finish-treatments are grouped according to function, demonstrates the successful outcome of the research undertaken:

Mildew, mold, moth, bacteria, and rot-proof treatments.
Perspiration, moisture, and water-repellent treatments.
Fire, flame, corrosion, and abrasion-proof treatments.
Shrink, stretch, wrinkle, and crease-resistant treatments.
Permanent weighting, crisping, pleating, stiffening, and softening treatments.
Permanent polishing and glazing treatments.
Embossing, texturizing, and crêping treatments.

These finishes are now produced by a number of commercial establishments and are generally known by a host of particular trade names. No attempt is made to present such a list here; the reader interested in such information should consult any of a number of textile trade journals. Many pages in these publications are devoted to advertising new fabric-finish products.

New discoveries in the field of textile finishes are being made daily. Indeed, a veritable new textile world is being opened up by the use of two closely related products: new synthetic fabric finishes and new synthetic textile fibers. Most textiles produced today are influenced by these synthetic products. What progress the future holds in textile production is un-

465

certain, but the direction in textile trends is definitely noticeable. Textile fibers, dyes, printing inks, and finishes are all being made synthetically. The hand and appearance of synthetic fibers is being made to simulate that of natural fibers, and at the same time the functioning of natural fibers, by means of special synthetic finishes, is being made to match the performance of the synthetic fibers.

GLOSSARY

Weaving Equipment and Woven Fabrics

ABACA. A hemplike fiber used for cordage. Chiefly grown in the Philippine Islands.

ABASSI. A fine, Egyptian, silklike cotton cloth.

ABBOT'S CLOTH. See *Monk's cloth.*

ABBOTSFORD. A light twilled woolen cloth with a subdued check pattern.

ABROME. A fine silklike fiber from the East Indian abrome plant. Used to be a substitute for jute, and sometimes for silk.

ABUTILON. A Chinese jutelike fiber.

ACCIDENTS. A weave made differently than the planned pattern draft.

ACETATE. A synthetic fiber made from cotton or cellulose and the products of acetic acid; commonly known as cellulose acetate.

ACRILON. An acrylic fiber used for clothing manufacture. Dries rapidly and is crease-resistant.

ACTIVE WARP. The warp yarns interlaced in braiding. See also *Passive warp.*

ADA or AIDA CANVAS. A stiff, basket-weave fabric used in art needlework.

ADMIRALTY CLOTH. Melton cloth used for uniforms.

ADRIANOPLE TWILL. A right-hand 2-up, 1-down twill.

AFGHAN STITCH. A crochet stitch used in making Afghans.

AGARIE. A fine terry-toweling used as a dress fabric.

AGAVE. A bast fiber used for cordage.

AGRA GAUZE. A pure silk stiffened gauze.

AIGUILLETTE. Cord, usually gold braid, used for trimming.

AIRPLANE CLOTH. Plain-weave cloth, usually cotton, formerly used on airplane wings, now used for shirts.

ALASKA YARN. A cotton-and-wool mixed fiber yarn used in knitting.

ALBATROSS. A lightweight plain-weave crepy surface wool fabric.

ALOE. A fiber from the leaf of the aloe plant which is related to the century and yucca plants.

ALPACA. A fabric of any weave made from the wool of the Alpaca, an animal related to the South American Llama.

ANDALUSIAN YARN or ANGLED DRAFT. A four-ply worsted knitting yarn used in Great Britain.

ANGORA. A mixed fabric of rabbit hair and wool.

ANGORA GOAT. A goat with long silky hair from a city and province of that name in Asia Minor. Now raised in Southwest United States. Fiber is known as mohair.

APOU. A ramie fabric of high luster made in China.

APPENZELL. An openwork Swiss embroidery, usually made in pale blue thread.

APPLIQUÉ. Pieces of fabric sewed above and onto another piece of fabric. See page 357.

469

GLOSSARY

APRON. Canvas sheet attached to cloth and warp beams; used instead of a fly rod.

APRON LOOM. See *Bow loom.*

ARGENTINE CLOTH. A vat-dyed cotton suiting; also a glazed tarlatan.

ARGYLE BOBBIN. Bobbin used in knitting; a small opening for the thread prevents the bobbin from unwinding.

ARMURE. A warp satin pattern on a rep background. Used for drapery and upholstery.

ARTIFICIAL LEATHER. A plastic fabric made by coating cotton with a plastic solution.

ART LINEN OR EMBROIDERY CRASH. A plain-weave fabric of coarse "round" linen.

ASBESTOS. Cloth woven of asbestos mineral fibers. Usually woven with cotton, which is then burned out.

ASTRAKHAN. Heavy coating material, usually cotton-backed, with a curled pile surface resembling Astrakhan or Karakul fur.

AUBUSSON. See *Tapestry.*

AUSTRIAN SHADE CLOTH. A cloth of any fiber made with a wide crêpe or crinkled stripe.

AWNING. A heavy cotton canvas, usually painted in stripes.

AXMINSTER. A type of carpet weave. See page 188.

AXMINSTER LOOMS. Looms for weaving Axminster carpets.

BACK BEAM. Beam or bar above warp beam. Also called slab stick and whiproll.

BACK STRAP. Strap attached to cloth beam which runs around hips of weaver.

BACK-STRAP LOOM. A two-stick body loom, attached to the weaver by a back strap. See *Girdle-Back Loom,* and page 88.

BAGHEERA. Uncut fine velvet.

BAIZE. A plain-weave wool fabric made to imitate felt.

BALBRIGGAN. A jersey knit cotton fabric usually used for men's underwear.

BASKET CLOTH. A cloth made usually of paired warps and paired wefts.

BATHROBE CLOTH. A thick, soft, double-woven, napped cotton that feels like outing flannel.

BATIK. Printed cloth made by the wax-resist dyeing process, especially in India and Java.

BATISTE. Very fine thin cotton cloth in plain weave. (A very fine wool cloth is also sometimes called batiste.)

BATTEN. The frame of the reed.

(To) BATTEN. To beat and firm the fabric with a reed, comb, spathe, stick, or sword.

BAYADERE. Bright horizontal striped material from India.

BEAM. End bars of loom, which hold the warp in the back of the loom and the cloth in front.

BEAM CRANK. Crank used to roll warp onto the warp beam.

BEAMING THE LOOM. Winding the warp onto the warp beam.

BEAT. To use the reed.

BEATER. A reed or batten.

BEATER-IN. A reed.

BEAVER. A silky napped woolen fabric made on a felt or a twill base, the former used for hats, the latter for coating.

BEDFORDCORD. A warpwise rep fabric.

BEMBERG. Manufacturer's name for a cuprammonium fabric.

BENGALINE. A plain-weave warp ribbed fabric.

BINDER. Tabby thread holding down loose floating wefts.

BIRD'S EYE. A small allover pattern weave, usually a geometric diamond-shaped twill.

BLOCK PRINTS. A fabric printed with carved wood or linoleum blocks.

BOAT SHUTTLE. A boat-shaped shuttle with flat bottom and sides. Holds a bobbin on an inside fine rod.

BOBBIN. A small stick, card, special quill, or tube on which thread is wound. There are various kinds of bobbins: stick, tube, argyle, lace, match case, etc.

BOBBIN BOARD. See *Spool board*.

BOBBIN CARRIER. A bobbin holder held in the hand and used in warping. See *Spool frame*.

BOBBIN WINDER. A hand- or machine-turned spindle which when turned facilitates the winding of the bobbin which it holds.

BODKIN. A shuttle.

BODY LOOM. See *Girdle-back loom* and *Back-strap loom*.

BOLTING CLOTH. A leno-weave silk (not degummed) made in Europe.

BOOKBINDING CLOTH. A plain-weave heavy-coated cloth for book binding.

BOTANY WOOL. Extra fine wool. Formerly wool from the merino sheep, Botany Bay, Australia.

BOUCLÉ. Fabric made of bouclé yarns. These are uneven, looped, wide and narrow yarns, sometimes made on a cotton core. Also fabrics made of these yarns.

BOW LOOM. Sometimes called an apron loom. Warp yarns are strung crosswise of a willow branch bent into a horseshoe-shaped arch. See page 80.

BRAID. A narrow strip of fabric used for trimming, made in any weave. Also a fabric construction known as braiding.

BREAST BEAM. Front beam on loom, level with waist of weaver, over which woven fabric passes before being rolled onto cloth beam.

BRILLIANTINE. Plain- or twill-weave wiry material similar to alpaca or mohair.

BROADCLOTH. Twill-weave woolen fabric resembling, but much finer than, sateen. Used for shirts, coats, and suits. Also a plain ribbed weave for cotton shirts.

BROCADE. A weave and also a type of fabric. The weave is an inlaid weave; the yarns not on the surface float on the back of or are concealed in the fabric; made by hand in Guatemala and other places. Made on the Jacquard loom for commercial distribution. The fabric is beautiful, especially when made in silk. Sometimes used for upholstery material. The ground weave may be damask, twill, satin, or plain.

BROCADE STICKS. Also called pick-up sticks and warp lifters.

BROCATELLE. A lustrous repoussé fabric made with two sets of warps and two sets of wefts. The pattern is bold and raised and in the satin weave against a contrasting weave ground (usually twill). Used for upholstery material. The surface may be of rayon, cotton, or silk with a cotton or linen backing. Woven on the Jacquard loom.

BROCHÉ. A silk fabric with small floral designs which resembles embroidery.

Made similar to brocade, but the filler threads do not float across the back; each little pattern is complete. A swivel weave.

BUCKRAM. A plain-weave jute cloth very openly woven. Used for stiffening.

BUNTING. Plain-weave cotton or wool very open fabric used for flags and for decorating. Bright, gay colors.

BURLAP. Plain-weave coarse cotton, jute, or hemp fabric used for sacks and backing.

BUTCHER'S LINEN. A cotton material finished with a resin to resemble linen.

CALICO. A plain-weave cotton print material named after Calicut, India. Formerly a fine print from India; now a cheap, narrow, printed cotton.

CAM. An irregular revolving disc, usually heart-shaped, attached to a shaft, used to control the raising of harnesses on a mechanical loom.

CAMBRIC. A plain-weave cotton or linen, named after Cambrai, France. Fine cambric is used for underwear, etc.; very fine is used for handkerchiefs, collars, etc.; inferior qualities (heavily starched and usually dyed in bright colors) for linings, costumes, etc.

CAMEL'S HAIR. A twill-weave fabric with a napped surface of fine underhair of camels. Sometimes mixed with wool.

CANDLEWICK. A cotton fabric in which tufts are added to a ground fabric.

CANE STICKS. Same as fly rod.

CANTON CRÊPE. A silk fabric, heavier than crêpe de Chine; also a lightweight wool crêpe.

CANTON FLANNEL. A twill-weave heavy flannel, first made in Canton, China.

CANVAS. There are two types of canvas, regular plain-weave heavy cotton or jute, used for awnings, tents, etc., and art canvas made in special basketlike weave and used for rug backings, bags, etc.

CAPES. Vertical members at center of loom; holds heddle harnesses, etc.

CARDING. Combing fibers on cards.

CARDS. Brushes, usually with metal bristles, used to straighten fibers before spinning.

CARD WEAVING. Weaving on cardboard base or with cardboard heddles.

CAROSEL. Dish-toweling made of 80 percent cotton and 20 percent asbestos. Manufacturer's name.

CASEMENT CLOTH. A translucent cloth of any weave and any fiber used for window coverings.

CASHMERE. The soft wool of goats of Kashmir, India. A beautiful wool used in shawls, fine woolen fabrics, and knitted fabrics.

CASSIMERE. A thin cloth of wool or other fibers in plain or twill weave with a soft finish.

CASTLE. Top beam of the loom, which holds up jacks and harnesses.

CELANESE. See *Acetate*. Manufacturer's trade name.

CELLOPHANE. A plastic made like rayon. Sold in sheets, ribbons, etc.

CHADDER or KADDER CLOTH. Homespun cotton cloth made in India.

CHAIN. Another name for warp. A warp chain is a column of warp crocheted ready for beaming.

CHALLIE or CHALLIS. Plain-weave lightweight wool, sometimes printed. Formerly a silk and wool mix made in Norwich, England.

CHAMBRAY. A plain-weave fine gingham, usually in plain colors.

CHARMEUSE. A satin weave with a cotton back. Also a mercerized cotton twill weave used for linings.

CHEESECLOTH. A plain-weave, open-mesh, loosely woven, thin cotton, used for dust cloths, bandages, etc.

CHENILLE. A type of pile formed by using prewoven "fur" strips as weft and weaving them into the warp. Used for carpeting, fringes, and upholstery.

CHEVIOT. A twill-weave, rough-surfaced fabric, usually of worsted and heavy wool. Similar to serge, but heavier and with a slight nap. Also a strong cotton shirting, plain weave in stripes or checks.

CHIFFON. Thin, plain-weave, gauzelike silk fabric; may also be of cotton, like fine voile.

CHINA SILK. A plain-weave thin silk. Used for underwear, lampshades, etc.

CHINCHILLA CLOTH. A twill-weave wool coating material with a napped surface; the napping is in little tufts.

CHINTZ. A plain-weave cotton fabric with a glossy surface and a printed design. Originated in India, it was one of the India prints imported into Europe in the seventeenth century. Chintz means "spotted," indicating the pattern. Now may have a permanent resin finish.

CIRE. Brilliant surface treatment of satin by heat, wax, and pressure.

CLOTH BEAM. Front beam on a loom on which woven fabric is rolled.

COMB. Wooden comb with fairly coarse teeth and often with a handle at the back, used instead of a reed to batten weft down.

COMBING. Cotton fibers are combed to separate better quality fibers.

COMBER BOARD. Heddle control for draw looms.

CONTINUOUS WARP. Warp not attached to cloth and warp beams, but passing around the outside of the lengths of each.

COP. A paper tube bobbin on which thread is wound.

CORDUROY. An extra weft-cut pile fabric, usually of cotton, having a velvet appearance. The pile is in rows or ridges. Named in France from "corde du Roi" (cord of the king).

COUCH. To hold a yarn or cord to a fabric by means of stitching.

COUNT. Threads per inch: warp count and weft count per square inch.

COUNTERBALANCED LOOM. A loom on which the heddles operate with cords revolving over rods, or pulleys, with or without heddle-horses for support.

COUTIL. A stout cotton fabric used in foundation garments. May be a plain and twill combination weave or other weaves.

COVERT. Twill- or satin-weave woolen or worsted fabric. White twisted into the yarn gives a pebbled appearance. Used for overcoats, raincoats, etc.

CRASH. Usually a plain-weave fabric made of uneven yarns. May be of linen, cotton, or combined yarns. Used for toweling, drapery, art linen, or dresses.

CREEL. A framework for holding bobbins in a spinning machine.

CRÊPE. A plain-woven crinkly fabric. A balanced crêpe is formed by alternating two rows of hard S-twisted yarns with two rows of hard Z-twisted yarns in both the warp and weft.

CRÊPE DE CHINE. A silky, usually shiny, fabric made up of tightly twisted S- and Z-twist yarns. Gum is removed from silk after weaving.

473

CRÊPE-BACK SATIN. Satin-weave fabric with a dull crêpe back.

CRETONNE. Plain, twill, or fancy weave in cotton or linen, printed with a rather bold pattern. First produced in Creton, a village in Normandy.

CREWEL. A form of embroidery, done in wool, usually accenting the chain stitch.

CRINKLE CRÊPE or JAPANESE CRÊPE. A heavy cotton crêpe. See *Crêpe*.

CRINOLINE. A plain-weave, stiff, coarse cotton used for stiffening hats, under-skirts, etc.

CROCHET. A chain of one thread or a group of threads, made by continuously looping it upon itself.

CROSS. A crossing of the warp made on the warping board to keep the threads in proper order. The cross is usually preserved at the back of the warp of primitive looms. Also called a lease.

CROSS STICKS. Sticks placed on either side of cross and tied together to secure cross. See *Lease rods*.

CUT VELVET. A Jacquard weave, brocaded velvet on georgette. Used for dresses.

DAISY-BELLE. A plain-weave solid-color fine fabric.

DAMASK. A Jacquard weave; a reversible warp-faced satin pattern with weft-faced sateen background. Named after Damascus, an ancient city in the Near East, where patterns were once woven in silk. Depending on weight and type of fiber, damask is used for table linen, drapery material, and upholstery.

DENIM. A twill weave of heavy tightly twisted cotton yarns. Named from the French town of Nîmes, "de Nîmes."

DENT. The space between the teeth of the reed.

DIAPER CLOTH. Plain or bird's-eye weave; close-weave soft cotton cloth, napped on one side.

DIMITY. Plain-weave fine cotton cloth containing cords, crossbars, stripes, or checks.

DISTAFF. A forked stick for holding fiber slivers.

DOBBY. Mechanical wooden (chain) heddle-harness hoist. Many harnesses possible on this loom.

DOBBY ATTACHMENT. A mechanism for dobby weaving.

DOESKIN. A twill-weave heavy cotton or woolen fabric, napped on one side.

DOG. Catch which holds rachet wheel.

DOTTED SWISS. See *Swiss*.

DOUBLE-BOBBIN SHUTTLE. A shuttle which holds two bobbins for basket weaving, etc.

DOUBLE CLOTH. May be almost any weave, but contains at least two sets of warp and at least two sets of weft.

DOUP. A half-handle for gauze weaving. See page 258.

DRAFT. There are several types of drafts: pattern draft—the design; chain draft—the threading plan for heddles; lifting draft, peg draft, and tying-up draft—terms for tying harnesses to treadles; weaving draft—order of manipulation of levers or treadles to make pattern.

DRAW BOY. A boy who stands at the side of draw looms and lifts the pattern sheds by manipulating draw cords.

DRAWING IN. Entering warp into heddle eyes.

DRAW LOOM. Loom with multiple heddles for ornate pattern weaving. The heddles are drawn up by hand by a draw boy who stands beside or behind loom.

DRESS OR DRESSING. A starch made of boiled strained flax seed, put on most woolen and linen yarns to make weaving easier.

DRILL. A twill cotton in a stout weave. Used for uniforms, heavy shirts, suits, etc.

DRUGGET. A thick felted or woven rug from India, suitable for interiors of rustic quality. Cotton warp with weft of jute or camel's hair. A coarse cloth of part wool.

DRUID'S CLOTH. Similar to monk's cloth, but coarser.

DRUM. A large warp beam. Also a revolving disc, part of the spinning wheel of Africa.

DRUM DYED. Warp yarns wound on a drum and dyed with a pattern before weaving.

DUCK. A plain close-weave heavy cotton, similar to canvas, but not as coarse. Used for trousers, pressing cloths, butcher's aprons, etc.

DUNGAREE. Blue denim.

DURETTA. See *Drill.*

DUVETYN. A twill-weave soft napped wool fabric with a cotton back.

DYES. See page 379.

EIDERDOWN. A knitted cotton fabric with a nap on one or both sides. Used for infants' wear and bathrobes.

EMBROIDERED WARP. The pattern yarns are put in the warp during weaving with a needle.

EMBROIDERY. See page 344.

END. Synonymous with warp.

END-TO-END CLOTH. A plain-weave quality cotton cloth used for men's shirts. A plain-weave broadcloth.

ENTERING. Threading in the heddles and the reed.

ENTERING HOOK. See *Heddle hook.*

EPONGE. A plain-weave soft loose cloth similar to ratiné.

EYE OR EYELET. Center hole of heddle.

FACONNÉ. A small allover pattern in same color as background.

FEATHER CLOTH. Little feathers woven or knitted in fabric.

FEELER. Trial woven pattern.

FELT. A fabric formed by suspending fibers in water, allowing them to settle then draining and pressing (matting) the fibers. Usually of wool, but now also of synthetic fibers.

FIBERGLAS. A fabric made of fine filaments of spun glass. Must not be worn as clothing.

FILET. A filled or embroidered square net.

FILLER. Weft yarns.

FILLING. Weft yarns.

FIXED-HEDDLE LOOM. A fixed hole-and-slot heddle, a fixed string heddle, or a fixed half-heddle (inkle loom). One set of heddles remains stationary.

FIXED WARP. A warp which is stabilized in one position. The alternate warp is moved above and below this warp to form sheds.

FLAG. Trial woven pattern.

FLANNEL. A twill or plain soft loose weave of cotton or wool, napped on one side.

FLANNELETTE. A striped or printed flannel.

FLAT CRÊPE. A crêpe fabric smoother and duller than crêpe de Chine.

FLEECE. A skin from an animal or a furlike cloth, napped on one side.

FLEXIBLE NET. A leno-weave, soft yet wiry, net used in hat making for rolled brims, etc.

FLOAT. Warp or weft may float (or skip) across the top of the weft or warp respectively.

FLOUR SACK. A plain-weave rough cotton of medium weight.

FLOWER. The pattern of lace.

FLYING SHUTTLE. A shuttle propelled from boxes on either side of shed by a lever pull. Has pointed metal tips.

FLY ROD. Two rods, one attached to the cloth beam and one to the warp beam to which, respectively, the cloth and warp are fastened to prevent slipping on the beam.

FOOT PEDDLES. Treadles tied to heddle harnesses to control their operation.

FOOT POWER. Treadles or levers which control heddle harnesses, operated by foot pressure.

FORTUNY PRINT. A secret process of printing cotton to resemble brocade. Made in Venice. Printed on plain or twill weave.

FOULARD. A twill-weave soft printed silk fabric. A mercerized cotton foulard is made in the satin weave.

FREE-RIGID HEDDLE. See *Single-heedle harness.*

FREE WARP. Warp not attached to cloth beam or to weights.

FRENCH CRÊPE. A lightweight crêpe used for lingerie.

FRIAR'S CLOTH. A basket-weave coarse fabric of cotton with hemp or jute mixture, similar to monk's cloth.

FRINGE. Trimming for draperies, upholstery, rugs, table runners, etc.

FRINGING FORK. See *Hairpin frame.*

FRISÉ OR FRIEZÉ. An uncut pile fabric. The best grade is finely woven mohair, but it may be woven of cotton, rayon, etc.

GABARDINE. A twill-weave hard-finished fabric. The name of a Jewish cloak of the Middle Ages.

GALATEA. A warp-faced 5-shaft twill, stout, heavy fabric used for children's play clothes.

GATING OR GAITING. The act of adjusting the harnesses.

GAUZE. A leno-weave loose open fabric used for curtain material. See *Cheesecloth.*

GEORGETTE. A plain-weave thin crepy dull silk fabric in which S- and Z-twisted yarns alternate.

GIMP. A narrow edging with heavy cord running through it, used for trimming.

GINGHAM. A plain- or fancy-weave yarn-dyed medium fine cotton fabric, usually woven in plaids or checks.

GIRDLE-BACK LOOM. A primitive loom sometimes called body loom, stick loom, back-strap, and strap loom. The front bar is fastened to a belt which goes around the waist or the thighs. The other end of the warp is fastened to another bar, which in turn is fastened to a tree or support.

GLEN PLAID.   A 4, 4 or 2, 2 (warp and weft) plaid.

GLORIA.   A fine twill umbrella fabric, usually of silk warp and cotton weft.

GLOVE SILK.   A warp-knit fabric of silk, acetate, or rayon.

GOLF CLOTH.   Fine woolen fabric used for sportswear.

GRANITE CLOTH.   A fancy irregular weave with pebbly hard-finished surface: usually a wool worsted cloth used for dresses.

GRAPH PAPER.   Squared paper used for making drafts. See *Draft*.

GRASS CLOTH.   A fine linenlike plain-weave cloth woven from ramie fiber.

GRAY GOODS.   Goods as it comes from the loom, before being given any finishing processes.

GREIGE-GRAY GOODS.   Rayon and silk before dyeing and finishing.

GRENADINE.   A leno weave similar to marquisette, only finer. Used as curtain and dress material.

GRIST.   Circumference of a yarn.

GROSGRAIN.   A plain-weave ribbed or rep fabric, heavier than poplin, usually made with silk or rayon warp and cotton weft. Used for ribbons, etc.

GROUND.   The background; usually a plain weave which fills in between design units. Also the net background of lace.

GUIMPE.   Narrow edging, with heavy cord running through it, used for trimming.

GUIPURE.   See *Lace*.

GULF COTTON.   Cotton raised along the Gulf of Mexico.

GUM.   Natural gum from tropical trees, as tragacanth, used to thicken dyes.

GUN CLUB CHECK.   A large check over a smaller one; used in tweeds.

GUNNY SACK.   A heavy, open, plain-weave fabric made of hemp or jute.

GYPSY CLOTH.   A plain-weave flannelette cloth, used for sportswear.

HAIR CLOTH.   A plain- or twill-weave cloth made of cotton, woolen, worsted, or linen warp and horsehair weft. Used for stiffening.

HAIRPIN FRAME.   A U-loop metal wire used for making hairpin lace.

HAIRLINE STRIPE.   A stripe in a fabric only about one yarn wide.

HAMMOCK FRAME.   A supported rectangular frame in which knotless-net hammocks are made.

HAMMOCK STITCH.   A 1–1 mesh—single-element process.

HAND or HANDLE.   The feel or drape of cloth.

HAND LOOM.   Any loom operated by man power.

HANDKERCHIEF LINEN.   Fine plain-weave cambric or linen.

HARD-TWIST.   A close tight twist given to some yarns.

HANK.   A skein or parcel of yarn. Hanks contain a standard number of yards, usually 840 yards for cotton and 560 yards for wool.

HARDANGER CLOTH.   A basket-weave soft mercerized cotton fabric used for Norwegian embroidery.

HARLEQUIN CHECK.   A plaid of three colors.

HARNESS.   The frame which holds the heddles.

HARVARD CLOTH.   A twill shirting.

HEADING CANES. These hold the cross at the back of primitive looms. Also called lease rods and laze rods.

HEADING CORDS. Cords which run through, or are entwined into, the warp and fasten it to the end beams of primitive looms. Also called loom strings.

HEADING RODS. May be used in place of heading cords.

HEADLE. See *Heddle*.

HEALD. See *Heddle*.

HEALD ROD. See *Heddle rod*.

HEATHER YARN. A multicolored fiber yarn.

HECK. A small heddle frame, specially threaded to spread the warp and to form a cross for the warping mill. Also a spinning attachment that guides the yarn on the bobbin.

HEDDLE. String loops or strips of metal, bone, or wood containing an eyelet through which the warp threads are strung. The threading of the heddles controls the pattern of the fabric; also called heald, headle, leash, and lease. String heddles are made over a special peg frame, the heddle board.

HEDDLE BOARD. A bar with pegs projecting upward on which string heddles are made.

HEDDLE EYES. Holes or eyelets in heddles through which warp is threaded.

HEDDLE FRAME. Heddle harness.

HEDDLE HARNESS. A harness which holds the heddles; sometimes called a frame, a stave, or a shaft. Sheds are formed when the harnesses are raised or lowered.

HEDDLE HOOK. A small flat hook used to assist in pulling the warp through the heddle eyes.

HEDDLE HORSES. Supports placed above the heddle harness which attach it to the pulley on counterbalanced looms.

HEDDLE REED. A fine metal single-heddle harness which is a reed and heddle frame.

HEDDLE ROD. A rod hung with looped heddle strings; used on primitive looms.

HEDDLE STANDARD. Doups for leno and gauze weaving.

HEDDLE STICKS. The two bars that hold the heddles in the harness of a foot power loom. Also the sticks which hold the string heddles on back-strap looms.

HEDDLE SWORD. See *Sword*.

HENEQUEN. A sisal fiber related to maguey, chiefly from Yucatan.

HERRINGBONE. A broken-twill wavelike pattern in continuous chevron zigzags.

HICKORY SHIRTING. A twill-weave heavy striped cotton fabric resembling ticking. Used for play clothes and shirting.

HIGH TENACITY. Reinforced, strong yarns.

HILDA. A twill-weave cotton warp and alpaca weft lining fabric.

HOLE BOARD. See *Single-heddle harness*.

HOLE AND SLAT BOARD. See Single-heddle harness.

HOLLAND SHADE CLOTH. A plain-weave linen with a sizing of oil and starch which makes cloth opaque.

HOLLOW-CUT VELVETEEN. A velveteen very similar to corduroy.

HOLLYWOOD CLOTH. A leno-weave cloth used for preliminary draping.

HOMESPUN. A rather coarse uneven spun yarn, which makes a slight uneven weave when woven. Used for early American furnishings.

HONAN. A wild silk from Honan, China, that takes dye evenly. Woven into pongee.

HONEYCOMB. A waffle cloth; a pattern weave which alternates warp and weft floats to form small squared honeycomb patterns. Used for toweling, baby blankets, etc.

HOPSACKING. A fine grade of burlap used in dresses, drapery, etc.

HOSPITAL GAUZE. Sterilized cheesecloth.

HUCK or HUCKABACK. A pattern weave in small patterns made up of warp floats at even intervals. Used principally for toweling.

IMPERIAL BROCADE. An Italian brocade in which gold and silver yarns are used.

IMPERIAL COATING. A 2-up, 2-down twill worsted of fine Botany yarns.

INDIA MUSLIN. A high-quality muslin.

INDIA PRINT. Usually a plain-weave printed fabric from India. May be a chintz, a block print, or a batik. Used for clothing and home furnishings.

INDIAN HEAD. A plain-weave moderately heavy cotton, vat-dyed, with a permanent finish. Used for clothing, towels, table cloths, etc.

INDIENNE. French interpretation of India prints made in the seventeenth and eighteenth centuries.

INKLE LOOM. A loom for belt weaving. See page 101.

INLAY WEAVES. See *Brocade* and *Swivel*.

ITALIAN CLOTH. A cotton-back satin.

JACK LOOM. A loom operated by a lever system; when the lever is pushed down, the harness is raised.

JACQUARD. Type of loom for intricate weaving; each warp is controlled by a needle which in turn is controlled by holes in the punched pattern cards.

JANUS CLOTH. A double-faced worsted fabric; each side is a different color.

JAPANESE CRÊPE. A cotton crêpe.

JARDINIERE VELVET. A Jacquard intricate-weave varied-height cut-silk velvet. The pile (cut and uncut) is set against a plain twill or satin weave in a flowerlike pattern grouping.

JASPÉ. Uneven dyed warp or weft threads; a form of tie and dye work.

JEAN. A twill-weave heavy cotton fabric similar to drill, but finer. Used for suiting, children's clothes, underwear, etc.

JERSEY. A plain knit fabric, not ribbed.

JERSEY TWEED. A soft woolen tweed in plain colors.

JESUIT CLOTH. Black thin hard-twist worsted fabric used by Catholic orders.

JUNGLE CLOTH. Heavy white cloth used for naval uniforms.

KARAKUL FABRIC. A wool pile fabric made to imitate Persian lamb fur.

KASHA CLOTH. A soft napped fabric of Tibet goat hair.

KHAKI. A twill weave in tawny khaki color.

KERSEY. A twill-weave heavy napped woolen cloth, similar to broadcloth but with shorter nap. Used for overcoats.

KEY LEVERS. Small lever knobs on the top of the frame of table looms which, when lowered, hoist the heddle harnesses. A loom equipped with key levers is also classified as a jack-type loom.

KNIFE SHUTTLE. A small hand shuttle for belt looms, similar to a stick shuttle except that one edge is sharp to assist in beating.

KNITTED FABRIC. A fabric made by interlooping yarns.

KNOT. Weaver's knot, slip knot, reef knot, etc. See description, page 52.

KNOTTED PILE. An oriental technique used in rug making.

LACE. An openwork fabric containing a ground and a flower (pattern); made with bobbins or needles, or by machinery.

LAID-IN WEAVE. See *Brocade* and *Swivel*.

LAMÉ. A silk fabric ornamented with metal threads.

LAMPAS. A fabric with a compound weave, having two warps and two or more wefts. It is similar to damask, in that pattern and background are in different weaves.

LAMS. Intermediate bars placed between and connecting harnesses and foot treadles on a foot-power loom. Sometimes spelled lamms. Two or more harnesses may be attached to one lam.

LAPPET. A weave with a floating-warp swivel pattern.

LAPPET ATTACHMENT. Attachment for loom for lappet insets.

LASH. Throw of weft.

LASTEX. A cloth woven of rubber filaments covered with silk, cotton, or rayon.

LATEX. Rubber filaments.

LAWN. A plain-weave soft fine polished cotton fabric.

LAY. The frame which holds the reed. It is located between the harnesses and the breast beam and usually pivots from the base of the loom.

LAZE RODS. See *Heading canes*.

LEASE. The cross made in the warp when warping on a warping board to keep the warp in order.

LEASE PEGS. Pegs in a warping board over which a lease is formed.

LEASE RODS. Rods slipped into the lease and tied together at the ends to prevent the cross or lease from getting lost.

LENO. Warp threads twisted in half-twists around each other between the weft threads.

LENO DOUPS. The leno heddles on skeleton harnesses for leno weaving.

LENO LOOMS. Looms on which the heddles are arranged for leno weaving.

LENO HEDDLES. Special slit heddles for leno weaving. The regular heddles can operate through the leno heddles.

LINEN MESH. A knit fabric of linen and cotton used for infants shirts.

LINGETTE. A satin weave in soft mercerized cotton, with self-colored stripes containing right- and left-hand twist warp.

LINGO. Long thin weights on warp ends on some looms (Draw and Warp-weighted).

LINSEY WOOLSEY. A colonial and Civil War fabric of handwoven material containing a linen warp and wool weft. Originated in England.

LINTON TWEED. Summer tweeds.

LISLE. A knitted fabric of smooth fine linen or cotton yarns, for underwear.

LONGCLOTH. A plain-weave unfinished bleach muslin.

LOOM STRING. See *Heading cords*.

LOOM. A frame for weaving which is equipped with devices for forming sheds.

LORETTE. A fabric which is 55 percent orlon and 45 percent wool; used for sportswear.

480

Lump. 120 yards of woven cloth.

Luster pile. Wool pile specially washed in alkali to give luster.

Lustrine. A satin-weave smooth polished cotton lining fabric.

Machinaw. A twill or double-weave heavy woolen napped fabric, often with two different design faces.

Madras. A plain- or fancy-weave soft cotton fabric, usually with a pattern in the weave. First made in Madras, India. Also a thin drapery fabric of leno and Jacquard weave, with figures on a leno ground and floats between figures cut to leave shaggy appearance.

Mail. Glass or metal eye of a heddle.

Maline. A net similar to bobbin net, but thinner and stiffer, usually made of silk.

Marquisette. A leno-weave open loose fabric of mercerized cotton, rayon, wool, or silk. Used for curtains and for dress material.

Marceline. A thin plain-weave silk.

Matelassé. A Jacquard-weave double cloth having a pattern made of a raised, quilted, or blistered surface.

Melton. A twill-weave heavy smooth woolen fabric resembling felt. Used in overcoats, sports jackets, etc. Named from Melton, England.

Mercerized. Cotton thread treated with alkali under pressure to give a silky finish.

Merveilleux. A twill-weave silk (or silk and cotton) used in lining men's coats.

Metal cloth. A plain- or satin-weave fabric of cotton warp with metal weft yarns; the metal yarns are formed by winding metal tinsel around cotton yarn.

Middy twill. See *Drill*.

Mignonette. A knitted rayon or silk fabric.

Milanese. A warp-knit fabric of silk or rayon with a crosswise effect. Used in gloves and women's underwear.

Mogador. Heavily ribbed varicolored striped material used in turbans in Mogador, Morocco. Name now given to fine faille tie-silk.

Mohair. Hair of the Angora goat. Cut or uncut pile fabric made with cotton or wool back. Used for upholstery.

Moiré. A water-weave surface finish on silk, rayon, acetate and sometimes cotton, made by engraved rollers pressed on the material under heat and steam. Pattern washes off of all material except acetate.

Moleskin. A twill-weave heavy cotton fabric, napped.

Monk's cloth. A basket-weave heavy cotton and jute fabric used for drapery material; may contain linen tow.

Moquette. A carpet resembling Axminster.

Moscow. Heavy shaggy wool coating.

Mosquito net. Coarse leno-weave starched cotton net.

Mousseline de soie. Silk organdy. A plain-weave silk muslin.

Multifilament yarn. Synthetic yarn with two or more filaments.

Mummy cloth. A fancy-weave irregular pebbly surface in linen or cotton for toweling. In wool the same weave is called granite cloth.

MUSLIN. A stout plain-weave white cotton fabric, stronger and heavier than longcloth. First made in ancient Mosul.

NACRE. Multicolor or irridescent; contrasting colors in warp and weft.

NAINSOOK. A plain-weave fine soft white cotton fabric with a polish on one side. Not so closely woven as cambric, but heavier than batiste.

NECKING CORDS. Cords joining pulley cords and heddle harnesses.

NEEDLE POINT. A cross-stitch design on specially prepared backing cloth. Petit-point has about 20 stitches to the inch, gros-point about 12 to the inch.

NEEDLE-POINT CLOTH. A wool fabric that looks like bouclé.

NET. An open-weave warp-twisted mesh-made fabric. Handmade meshwork nets are warp-structured fabrics. Machine-made nets are usually formed by twisting together both warp and weft yarns. The term *net* is usually loosely used to include knotted nets. The openings in the mesh may be square, hexagonal, or diamond-shaped; there are also many fancy meshes. May have filet or tufted ornamentation.

NETTING NEEDLE. A form of stick shuttle with one pointed end, containing an inner prong, and one indented end.

NIDDY-NODDY. A hard skein-winder frame in the shape of a T with a bottom rod at right angles to the top rod.

NINON. Various weaves of sheer voile, often called triple voile.

NOTTINGHAM. A machine-made lace curtain.

NUMDAH. A type of embroidered rug from India, made on a felted wool base.

NUN'S VEILING. A plain-weave soft lightweight fabric, finer than voile; made of worsted wool, silk, or rayon.

OATMEAL CLOTH. A soft heavy linen with a pebble surface.

OILCLOTH. A plain-weave cotton fabric, coated with linseed oil and filler, printed, and varnished.

OILED SILK. A plain-weave fine silk, boiled in linseed oil and dried. Used for waterproofing.

ONDINE. A bengaline cord; every third weft is crinkled.

OPPOSITES. A weave treadled opposite to the planned pattern threading.

ORGANDY. A plain-weave lightweight crisp fabric made of fine hard-twisted cotton yarns.

ORGANZA. Thin transparent silk.

ORLEANS. Cross-dyed dress goods with cotton warp and wool weft.

OSNABURG. A plain-weave heavy cotton sacking used for cement, coarse clothing, and drapery material.

OTTOMAN. A plain-weave heavy corded fabric (cotton warp, silk weft).

OUTING FLANNEL. See *Flannel.*

OXFORD CLOTH. Cotton cloth with twice as many warps as wefts.

PADDLE. A paddle-shaped hand stick perforated with two rows of holes. Warp yarns passing through these holes can be carried around the warping board in groups of 8, 10, 12, or 16 yarns. This facilitates the warping process.

PAISLEY. Printed or woven shawls imitating the original paisley shawls made in Paisley, Scotland, to imitate shawls from Kashmir, India.

PAJAMA CHECK. Barred dimity or nainsook used in underwear.

PALAMPORE. Hand-printed batik, chintz, or calico made before the invention of hand block printing.

PALM BEACH. A plain-weave cotton-warp fabric with mohair filling. For summer wear clothing.

PAMICO. Colorfast plain-weave cotton fabric.

PANAMA CLOTH. A basket-weave fabric for supporting crowns and brims in millinery work.

PANAMA. A plain-weave cotton warp and wool weft fabric for summer suits.

PANNE. A pile fabric with a shiny surface made by pressing the pile flat.

PARAMATTA. Dress goods with cotton-warp wool-weft, 1-up, 2-down weave.

PARACHUTE CLOTH. Fabric of silk or nylon. Rayon used for cargoes.

PASSEMENTERIA. Heavy edging or trimming.

PASSIVE WARP. Warp yarns which act as wefts in some braids.

PAWL. The catch which holds the racket wheel on a loom. Also called "dog."

PEAU DE SOIE. A twill-weave strong leather-like fabric with a shiny surface. Has a fine grain. Used for dresses, collars, trimmings, etc.

PEDAL. Foot treadle.

PERCALE. A plain-weave closely woven stiff-finish cotton fabric, printed or plain.

PERCALINE. A plain-weave highly sized lining or book-binding material.

PERSANE. Printed cottons of the eighteenth century, which imitated Persian originals.

PERSIAN LAWN. A plain-weave thin sheer white cotton fabric.

PETIT-POINT. See *Needle point*.

PICK. Synonymous with weft.

PICK-UP STICK. A small smooth hardwood stick used for picking up warp threads for certain pattern weaves. Sometimes has a hook at one end. Also called brocade stick and warp lifter.

PICOTE. An allover floral design interspersed with dots.

PIECE. Finished cloth 60 yards long. A half-piece is 30 yards long.

PILE. A raised cut or uncut furlike surface on a fabric.

PILOT CLOTH. A twill-weave heavy woolen coating used by seamen.

PIÑA CLOTH. A plain-weave open fabric made of the pineapple fiber.

PIN STRIPES. Narrow stripes.

PIQUÉ. A fancy-weave, corded or raised-weft fabric with geometric surface designs. Usually in white, but can be colored or printed. A stiff, trim tailored material used for dresses, infants coats, etc.

PLAID. See *Tartan*.

PLAIN WEAVE. Alternate over-and-under weaving of weft.

PLAIT. A braid or mat of vegetable fiber.

PLISSÉ. A plain-weave fabric, printed with a chemical which gives it a puckered or crinkled appearance.

PLUSH. A deep-cut or uncut pile fabric rather openly woven.

PLY. The number of threads or yarns twisted together.

POIRET TWILL. A fine twill, usually of worsted.

POKE SHUTTLE. A stick shuttle.

POMPADOUR. A delicate printed or woven material containing a dainty floral design. Named after Madame de Pompadour.

PONGEE. A silk, rayon, or cotton-and-rayon fabric made to imitate the original wild-silk irregular-spun ecru-colored fabric from Shantung and Honan.

POODLE CLOTH. A pile fabric which resembles the fur of a French poodle.

POPLIN. A fine plain-weave horizontally ribbed cotton. Used for children's suits and dresses. Also made in silk and wool.

PORTEE CROSS. A cross in the warp on the warping board.

PULLEY. The revolving bar or pulley above heddle harnesses on a counterbalanced loom.

PUSSY WILLOW. Silk plain weave with a dull surface.

QUADRIGA CLOTH. A silky finished percale.

QUILL. The tube bobbin on which the weft is wound for a hand shuttle.

RACE. See *Shuttle race*.

RACHET WHEEL. A cogged wheel with a rachet bar, which is placed on one end of the cloth and warp beams to prevent unrolling of beam except as wanted. Also called pawl.

RADDLE. A toothed frame, the teeth projecting upward approximately 3 inches, placed temporarily on the back of the loom. The warp passes through it as it is being transferred from the warping board (crocheted chain) to the warp beam. Used to spread warp. The raddle has a removable cap over the top of the teeth.

RADIUM. A plain-weave fine soft silk ("Pussy Willow").

RADNOR. A fancy weave with corded checks. Used for upholstery.

RAMONA CLOTH. A plain-weave linen-finish cotton.

RATINÉ. A nubby knotlike yarn. Also the name of the fabric woven from the yarn.

RAYON. A synthetic silklike filament made from regenerated cellulose. Its short staple fibers can be made to imitate wool and cotton.

REED. A frame containing finely spaced metal partitions separated by slits or dents through which the warp fibers pass and which, when battened against the newly thrown weft, firms the fabric.

REED HOOK. Same as heddle hook, but sometimes wider; used to assist in pulling warp through dents in reed.

REEF KNOT. A square knot. A method of joining broken warp, though the weaver's knot is better.

REEL. A swivel type of warping board. May also hold yarn as it is being spun.

REP. A plain-weave heavily corded fabric.

REVERSIBLE. A fabric which has a reversible pattern, i.e., the same design in opposite colors on the back.

RHYTHUM CRÊPE. A rayon seersucker.

RICE NET. A leno-weave square-mesh fabric which is highly starched. Used for millinery construction.

RING WARP. Warp forming an unbroken loop around the end bars of a two-stick loom.

RIPPLESHEEN. A plain-weave firm cotton fabric with a slight rib.

RISING-SHED LOOM. A jack loom.

ROLLERS. Loom beams.

ROMAN STRIPES. Wide brightly colored warp stripes.

ROSHANARA. Manufacturer's name for a heavy crepy rib-silk fabric.

ROVING. A soft cord or a roll of fibers; the process between the sliver and spinning.

RUBBER SHEETING. A plain-weave cotton fabric heavily coated with cured rubber.

RUG SHUTTLE. A frame shuttle. The two side pieces are pointed at both ends and are connected with two rods.

SAILCLOTH. Similar to canvas, but of finer quality. Used for couch covers, etc.

SAMITE. A fabric which contains gold and silver threads; silk 6-thread warp fabric.

SATEEN or SATINE. Satin-weave mercerized cotton with weft floats.

SATIN. Satin-weave silk fabric (five or more heddles), woven of rayon or acetate, with warp floats. Comes in various weights, sometimes cotton-backed.

SCRIM. A plain-weave coarse open marquisettelike cotton. Used for curtains.

SEALSKIN CLOTH. A fabric made of wild silk or mohair pile with a cotton ground; usually dyed black.

SECTION. A trial woven pattern.

SECTIONAL WARPBEAM. A warp beam, ideally one yard around, sectioned by pegs (usually wooden) usually 2 inches apart from centers, located along each quarter of the beam; beams may be in four or six cogs. The warp for the loom is wound on one section at a time.

SEERSUCKER. A plain-weave lightweight crinkle-striped cotton fabric which does not need ironing.

SELVAGE. Reinforced side edges of fabric. Sometimes cloth has selvages on four sides.

SERGE. A twill-weave hard-twisted wool worsted fabric. Also made in silk, mercerized cotton, mohair, or alpaca.

SETT. Number of dents to an inch in a reed.

SETTING UP THE LOOM. Putting the warp on the loom preparatory to weaving.

SHADE CLOTH. A plain-weave heavily oiled cloth for window shades.

SHADOW PRINT. A warp-printed fabric.

SHAFT. A heddle harness.

SHAKER. Heavy jersey used for school athletic sweaters.

SHANTUNG. See *Pongee.*

SHARKSKIN. A fancy weave with a tight durable finish of worsted yarns. Rayon is also used.

SHED. A space in the warp formed by raising up a heddle harness. The space through which the shuttle is thrown.

SHED CORD. A cord slipped through a shed to preserve it.

SHED ROLL. A round rod (about 3/4 of an inch in diameter) placed behind the cross and used on primitive looms to lift odd-numbered warp yarns.

SHED STICK. A wide flat smooth stick which opens a shed when turned on its side. Sometimes called shed sword.

SHED SWORD. See *Shed stick.*

SHEER. A general name for any semitransparent fabric.

485

SHEETING. Plain- or twill-weave wide firm cotton or linen for bed linen. May be of bleached or unbleached muslin, fine linen, mercerized cotton, or finest grade combed cotton (percale).

SHEPHERD'S CHECK. Black-and-white-checked fabrics.

SHIKI REP. A plain-weave corded fabric woven with irregular yarns.

SHOOT. A weft thread. Also spelled Shute.

SHOT. A throw of the weft through the shed.

SHUTTLE. A container for the bobbin. The shuttle is usually boat-shaped and slips easily through the shed. There are poke shuttles, rug shuttles, draw shuttles, shuttle sticks, roller shuttles, knife-edged shuttles, etc.

SHUTTLE BOXES. Two boxes, located opposite one another at the ends of the warp shed, that hold the shuttle as it passes from one side of the loom to the other. A jerk of cord drives the shuttle through the shed and into the opposite shuttle box.

SHUTTLE RACE. A bar on the front of the reed to support the passage of the shuttle.

SIGN CLOTH. A plain-weave heavily sized muslin. Sometimes the name is given to leno mesh for silk screen work.

SILESIA. A twill-weave closely woven smooth lightweight cotton fabric. Used for lining. Originally made in Silesia, Prussia.

SIMPLE. A cord on a draw loom to which a number of heddles are attached.

SILKALINE. A plain-weave luster-surfaced thin cotton used for linings, etc.

SINGLE-ELEMENT PROCESS. Fabric structures made by a single yarn, as knitting.

SINGLE-HEDDLE HARNESS. A board or frame containing holes alternating with slots through which the warp is drawn. By raising or lowering this harness two different sheds are made.

SINGLES. A single-twist yarn.

SINKING-SHED LOOM. A counterbalanced loom.

SIZING. Application of size or starch to warp yarns.

SKEIN HOLDER. See *Swift*.

SLAB BEAM. Beam on back of loom over which warp from warp beam passes. Sometimes called slab stock or stock.

SLEY. To thread reed. Also called reeding.

SLICKER CLOTH. Cotton cloth treated with wax or oil to waterproof it.

SLIP KNOT. A useful knot which can easily be untied.

SLIVER. A loose ball of carded fibers before spinning. Usually placed on a distaff.

SNITCH KNOT. See *Slip knot*.

SOFT TWIST. A lightly or loosely twisted yarn.

SOIESETTE. Manufacturer's name for a smooth mercerized cotton used for lining, curtains, etc.

SOLEIL. Any fabric with a high luster.

SPATHE. Heddle sword or heddle sticks.

SPINDLE. A small slender stick, usually weighted with a spindle whorl, which assists in spinning yarn and on which yarn is wound as spun.

SPINDLE WHORL. A small spindle weight, usually disc-shaped.

SPINNING. A process of twisting the sliver (or the roving) into yarn.

SPINNING JENNY. A power spinning wheel.

SPINNING MULE. Mule-power spinning wheels.

SPINNING WHEEL. A foot-treadle wheel which operates a spindle.

SPLITS. Two narrow cloths woven on one loom.

SPOOL BOARD. A horizontal board with spikes projecting upward; usually holds 30 spools or bobbins.

SPOOL FRAME. A hand-held spool rack. See *Bobbin carrier*.

SPOOL RACK. A rack holding many spools, one for each warp thread, on crosswise metal bars.

SPUN. See *Spinning* and *Twist*.

SPUN SILK. Silk cloth made from waste silk from damaged cocoons, mill waste, etc.

STAFFORD. Heavy cotton in plain or rep weave. Used for curtains.

STAVE. A heddle harness.

STICK SHUTTLE. A long narrow flat smooth stick with a horseshoe-shaped notch in each end. The weft thread is wound lengthwise from notch to notch in a figure 8 twist from front to back on each side. Used in weaving narrow fabrics.

STOCK. Slab beam.

STRIE. Same as Jaspé.

STRING HEDDLE. See *Heddle*.

STUFFER YARNS. Yarns layed between face and back of the fabric to give added thickness.

SUDANETTE. A plain-weave fine mercerized cotton fabric made of long-staple Pima cotton. Resembles fine broadcloth.

SUÈDE. A warp-knit lightly napped fabric. Sometimes a woven fabric with soft nap.

SURAH. A silk serge.

SWAMI. A warp-knitted fabric of cotton or rayon used for foundation garments.

SWATCH. A small sample of fabric.

SWIFT. A turning wheel 6 to 12 inches thick with an adjustable diameter; used for holding and unwinding a hank of yarn while rolling it into a ball.

SWISS. A plain-weave sheer cotton, originally made in Switzerland; may have swivel or lappet designs or flock patterns.

SWIVEL WEAVING. See *Broché, Lappet*, and *Swiss*. An inlaid pattern on a ground weave. The pattern yarn is carried back and forward in each pattern area.

SWORD. Battening stick. See *Shed stick*.

TABBY (verb). To throw in the tabby yarn.

TABBY (noun). Plain weaving with the same count of warp and weft to the inch. A 50/50 weave. Tabby is also a term used by some weavers to denote the alternate throws of the foundation plain weave which is placed between throws of pattern weft in overshot, brocade, and other weft-faced patterns, to prevent long warp floats.

TABBY YARN. A yarn used to weave tabby or to stabilize a throw of pattern weft.

TABLE LOOM. A loom which sits on the table and is operated by hand motion. Heddle harnesses are operated by key levers or counterbalanced beams. The key levers operate as a jack loom.

TABLET WEAVING. Weaving with tablet or card heddles.

TABORET. A strong silk dapery fabric with satin and moiré stripes.

TAFFETA. A plain-weave closely woven fine-quality stiff silk fabric. May be woven of rayon or acetate.

TAGS. Ends of yarn which hang free of a woven fabric.

TAMBOUR. Chain-stitch embroidery on net.

TAPA CLOTH. A bark cloth made from the paper mulberry tree. Made and used for clothing in some tropical areas. Usually printed in brown patterns with gum-like resin.

TAPESTRY. A special weave, made in the plain weave, but in sections across the warp. The weft yarns have different ways of joining: interlocking into one another, interlocking around the same warp, or interlocking around adjacent warps to leave a narrow slit (kimlin tapestry). Renaissance tapestries had a coarse warp and fine weft which gave a corded effect. Navaho rugs and French Aubusson rugs are in the tapestry weave.

TARLATAN. A plain-weave highly sized open gauzelike cotton usually highly colored. Used for costumes. Cannot be washed.

TARTAN. A name given to Scotch plaids.

TEASELS. Plant burrs used to raise nap on fabric.

TEMPLE. An instrument for stretching fabric while weaving. It is an adjustable bar with a pronged fork at either end. Also called template and warp stretcher.

TENSION BOX. Used to put a tension in warp for sectional warp beam.

TERRY CLOTH. A looped-pile knit or woven fabric of cotton. Used for towels, beach wear, etc. Also called Turkish toweling.

THEATRICAL GAUZE. A plain-weave open ecru coarse linen. Used for drapery.

THREAD. Tightly twisted fibers twisted into a long strand.

THREADING DRAFT. A graph pattern for threading the heddles.

THREADING THE LOOM. Threading the warp into the heddle eyes and the dents.

THROW. A shot through the shed with the shuttle.

TICKING. A plain, twill, or satin close weave used for holding feathers for pillows, or mattresses.

TIE-SILK. See *Foulard*.

TIE-UP DRAFT. A pattern for tying up heddle harnesses, lams, treadles, etc. Also called peg plan and lifting plan.

TISSUE. Any filmy stiff transparent fabric.

TOILES DE JOUY. Fabric made at Jouy by Oberkampf in the late eighteenth and early nineteenth centuries. Usually of cotton, printed in monochrome, showing Chinese or rural French scenic designs.

TOP CASTLE. Top brace of superstructure of loom, above heddle harnesses.

TRANSPARENT VELVET. A rich fine thin velvet.

TRICOT. A warp-knit fabric, containing an extra warp which travels diagonally, to prevent runs.

488 TRICOT MACHINE. A machine for interlocked knitting.

TREADLES. Foot pedals which control the operation of the heddle harnesses on a foot-power loom.

TROPICAL. Summer-weight worsted for men's suits.

TUBING. Cotton or linen fabric woven in a tube shape.

TUBULAR WARP. Continuous warp.

TULLE. A fine but stiff net, soft to the feel, usually of silk.

TURKISH TOWELING. See *Terry cloth*.

TURNING ON. Beaming the warp.

TUSSAH SILK. See *Pongee*. A variety of wild silk which is stronger and rougher than cultivated silk. It comes in ecru colors.

TWEED. Plain or twill weave of rough mixed fibers (black, white, grey). Looks like homespun. Sometimes in checks.

TWILL. A basic diagonal weave. Warps or wefts skip two, three, four, or five wefts or warps respectively; serge, etc.

TWIST. Fibers are twisted together in the spinning process to make a yarn. There are two twists: clockwise (also called S-twist), and counterclockwise (also called Z-twist, twistaway and weft-way).

TWO PLY. Two yarns twisted together.

TYING UP LOOM. Fastening up heddle harness to treadles, etc. Also called gating the loom.

UNION CLOTH. Cloth of mixed fibers.

UPHOLSTERY WEBBING. Usually a twill-weave jute banding used in upholstery to hold tied springs. Plain webbing is used for backing, etc., in upholstery work.

VARICOLORED. Yarns dyed in more than one color.

VELOUR. A pile weave. Used for upholstery or for dress goods, depending on height of pile.

VELVET. A fabric having a short thick warp pile. May be of any fiber content. Depending on the type of velvet, may be used for drapery, upholstery, and dress goods. Plush has a pile longer than 1/7 inch.

VELVETEEN. A weft pile fabric with short pile, usually of cotton.

VICUÑA. A name given to a high-quality fabric made from the expensive hair of the vicuña, a South American wild cameloid.

VOILE. A plain-weave sheer clinging cotton fabric. May be made of silk, rayon, or wool.

WAFFLE CLOTH. See *Honeycomb*.

WALL CANVAS. Fabric used as a wall covering as a base for paint. A thin canvas.

WARP. The longitudinal yarns in the loom into which the crosswise weft yarns are woven. Also called "end."

WARP (CONTINUOUS). Warp which passes over the two end bars or beams but is not attached to either.

WARP (FIXED). Short warp secured to two end bars.

WARP (ROLLED). Warp rolled from the end bar or beam to the cloth roll.

WARP BEAM. Drum at back of loom which holds warp.

WARP-FACED. Fabric with closely spaced warps. Weft does not show.

WARP KNIT. A nonrunning knit of special construction. See *Tricot*.

WARP LIFTER. See *Pick-up stick*.

WARP PRINT. See *Shadow print*.

WARPING. Process of winding the warp on the warp beam. As used in this book, the process of putting warp on the loom.

WARPING BOARD. A board with projecting pegs upon which the warp is strung preparatory to putting it on the loom.

WARPING THE LOOM. Putting the warp onto the loom. When a warp beam is on the loom, the process is often called beaming.

WARP SPREADER. See *Raddle*. On some primitive looms the warp was sewed through a piece of leather to keep it spread out.

WARP STRETCHER. A flat wooden strip with spikes at both ends, which holds the cloth a given width during weaving to insure even margins.

WARP-WEIGHTED. Weights attached to hanging warp.

WAY. Color scheme (4 ways = 4 colors).

WEAVER'S KNOT. A knot indispensable to a weaver. See page 53.

WEAVES. A manner of manipulating the sheds to obtain a pattern.

WEAVING. The use of the loom to fabricate cloth. The interweaving of warp and weft.

WEB. The finished weaving. The cloth.

WEFT. The crosswise filling yarns; woof; pick.

WEFT-FACED. Fabric with closely spaced wefts. Warp does not show.

WEFT KNIT. The usual knitting process.

WHIPCORD. A twill weave with a pronounced diagonal rib on right side.

WHIPROLL. Rod above warp beam over which warp passes.

WIGAN. A plain-weave canvaslike cotton fabric used to line men's coats.

WILD SILK. Sometimes called Tussah.

WILLOW. A special double hat-frame fabric made of a crinoline material and cellulose fibers.

WILTON. A carpet weave.

WILTON LOOM. Jacquard looms on which cut-pile or looped-pile rugs are woven.

WINDER. See *Bobbin winder*.

WINDING FRAMES. See *Warping board*.

WOOF. Another term for weft or filling thread.

WOOLEN. Fabric made of second-grade wool fibers.

WORSTED. Fabric made of long-staple multiple-combed yarns of wool.

YARN. A twisted strand or cord, usually of cotton, wool, or linen.

YARN-OVER. To throw the yarn in front of the point of the knitting needle or the crochet hook.

ZEPHYR. Fine gingham, usually plain weave. Also the name given to fine wool yarn.

REFERENCES

Weaving, Twining, and General Textiles

1. Amsden, Charles A., *Navaho Weaving*, University of New Mexico Press, Albuquerque, 1949.
2. Atwater, Mary M., *Byways in Hand-Weaving*, The Macmillan Company, New York, 1954.
3. Atwater, Mary M., *Guatemala Visited*, by author, Salt Lake City, 1946.
4. Atwater, Mary M., *The Shuttle Craft Book of American Hand-Weaving*, The Macmillan Company, New York, 1951.
5. Baity, Elizabeth Chesley, *Man is a Weaver*, George Harrap & Co., Ltd., London, 1947.
6. Bellinger, Louisa, *Textile Analysis* (Egypt and Near East), #2, Textile Museum, Washington, D.C., 1950.
7. Bendure, Zelma, and Pfeiffer, Gladys, *America's Fabrics*, The Macmillan Company, New York, 1947.
8. Bennett, Wendell C., and Bird, Junius B., *Andean Culture History*, American Museum of Natural History, New York, 1949.
9. Beriau, Oscar, *Home Weaving*, Arts and Crafts of Gardenvale, Inc., Gardenvale, Quebec, 1947.
10. Bird, Junius, "Textile Notes," in W. D. Strong, and C. Evans, Jr., *Viru Valley*, Columbia University Press, New York, 1952.
11. Bird, Junius, and Mahler, Joy, "America's Oldest Fabrics," *American Fabrics*, Reporter Publications, Inc., New York, Winter, 1951–52.
12. Black, Mary E., *Key to Weaving*, Bruce Publishing Co., Milwaukee (Wis.), 1949.
13. Breck, Joseph, *Peruvian Textiles*, Metropolitan Museum, New York, 1930.
14. Brown, Harriette J., *Hand Weaving*, Harper & Brothers, New York, 1952.
15. Candee, Helen, *The Tapestry Book*, Tudor Publishing Co., New York, 1935.
16. Clifford, Lois I., *Card Weaving*, Manuel Arts Press, Peoria (Ill.), 1947.
17. Coates, Helen, *Weaving for Amateurs*, Studio Publishing Co., London, 1946.
18. Crawford, M. D. C., *Peruvian Fabrics*, Anthropology Papers, American Museum of Natural History, New York, 1916.
19. Crowell, Ivan H., *Popular Weaving Crafts*, Charles A. Bennett Co., Peoria (Ill.), 1950.
20. Denny, Grace G., *Fabrics*, J. B. Lippincott Co., Philadelphia, 1936.
21. Evans, Mary, and McGowan, E. B., *Guide to Textiles*, John Wiley & Sons, New York, 1939.
22. Forbes, R. J., *Studies in Ancient Technology*, E. J. Brill, Leiden, Netherlands, 1956.

REFERENCES

23. Gayton, A. H., *The Uhle Pottery Collections from Nieveria*, University of California Press, Berkeley, 1927.

24. Gilroy, Clinton G., *Art of Weaving*, George D. Baldwin, New York, 1844.

25. Glazier, Richard, *Historic Textile Fabrics*, B. T. Batsford, Ltd., London, 1923.

26. Harcourt, Raoul d', *Les Textiles du Anciens du Perou*, Les Editions d'Art et d'Histoire, Paris, 1934.

27. Hess, Katharine Paddock, *Textile Fibers and Their Use*, J. B. Lippincott Co., Philadelphia, 1954.

28. Hooper, Luther, *Hand Loom Weaving*, Sir Isaac Pitman & Sons, Ltd., London, 1936.

29. House, Florence E., *Notes on Weaving Techniques*, Columbia University Press, New York, 1956.

30. I.C.S. Staff, *Advanced Textile Designing*, International Textbook Co., Scranton (Pa.), 1950.

31. I.C.S. Staff, *Fundamentals of Textile Designing*, International Textbook Co., Scranton (Pa.), 1949.

32. James, George Wharton, *Indian Blankets*, Tudor Publishing Co., New York, 1937.

33. Kent, Kate Peck, *Montezuma Castle Archaeology*, Part 2, Textiles, Southwest Monuments Association, Globe (Ariz.), 1954.

34. Kissell, Mary L., *Basketry of Papago and Pima*, Anthropology Papers, American Museum of Natural History, New York, 1916.

35. Kissell, Mary L., *Yarn and Cloth Making*, The Macmillan Company, New York, 1918.

36. Lee, Julia S., *Elementary Textiles*, Prentice-Hall, Inc., New York, 1953.

37. Lewis, Ethel, *The Romance of Textiles*, The Macmillan Company, New York, 1938.

38. Lyford, Carrie A., *Crafts of the Ojibwa*, Education Division, U.S. Office of Indian Affairs, Washington, D.C., 1943.

39. Lyford, Carrie A., *Iroquois Crafts*, Education Division, U.S. Office of Indian Affairs, Washington, D.C. 1945.

40. Matthews, J. Merritt, *Matthew's Textile Fibers*, 5th ed., H. R. Mauersberger (ed.), John Wiley & Sons, New York, 1947.

41. Matthews, Washington, "Navaho," *Third Annual Report, Bureau of Ethnology*, Washington, D.C., 1884, pp. 371–391.

42. Miner, Horace, "Importance of Textiles in Archaeology," *American Antiquity*, Vol. I, 1935–1936.

43. Mohr, Albert, and Sample, L. L., "Twined Water Bottles of the Cuyama Area, Southern California," *American Antiquity*, April, 1955.

44. Mumford, John Kimberly, *Oriental Rugs*, Charles Scribner's Sons, New York, 1902.

45. Oelsner, G. H., *Handbook of Weaves*, Dover Publications, New York, 1950.

46. O'Neale, Lila M., *Archaeological Explorations in Peru* (III), University of California Press, Berkeley, 1937.

47. O'Neale, Lila M., *Textiles of Highland Guatemala*, Carnegie Institute, Washington, D.C., 1945.

494

48. O'Neale, Lila M., *Textile Periods of Ancient Peru* (Paracas), University of California Press, Berkeley, 1942.

49. O'Neale, Lila M., *Textile Periods of Ancient Peru* (Gauze Weaves), University of California Press, Berkeley, 1948.

50. O'Neale, Lila M., "Weaving," *Handbook of South American Indians,* Vol. 5, B.A.E., 1949.

51. O'Neale, Lila M., "Textiles," in Gordon R. Willey, and John M. Corbett, *Early Ancon and Early Supe,* Columbia University Press, New York, 1954.

52. Paul, Frances, *Spruce Root Baskets of Alaskan Tlingit,* Education Division, U.S. Office of Indian Affairs, Washington, D.C., 1944.

53. Potter, M. D., and Corbman, Bernard P., *Fiber to Fabric,* McGraw-Hill Book Company, New York, 1954.

54. Read, John, *Elementary Textile Design and Fabric Structure,* The Textile Institute, Manchester, England, 1950.

55. Rodier, Paul, *The Romance of French Weaving,* Tudor Publishing Co., New York, 1936.

56. Roth, Ling, *Studies in Primitive Looms,* Bankfield Museum, Halifax, England, 1950.

57. Schinnerer, Louise, *Antike Handarbeiten,* Wien, 1896.

58. Small, Cassie, *How to Know Textiles,* Ginn and Company, Boston, 1932.

59. Start, Laura E., *McDougall Collection of Indian Textiles from Guatemala and Mexico,* Oxford University Press, Oxford, 1948.

60. Strong, John H., *Fabric Structure,* Chemical Publishing Co., New York, 1947.

61. Taullard, Alfredo, *Tjidos y Ponchos Indigenas de Sudamerica,* Guillermo Kraft, Ltd., Buenos Aires, 1949.

62. Thomson, W. G., *A History of Tapestry,* Hodder and Stoughton, London, 1906.

63. Tidball, Harriet D., *The Inkle Weave,* Shuttle Craft Guild, Virginia City (Mont.), 1952.

64. Walton, Perry, *The Story of Textiles,* Tudor Publishing Co., New York, 1937.

65. Watson, William, *Advanced Textile Design,* Longmans, Green & Co., New York, 1925.

66. Whiton, Sherrill, *Elements of Interior Decoration,* J. B. Lippincott Co., Philadelphia, 1951.

67. Wingate, Isabel, *Textile Fabrics,* Prentice-Hall, Inc., New York, 1949.

68. Woolman, M. S., and McGowan, E. B., *Textiles,* The Macmillan Company, New York, 1926.

69. Worst, Edward F., *Foot-Power Loom Weaving,* Bruce Publishing Co., Milwaukee, (Wis.), 1924.

Embroidery

70. Bird, Junius, and Bellinger, Louisa, *Paracas Fabrics and Nasca Needlework,* National Publishing Co., Washington, D.C., 1954.

71. Brooks, Helen, *Your Embroidery,* Charles A. Bennett Co., Peoria (Ill.), 1949.

72. Cox, Hebe, *Simple Embroidery Design*, Studio Publications, New York, 1948.

73. Christie, A., *Embroidery and Tapestry Weaving*, Sir Isaac Pitman & Sons, Ltd., London, 1935.

74. Christie, A., *Samplers and Stitches*, B. T. Batsford, Ltd., London, 1920.

75. Harbeson, Giorgiana Brown, *American Needlework*, Coward-McCann, Inc., New York, 1938.

76. Hawley, Willis Meeker, *Chinese Folk Design and Embroidery*, published by author, Hollywood, 1949.

77. Jones, Anne Brandon, *Stitch Patterns and Design for Embroidery*, Manual Arts Press, Peoria (Ill.), 1929.

78. Karasz, Mariska, *Adventures in Stitches*, Funk & Wagnalls Co., New York, 1949.

79. Langenberg, Ella L., *The Beginner's Book of Needle Craft*, Hobby Book Mart, New York, 1948.

80. Lefeburke, Ernest, *Embroidery and Lace*, G. P. Putnam's Sons, New York, 1899.

81. Stafford, Cora, E., *Paracas Embroideries*, J. J. Augustin, New York, 1941.

82. Thomas, Mary, *Mary Thomas' Embroidery Book*, William Morrow & Co., New York, 1936.

83. Villalba, J. de, *Broderies populaires espagnoles*, Henri Ernst, Paris, 1928.

Rugs

84. *American Fabrics*, Reporter Publications, Inc., Winter 1951–1952.

85. *American Fabrics*, Reporter Publications, Inc., Winter 1952–1953.

86. *Carpets and Rugs*, Hoover Home Institute, Hoover Co., North Canton (Ohio), 1951.

87. *A Century of Carpets and Rugs*, Bigelow-Hartford Carpet Co., New York, 1925.

88. Dilley, Arthur Urban, *Oriental Rugs and Carpets*, Charles Scribner's Sons, New York, 1939.

89. Hawley, Walter A., *Oriental Rugs*, Tudor Publishing Co., New York, 1937.

90. Lewis, G. Griffin, *Practical Book of Oriental Rugs*, J. B. Lippincott Co., Philadelphia, 1921.

91. *Minerva Hooked Rug Manual*, James Lees and Sons Co., Chicago, 1950.

92. O'Brien, Mildred Jackson, *The Rug and Carpet Book*, McGraw-Hill Book Company, New York, 1951.

93. Underhill, Vera Bisbee, *Creating Hooked Rugs*, Coward-McCann, Inc., New York, 1952.

Lace and Other Single-Element Processes

94. Bültzengslöwen, Regina A., and Lehmann, Edgar, *Nichtgewebe Textilien vor 1400*, Verlag dr. ell., Tübingen, Germany. (Manuscript information by communication.)

95. Caplin, Jessie F., *The Lace Book*, The Macmillan Company, New York, 1932.

96. Clifford, C. R., *The Lace Dictionary*, Clifford & Lawton, New York, 1913.

97. Davidson, D. S., "Knotless Netting in America and Oceania," *American Anthropologist*, Vol. 37, 1935, pp. 117–134.

98. Evans, Ethel, *This is Crocheting*, The Macmillan Company, New York, 1949.

99. Evans, Ethel, *This is Knitting*, The Macmillan Company, New York, 1948.

100. Graumont, Raoul, and Hensel, John, *Encyclopedia of Knots*, Cornell Maritime Press, Cambridge, 1946.

101. Hald, Margrethe, *Olddanske Tekstiler*, Köbenhavn, 1950.

102. Johnson, Irmgard Weittander, *Twine Plaiting*, Thesis, University of California, Berkeley, 1950.

103. Johnson, W. H., and Newkirk, L. V., *The Textile Arts*, The Macmillan Company, New York, 1948.

104. Kellogg, Charlotte, *Bobbins of Belgium*, Funk & Wagnalls Co., New York, 1920.

105. *Knitting for Young America*, Institute for Hand Knitting, New York, 1948.

106. Laird, Elizabeth, *The Complete Book of Knitting*, World Publishing Co., New York, 1947.

107. Mincoff, Elizabeth, and Marriage, Margaret, *Pillow Lace*, John Murray, London, 1907.

108. Moore, N. Hudson, *The Lace Book*, Frederick A. Stokes Co., New York, 1904.

109. Palliser, Bury, *History of Lace*, Lampon Low, Marston, London, 1875.

110. Powys, Marian, *Lace and Lace Making*, Charles T. Brandford Co., Boston, 1953.

111. Rogge, Elis M., *Egyptish Vlechtwerk* (Meshwork), V. Holkema & Warendorf, Amsterdam, 1928.

112. Spencer, Charles L., *Knots and Fancy Work*, Dodd, Mead and Co., New York, 1942.

113. Whiting, Gertrude, *Tools and Toys of Stitchery*, Columbia University Press, New York, 1928.

Printing, Painting, and Stenciling

114. *American Fabrics Magazine*, Reporter Publications, Inc., New York, Spring, 1954.

115. Biegeleisen, J. I., *The Silk Screen Printing Process*, McGraw-Hill Book Company, New York, 1938.

116. Brooks, Evelyn, *Your Textile Printing*, Charles A. Bennett Co., Peoria (Ill.), 1950.

117. Clouzot, Henri, *Painted and Printed Fabrics*, Metropolitan Museum of Art, New York, 1927.

118. Hall, Herbert J., and Buck, Mertice M. C., *Handicrafts for the Handicapped*, Moffat, Yard & Co., New York, 1917.

119. Hielt, Harry L., and Middleton, H. K., *Silk-Screen Process Production*, Blandford Press, Ltd., London, 1950.

120. House, Florence, *Creative Expression through the Block Print*, Progressive Education Association, Washington, D.C.

121. Kosloff, Albert, *Screen Process Printing*, Signs of the Times, Cincinnati, 1950.

122. Michel, Adelaide, *Stenciling*, Manual Arts Press, Peoria (Ill.), 1920.

123. Middleton, H. K., *Practical Silk Screen*, Blandford Press Ltd., London, 1947.

124. Perry, Raymond W., *Block Printing Craft*, Manual Arts Press, Peoria (Ill.), 1938.

125. Polk, R. W., *Essentials of Linoleum Block Printing*, Manual Arts Press, Peoria (Ill.), 1927.

126. Porte, R. T., *Printing Throughout the World*, Porte Publishing Co., Salt Lake City, 1929.

127. Sipley, L. W., *A Half Century of Color*, The Macmillan Company, New York, 1953.

128. Teplitz, Irving, *Principles of Textile Converting*, Textile Book Publishers, Inc., New York, 1947.

Dyeing and Batik

129. Baker, Walter, and Baker, Ida, *Batik and other Pattern Dyeing*, Atkinson Mentser and Co., 1929.

130. Bühler, A., article on pattern dyeing, *Ciba Review*, Ciba Co., New York, June, 1954.

131. Diserens, Louis, *The Technology of Dyeing and Printing*, Reinhold Corp., New York, 1948.

132. Fraps, G. S., *Principles of Dyeing*, The Macmillan Company, New York, 1921.

133. Hollen, Mary, and Saddler, Jane, *Textiles*, The Macmillan Company, New York, 1955.

134. Haddon, A. C., and Start, Laura E., *Iban or Sea Dayak Fabrics*, Cambridge University Press, Cambridge, 1936.

135. Henschen, I., "Weaving Techniques," *Ciba Review*, Ciba Co., New York, October, 1951.

136. Heusser, Albert H., *The Silk Dyeing Industry in the United States*, Silk Dyers' Association, Paterson (N.J.), 1927.

137. Horsfall, R. S., and Lawrie, L. G., *The Dyeing of Textile Fibers*, Chapman & Hall, Ltd., London, 1949.

138. Lubs, H. A., *The Chemistry of Synthetic Dyes and Pigments*, Reinhold Corp., New York, 1955.

139. Mijer, Pieter, *Batiks and How to Make Them*, Dodd and Mead & Co., New York, 1919.

140. Owen, F. A., *Dyeing and Cleaning of Textile Fabrics*, John Wiley & Sons, New York, 1909.

141. Pellew, Charles E., *Dyes and Dyeing*, Robert M. McBride and Co., New York, 1918.

142. Pope, F. Whipple, *Methods in Dyeing by Vegetable Dyes*, North Bennet State Industrial School, Boston.

143. Young, Stella, *Navajo Native Dyes*, Indian Handcrafts, No. 2, Education Division, U.S. Office of Indian Affairs, Washington, D.C., 1940.

Design

144. *American Fabrics Magazine*, various issues, Reporter Publications, Inc., New York.

145. Birrell, Verla, *Portfolio of Historic Design*, Salt Lake City, 1947.

146. *Design in Scandinavia*, American Federation of Art, New York, 1956.

147. Glazier, Richard, *Historic Textile Fabrics*, B. T. Batsford, Ltd., London, 1923.

148. Haddon, A. C., *Evolution in Art*, Charles Scribner's Sons, New York, 1910.

149. Hunt, Anthony, *Textile Design*, Studio Publications, New York, 1951.

150. Képes, György, *Language of Vision*, P. Theobold, Chicago, 1944.

151. Knapp, Harriet E., *Design Approach to Crafts*, Holden Publishing Co., Springfield (Mass.), 1945.

152. Moholy-Nagy, Laszlo, *The New Vision*, Wittenborn, Schultz, Inc., New York, 1949.

153. Noyes, Eliot E., *Organic Design*, Museum of Modern Art, New York, 1941.

154. Rasmusen, Henry N., *Art Structure*, McGraw-Hill Book Co., New York, 1950.

155. Scott, Robert Gillam, *Design Fundamentals*, McGraw-Hill Book Co., New York, 1951.

156. Smith, Janet K., *Design*, Reinhold Corp., New York, 1950.

157. Snelgrove, Isabel P., *Practice and Appreciation of Design*, Burgess Publishing Co., Minneapolis, 1947.

158. Speltz, Alexander, *Styles of Ornament*, B. T. Batsford, Ltd., London, 1910.

159. Watson, William, *Advanced Textile Design*, Longmans, Green & Co., New York, 1925.

160. Weltfish, Gene, *The Origins of Art*, Bobbs-Merrill Co., Inc., Indianapolis (Ind.), 1953.

161. Wright, R. H., *Modern Textile Design and Production*, National Trade Press, London, 1949.

Textile Fabric Glossaries and Dictionaries

162. *Davidson's Textile Year Book*, Davidson Publishing Co., Ridgewood, New Jersey, 1953.

163. Denny, Grace G., *Fabrics*, J. B. Lippincott Co., Philadelphia, 1926.

164. Hoye, John, *Staple Cotton Fabrics*, McGraw-Hill Book Company, New York, 1942.

165. Linton, George E., *The Modern Textile Dictionary*, Duell, Sloan and Pearce, New York, 1954.

166. Linton, George E., Pizzuto, J. J., *Applied Textiles*, Lifetime Editions, Inc., New York, 1948.

167. Maerz, A., and Paul, M. Rea, *A Dictionary of Color,* McGraw-Hill Book Company, New York, 1950.
168. Pritchard, M. E., *A Short Dictionary of Weaving,* Philosophical Library, New York, 1954.
169. *Webster's New International Dictionary,* G. & C. Merriam Co., Springfield (Mass.), 1955.

REFERENCES

Index

503

INDEX

504

INDEX

INDEX

509

INDEX

511

INDEX